Auto
Air Conditioning
TECHNOLOGY

by

JOHN V. ALTHOUSE

and

MILTON RABBITT

South Holland, Illinois

THE GOODHEART-WILLCOX COMPANY, INC.

Publishers

Library of Congress Catalog Card Number 90-34671
International Standard Book Number 0-87006-815-6

1234567890-91-9876543210

Library of Congress Cataloging in Publication Data

Althouse, John V.
   Automotive air conditioning technology / by John V. Althouse, Milton Rabbitt.
      p. cm.
   Includes index.
   ISBN 0-87006-815-6
   1. Automobile—Heating and ventilation. 2. Automobiles—Heating and ventilation—Maintenance and repair. 3. Automobiles—Air conditioning. 4. Automobiles—Air conditioning—maintenance and repair. I. Rabbit, Milton. II. Title.
TL271.A48   1991
629.27'7--dc20   90-34671
                                                  CIP

INTRODUCTION

Automotive work requires a thorough knowledge of the basic principles of a specific system. Air conditioning, ventilation, and heating work is no exception. AUTO AIR CONDITIONING TECHNOLOGY explains and illustrates the related principles involved in the operation of these systems. The book also discusses troubleshooting and service procedures.

AUTO AIR CONDITIONING TECHNOLOGY contains the latest technical advances in the field. Many different car manufacturers are now using variable displacement compressors. Theory, parts identification, and testing of this compressor are discussed. The fluidic defroster, which is used on some new vehicles, is also discussed. The refrigerants currently used in automotive systems contain ozone-destroying chlorinated fluorocarbons. These refrigerants will be phased out and replaced in coming years with less harmful materials. During the transition, refrigerant recovery and recycling will be important. It is explained in detail.

AUTO AIR CONDITIONING TECHNOLOGY has many features that make it easy to understand. The focus of this text is on the needs of the automotive student in high school, adult classes, technical schools, and community colleges. The book is highly illustrated with photographs and line drawings to aid understanding. Each chapter begins with learning objectives that emphasize the important topics; a summary at the end of each chapter reviews those same topics. Immediately after the summary is a list of words that have been defined in each chapter. All defined words are italicized in the text for easy recognition. The review section, at the end of each chapter, consists of essay, true-false, multiple choice, fill-in-the-blank, and ASE-type questions.

Since many automotive air conditioning service and repair operations can be dangerous, safety precautions are stressed. They are printed in color for emphasis.

AUTO AIR CONDITIONING TECHNOLOGY is a valuable guide. It explains to the car owner how automotive heating and air conditioning operates and how to service the system. It will help an interested student prepare for a career. It will also act as a reference for the experienced technician, providing the latest auto heating, ventilation, and air conditioning technology.

John V. Althouse
Milton Rabbitt

CONTENTS

SECTION 4—ON-THE-JOB SKILLS

IMPORTANT SAFETY NOTICE

Proper service and repair methods are critical to the safe, reliable operation of automobiles. The procedures described in this book are designed to help you use a manufacturer's service manual. A service manual will give the how-to details and specifications needed to do competent work.

This book contains safety precautions which must be followed. Personal injury or part damage can result when basic safety rules are not followed. Also, remember that these cautions are general and do not cover some specialized hazards. Refer to a service manual when in doubt about any service operation!

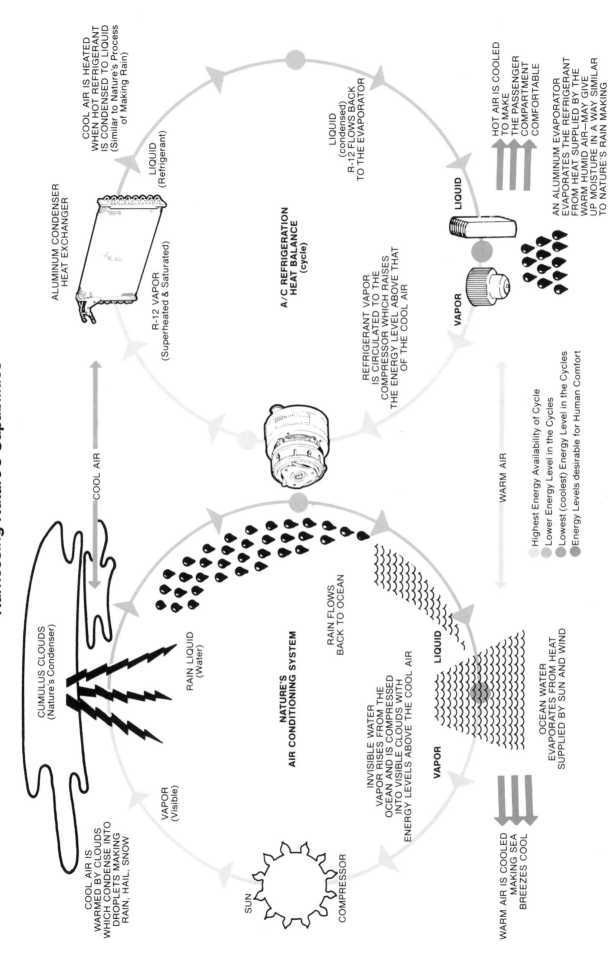

AIR CONDITIONING
Harnessing Nature's Capabilities

CUMULUS CLOUDS
(Nature's Condenser)

COOL AIR IS WARMED BY CLOUDS WHICH CONDENSE INTO DROPLETS MAKING RAIN, HAIL, SNOW

COOL AIR

RAIN LIQUID (Water)

VAPOR (Visible)

SUN

COMPRESSOR

RAIN FLOWS BACK TO OCEAN

NATURE'S AIR CONDITIONING SYSTEM

INVISIBLE WATER VAPOR RISES FROM THE OCEAN AND IS COMPRESSED INTO VISIBLE CLOUDS WITH ENERGY LEVELS ABOVE THE COOL AIR

LIQUID

VAPOR

OCEAN WATER EVAPORATES FROM HEAT SUPPLIED BY SUN AND WIND

WARM AIR IS COOLED MAKING SEA BREEZES COOL

ALUMINUM CONDENSER HEAT EXCHANGER

COOL AIR IS HEATED WHEN HOT REFRIGERANT IS CONDENSED TO LIQUID (Similar to Nature's Process of Making Rain)

LIQUID (Refrigerant)

R-12 VAPOR (Superheated & Saturated)

A/C REFRIGERATION HEAT BALANCE (cycle)

REFRIGERANT VAPOR IS CIRCULATED TO THE COMPRESSOR WHICH RAISES THE ENERGY LEVEL ABOVE THAT OF THE COOL AIR

WARM AIR

LIQUID (condensed) R-12 FLOWS BACK TO THE EVAPORATOR

HOT AIR IS COOLED TO MAKE THE PASSENGER COMPARTMENT COMFORTABLE

LIQUID

VAPOR

AN ALUMINUM EVAPORATOR EVAPORATES THE REFRIGERANT FROM HEAT SUPPLIED BY THE WARM HUMID AIR—MAY GIVE UP MOISTURE IN A WAY SIMILAR TO NATURE'S RAIN MAKING

Highest Energy Availability of Cycle
Lower Energy Level in the Cycles
Lowest (coolest) Energy Level in the Cycles
Energy Levels desirable for Human Comfort

Air conditioning cycles.   (Harrison Radiator Div., GM)

INTRODUCTION TO AIR CONDITIONING

After studying this chapter, you will be able to:
- *List the advantages of air conditioning (A/C) systems.*
- *Explain the basics of how an air conditioning system works.*
- *Describe the different types of A/C systems.*
- *List the components of the modern A/C system.*
- *Explain how the mode doors direct airflow to the passenger compartment.*

INTRODUCTION

Air conditioning is the controlled environment of ar enclosed space, such as inside an auto. Air conditioning involves dehumidifying, cleaning, and cooling the air inside the car. This provides comfort to the driver and passengers alike.

Comfort affects driver responsiveness and reaction time to a given situation. Air conditioning provides greater safety by reducing driver fatigue. In addition, interior noise level is reduced when all windows are closed and the air conditioner is on. Air conditioning also eliminates windshield fogging. This allows the driver to maintain good visibility of the road and other cars.

Air contains dust, pollen, and other airborne contaminants. The temperature of the evaporator is below the dew point. This causes the moisture in the air to condense, on the evaporator core, and turn into water. The water collects the dust and pollen as the air passes through the evaporator. The water then carries the dust and pollen as it leaves the evaporator housing through the drain. Very little dust and pollen can enter the passenger compartment of the car when the air conditioner is on.

HISTORY OF AUTOMOTIVE AIR CONDITIONING

Automotive air conditioning, that used a refrigerant, was first introduced on the 1940 Packard. Since then, it has become one of the most popular accessories found on cars today.

Early attempts at automotive air conditioning consisted of *evaporative coolers* that were hung from the passenger side window, Fig. 1-1. Water was fed by gravity or capillary action over a filter/screen. Incoming air flowed through the screen into the passenger compartment. The evaporating water absorbed heat from the incoming air. However, the disadvantage of this system is that it raised the humidity level inside the car. This made the coolers only practical in the dry, desert climates of the southwestern region of the United States.

The first air conditioners to use a refrigerant were *hang-on units*, Fig. 1-2. The assembly was mounted

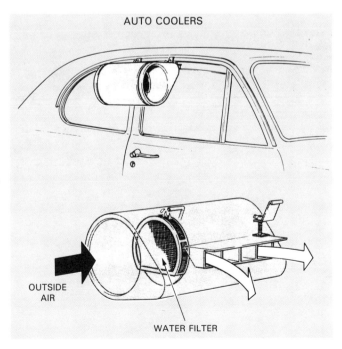

Fig. 1-1. Early auto air conditioners were hung from the passenger side window and cooled only while the car was moving. (Ford)

under the instrument panel. This unit was independent of the heating, defrosting, and ventilation system. The heater core was in a separate housing from the evaporator, Fig. 1-3. Operation involves recirculating the air from inside the car instead of fresh air from the outside.

The next advancement in air conditioning came when the evaporator core was combined in the same housing as the heater core. This is referred to as an *integrated heating and cooling system,* Fig. 1-4. This system allowed the outside air to enter or be recirculated inside the car.

The latest advancement incorporates an *automatic temperature control* (ATC), Fig. 1-5. Sensors provide information to a computer which controls the system automatically to maintain the desired temperature setting

THE PRESENT AND FUTURE

Currently, about 90 percent of all cars made today come equipped from the factory with air conditioning, Fig. 1-6. The market is almost at the saturation point (100 percent) with automotive air conditioners. The effects of automotive air conditioning pose many concerns.

Cars with air conditioning are not as fuel efficient with the system in operation. With continuing concern about fuel economy, manufacturers make components as light as possible to reduce the weight. With the elimination and integration of various air conditioning parts, less space is needed. The refrigerant used in automotive air

conditioners is also of concern.

The refrigerant used in cars today, R-12, is becoming an environmental concern. Some scientists believe that chlorine in the refrigerant causes ozone (at the ozone layer) to disintegrate. The ozone layer protects the earth from ultraviolet rays. Some scientists fear the result could be an average ambient temperature increase. Substitute refrigerants that are ozone-friendly are being tested and evaluated for use in the near future.

AUTOMOTIVE AIR CONDITIONING

A complete air conditioning system from the factory consists of an evaporator, heater core (inside the evaporator housing), condenser, compressor, and a receiver/drier, Fig. 1-7. The refrigerant used in automotive air conditioners today is R-12. The main purpose of an air conditioning system is to transfer heat from inside the passenger compartment, to the surrounding outside air.

Temperature control

Outside air is routed through ducts to a cooling core (evaporator) inside the car. As the air passes through the evaporator, the air is cooled and dehumidified. When maximum cooling is needed, no outside air enters the car. Inside air is recirculated across the evaporator, Fig. 1-8A. However, the driver may elect to make the passenger compartment warmer by having some of the airflow pass through the heater core. A mixture of cold

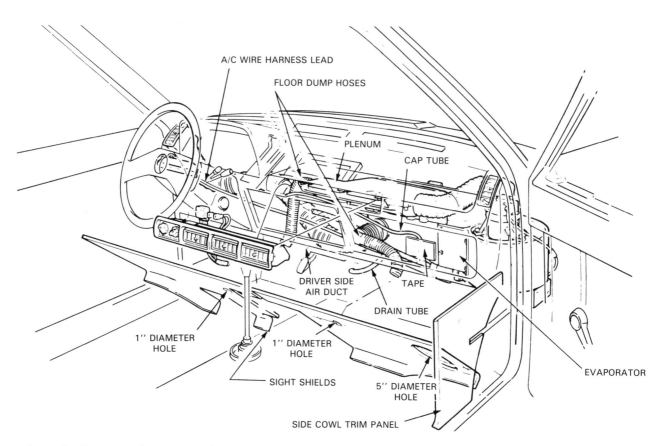

Fig. 1-2. Hang-on units attach to the underside of the instrument panel. Evaporator core is in a separate location from heater core.   (Mark IV)

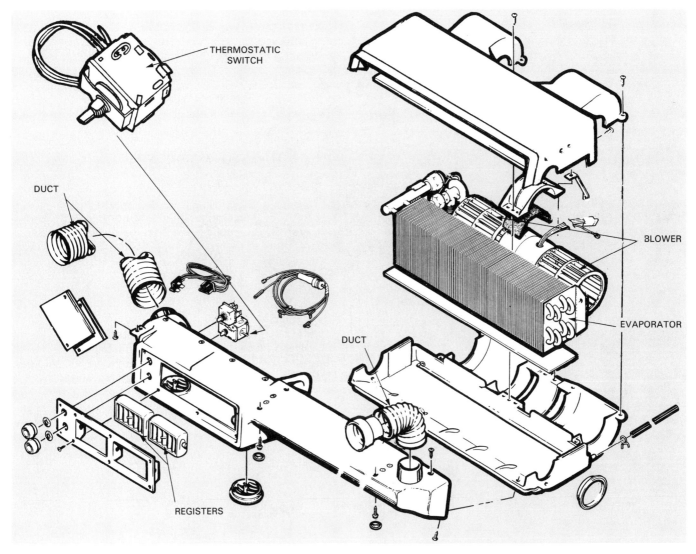

THERMOSTATIC SWITCH

DUCT

BLOWER

EVAPORATOR

DUCT

REGISTERS

Fig. 1-3. One of the first type of auto air conditioners using a refrigerant. Only the evaporator is contained within the unit.

and heated air then enters the passenger compartment. The *temperature blend-air door* directs the airflow, Fig. 1-8B and 1-8C.

Humidity control

Humidity, the moisture in the air, combined with heat is very uncomfortable. High heat and high humidity cause fatigue. The problem is increased by the fact that ''the hotter the air, the more moisture the air can hold.'' The air conditioner is less effective during times of high humidity, as the moisture accumulation on the evaporator reduces heat transfer efficiency.

The temperature of the evaporator core is below the dew point. The moisture in the air is cooled and condenses when it comes in contact with the evaporator. The moisture condenses on the evaporator and turns into water, Fig. 1-9. Therefore, on extremely humid days, the effectiveness of the air conditioner is reduced.

TYPES OF SYSTEMS

There are several types of air conditioning systems available today. They include:

1. Hang-on or add-on.
2. Integral with manual controls.
3. Integral with automatic controls.

Add-on

The add-on unit is so called because there is no air conditioner on the car when it comes from the factory. It is ''added on'' to the car at some point after it arrives at a new car dealership. This means the car owner may wait up to several years before deciding to have air conditioning added. The unit is installed under the dash, Fig. 1-10. The unit recirculates the air within the passenger compartment to the evaporator. An integral system cools the incoming air from outside the car, and recirculates in-car air, as well.

Integral/manual temperature controls

An integral system combines the heater core and evaporator core inside one housing and shares the same fan. The air from outside the car, if so desired, is routed to the housing where it is cooled or heated and then distributed through the ducts. The controls are mounted on the dash, Fig. 1-11.

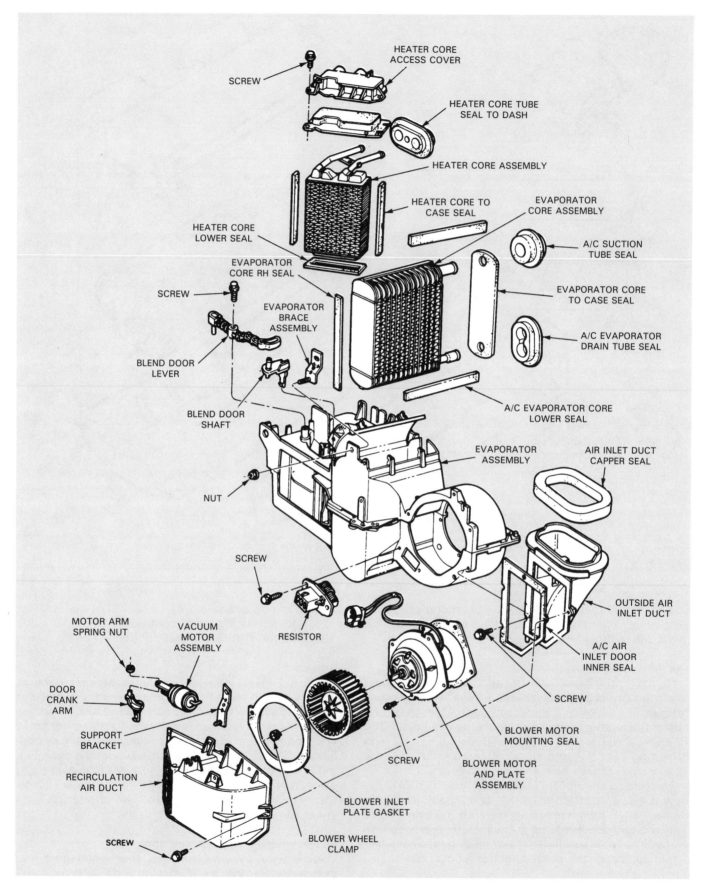

Fig. 1-4. Integral system combines heater core, evaporator core, and blower motor in one housing. (Ford)

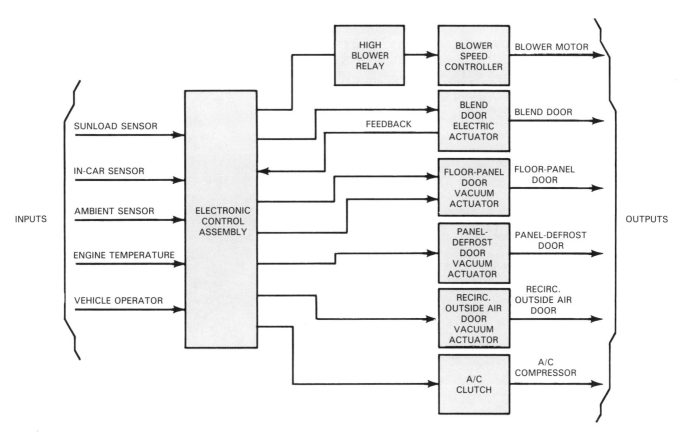

Fig. 1-5. With automatic temperature control, sensors provide input to computer. Computer then decides when to turn on air conditioner, which vacuum motors to actuate, and sets the blower motor speed. (Ford)

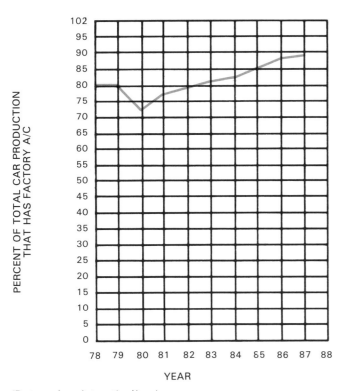

(Facts are from Automotive News)

Fig. 1-6. Approximately 90 percent of all cars made today roll off the assembly line with air conditioning.

MODE

The *mode selector* determines where the airflow will enter the passenger compartment. If the "heat" or "floor" position is chosen, 80 percent of the airflow enters the passenger compartment near the driver's feet while 20 percent is directed to the windshield. However, when the "defroster" is selected, 80 percent of the airflow is directed to the windshield while 20 percent is directed near the driver's feet. When the "panel" or "air conditioning" position is selected, the airflow comes through the dash panel. When the "mix" or "bi-level" is chosen, the airflow is routed to the dash panels and to the floor.

Temperature

A temperature blend-air door is controlled by an electric or vacuum motor or Bowden cable. This determines the temperature inside the passenger compartment.

A/C

When the MAX A/C mode is selected, outside air is blocked off by the outside/recir door because vacuum motor number three, Fig. 1-8B, has vacuum applied to it. Vacuum motor number one also has vacuum applied. This positions the panel/defrost door to block the airflow to the defroster outlets. Vacuum motor number two has no vacuum applied to it. This positions the floor/panel door to allow the airflow to the dash panel, while at the same time blocking the airflow to the floor

11

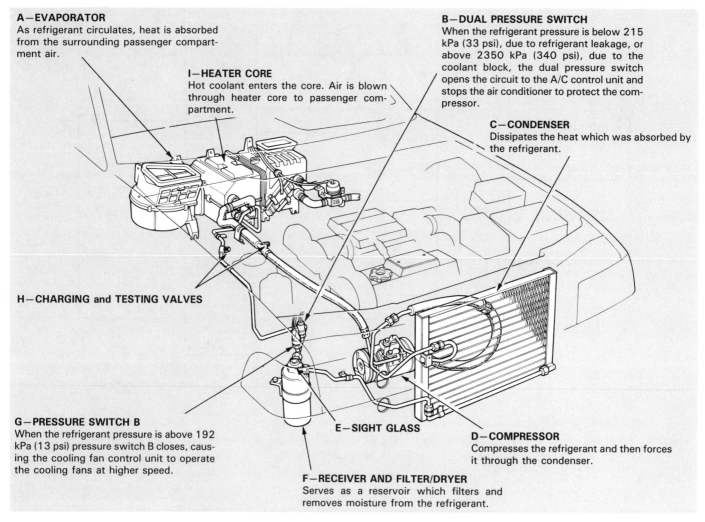

A—EVAPORATOR
As refrigerant circulates, heat is absorbed from the surrounding passenger compartment air.

I—HEATER CORE
Hot coolant enters the core. Air is blown through heater core to passenger compartment.

B—DUAL PRESSURE SWITCH
When the refrigerant pressure is below 215 kPa (33 psi), due to refrigerant leakage, or above 2350 kPa (340 psi), due to the coolant block, the dual pressure switch opens the circuit to the A/C control unit and stops the air conditioner to protect the compressor.

C—CONDENSER
Dissipates the heat which was absorbed by the refrigerant.

H—CHARGING and TESTING VALVES

G—PRESSURE SWITCH B
When the refrigerant pressure is above 192 kPa (13 psi) pressure switch B closes, causing the cooling fan control unit to operate the cooling fans at higher speed.

E—SIGHT GLASS

D—COMPRESSOR
Compresses the refrigerant and then forces it through the condenser.

F—RECEIVER AND FILTER/DRYER
Serves as a reservoir which filters and removes moisture from the refrigerant.

Fig. 1-7. Factory installed integral air conditioning system. Note the functions of the major parts.   (Honda)

outlets. The air inside the passenger compartment is then recirculated, when maximum cooling is desired on hot, humid days.

When the mode selector is moved off MAX A/C, some fresh air from the outside passes through the evaporator. This is because vacuum is no longer applied to vacuum motor number three. The outside/recirc door no longer blocks the outside air from entering the car. This setting is selected when maximum cooling is not needed.

Heat/defrost

When the temperature selector is at the extreme right, all airflow is routed through the heater core for maximum heating. A Bowden cable or motor positions the blend-air door to route all ambient air through the heater core. Motor number two positions the floor/panel door to direct the heated airflow to the floor and blocks it from going to the defroster outlets. No vacuum is applied at motor number one during the heat or defrost mode. When the defrost mode is selected, the floor/panel door blocks the airflow to the floor outlets.

Fan

The *fan* or blower motor creates an airflow past the evaporator and/or heater core and into the passenger

compartment. The higher the speed of the fan, the more air that can be heated or cooled. The higher fan speed also creates more noise, which some people find objectionable.

The speed of the fan is controlled at the dash. Current is then sent to the blower motor through a resistor, Fig. 1-12. The voltage out of the resistor determines the fan speed. This resistor is usually located on the outside of the evaporator/heater housing.

Integral/automatic temperature control

An integral automatic temperature control (ATC) system combines the evaporator and heater core in one housing. The temperature and mode is set by the driver and the system maintains that specific temperature inside the car.

For example, if the driver sets the temperature for 74 °F (23 °C) inside the car and the outside temperature is 35 °F (2 °C), Fig. 1-13, the heater automatically comes on and stays on until it is 74 °F (23 °C) inside the car. However, if the outside temperature should suddenly increase to 80 °F (27 °C), the heat is automatically turned off and the air conditioner is automatically turned on to maintain the temperature inside the car at 74 °F (23 °C). The system can also blend heated and cooled air to satisfy a desired temperature setting.

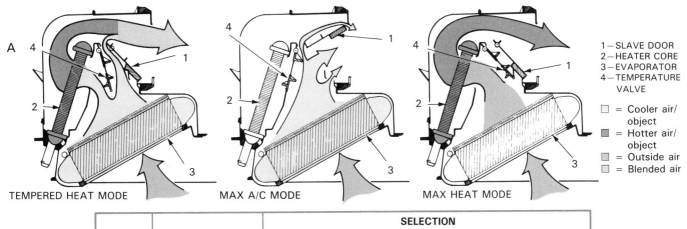

A

1 — SLAVE DOOR
2 — HEATER CORE
3 — EVAPORATOR
4 — TEMPERATURE VALVE

☐ = Cooler air/object
▨ = Hotter air/object
▨ = Outside air
▨ = Blended air

TEMPERED HEAT MODE   MAX A/C MODE   MAX HEAT MODE

VACUUM PORT	FUNCTION	SELECTION						
		OFF	DEFROST	FLOOR—PANEL (MIX)	FLOOR	FLOOR—PANEL (HI-LO)	PANEL	RECIRC.
1	Outside—Recirc.	V	NV	NV	NV	NV	NV	V
2	Full Floor	NV	NV	NV	V	NV	NV	NV
3	Floor—Panel (Partial)	NV	NV	V	V	V	NV	NV
4	Panel—Defrost	NV	NV	NV	NV	V	V	V
5	Source	V	V	V	V	V	V	V
6	Plugged	—	—	—	—	—	—	—

SYMBOLS
V — VACUUM
NV — NO VACUUM
PV — PARTIAL VACUUM

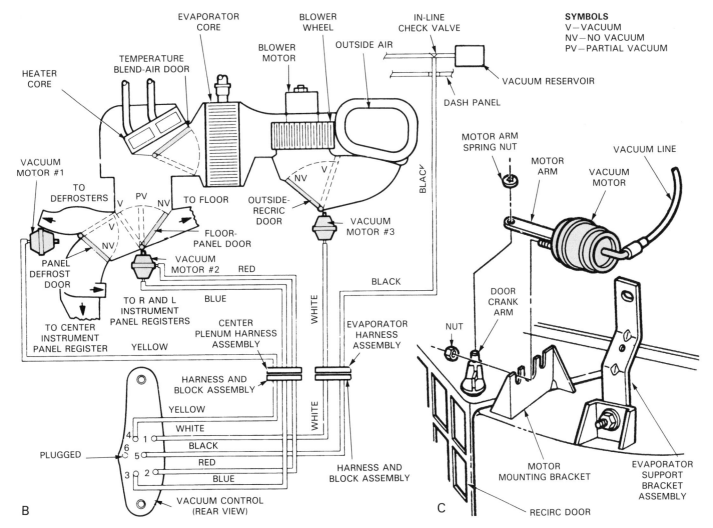

Fig. 1-8. Outside air flows into evaporator housing. A—Temperature blend-air door directs airflow. Note on tempered heat mode that air flows through evaporator before passing through heater core. This removes moisture from the air before it is heated. This action reduces windshield fogging. Also, the only time the air conditioner is not operating is during the maximum heat mode. B—Vacuum motors control the position of the mode doors, based on driver input. C—When vacuum is applied to vacuum motor, the motor arm pulls rearward, moving the door arm with it.   (Ford and Oldsmobile)

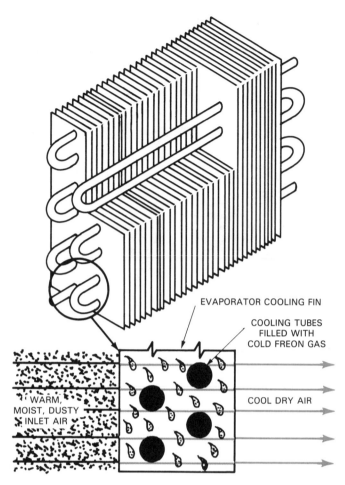

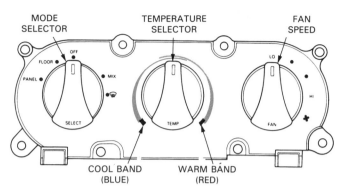

Fig. 1-11. Heater/air conditioning controls for a manual integral system are mounted on dash. Driver must adjust these controls to obtain desired temperature. With manual controls, the driver must readjust the settings if passenger compartment becomes too hot or too cold.

Fig. 1-9. Warm, moist air passes through the cooler evaporator core and the moisture condenses on it. This action dehumidifies the air before it enters the passenger compartment.

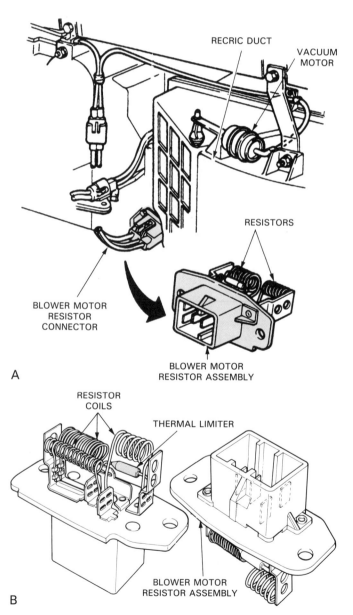

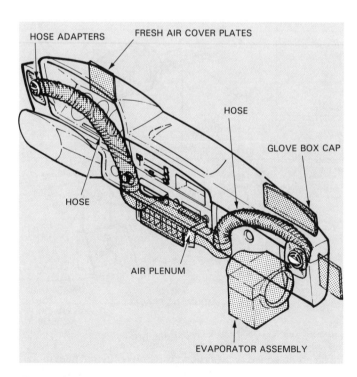

Fig. 1-10. Hang-on unit showing ductwork through dash panel. (Frigiking)

A

B

Fig. 1-12. Blower motor resistor. A—Located on evaporator/heater housing. B—Thermal limiter. Excessive heat, due to high amperage, causes circuit to open. (Ford)

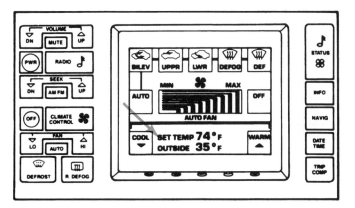

Fig. 1-13. With automatic temperature control, the driver sets the temperature and the system maintains that temperature. (Oldsmobile)

ATC operation

The automatic temperature control system contains sensors, actuators, and a computer in addition to the compressor, evaporator, and condenser. The temperature sensors, Fig. 1-14, send inside and outside temperature information to the computer. The computer then compares the temperatures and decides which actuators to turn on and off, Fig. 1-15. An *actuator* is an output device that is electrically controlled by the computer. This can be a vacuum motor that opens and closes temperature blend-air and mode doors, just like the manual system, to obtain the desired temperature and can automatically control the fan speed as well.

FORCED VENTILATION

Most cars today, regardless if a system is automatic or manual, have forced ventilation. When the windows are rolled up and the car is in motion, fresh air from the outside enters the car even if the temperature controls remain in the OFF position, Fig. 1-16. As fresh air enters the inlet, it passes through the evaporator housing, Fig. 1-17. The fresh air circulates through the entire car, Fig. 1-18. The fresh air then exits the car through pressure relief valves located in the door posts, Figs. 1-19 and 1-20.

TINTED GLASS

Tinted glass is used for all windows when air conditioning is installed at the automotive assembly plant. This reduces the amount of radiant heat that enters the car. Therefore, the tinted glass reduces the work load of the air conditioner. Windshields are gradient (gradual change) density tinted which allows the upper portion

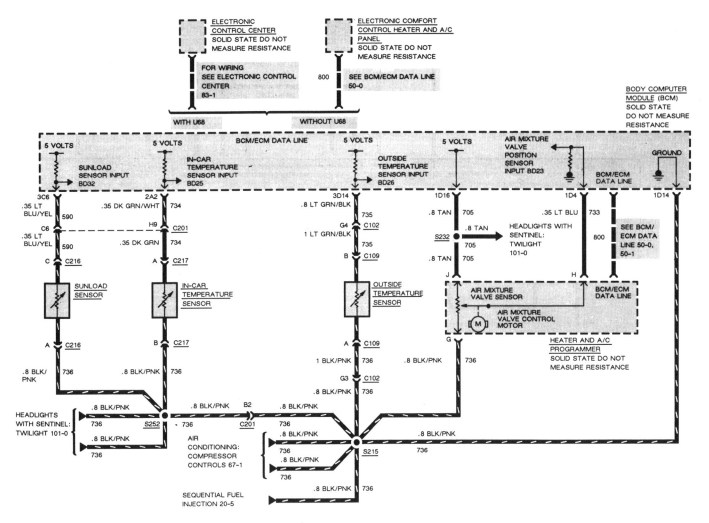

Fig. 1-14. Sensors in the automatic temperature control system provide input to the computer. (Oldsmobile)

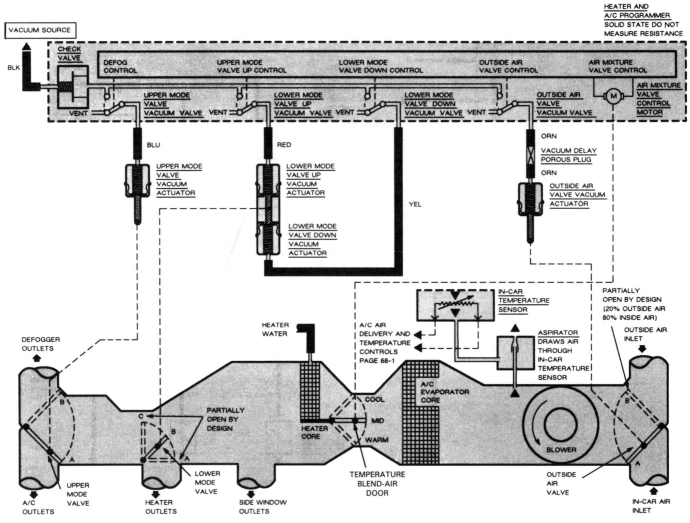

Fig. 1-15. Actuator opens and closes the temperature blend-air door while another actuator controls the fan speed. (Oldsmobile)

to have a darker tint than the rest of the windshield. This provides greater protection against radiant heat for areas that do not affect driver visibility.

GAS MILEAGE

When the air conditioner is turned on, the fuel economy is affected. This effect varies directly with the amount of horsepower the A/C compressor takes away from the engine to run the car. The more horsepower needed to run the compressor, the more fuel economy drops. Other factors that affect fuel mileage are:

1. An air conditioning system designed with a smaller condenser and/or evaporator than needed. If the evaporator is smaller than needed, not enough heat will be absorbed from within the passenger com-

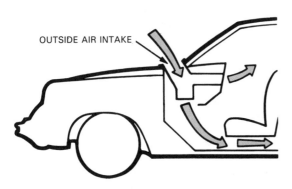

Fig. 1-16. Outside air enters the car below the windshield.

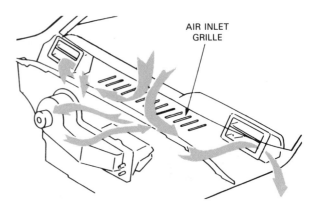

Fig. 1-17. After outside air enters through the inlet grille, it passes through evaporator housing. (Oldsmobile)

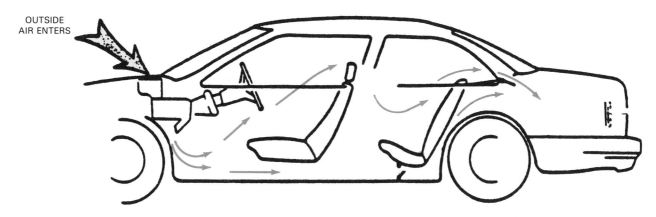

Fig. 1-18. After outside air passes through evaporator housing, it circulates through the entire car.

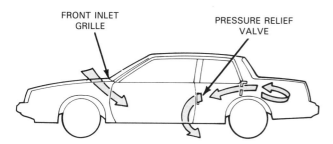

Fig. 1-19. Outside air exits through a pressure-relief valve located at each front door post on two-door models and rear door posts on four-door models. (Oldsmobile)

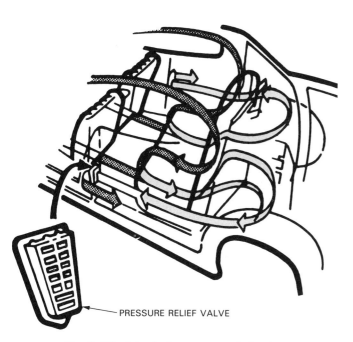

Fig. 1-20. A typical pressure relief valve.

partment. If the condenser is smaller than needed, it will not be able to dissipate the heat picked up from within the passenger compartment. Either condition will cause the air conditioning system to work harder and cause a drop in fuel economy.

2. Engine size. The percentage of horsepower the compressor "steals" from a large engine is less than from a small engine. For example, an air conditioning system can require eight horsepower at high speeds. With a small four-cylinder engine that can only put out a maximum of 100 horsepower, the air conditioner "absorbs" approximately eight percent of the total available horsepower. However, with a large V-8 engine that produces 300 horsepower, the air conditioner steals only about two and one-half percent of the total available horsepower. Therefore, an air conditioning system has less effect on fuel economy and power of a large engine.

3. Area of glass. A vehicle that has a large square footage of windows is much harder to keep cool. This means the air conditioner has to work harder and causes a drop in fuel mileage.

SUMMARY

Air conditioning not only cools the air within the passenger compartment, but controls the humidity and cleans the air. Factory installed air conditioning systems today are integrated, which means the evaporator and heater core are combined in one housing. Hang-on units have the evaporator in a separate location from the heater core.

Air conditioning controls can be manual or automatic. Vacuum motors open or close doors, depending on driver selection. Automatic temperature controls include a computer that controls the actuator/transducers based on information from the inside and outside temperature sensors, and a power servo that controls the fan speed.

Air conditioning may be affecting the environment, according to some scientists. When the chlorine from the refrigerant used in cars, R-12, enters the atmosphere, it may affect the ozone layer. Because of this much effort is being expended to develop an ozone-friendly substitute for R-12. Despite these facts, more cars than ever come equipped with air conditioning.

KNOW THESE TERMS

Air conditioning, Evaporative coolers, Hang-on units, Integrated heating and cooling system, Automatic temperature control. Temperature blend-air door, Humidity, Mode selector, Actuator, Fan.

17

REVIEW QUESTIONS — CHAPTER 1

1. Name the two types of air conditioning systems.
2. Humidity control is achieved by:
   a. Moisture removal at the condenser.
   b. Trapping the moisture in the drier.
   c. Moisture condensing on the coil surface of the evaporator.
3. Aftermarket air conditioning systems are of the recirculating type. True or false?
4. The load on the air conditioning system is affected by:
   a. Humidity.
   b. Ambient air temperature.
   c. Amount of glass area.
   d. All of the above.
5. Explain the important differences between manual and automatic temperature control.
6. One of the early attempts at air conditioning in an automobile consisted of an _____ cooler in the car window.
7. With the air conditioner in operation, the fuel economy _____.
8. What does ATC mean?
9. List four advantages of automotive air conditioning.
10. Explain the meaning of recirculating air conditioning.
11. Tinted glass is used to:
    a. Match the color of the car.
    b. Reduce glare.
    c. Increase radiant heat.
    d. Decrease radiant heat.
12. List the factors affecting fuel economy with the a/c in operation.
13. Reducing the _____ of air conditioning components reduces fuel consumption.
14. Air filters are used to filter the air flow from air conditioning systems. True or false?
15. The desired outlet air temperature of an integrated system is controlled by:
    a. Condenser pressure.
    b. Evaporator.
    c. Heater.
    d. Blend-air door.
16. Fully integrated heating and air conditioning systems share common _____.

SPECIAL SERVICE TOOLS AND EQUIPMENT

2

After studying this chapter, you will be able to:
• Identify the various special tools.
• Describe the purpose of the different special tools.
• Explain various methods of refrigerant leak detection.
• List the different performance test equipment and describe its purpose.

INTRODUCTION

Automotive technicians must furnish their own hand tools and some power tools. A person specializing in automotive air conditioning work needs special tools above and beyond the standard ratchets, sockets, wrenches, screwdrivers, and pliers, Fig. 2-1. Some shops purchase the special tools needed for air conditioning work while others insist the technician purchase them. Every air conditioning system has a slightly different design of the same part. This means a different special tool may be needed for servicing the same type of part on various systems. Special tools are needed when working on air conditioning compressors.

SNAP-RING PLIERS

External and internal *snap-ring pliers* are needed to remove and/or install snap rings, Fig. 2-2. Snap rings are found in the A/C clutch and compressor. Snap rings are made of spring steel and therefore can be spread apart. A snap ring is a horseshoe or circular shaped washer with tiny holes at each end to accept pliers. When mounted around a shaft to hold it in place, they are called external snap rings. However, when positioned inside a cylinder-like object to retain other items within, they are called internal snap rings.

SEAL TOOLS

Seal tools are required to remove and install compressor shaft seals. Fig. 2-3 illustrates the seal-seat

Fig. 2-1. Special tools are needed when working on automotive air conditioning systems. (Snap-on Tools)

remover and installer in use. Once the snap ring is removed, the seal-seat installer grabs the lip of the seat. The tool is then pulled to bring the seat out of the compressor so that the seal can be removed.

When the notches in the seal remover/installer align with the tangs of the seal assembly, rotating the tool slightly locks it to the assembly. This allows the seal assembly to be pulled out of the compressor.

FLARE-NUT WRENCH

Tubing flare nuts require the use of a flare-nut wrench, Fig. 2-4. The *flare-nut wrench* is a box-end wrench with

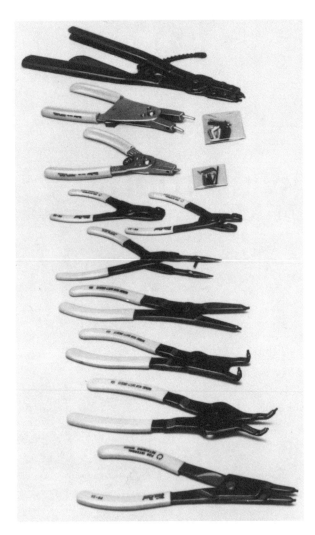

Fig. 2-2. An assortment of snap-ring pliers. (Snap-on)

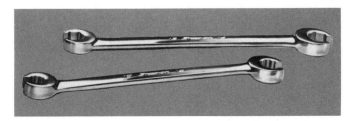

Fig. 2-4. Flare-nut wrenches are used on line fittings. (Snap-on)

a section removed allowing the wrench to slip over tubing so it can fit on the hex nut. Open-end wrenches should not be used to remove flare nuts because they may slip off and round the hex. A crowfoot wrench is a flare-nut wrench that must be attached to a ratchet, Fig. 2-5.

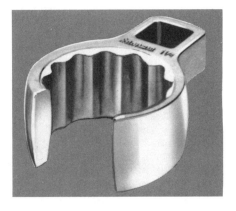

Fig. 2-5. Crowfoot wrench is usually used with torque wrench to torque line fittings to specification. (Snap-on)

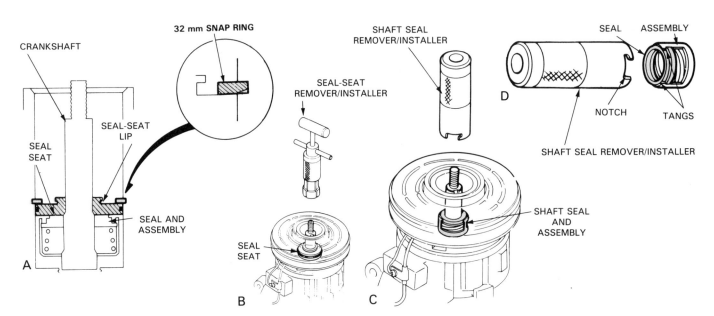

Fig. 2-3. A seal-seat remover/installer and seal assembly remover/installer are both needed. A—After removing the snap ring, the seal seat must be removed to gain access to the seal assembly. Note the lip on the seal seat. B—The seal-seat remover/installer must grab the lip of the seal seat so it can be extracted. C—The seal assembly requires the use of another tool. D—The notches in the tool must align with the tangs of the seal assembly. The tool is then rotated to lock the two together. (Honda)

SERVICE VALVE RATCHET AND WRENCH

Air conditioning compressor service valves, when used, are usually square and require a special wrench to turn them. Fig. 2-6 shows this tool which usually has a ratchet at one end and a fixed square opening at the other end. The fixed end should be used when "cracking" (slightly opening) the service valve.

ORIFICE TUBE SERVICE TOOL

A special tool is required to remove and install fixed orifice tubes. Fig. 2-7 shows this tool being used to remove an orifice tube. Fig. 2-8 shows the tool installing the orifice tube.

TORQUE WRENCH

Torque wrenches, Fig. 2-9, are used to ensure proper tightness of fittings and fasteners. If a fastener or fitting is too loose, a leak could develop. If a fastener is too tight, it could strip the threads of the fastener or

damage the seal. The wrenches are calibrated in either in. lbs. or ft. lbs., (kg-cm or kg-m) in order to tighten fasteners and line fittings to manufacturer's specifications. Line fittings are torqued by using a torque wrench and a flare nut wrench.

OTHER SPECIAL TOOLS

Special air conditioning tools are designed for particular car models, Fig. 2-10. These special tools are shown and described in the shop manuals for the individual car models.

AIR CONDITIONING SYSTEM LEAK DETECTORS

Flame leak detector

The *halide leak detector* is a gas-burning torch that is available in several different sizes and provides an accurate, simple method of leak detection. The torch consists of a propane tank and a special burner incorporating a valve, a pick-up tube, a reaction plate and chimney, Fig. 2-11. In operation, the refrigerant, when burned in

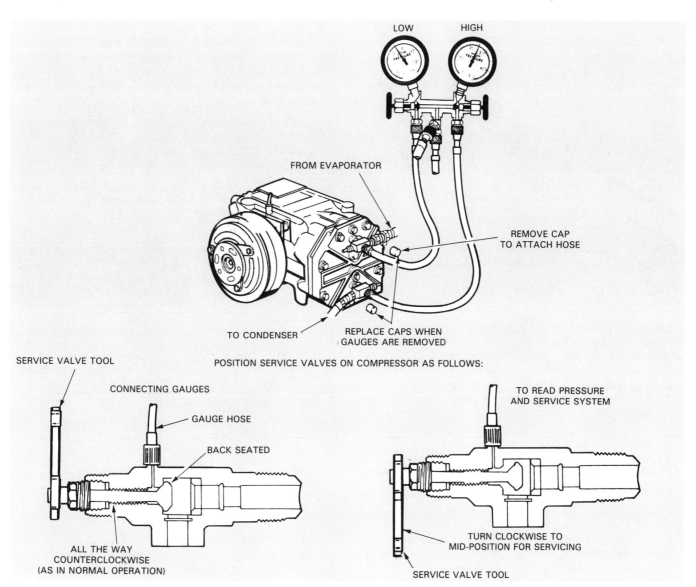

Fig. 2-6. Some service valve stems are square and require a wrench with a square opening.

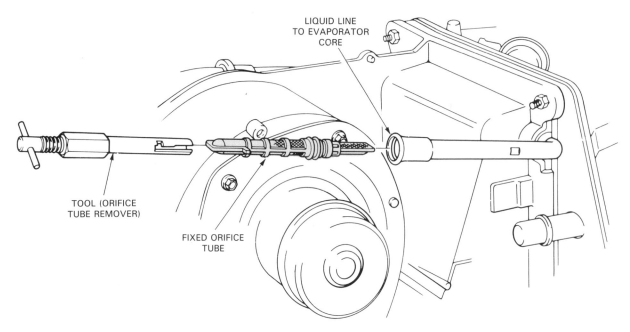

Fig. 2-7. Orifice tube remover/installer must be twisted as it is pulled to remove orifice tube.   (Ford)

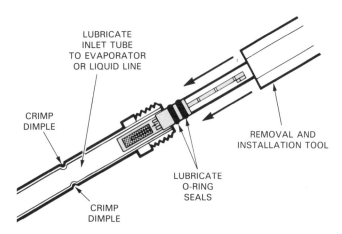

Fig. 2-8. Push orifice tube in place with the remover/installer.
(Ford)

a controlled flame over a heated copper plate, will cause the flame to change color. The color of the flame changes in proportion to the size of the leak, Fig. 2-12.
1. Blue flame indicates no leak.
2. Yellow-green flame indicates a small leak.
3. Bright blue-purple flame indicates a large leak.
4. Solid yellow flame indicates a malfunction in the leak detector caused by insufficient air being aspirated, or a dirty reaction plate.

Prior to operating the propane leak detector, it is necessary to observe the following safety precautions:

1. Do not inhale fumes produced by the detector. They are a poisonous gas (phosgene).
2. Do not use detector near carburetor or battery. Keep a fire extinguisher close at hand.
3. Keep flame from contacting any parts which can be easily damaged by heat.
4. Use in a well-ventilated area.

To operate torch, open the valve until a slight hiss of gas is heard. Then, light the gas at the chimney opening. Adjust the flame to the desired volume. A pale-blue flame just touching the reaction plate is best for detect-

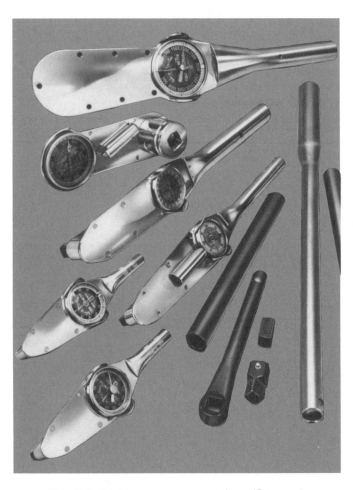

Fig. 2-9. Dial-type torque wrenches. (Snap-on)

22

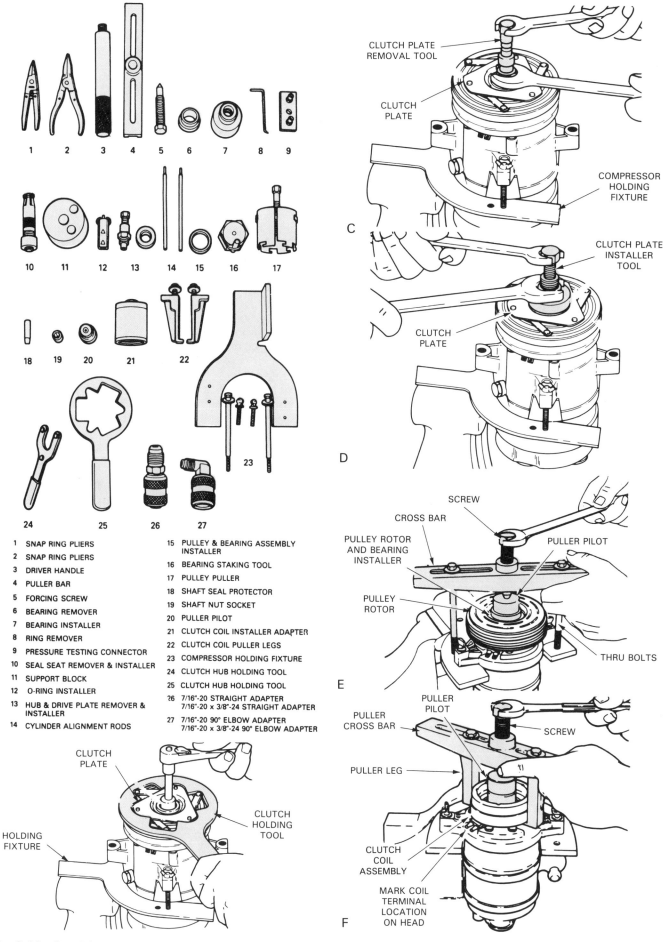

C — CLUTCH PLATE REMOVAL TOOL

CLUTCH PLATE

COMPRESSOR HOLDING FIXTURE

D — CLUTCH PLATE INSTALLER TOOL

CLUTCH PLATE

A

1 SNAP RING PLIERS
2 SNAP RING PLIERS
3 DRIVER HANDLE
4 PULLER BAR
5 FORCING SCREW
6 BEARING REMOVER
7 BEARING INSTALLER
8 RING REMOVER
9 PRESSURE TESTING CONNECTOR
10 SEAL SEAT REMOVER & INSTALLER
11 SUPPORT BLOCK
12 O-RING INSTALLER
13 HUB & DRIVE PLATE REMOVER & INSTALLER
14 CYLINDER ALIGNMENT RODS

15 PULLEY & BEARING ASSEMBLY INSTALLER
16 BEARING STAKING TOOL
17 PULLEY PULLER
18 SHAFT SEAL PROTECTOR
19 SHAFT NUT SOCKET
20 PULLER PILOT
21 CLUTCH COIL INSTALLER ADAPTER
22 CLUTCH COIL PULLER LEGS
23 COMPRESSOR HOLDING FIXTURE
24 CLUTCH HUB HOLDING TOOL
25 CLUTCH HUB HOLDING TOOL
26 7/16"-20 STRAIGHT ADAPTER
   7/16"-20 x 3/8"-24 STRAIGHT ADAPTER
27 7/16"-20 90° ELBOW ADAPTER
   7/16"-20 x 3/8"-24 90° ELBOW ADAPTER

B — CLUTCH PLATE

HOLDING FIXTURE

CLUTCH HOLDING TOOL

E — SCREW

CROSS BAR

PULLEY ROTOR AND BEARING INSTALLER

PULLER PILOT

PULLEY ROTOR

THRU BOLTS

F — PULLER PILOT

PULLER CROSS BAR

SCREW

PULLER LEG

CLUTCH COIL ASSEMBLY

MARK COIL TERMINAL LOCATION ON HEAD

Fig. 2-10. Special tools vary from one car model to another. A—Set of special tools needed to work on a specific compressor. B—Clutch holding tool prevents clutch from turning while removing nut. C—Clutch plate removal tool can now be positioned in place. D—Clutch plate is installed with the use of installer. E—Clutch pulley must be removed from compressor with a special puller and fixtures. F—Same tool is used to remove/install coil.   (Oldsmobile)

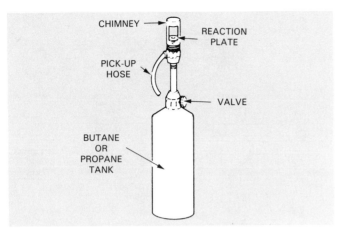

Fig. 2-11. Halide detector flame shows if refrigerant is leaking. Do not use it near fuel system or battery.   (Ford)

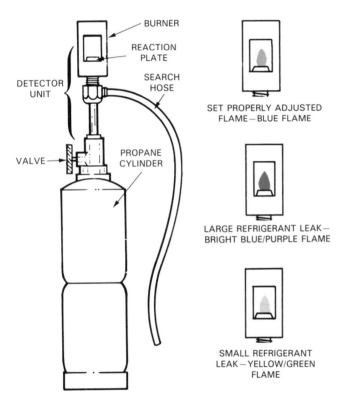

Fig. 2-12. The color of the flame indicates the size of the leak. (Volkswagon)

ing leaks. The reactor will be ready for use when it becomes red hot.

Hold the torch in an upright position. Inspect for leaks by slowly moving the pick-up hose around all connections and points of possible leakage. It is important to move the pick-up hose slowly to accurately pinpoint the leak. Since refrigerant is heavier than air, the leak will be more apparent at the underside of the line fittings.

Electronic leak detectors

The electronic leak detector, Fig. 2-13, is the most widely used as it is the safest and most accurate method of locating even the smallest of refrigerant leaks. It is capable of detecting leaks with a rate as low as one-half

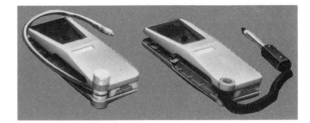

Fig. 2-13. Electronic leak detectors.   (Snap-on)

ounce of refrigerant per year. It is important that the leak detector be calibrated and/or sensitivity adjusted before using. Manufacturer's instructions must be followed to the letter for setting sensitivity. The electronic detector may use a flashing light and/or a loud, steady audible signal when a large leak is found, and a fast-ticking sound for small leaks. The first step in operating is to turn it on and calibrate to the manufacturer's instructions. This involves setting the flashing light or ticking rate, using a calibrated sample. In operation, the probe, Fig. 2-14, should be moved slowly, approximately one inch per second. Remember that the refrigerant is heavier than air and the probing should be directly below the potential leak areas. The electronic detector is recommended over all other types of detectors because of safety and accuracy.

Dye-type leak detector

The use of a *leak-detecting dye* involves adding a colored dye to the compressor oil. This method is not recommended, because of the following reasons:
1. A leak can exist without any oil leakage.
2. The chemical stability of the refrigerant may be altered or the dye may curdle and block the inlet screen in the expansion valve or orifice tube.

Visual inspection

Some leaks may be quite obvious. When refrigerant leaks at the condenser, a fitting, or the compressor for

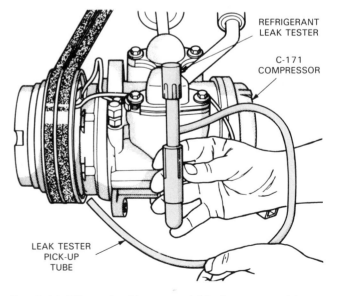

Fig. 2-14. When checking potential leak areas, position test probe or tube at lowest point of part being checked.

a length of time, dirt usually gathers at this point. The refrigerant also carries the refrigerant oil as it circulates through the A/C system. When a leak occurs, the oil sometimes escapes. The oil collects at the point of the leak. Dirt then collects on the oil, therefore, a visual inspection will detect some leaks.

Liquid bubble test

If either torch or electric detectors are not available, the simplest leak test method involves brushing a soapy liquid solution over a suspected leak area. Watch for the bubbles that indicate a leak is present. NOTE: Always leak test after making repairs.

SAFETY TOOLS AND EQUIPMENT

Safety glasses

Safety glasses or safety goggles, Fig. 2-15, provide eye protection and must be worn whenever working on air conditioning systems. Eye protection must be used to prevent refrigerant from contacting the eyeball, resulting in injury of the possible loss of sight. Safety glasses also protect the eyes from dirt and contamination blown by the engine fan.

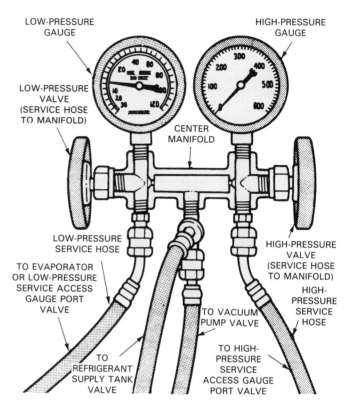

Fig. 2-16. Manifold gauge set is needed to troubleshoot the a/c system. (Ford)

Fig. 2-15. Wear safety glasses when using refrigerant.

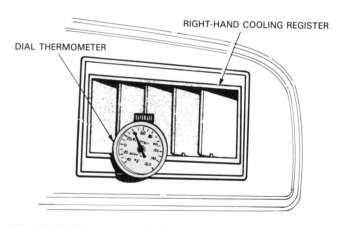

Fig. 2-17. Thermometer is placed at dash register to evaluate air conditioning system performance.

Protective gloves and clothing

To protect the skin from contacting the refrigerant, resulting in frostbite, protective clothing must be worn. Gloves and long sleeved shirts, buttoned at the collar, provide ample protection.

PERFORMANCE TEST TOOLS AND EQUIPMENT

Tools used in testing the overall system performance include the manifold gauge set, Fig. 2-16, and thermometer, Fig. 2-17. Referring to Fig. 2-16, note the low-pressure gauge and valve on one side of the manifold and the high-pressure gauge and valve on the other side. The test hoses and their functions are also identified.

The *hygrometer* or *psychrometer,* Fig. 2-18, is a tool

for measuring relative humidity of the ambient air. High humidity and evaporator control malfunction are factors in reducing system cooling performance, resulting in temperature loss of A/C cooling or evaporator freeze-up. To evaluate air conditioning performance, graphs of the relationship between system pressure, humidity, ambient air temperature, and discharge air temperature can be found in the service manuals for the given system.

Vacuum pump

The *vacuum pump,* Fig. 2-19, is used to remove air and moisture from the air conditioning system during evacuation. In use, the vacuum pump is connected to the system with a charging station or manifold gauge.

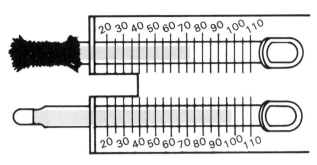

WET BULB 72 °F.

DRY BULB 98 °F.

Fig. 2-18. Relative humidity affects air conditioning performance and must be checked prior to its evaluation. (Chrysler)

Fig. 2-19. Vacuum pumps. They are used to evacuate moisture from A/C system. (Snap-on)

Run the vacuum pump until the pressure gauge reads as close to 30 in. Hg as possible.

If a steady gauge reading, after shutdown, cannot be maintained, there is a leak in the system that first must be repaired before going any farther. Let the pump run for 30 minutes after the reading is obtained. This will boil all moisture out of the system, since the vacuum has lowered the pressure, causing the water to boil at a lower temperature. Shut off the pump and close the hand valves. The pump can be removed and the system is ready for recharge.

Dispensing valve

The *dispensing valve* is a shutoff valve that has a special relief and flow check feature. The purpose of this valve is to prevent explosive pressures from reaching the R-12 supply can if the dispensing hose is inadvertently connected to the high pressure side of the air conditioning system.

To use the dispensing valve, engage the tabs on the retainer lip of the R-12 can top, Fig. 2-20. Be sure the valve is closed before screwing the valve assembly down to the container top. Screw the manifold gauge center hose to the dispensing valve, Fig. 2-21. When the container empties, close the valve and remove the container.

Portable charging station

The *portable charging station* is designed for mobility, Fig. 2-22. It is used for charging A/C systems. It has a manifold gauge set, vacuum pump, heater (for refrigerant), and a charging cylinder.

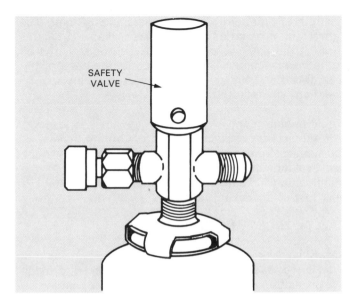

Fig. 2-20. Safety-dispensing valve prevents high-pressure R-12 from A/C system flowing into can.

Portable service center

The *portable service center,* Fig. 2-23, is used to perform system troubleshooting, system servicing, and system maintenance tests.

SUMMARY

Air conditioning service hand tools are required to provide the mechanic with an efficient means to service and repair an A/C system. With proper use of these tools, servicing can be performed in the least amount of time, with maximum safety, by the mechanic.

Due to the properties of R-12 refrigerant, the mechanic must wear safety goggles or glasses, gloves, and shirts with long sleeves. Work should be done in a well lighted and ventilated area. Along with these precautions, first aid supplies should be readily available.

A leak detection device must be used before and after servicing any system to ensure the system is properly sealed.

System performance is determined by measuring temperatures and pressures. Temperatures and pressures measured can be compared to specific manufacturer's charts and tables for system diagnosis.

Evacuating, charging, and purging servicing equipment is necessary to bring an A/C system to proper refrigerant and oil levels.

KNOW THESE TERMS

Snap-ring pliers, Seal tools, Flare-nut wrench, Torque wrench, Halide leak detector, Leak-detecting dye, Safety glasses, Hygrometer or psychrometer, Vacuum pump, Dispensing valve, Portable charging station, Portable service center.

REVIEW QUESTIONS—CHAPTER 2

1. Name the three most important items of apparel to be worn when servicing an automotive air conditioning system.

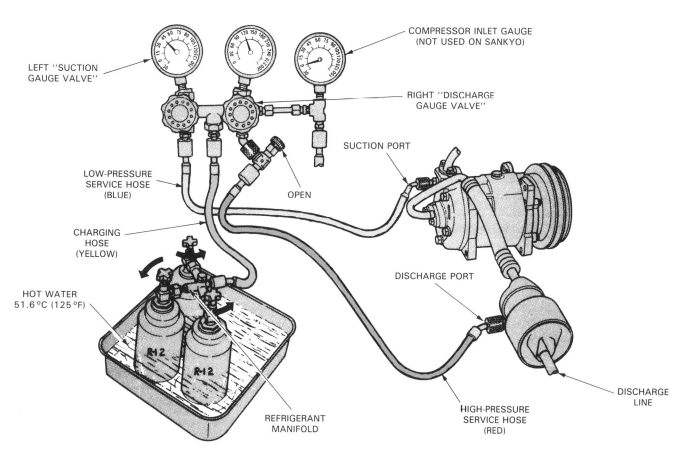

LEFT "SUCTION GAUGE VALVE"

COMPRESSOR INLET GAUGE (NOT USED ON SANKYO)

RIGHT "DISCHARGE GAUGE VALVE"

SUCTION PORT

LOW-PRESSURE SERVICE HOSE (BLUE)

OPEN

CHARGING HOSE (YELLOW)

DISCHARGE PORT

HOT WATER 51.6 °C (125 °F)

R-12

R-12

DISCHARGE LINE

REFRIGERANT MANIFOLD

HIGH-PRESSURE SERVICE HOSE (RED)

Fig. 2-21. The center or yellow hose connects the gauges to the supply of refrigerant. The blue hose connects to the low-pressure side of the A/C system while the red hose connects to its high-pressure side.   (Chrysler)

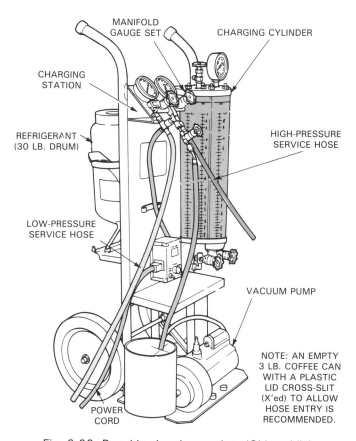

MANIFOLD GAUGE SET

CHARGING CYLINDER

CHARGING STATION

REFRIGERANT (30 LB. DRUM)

HIGH-PRESSURE SERVICE HOSE

LOW-PRESSURE SERVICE HOSE

VACUUM PUMP

NOTE: AN EMPTY 3 LB. COFFEE CAN WITH A PLASTIC LID CROSS-SLIT (X'ed) TO ALLOW HOSE ENTRY IS RECOMMENDED.

POWER CORD

Fig. 2-22. Portable charging station. (Oldsmobile)

Fig. 2-23. Portable air conditioning service center. (Snap-on)

2. The vacuum pump is used for:
   a. Operating the pressure gauge set.
   b. Detecting a refrigerant leak.
   c. Charging an air conditioning system.
   d. Evacuating an air conditioning system.
3. Operation of the halide leak detector is based on:
   a. Electronic circuit.
   b. Hydraulic pressure.
   c. Vacuum-pressure.
   d. Flame combustion.
4. Air conditioning service tools should be used to minimize damage to _____ and injury to _____.

5. Describe a flare-nut wrench and how it is used.
6. A service valve ratchet wrench has a fixed square socket for ''cracking'' the valve. True or false?
7. Explain the difference between a portable charging station and a portable service center.
8. A hygrometer or psychrometer is used to measure _____.
9. In an emergency, _____ water can be used to find a refrigerant leak.
10. List the three items found on a portable charging station.

3

PHYSICS FOR HEATING AND AIR CONDITIONING

After studying this chapter, you will be able to:
* *Explain the natural laws that affect the operation of a heating and air conditioning system.*
* *Describe the three states of matter.*
* *Define the terms "hot" and "cold."*
* *Summarize the three methods of heat transfer.*
* *Compare the different forms of heat.*
* *Use conventional and metric temperature scales.*
* *Explain the different types of pressure and vacuum measurements.*
* *Describe the effect of pressure on gases, liquids, and solids.*
* Explain the effect of humidity on an air conditioning system.

INTRODUCTION

This chapter explains the underlying principles that govern the operation of a heating and air conditioning system. It discusses the physical laws of nature and effects that allow the passenger compartment to be cooled and heated. As a result, you will learn about the basic terms that will be used throughout the rest of this text.

LAWS OF NATURE

It is very important to have a thorough knowledge of the laws of nature that govern our universe. These laws or principles will help you understand why things happen as they do in a refrigeration system. This will enable you to troubleshoot tough problems in the field.

Physical states

A substance can exist in one of three states. The state of the substance depends on the temperature and pressure it is exposed to and the heat content of the substance. The three states of a substance are:
1. Solid (for example, ice).
2. Liquid (for example, water).
3. Vapor (for example, steam).

Solid

A *solid* is defined as a substance that maintains its shape without the aid of a container that must be supported by an upward force. For example, an ice cube no longer needs its tray (container) when frozen. When it is placed on a table top, the table is the upward force that supports the ice cube.

Liquid

A *liquid* is defined as a substance that takes the shape of its container and seeks its own level. For example, when a liquid is placed in a U-shaped tube, the liquid is at the same height on each side of the "U." Also, a liquid can be pressurized, but it cannot be compressed. This is from Pascal's Law which states that "pressure applied upon a confined fluid is transmitted equally and in all directions." A liquid that remains in an uncovered container will eventually evaporate (turn into a vapor).

Vapor

A *vapor* (gas) is defined as a substance that must be placed in a sealed container to prevent it from escaping into the atmosphere. By placing it in a sealed container, a vapor can be pressurized and compressed. This fact comes from Boyle's Law which states "when the temperature is constant, the volume of the gas varies inversely to the pressure." This means when pressure is applied to a gas, the volume of the gas decreases; when the volume of gas increases, less pressure is exerted on its container.

HEAT OF COMPRESSION

Compressing a vapor causes the temperature of the gas to increase. This is because the number of gas molecules remains the same, but the space they occupy decreases. The molecules are forced to "collide" with each other faster because of the reduced distance they must travel. This results in a chain reaction, Fig. 3-1.

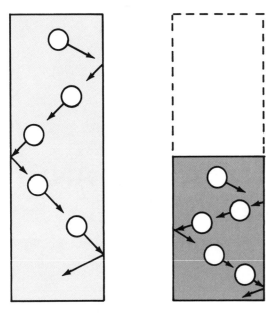

Fig. 3-1. Molecules travel less distance when compressed. This causes the speed of molecules to increase and, thus, the temperature and pressure of the gas to increase.

On the other hand, by increasing the temperature on a sealed container of a vapor (gas), the pressure inside the container increases. It is for this reason that aerosol cans are to be kept away from heat or they will explode. Any substance can be made into a solid, liquid, or a vapor.

CHANGE OF STATE

To learn how an air conditioning system works, you must understand how a substance changes state. A change of state can be from a:
1. Solid to a liquid.
2. Liquid to a vapor.
3. Vapor to a liquid.
4. Liquid to a solid.

Effects of heat

When heat is applied to any substance, the molecules of that substance speed up. The faster the molecules move, the easier it is for a substance to change state. For example, heating ice (a solid) at any temperature above 32 °F (0 °C) causes it to melt and turn into water (a liquid). Heating water after it reaches 212 °F (100 °C) causes the water to boil. The water then changes from a liquid to a vapor (steam), Fig. 3-2. When the heat is removed and the vapor cooled, the vapor condenses back into a liquid. Reducing the temperature on a liquid causes it to turn into a solid. However, further reduction in temperature will not have an effect on a solid. During a change of state, large amounts of heat are absorbed by the substance or released into the atmosphere. By varying the pressure, the boiling point of a liquid can be raised or lowered.

Effects of pressure

The ease in which a liquid evaporates depends on the pressure applied to it. When water is placed in a sealed

Fig. 3-2. The three states of water. When ice is heated, it turns into water. Further heating causes the water to turn into a gas or vapor.

container and pressurized, the water boils at a temperature higher than 212 °F (100 °C). The boiling temperature depends on the amount of pressure; the greater the pressure, the higher the boiling point. The higher pressure decreases the speed at which the molecules move.

On the other hand, if water is placed in a sealed container and the air pumped out to create a vacuum, the water would boil at a temperature that is lower than 212 °F (100 °C). The boiling point depends on the amount of vacuum; the greater the vacuum, the lower the boiling point. It is possible to boil water at room temperature (72 °F) in a vacuum. Therefore, the less pressure that is placed on a liquid, the easier it is to turn it into a vapor.

HUMIDITY

Humidity is the water vapor or moisture in the air. The amount of humidity depends on the temperature. When the weather is hot, the air can hold more moisture than when it is cold. Humidity is measured in terms of the amount of water the air can hold, and is expressed as a percentage. A relative humidity of 75 percent means the air can hold an additional 25 percent water vapor before it is saturated (100 percent relative humidity).

Effects of humidity

Before an air conditioner can be fully effective in transferring heat from the inside of a car, moisture in the air is reduced. It is for this reason the air conditioning system works harder on a humid day and is less effective.

As a liquid evaporates, there is a temperature reduction. For example, after you leave a swimming pool on a hot day, you immediately feel cooler than before you entered the pool. It is the water evaporating from your skin that provides the cooling effect. However, if it is an extremely humid day, it is not easy for the water to evaporate because the air already contains a large amount of water vapor. Therefore, there is less cooling effect on a humid day.

Wet bulb temperature

The relative humidity is measured with a wet bulb or *psychrometer.* A wet cloth sock is placed over the bulb of a thermometer. As the psychrometer spins, the wet bulb is cooled by evaporation. When the humidity is low, it registers a lower temperature than a dry bulb thermometer. When humidity is high, there is less evaporation, and therefore, less of a cooling effect. The temperature difference is less between the wet and dry bulb. When there is no difference, or the readings are the same, humidity is 100 percent (the air is saturated with water vapor).

HEAT

All substances are composed of molecules. A *molecule* is the smallest possible particle of material that retains the properties of that material. Molecules are constantly in motion in all substances. Adding heat to a substance increases the speed of the molecules. The speed of the molecules determines whether the substance is a solid, liquid, or a gas. Temperature is an indication of the speed of the molecules.

When mechanical work is done, heat is produced. For example, mechanical work done by the A/C compressor results in a temperature rise. Therefore, mechanical energy is transformed into heat energy.

HEAT TRANSFER

Heat can be transferred any one of three ways. They are:

1. Conduction.
2. Convection.
3. Radiation.

Sometimes one, two, or all three methods may apply in a situation.

Conduction

Conduction is when there is direct contact with the heat, which is then transferred from one molecule to the next, Fig. 3-3. Some components of an air conditioning system are made of materials (aluminum) that are excellent conductors of heat. This allows the heat to readily transfer to the refrigerant.

Convection

Convection is when heat is transferred by circulation of a liquid or a gas. The circulation is caused by changes in the density of the liquid or gas. For example, warm air is less dense than cold air. Therefore, the warm air rises while the cold air sinks, Fig. 3-4. The same is true for a liquid.

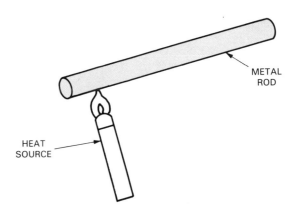

Fig. 3-3. Heating by conduction. Flame is in direct contact with the metal rod.

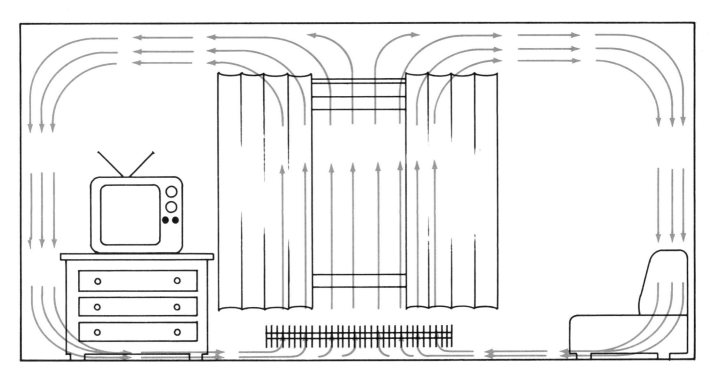

Fig. 3-4. Heating by convection. Hot air rises. As the hot air is cooled, it sinks to the floor, where it is again heated.

Radiation

Radiation is when heat is transmitted through electromagnetic waves or rays. Radiation is the process by which heat from the sun reaches the earth. All objects contain heat and give off some radiant energy. When the radiation wave strikes an object, the wave is either reflected or absorbed by the object. Light colors or shiny surfaces reflect the rays. However, dark colors and dull surfaces absorb the rays. This means any object can be heated by another object without contacting one another, Fig. 3-5. It is for this reason that a light-colored car is easier to cool than a dark-colored car.

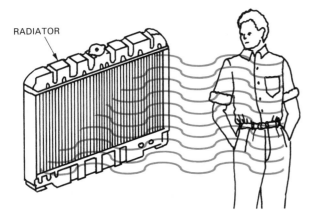

Fig. 3-5. Heating by radiation. Invisible heat waves radiate outward from the heat source. Heat can be felt when standing near, but not touching, the heat source.

COLD

Cold is the absence of heat. Heat, as a form of energy, cannot be destroyed. Cold is not something that is produced.

Air conditioning is the process of transferring heat from one place to another. For example, when there are two objects of different temperatures either in direct contact or near each other, the cooler of the two objects increases its temperature as it absorbs heat from the hotter object. While this happens, the hotter of the two objects decreases its temperature.

Direction of travel

Heat always travels from a hotter object to a cooler object. An example of this can be observed when a spoon is placed in a cup of hot coffee. Heat flows from the hot coffee to the cooler spoon until the spoon approaches the temperature of the coffee. The fast moving molecules of the hot coffee impart some of their energy to the slower moving molecules in the cooler spoon. Once the molecules of the spoon are moving as fast as the coffee, there is no further heat transfer.

UNIT OF HEAT

The measure of the quantity or amount of heat is a *calorie* (metric system) or *BTU* (British Thermal Unit). One calorie (BTU) is the amount of heat required to raise the temperature of one gram (pound) of water one degree

Celsius (Fahrenheit), Fig. 3-6. Therefore, it requires 100 calories of heat to raise the temperature of one gram of water from 0°C to 100°C.

The BTU is the amount of heat necessary to heat one pound of water one degree Fahrenheit. It requires 970 BTU to change 1 lb. of water at 212°F to 1 lb. of steam at 212°F (latent heat of vaporization).

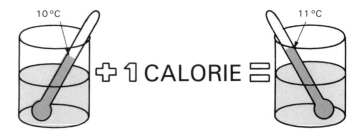

Fig. 3-6. A calorie is the amount of heat needed to raise the temperature of one gram of water one degree Celsius.

SENSIBLE HEAT

Sensible heat is measurable on a thermometer. For example, a container of water being heated by a flame, Fig. 3-7. When heat is added to bring the water to 212°F (100°C) it is sensible heat that can be measured by a thermometer. Once the water boils, it cannot be made hotter by applying more heat. This is the point at which latent (hidden) heat must be considered.

LATENT HEAT

Latent heat (hidden heat) causes a change of state without a change in temperature.

Latent heat of fusion is when a solid changes to a liquid when heat is added, without an increase in temperature. For example an ice cube melts at a constant temperature of 32°F (0°C). The latent heat, 79.7 calories per gram, is absorbed by the ice causing it to melt, Fig. 3-8.

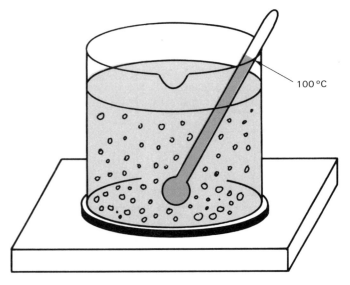

Fig. 3-7. Sensible heat is measured with a thermometer.

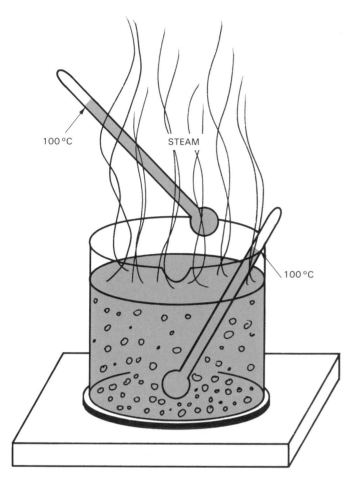

Fig. 3-8. Latent heat of vaporization turns a liquid into a gas, or vapor, without increasing the temperature of the liquid or vapor.

Latent heat of vaporization

Latent heat of vaporization is when a liquid changes to a vapor without an increase in temperature when heat is added, Fig. 3-8. When water reaches 212 °F (100 °C), the water temperature cannot increase further and therefore it vaporizes or turns to steam. When a liquid changes to a vapor, the vapor absorbs a massive amount of latent heat. It requires 540 calories, or five times more than that amount of heat, to change one gram of water at 100 degrees Celsius to one gram of steam at 100 degrees Celsius (latent heat of vaporization). This is because the vapor has expanded many times its original liquid state. When refrigerant changes from a liquid to a vapor, inside the evaporator, it absorbs massive amounts of heat from the air flowing past the evaporator as the refrigerant changes state.

Latent heat of condensation

Latent heat of condensation is when the vapor condenses and turns back into a liquid. As the liquid condenses, it releases a massive amount of latent heat without increasing the temperature, Fig. 3-9.

Latent heat of solidification

Latent heat of solidification is when a liquid changes into a solid. For example, when water changes into ice, a massive amount of latent heat is released into the at-

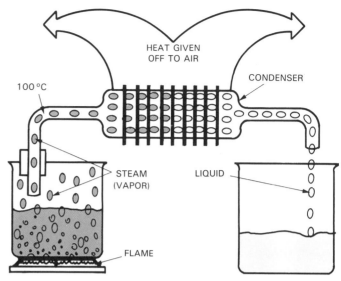

Fig. 3-9. Heat is given off when the vapor condenses.

mosphere without a change in temperature. The latent heat released, while freezing, is 79.7 calories per gram.

SUPERHEATED VAPOR

Superheated vapor continues to absorb heat. Consider what happens to water in a sealed container. As this container is heated, the pressure inside increases, Fig. 3-10. The vapor and liquid in the container are at the same temperature. With continued heating:
1. All the liquid becomes vapor.
2. Pressure ceases to increase.
3. The vapor continues to increase in temperature.

SPECIFIC HEAT

Specific heat is the ability to absorb or expel heat. Every substance has a different ability or capacity for absorbing or expelling heat. The measurement of specific heat is the amount of heat required to change one pound (gram) of a substance one degree Fahrenheit (Celsius).

The specific heat of all substances measured is relative to water, considered the standard. Water is given a value of 1.00. Most materials require less heat per given

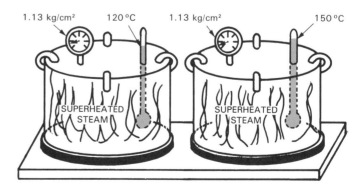

Fig. 3-10. When vapor temperature increases, it is superheated. Vapor temperature may increase without increasing vapor pressure.

weight (lower specific heat value) than water. Two exceptions are: ammonia, with a specific heat of 1.10; and hydrogen, with a specific heat of 3.41. These and specific heats of other materials are given in the following table:

SPECIFIC HEAT VALUES

Air .240	Hydrogen 3.41
Ammonia 1.10	Rubber .481
Aluminum .230	Steel .118
Brass .086	Tin .045
Copper .093	Water 1.00
Gasoline .700	
Glass .194	

The specific heat of water is 1.00. It requires one calorie to raise its temperature one degree Celsius per gram of water. It is possible to determine the number of degrees Celsius per gram that other materials will be raised by dividing the values in the table into 1.00.

TEMPERATURE

Critical temperature

All substances have a *critical temperature.* This is the maximum temperature at which a substance can be made to change from a vapor to a liquid, no matter what pressure is applied. For example, the critical temperature of water is 705 °F (374 °C). Above this temperature, it is impossible to turn steam back into water, regardless of pressure.

This is an important consideration in choosing a refrigerant, because the change of state must occur within the temperature range found in an air conditioning system. For example, the critical temperature of R-12, the most commonly used refrigerant, is 232.5 °F (111.4 °C), which is above the temperatures encountered in automotive air conditioning.

Temperature scales

The *Celsius* or *centigrade* scale, in the metric system, divides the difference from the melting point of ice to the boiling point of water into 100 equal divisions. The Celsius scale sets the melting point of ice at 0 °C and where water boils at 100 °C.

The *Fahrenheit scale,* in the customary (U.S. Conventional) system, divides the difference from the melting point of ice to the boiling point of water into 180 equal divisions, each being one degree. The Fahrenheit scale sets the melting point of ice at 32 °F and the boiling point of water at 212 °F, Fig. 3-11.

Absolute zero

Absolute zero is the complete absence of heat. At this point, there is absolutely no molecular movement in a substance. Scientists have computed this temperature to be − 460 °F (−273 °C). When extremely cold temperatures are measured, a different scale is used. When using the customary (Fahrenheit) measurement system, the Rankin scale is used. However, if the metric system is being used, the Kelvin scale is used. The Rankin and Kelvin are both 0° (absolute zero) at the lower end of the scale, Fig. 3-12.

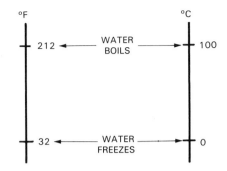

Fig. 3-11. Comparing the metric and customary scales for measuring temperature. Metric scale uses Celsius or Centigrade. The customary scale uses Fahrenheit.

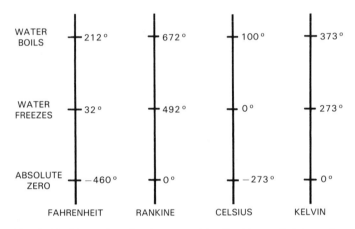

Fig. 3-12. Measuring absolute zero. The Rankine or Kelvin scale is used to avoid measuring with minus signs in front of temperature readings. The Rankine scale is used for the customary unit of measuring temperature. The Kelvin scale is used for the metric unit of measuring temperature.

Ambient temperature

Ambient temperature refers to the temperature of the surrounding air. In air conditioning work, ambient temperature refers to the temperature outside the car, as opposed to inside the car.

PRESSURE

Pressure is an external force acting on another body that is in direct contact with it. Atmospheric pressure is the weight of the air in the atmosphere acting on the surface of the earth. A barometer measures atmospheric pressure. Atmospheric pressure is 14.7 psi. at sea level. As you go up in elevation, atmospheric pressure decreases.

To understand atmospheric pressure, look at Fig. 3-13. As atmospheric pressure increases, it forces the mercury (a liquid at normal temperatures) in the container to rise in the tube. However, as atmospheric pressure decreases, the mercury in the tube falls. The height the liquid rises or falls corresponds to atmospheric pressure.

Vacuum

A pressure less than atmospheric is what is referred to as a *vacuum* or partial vacuum. A pressure gauge

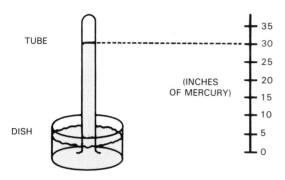

Fig. 3-13. Atmospheric pressure forces mercury in bowl upward through tube. When atmospheric pressure is reduced, due to weather or elevation, the height of the mercury in the tube decreases.

reads a value only if a pressure is greater than atmospheric. To read a pressure less than atmospheric, a vacuum gauge is needed. Vacuum is calibrated in inches or centimeters of mercury (Hg). A partial vacuum is somewhere between 0 and 29 inches Hg. A complete vacuum, void of all air, is 29 inches Hg. Separate gauges are needed to measure pressure or vacuum unless the gauge is compound (can measure both). With an absolute pressure scale, only one gauge is needed.

Absolute pressure

Gauge pressure does not include atmospheric pressure as part of the reading. This means that gauge pressure is calibrated to read zero although atmospheric pressure is present. An *absolute pressure* scale includes atmospheric pressure as part of the reading, Figs. 3-14 and 3-15. This means that a pressure less than atmospheric is read as a reduced pressure and not as a vacuum and that only one gauge is needed. When a reading of zero is obtained, a complete absence of pressure exists (vacuum).

Critical pressure

Critical pressure is the least amount of pressure needed to cause a vapor to turn into a liquid at its critical

KG/CM² KILOGRAMS PER SQUARE CENTIMETER	PSIG POUNDS PER SQUARE INCH GAUGE	KG/CM²A KILOGRAMS PER SQUARE CENTIMETER ABSOLUTE	PSIA POUNDS PER SQUARE INCH ABSOLUTE
0	0	1.05	15
−.35	−5	.70	10
−.70	−10	.35	5
−1.05	−15	0	0

Fig. 3-15. Pressure/vacuum conversions.

temperature. Any pressure less than the critical pressure will cause the vapor to remain a vapor.

SPECIFIC GRAVITY

Specific gravity is the ratio of the mass of a volume of a liquid or solid, compared to a mass of an equal volume of water. This means that water has a specific gravity of 1.00. If an object is placed in a body of water and has a specific gravity higher than one, such as steel, the object sinks. However, if an object placed in the same body of water has a specific gravity less than one, such as oil or gas, the object floats.

The specific gravity of a liquid is measured with a hydrometer. The *hydrometer* consists of a graduated glass cylinder containing a float. The float rides higher in the cylinder when the liquid is heavier than water, Fig. 3-16. A hydrometer can be used to measure the specific gravity of different types of solutions found in a car, such as engine coolant and the electrolyte in batteries.

Density

Density is the mass of a substance per unit of volume. For example, one cubic foot of wood weighs less than one cubic foot of gold. Density is measured in cubic feet or kilograms per cubic meter.

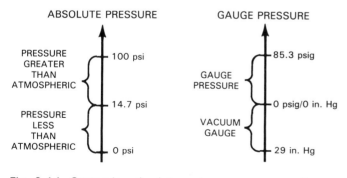

Fig. 3-14. Comparing absolute and gauge pressure. Gauge pressure does not include atmospheric pressure as part of reading. If gauge pressure is measured, a separate scale and gauge must be used when measuring pressures less than atmospheric. However, absolute pressure requires only one scale or gauge to measure pressure that is greater or less than atmospheric.

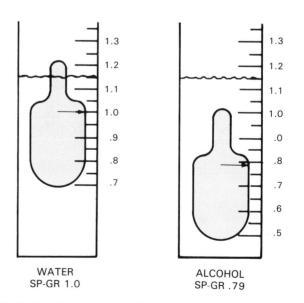

Fig. 3-16. A hydrometer is used to determine the specific gravity of a liquid. The specific gravity of water is 1.00. The specific gravity of alcohol, which is lighter, is 0.79.

BASIC AIR CONDITIONING

An air conditioning system transfers heat within the passenger compartment to the outside or ambient air. Heat is absorbed when the high-pressure refrigerant liquid changes into a low-pressure vapor inside the evaporator. The heat is carried away by the low-pressure refrigerant vapor to the compressor.

The compressor compresses and raises the temperature of the refrigerant vapor. The refrigerant now becomes a high-pressure vapor as it enters the condenser. As the high-pressure vapor enters the condenser, it begins to give off the heat that it absorbed inside the evaporator to the cooler surrounding area. As the high-pressure vapor inside the condenser cools, it turns into a high-pressure liquid. This cycle continually repeats while the air conditioner remains on.

SUMMARY

The following statements are a review of some of the fundamental principles of air conditioning discussed in this chapter.

Heat always moves from a hotter object to a cooler object. In air conditioning, heat is absorbed by the cooler refrigerant.

Heat is absorbed during a change of state from a liquid to a vapor. The absorption occurs during change of state of the refrigerant.

Conversely, heat is released during change of state from vapor to a liquid.

Temperature at which a liquid changes to a vapor varies directly with the pressure on it. High pressure requires high temperature to change state.

The operating principle for all refrigeration systems is based on heat transfer during the change of state of a refrigerant.

KNOW THESE TERMS

Solid, Liquid, Vapor, Humidity, Psychrometer, Molecule, Conduction, Convection, Radiation, Cold, Calorie, British Thermal Unit, Sensible heat, Latent heat, Latent heat of fusion, Latent heat of vaporization, Latent heat of condensation, Latent heat of solidification, Superheated vapor, Specific heat, Critical temperature, Celsius, Centigrade, Fahrenheit, Absolute zero, Ambient temperature. Pressure, Vacuum, Gauge pressure, Absolute pressure, Critical pressure, Specific gravity, Hydrometer, Density.

REVIEW QUESTIONS—CHAPTER 3

1. The amount of heat required to raise one gram of water one degree Celsius is called a:
   a. Fahrenheit.
   b. Btu.
   c. Calorie.
   d. None of the above.
2. Three methods in which heat is transferred are: _____, _____ and _____.
3. Sensible heat is measured by a _____.
4. The amount of heat required to change a liquid to a vapor is called _____ heat of _____.
5. The boiling point of a liquid _____ as the pressure on that liquid increases.
   a. Decreases.
   b. Remains unchanged.
   c. Increases.
   d. None of the above.
6. Explain the direction in which heat flows between two temperature levels.
7. Latent heat is the heat _____ or released during the change of state with no change in _____.
   a. Measured, vapor.
   b. Absorbed, temperature.
   c. Evaporated, pressure.
8. The temperature of a contained vapor will _____ with continued heating with no change in _____.
9. Warm air holds _____ moisture than cold air.
   a. More.
   b. Less.
   c. Same.
   d. None of the above.
10. The transmission of heat in the form of waves through space is called:
    a. Conduction.
    b. Convection.
    c. Radiation.
    d. Condensation.
11. The speed or motion of molecules decreases when a substance changes state from a liquid to a gas. True or false?
12. Comparing the weight of a volume of liquid to an equal volume of water determines _____.
13. A graduated glass cylinder with a float used to determine specific gravity of a liquid is called:
    a. Density gauge.
    b. Atmospheric pressure gauge.
    c. Mercury column.
    d. Hydrometer.
14. At absolute zero there is no _____ movement in a substance.
15. Radiator pressure caps are used on an automotive cooling system to:
    a. Increase coolant density.
    b. Lower coolant specific gravity.
    c. Control humidity.
    d. Raise the coolant boiling point.
16. Temperature readings indicate speed of molecular motion. True or false?
17. The terms calorie and BTU (British Thermal Unit) are used as measures of:
    a. Latent heat of fusion.
    b. Critical temperature.
    c. Density.
    d. Heat.
18. The complete absence of heat is defined as:
    a. Heat of compression.
    b. Critical temperature.
    c. Specific heat.
    d. Absolute zero.
19. Body cooling is promoted by reducing humidity. True or false?

20. Define the word "latent" as used in latent heat of vaporization.
21. Explain why a car painted a light color is easier to cool than a car that is painted a dark color.
22. When a liquid changes to a solid, it releases a quantity of heat. This is known as the heat of solidification. The reverse of this process is called:
    a. Heat of vaporization.
    b. Heat of condensation.
    c. Heat of liquidization.
    d. Heat of fusion.
23. The three states of matter are: _____, _____, and _____.
24. Removal of heat from one place and transferring it to another is the definition of refrigeration. True or false?
25. The handle of a spoon in a hot cup of coffee becomes hot because of heat transfer by:
    a. Radiation.
    b. Evaporation.
    c. Convection.
    d. Conduction.
26. The "specific heat" of a material is:
    a. The amount of heat it can store.
    b. The amount of heat it can absorb or expel.
    c. Measured with a hydrometer.
    d. Measured with a psychrometer.
27. Critical temperature of a substance is the temperature at which the substance solidifies. True or false?
28. When wet bulb and dry bulb temperatures are the same, relative humidity is _____.
29. Atmospheric pressure:
    a. is 14.7 pounds per square inch at sea level.
    b. Varies with altitude.
    c. Is the weight of the air in the atmosphere.
    d. All of the above.
30. Vacuum is any pressure less than atmospheric. True or false?

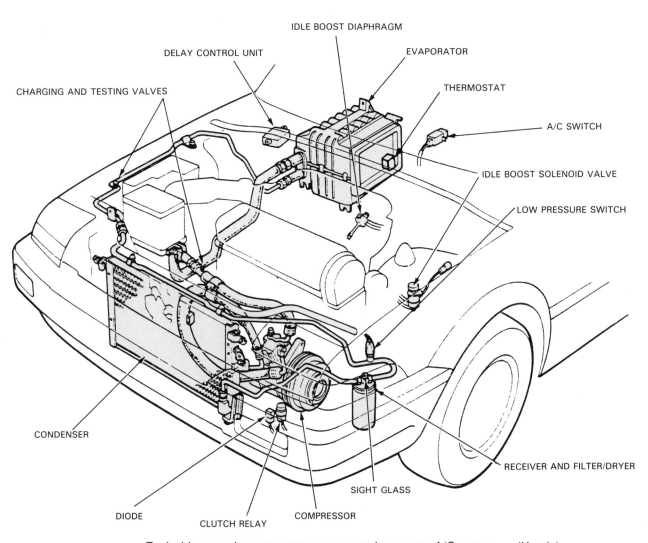

IDLE BOOST DIAPHRAGM

DELAY CONTROL UNIT

EVAPORATOR

THERMOSTAT

CHARGING AND TESTING VALVES

A/C SWITCH

IDLE BOOST SOLENOID VALVE

LOW PRESSURE SWITCH

CONDENSER

RECEIVER AND FILTER/DRYER

SIGHT GLASS

DIODE

CLUTCH RELAY

COMPRESSOR

Typical hose and component arrangement in an auto A/C system.   (Honda)

4 HOSES, LINES, AND FITTINGS

After studying this chapter, you will be able to:
• List the different types of A/C hoses.
• Name the different materials used in A/C lines.
• Describe the different types of a/c fittings.
• Explain the different ways in which O-rings are used.

AIR CONDITIONING HOSES

An *air conditioning hose* provides flexible routing for the refrigerant between components of the A/C system. Hoses also dampen pressure impulses and reduce compressor noises. Original equipment hose assemblies often consist of a combination of flexible hose and rigid tubing, Fig. 4-1.

There are two basic types of air conditioning hoses found on cars today. Some have a neoprene inner liner and a double-braided rayon outer core. A variation of this hose has a neoprene inner liner and outer core, Fig. 4-2. However, some A/C hoses are made of single-braided

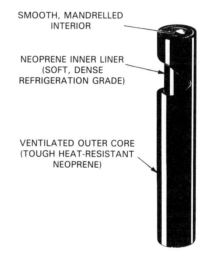

Fig. 4-2. Cutaway view shows a neoprene type A/C hose. (Everco)

nylon. Both hoses are designed to operate at 350 psi, but the neoprene A/C hoses have a burst pressure of 1500 psi, while nylon A/C hoses have a burst pressure of 3500 psi. When replacing A/C hose, make sure the replacement hose has the same burst strength and inside diameter.

A/C LINES

Air conditioning lines are rigid tubing, where no flexing is encountered, to carry the refrigerant between components of the A/C system. The A/C lines are made of aluminum or steel, Fig. 4-3. When removing an A/C line, two wrenches should be used. One wrench should hold the fitting at the component stationary, while the other wrench should turn the fitting on the line, Fig. 4.4. This procedure should be followed whether the

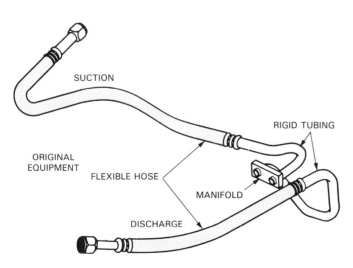

Fig. 4-1. Original equipment A/C hose assembly.

Metal Tube O.D.	Thread and Fitting Size	Steel Tubing Torque*	Aluminum Tubing Torque*
1/4	7/16	13	6
3/8	5/8	33	12
1/2	3/4	33	12
5/8	7/8	33	20
3/4	1 1/16	33	25
*Foot Pounds			

Fig. 4-3. The torque applied at the connections varies on the type of metal used for the A/C line and its diameter. (Delco)

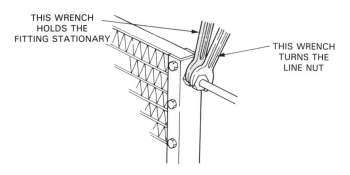

Fig. 4-4. One wrench is placed on the component fitting and is held stationary. The other wrench is placed over the A/C line fitting and is turned. This prevents damage to the A/C line, component, and connection. (Isuzu)

line is being loosened or tightened. When installing:
1. Avoid sharp turns or bend that might kink the A/C line. This would restrict the flow of refrigerant.
2. Always replace A/C lines with lines of the same material, wall thickness, and inner diameter.
3. Do not route A/C lines near the exhaust system.
4. The A/C lines must be secured to prevent rubbing against other hoses and sharp objects.
5. The replacement A/C line should have the same burst strength.

A/C FITTINGS

Fittings connect the lines to other lines or components of the A/C system. There are three basic types of connections, Fig. 4-5. A hose clamp for neoprene A/C hose is of a slightly different design than for nylon A/C hose, Fig. 4-6.

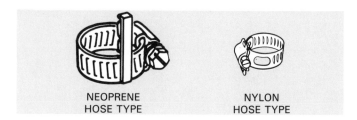

Fig. 4-6. The hose clamp used for neoprene A/C hoses has locating legs that correctly position the clamp on the hose. (Everco)

When a neoprene hose clamp is used, *barbs* are located at the end of the metal A/C line, Fig. 4-7. (The barbs are protrusions that help secure the A/C hose.) The A/C hose is placed over the barbs and butted against the shoulder of the A/C line. The clamp is positioned so that its legs touch the end of the A/C hose. This positions the clamp directly over the barbs, which promote a positive seal when the clamp is tightened, Fig. 4-7. Some A/C hoses can be repaired in a similar manner by splicing, Fig. 4-8.

O-RINGS

When O-rings are used, they must butt against the shoulder of the A/C line, Fig. 4-9. Some A/C lines have

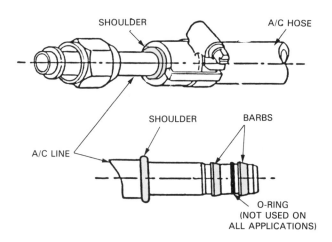

Fig. 4-7. Top. The A/C hose butts up against the shoulder of the A/C line. The legs of the clamp must touch the end of the A/C hose before it is tightened. This ensures the clamp is correctly positioned over the barbs of the A/C line. Bottom. The barbs on the A/C line promote a positive seal.

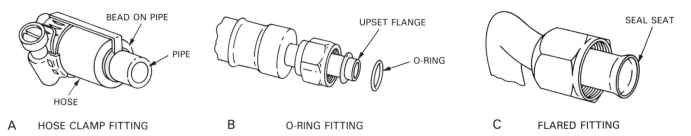

| A HOSE CLAMP FITTING | B O-RING FITTING | C FLARED FITTING |

Fig. 4-5. The different types of fittings. A—Clamp type. B—O-ring at connection. C—Flared fitting. This normally does not need any O-rings and is held in place by a nut.

A

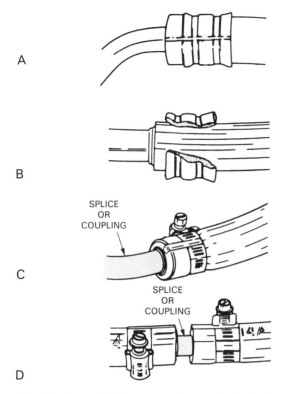

B

SPLICE
OR
COUPLING

C

SPLICE
OR
COUPLING

D

Fig. 4-8. Some A/C hoses can be repaired. A—Start repair by making a groove in original hose clamp with a fine tooth hacksaw. B—Break open clamp at groove. C—Install A/C hose, coupling, and clamp. Position clamp and tighten. D—Position the other end of A/C hose on coupling. Position clamp on A/C hose and tighten.   (Oldsmobile)

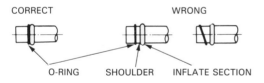

CORRECT   WRONG

O-RING   SHOULDER   INFLATE SECTION

Fig. 4-9. The O-ring must be placed squarely against the shoulder. (Isuzu)

a groove the O-ring must fit, Fig. 4-10. One car maker uses a fitting that requires the use of two O-rings, Fig. 4-11. A special tool is needed to remove and install the fitting, Fig. 4-12. Another car maker uses a dual O-ring joint. A special tool is also needed to remove this connection, Fig. 4-13.

Regardless of the type fitting, if an O-ring is used, it must be lubricated with refrigerant oil before it is installed, Fig. 4-14. When an A/C line is disconnected, always use new O-rings before installing the lines.

LIQUID LINE FILTERS

A liquid line filter contains a screen and filter. The screen traps large particles, while the filter traps small

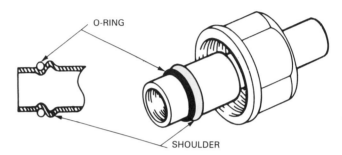

O-RING

SHOULDER

Fig. 4-10. Some A/C lines have a groove the O-ring must squarely sit in. (Ford)

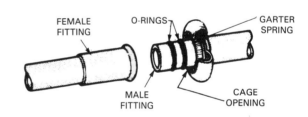

FEMALE
FITTING

O-RINGS

GARTER
SPRING

MALE
FITTING

CAGE
OPENING

Fig. 4-11. One car maker uses a flared end at one end of the A/C line and O-rings on the other end. A special spring device holds the two lines together. A special tool is needed to remove and install this special fastener. (Ford)

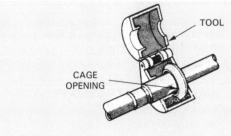

TOOL

CAGE
OPENING

1. Fit tool to coupling so that tool can enter cage opening to release the garter spring.

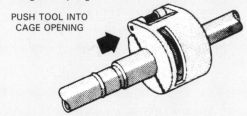

PUSH TOOL INTO
CAGE OPENING

2. Push the tool into the cage opening to release the female fitting from the garter spring.

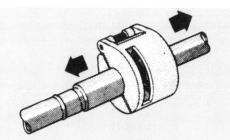

3. Pull the coupling male and female fittings apart.

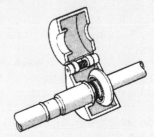

4. Remove the tool from the disconnected spring lock coupling.

Fig. 4-12. Special tool and sequence is shown removing and installing special fastener from A/C lines. (Ford)

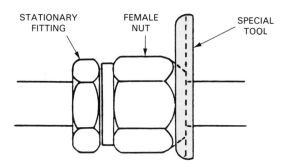

Fig. 4-13. Some A/C lines on GM products use a double O-ring. A special tool is needed to remove this connection. (Oldsmobile)

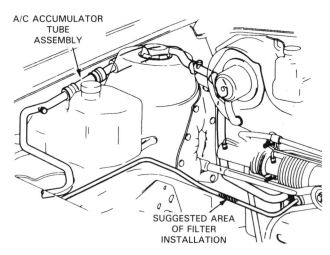

Fig. 4-15. Shaded area shows desired area of splice for liquid line filter. (Oldsmobile)

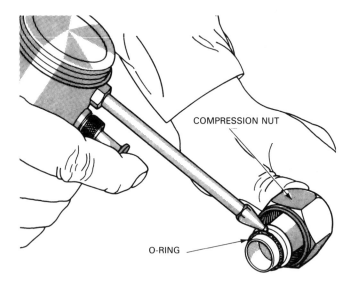

Fig. 4-14. O-rings must be lubricated with refrigerant oil, of the same viscosity used in the A/C compressor, before connections are made.

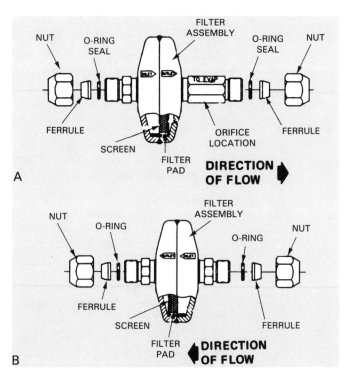

Fig. 4-16. Liquid line filters. A—Filter with orifice. B—Filter without orifice. (Oldsmobile)

particles. The *liquid line filter* eliminates the need to flush the A/C system with R-11 when:

1. The A/C compressor is replaced because it has seized.
2. The orifice tube repeatedly plugs.

The liquid line filter is spliced into the high pressure side between the evaporator and condenser (liquid R-12), Fig. 4-15. There are two types of liquid line filters, Fig. 4-16.

NOTE: When a liquid line filter with an orifice is installed in a system that uses an orifice tube, the original orifice tube must be removed from the A/C line.

SUMMARY

An A/C hose provides flexible routing, while an A/C line provides a rigid line to carry the refrigerant to the components. The A/C hose can be neoprene or nylon. The A/C line can be aluminum or steel tubing. When removing or installing A/C lines, always use two wrenches. The a/c fittings connect hoses to other hoses or components and can be of the clamp, O-ring, or flared type. The hose clamp, used on a neoprene A/C hose, is automatically positioned directly over the barbs of the A/C line before it is tightened. New O-rings must always be used when making repairs. Lubricate them with refrigerant oil before installing the A/C lines. Liquid line filters eliminate the need to flush the system with R-11 and are installed in the high-pressure side between the evaporator and the condenser.

KNOW THESE TERMS

Air conditioning hose, Air conditioning lines, Fittings, Barbs, Liquid line filter.

REVIEW QUESTIONS—CHAPTER 4

1. Lubricated A/C line O-rings are considered reusable. True or false?

2. Two wrenches must always be used in tightening or loosening an A/C hose fitting in order to:
   a. Provide support and keep fitting stationary during turning process.
   b. Prevent the damaging of the tubing and hose due to twisting forces.
   c. Reduces the chance of one wrench slipping.
   d. Both a and b.
3. Replacement A/C hose must be of the same _____ diameter and the same _____ strength.
4. List at least three precautions that must be observed when installing and routing A/C lines and hoses.
5. The burst strength of most neoprene hose is:
   a. 1500 psi.
   b. Higher than the burst strength of nylon hose.
   c. 350 psi.
   d. 3500 psi.

6. Hose between components are used to:
   a. Reduce noise and allow for relative movement.
   b. Change liquid refrigerant to a vapor.
   c. Reduce weight.
   d. Eliminate sharp bends.
7. List the two different materials commonly used in rigid line construction.
8. Air conditioning hose clamps have positioning legs to ensure the clamp is directly over the tubing barbs. True or false?
9. The spring-lock type tube coupling requires a special tool to couple and uncouple. True or false?
10. The liquid line filter is generally spliced into the:
    a. Low-pressure side between the evaporator and the accumulator.
    b. High-pressure side between the evaporator and the condenser.
    c. High-pressure side between the compressor and the condenser.
    d. None of the above.

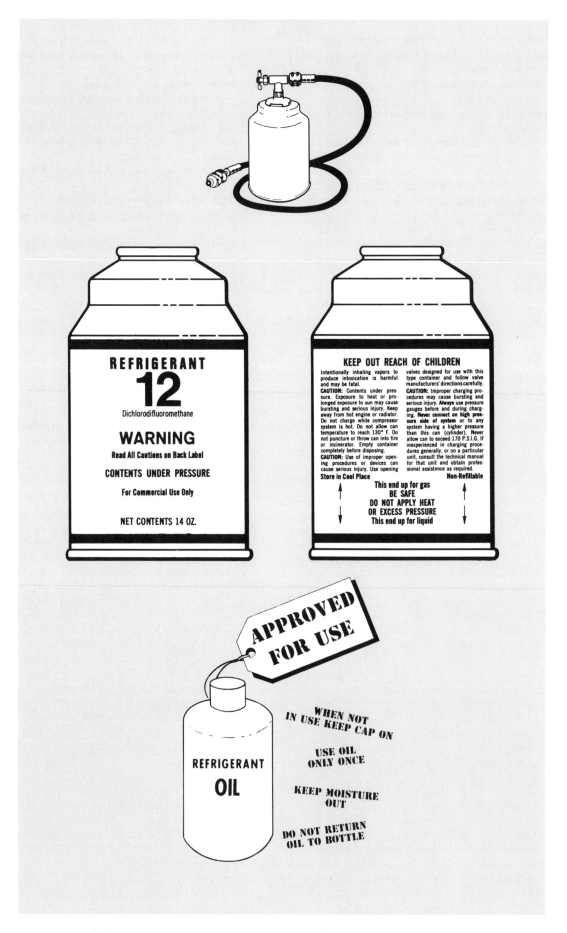

Refrigerant and refrigerant oil cautions.   (Harrison Radiator Div., GM)

5

REFRIGERANT AND REFRIGERANT OIL

After studying this chapter, you will be able to:
* *List the different types of refrigerants.*
* *Explain the temperature-pressure relationship of R-12.*
* *List the different characteristics of R-12.*

REFRIGERANT

A *refrigerant* is a substance used in an air conditioning system to remove heat. The substance must be stable and capable of withstanding high pressure and temperatures without deteriorating or decomposing.

The basic need for a refrigerant is to transfer heat from the inside to the outside of the car. The refrigerant is one of the most important elements of the entire air conditioning system. The mechanical components of the system simply circulate the refrigerant and cause it to change state from a liquid to a vapor and back to a liquid again. Refrigerant is the medium that carries the heat away from inside the car.

REFRIGERANT ACTION

The basic action in heat absorption takes place when the refrigerant changes state from a liquid to a vapor during rapid expansion. The heat-laden vapor is then transferred to a device where it is condensed back to a liquid, expelling the heat.

HALOGENS/REFRIGERANTS

Refrigerants are made up of halogens. The family of *halogens* consists of: chlorine, fluorine, iodine, and bromine. A halogen, by itself, is poisonous. However, in some compound forms it is harmless. As an example, the halogen chlorine combined with sodium produces table salt. A refrigerant does not react with most rubber or metals, but may discolor chrome or stainless steel. When any substance containing a halogen hits a hot copper object, a bright green color is produced.

TYPES OF REFRIGERANTS

There are many different types of refrigerants available. Some are best suited for larger refrigeration units. Others are best suited for automotive air conditioning.

1. *Monochlorodifluoromethane,* commonly called R-22, has a chemical symbol $CHCLF_2$. R-22 has a boiling point of $-40\,°F$ ($-40\,°C$) at atmospheric pressure. The latent heat of R-22 is 93.21 BTU/pound. It is stable, noncorrosive, nontoxic, and nonflammable. R-22 is generally used in large stationary systems using reciprocating compressors.

2. *Trichloromonofluoromethane,* commonly called R-11, has a chemical symbol of CCL_3F. R-11 has a latent heat of 84 BTU/pound. It is stable, nontoxic and nonflammable. R-11 is primarily used in large centrifugal compressor systems.

3. *Dichlorodifluoromethane,* commonly called R-12, has a chemical symbol of CCL_2F_2. *R-12* is a derivative of carbon tetrachloride (CCL_4), commonly called carbon tet. R-12 has a boiling point of $-21.7\,°F$ ($-29.8\,°C$) at atmospheric pressure, with a latent heat of 68.2 BTU/pound. It is the most common refrigerant in automotive use.

Refrigerant Classifications

There are two different organizations that categorize refrigerants. The National Refrigeration Safety Code (NRSC) uses three classifications. Group 1 is the safest. Group 2 is toxic and somewhat flammable, and Group 3 is flammable. R-11, R-12, and R-22 are all Group 1 refrigerants.

The National Board of Fire Underwriters uses six classifications, from Group 1 (most toxic) to Group 6 (least toxic). R-11 and R-12 are both in Group 6; R-22 is in Group 5.

R-12

Since 1955, R-12 has been the most widely used refrigerant for automotive air conditioning systems. The air conditioning system controls of automobiles produced since that time are specifically designed for the properties of R-12. As a result, these controls will not function properly and efficiently if another refrigerant is substituted.

Phasing out R-12

Because of scientific concern about damage to the Earth's ozone layer, R-12 is being phased out under an international agreement. R-12 will no longer be produced after the year 2000. Because of declining supplies, many shops will find it necessary to recycle R-12. A number of other refrigerants, such as R-11, R-113, and R-114, are also affected.

Auto air conditioning systems using a new environmentally safer refrigerant, R-134a, will become common on cars in the mid-1990s. R-134a systems must operate at higher pressure, and also use a different type of refrigerant oil.

R-12 and R-134a cannot be interchanged; they must be kept separate and used only in systems specifically designed for them. This means that for a period of years, A/C technicians will have to work with both systems. They will have to exercise caution to avoid contamination of refrigerants that could cause system damage and failure.

R-12 trade names

Many manufacturers of refrigerants produce R-12 under such trade names as Freon 12, Aircon 12, Genetron 12, Unicom 12, Prestone 12, Isotron 12, and Freeze 12. The "12" designation on refrigerant containers indicates that they contain R-12 that has been subjected to rigid inspection and that meets all specifications for use in automotive air conditioning systems.

R-12 temperature-pressure relationship

A mechanic can easily determine the temperature of the evaporating coil by noting the pressure of the low side. When the low-side pressure gauge indicates 35 psi, the evaporator temperature is approximately 35 °F (2 °C). This is true because the *pressure-temperature relationship* of R-12 is roughly one psi per one degree Fahrenheit. This is only true for the air conditioner low side. This is not true when pressures exceed 80 psi or fall below 20 psi, Fig. 5-1.

R-12 characteristics

R-12 is the most desirable of the refrigerants for automotive use because it is odorless in concentrations of less than 20 percent (greater than 20 percent smells like carbon tetrachloride), nonpoisonous, nonflammable, and noncorrosive. Other desirable qualities are:
1. Low operating pressure.
2. Stable at high and low temperatures.
3. Boiling point of −21.7 °F (−29.8 °C).
4. Compatible with refrigeration oil (does not separate from or change the oil).

R-12 is basically a safe refrigerant. However, there are some safety hazards that a technician should be aware of when handling R-12, Fig. 5-2:

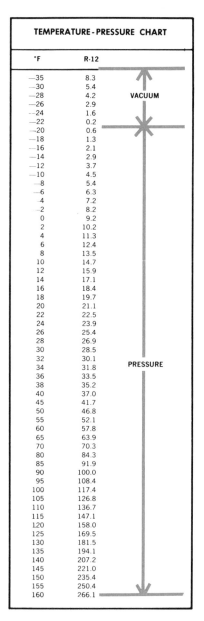

TEMPERATURE-PRESSURE CHART	
°F	R-12
−35	8.3
−30	5.4
−28	4.2
−26	2.9
−24	1.6
−22	0.2
−20	0.6
−18	1.3
−16	2.1
−14	2.9
−12	3.7
−10	4.5
−8	5.4
−6	6.3
−4	7.2
−2	8.2
0	9.2
2	10.2
4	11.3
6	12.4
8	13.5
10	14.7
12	15.9
14	17.1
16	18.4
18	19.7
20	21.1
22	22.5
24	23.9
26	25.4
28	26.9
30	28.5
32	30.1
34	31.8
36	33.5
38	35.2
40	37.0
45	41.7
50	46.8
55	52.1
60	57.8
65	63.9
70	70.3
80	84.3
85	91.9
90	100.0
95	108.4
100	117.4
105	126.8
110	136.7
115	147.1
120	158.0
125	169.5
130	181.5
135	194.1
140	207.2
145	221.0
150	235.4
155	250.4
160	266.1

Fig. 5-1. Temperature-pressure relationship for R-12 refrigerant.

1. R-12 is heavier than air and may cause asphyxiation if used in an enclosed or confined space. Make sure there is adequate ventilation.
2. When R-12 is exposed to heat or flame, a phosgene gas is produced that has a detrimental effect to the human nervous system. Also, the R-12 may break down into its base elements when heated and cause a sharp, pungent odor. Always use a leak detector, torch type, in a well ventilated area.
3. When water or moisture combines with R-12, hydrochloric acid forms that can dissolve metal. Prior to charging, always evacuate an air conditioning system after it has been opened, to remove moisture.
4. R-12 vaporizes so quickly at atmospheric temperatures that it can remove enough heat from the skin to cause frostbite. Always wear

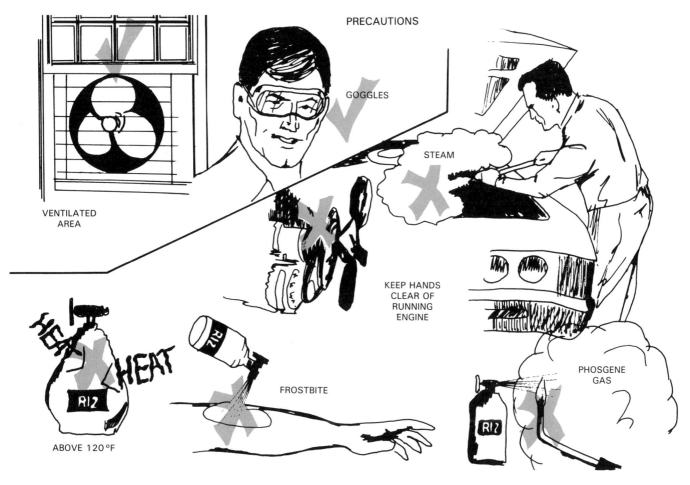

Fig. 5-2. Observe all safety precautions.

gloves and long sleeve shirts.

5. If R-12 contacts the eyeball, blindness may occur. Always wear safety goggles.

6. If a container of R-12 is subject to heat above 120°F (48.8°C), the container will explode due to the internal pressure. Keep containers of R-12 out of the sun and in a cool, dry storage place.

EMERGENCY FIRST AID

It is important to have and know the location of the first-aid cabinet. Among the supplies in the cabinet should be sterile mineral oil.

If R-12 gets in the eye, above all, DO NOT rub it. Flood with water to increase the temperature. Place a few drops of sterile mineral oil in the eye to absorb the R-12. This provides a protective film to reduce the possibility of infection. Seek a physician for immediate treatment.

If the skin is exposed to R-12, treat for frostbite by washing the area with cool water. This increases the temperature of the skin. Follow with a sterile dry bandage.

REFRIGERANT CYLINDERS

The common sizes of refrigerant cylinders range from 14 oz. to 150-pound capacity. The 14 oz.-cans, Fig. 5-3,

Fig. 5-3. Type of R-12 containers. A—30 lb. drum is used where large amounts of air conditioning work is done and is disposable. B—14 oz. can is thrown away after it is used.

are readily available through many retail stores for the small-volume user. Air conditioning repair shops use larger cylinders ranging from 10-pound to 150-pound capacity.

White is the color for cylinders containing R-12. Orange is the color for cylinders containing R-11. Green is the color for cylinders containing R-22.

Disposable types of nonrefillable 14-oz. cans are available in auto supply and retail stores. They are used with a simple valve device that punctures the can top, Fig. 5-4.

Refillable cylinders of a heavier construction are used in repair shops that involve large quantity usage. The regulations for refilling are established by the Interstate Commerce Commission. The ICC Regulations provide cylinder filling procedures and establish rules for periodic inspection of cylinder condition.

ICC Regulations also prescribe that cylinders over 4 1/2 inches in diameter and 12 inches in length must be equipped with some type of pressure-release protection, such as a *fusible plug* or *pressure-release valve.* The purpose of this is to provide a means of releasing excess pressure in the cylinder.

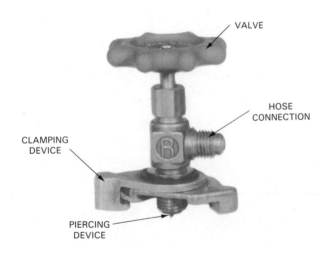

Fig. 5-4. Service valve is needed to pierce top of 14 oz. R-12 cans.

REFRIGERANT OIL

Refrigerant oil comes in different containers, Fig. 5-5. *Refrigerant oil* is odorless and clear in color (with a yellow tint). However, the refrigerant oil will turn black and have a strong odor when contaminated. When this occurs, the refrigerant oil should be changed. Some compressors do not have an oil pump and depend on the refrigerant oil circulating with the refrigerant. As in other oil applications, refrigerant oil:

1. Cleans by taking impurities with it.
2. Cools by dissipating the heat it has picked up.
3. Lubricates the moving parts of the compressor and keeps the thermostatic expansion valve (TXV) in proper operating condition.

4. Acts as a seal between piston ring and cylinder wall in the compressor.

A special oil

Refrigerant oil must be compatible with all parts of the system, including gaskets and seals. The wrong type of oil causes swelling and/or deterioration of the seals. Properties and characteristics of refrigerant oil:

1. Highly refined to ensure that it is moisture-free. Refrigerant oil has a high affinity for moisture and every precaution must be taken to keep it moisture-free.
2. Antifoaming agents which ensure liquid oil to moving parts.
3. Should have no or very little chemical reaction with refrigerant or any component of the system.
4. Refined to remove wax impurities which could plug orifices in the system.
5. Oxidation inhibitors are added to prevent corrosion from forming.
6. Sulphur is removed by refining to prevent sludge and gum from forming.
7. Good thermal stability minimizes the formation of carbon deposits on hot areas of the compressor.
8. Low pour point allows the oil to remain in its liquid state to provide adequate lubrication at lower temperatures.

Viscosity

Viscosity is the resistance to flow and is determined by the Saybolt test. This is the time in seconds for a specified quantity of oil to flow through a specified size orifice at 100°F (37.7°C). High-numerical viscosities will not flow through small oil passages when tempera-

A   B

Fig. 5-5. Refrigerant oils. A—In plastic quart-size bottles. B—In pressurized cans that require service valve to pierce its top.

tures are cold. Low-numerical viscosities will result in inadequate film strength, allowing metal-to-metal contact when temperatures are very high. The proper viscosity is important to maintain an adequate oil film on all bearing surfaces. The viscosity selected for air conditioners depends on:

1. Compressor temperature.
2. Evaporator temperature.
3. Type of refrigerant used.

The most common viscosities used with automotive air conditioners are 300, 525, or 1000. Always consult the service manual for the exact viscosity for the car's air conditioning system.

Oil level

The oil level in an air conditioning system (the quantity of oil retained in the compressor) should be checked when repairs are made to the system. If the oil level is too high, cooling will be inadequate. If the oil level is too low, the moving parts in the system will not have enough protection. Before checking the oil level, run the A/C compressor at least 15 minutes. This allows some of the oil that is carried with the refrigerant to return to the compressor sump.

The system must first be discharged of refrigerant to relieve the pressure. The A/C compressor is disconnected and removed from the engine. The drain plug is removed, Fig. 5-6A, and the oil poured out of the compressor into a drain pan and discarded. Install the drain plug. Fill the compressor with the correct type and amount of new oil as specified in the service manual, Fig. 5-6B. Replace and tighten the fill plug and reinstall the A/C compressor.

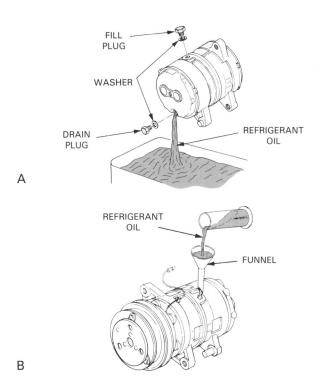

Fig. 5-6. Checking the oil level. A—Remove the drain plug and pour oil from compressor into drain pan. B—Remove fill plug and add specified amount of fresh oil. Consult the service manual. (Isuzu)

SUMMARY

R-12 is the refrigerant used today in automotive air conditioning systems. It possesses desirable properties and is the least dangerous when proper safety precautions are observed. It will be replaced in coming years with R134a, which is environmentally safer.

A special oil is needed to lubricate the A/C components. It must be compatible with the refrigerant and all components of the air conditioning system.

Efficiency of the system is greatly decreased when the refrigerant becomes contaminated and is no longer chemically stable.

KNOW THESE TERMS

Refrigerant, Halogen, Monochlorodifluoromethane, Trichloromonofluoromethane, Dichlorodifluoromethane, R-12, Pressure-temperature relationship, Throwaway cans, Refillable cylinder, Refrigerant oil, Viscosity.

REVIEW QUESTIONS—CHAPTER 5

1. When R-12 comes in contact with the skin, the result can be:
   a. A rash.
   b. Discoloration.
   c. Frostbite.
   d. Death.
2. Describe three different types and constructions of R-12 containers.
3. List the characteristics of R-12 refrigerant.
4. Basic need for a refrigerant is to transfer _____ from inside the car.
5. Explain refrigerant action during heat transfer.
6. What is the weight of refrigerant in throwaway-type containers?
7. The most frequently used refrigerant in automotive air conditioning is:
   a. R-11.   c. R-22.
   b. R-12.   d. None of the above.

8. If R-12 gets into an eye or on the skin, the following steps must be taken:
   a. Use sterile oil to absorb the refrigerant.
   b. Wash with water.
   c. Call a physician.
   d. All of the above.
9. The purpose of refrigerant oil is to lubricate, cool, _____, and seal.
10. Refrigerant oil must:
    a. Be moisture free.
    b. Be kept in a tight container.
    c. Never be reused.
    d. All of the above.

11. Used refrigerant oil contact with the skin should be avoided because:
    a. It contains acids.
    b. It causes dermititis.
    c. It could contain refrigerant causing frostbite.
    d. a and c are correct.
12. Refrigerant exposed to open flame forms a dangerous _____ _____.
13. Closed containers of R-12 refrigerant, when subjected to intense heat, can explode. True or false?
14. Oil viscosity is determined by the _____ test.

6 SHOP SAFETY

After studying this chapter, you will be able to:
* *List the safety rules that apply to any shop.*
* *Explain how to give first aid for frostbite.*
* *Describe treatment for frostbite to the eyeball.*
* *Relate the hazards of using R-12 in an unventilated shop.*
* *Show how to safely use jacks, jack stands, and lifts.*
* *Explain why the battery is disconnected when working on the electrical circuit.*

SAFETY

Shop safety must be practiced at all times. Safety is everybody's responsibility. Everyone is responsible for their own safety and the safety of their fellow workers. There are many areas where accidents can occur in the automotive shop. An accident can result in injury, loss of life, and/or property damage. Safety rules, which apply to all automotive repair shops, include:

1. Proper conduct of ALL individuals; running and horseplay results in accidents.
2. To prevent fires, place used rags in a sealed container, Fig. 6-1. Oily rags can ignite by careless smoking or spontaneous combustion.
3. All flammable chemicals should be kept in special closed flameproof containers, Fig. 6-2.
4. "NO SMOKING" signs should be prominently displayed and adhered to, Fig. 6-3.
5. Fire extinguishers must be provided and all personnel made familiar with their location, Fig. 6-4. Never throw water on a gasoline or oil fire. This will spread the fire instead of putting it out.
6. Shops should be well lighted and ventilated to exhaust toxic fumes and car emissions, Fig. 6-5.
7. Good housekeeping prevents accidents; keep aisles clear, floors clean, and tools stored in their proper locations, Fig. 6-6.

8. Remove all jewelry. This prevents burns from electrical shorts, or injury from being snagged on engine parts or caught in rotating mechanisms.
9. Have a first-aid kit, Fig. 6-7, readily available along with an emergency phone number.

Fig. 6-1. Always place oily rags in a sealed container. It seals out the air needed to support combustion.
(Automotive Encyclopedia)

Fig. 6-2. Flammable fluids must be kept in a sealed container. Store sealed containers away from heat, flames, and sparks that could ignite and cause an explosion. (Lab Safety)

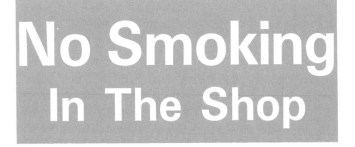

Fig. 6-3. No smoking signs should be displayed through the entire shop. Make sure all persons in the shop adhere to the warning.

Fig. 6-4. Class A fire extinguishers are for paper-type fires. Class B fire extinguishers are for grease and oil-related type fires. Class C fire extinguishers are for electrical-type fires. (Lab Safety)

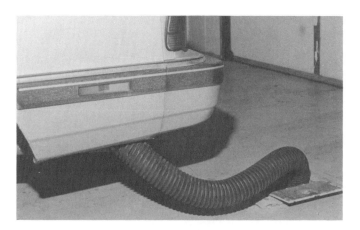

Fig. 6-5. When the engine must remain running for test purposes, the doors to the shop must remain open. If weather does not permit this, the car exhaust system must be hooked to a ventilation system.   (Automotive Encyclopedia)

Fig. 6-6. A clean shop should look like this before, during, and after working hours. There should not be any tools or grease on the floor the technician can slip and fall on. (Automotive Encyclopedia)

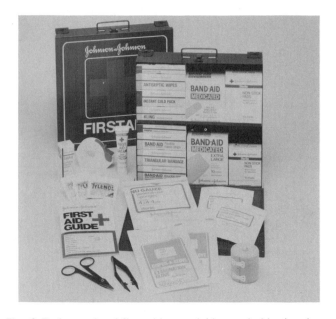

Fig. 6-7. A supply of first-aid material is needed in the shop. (Lab Safety)

A/C SAFETY

Working on air conditioning exposes the technician to the dangers of frostbite from the refrigerant. This could result in blindness if refrigerant contacts the eyeball or frostbite if it contacts the skin. Toxic fumes are given off when the refrigerant is exposed to an open flame. Some A/C leak detectors use a flame to detect a refrigerant leak. This can be hazardous to your health if used in an unventilated area. Also, refrigerant displaces the oxygen in an unventilated room and can lead to suffocation or asphyxiation.

REFRIGERANT AND FROSTBITE

When adding, discharging, or purging an air conditioning system, small amounts of refrigerant escape at the fittings. Therefore, safety glasses and gloves must be worn at all times, Fig. 6-8. Also, place a rag over the service fittings when removing and installing connections to absorb the escaping refrigerant.

Frostbite is one of the most common injuries in servicing air conditioners. R-12 evaporates at $-21.6\,°F$ $(-29.9\,°C)$. At this temperature, a drop on the skin immediately freezes it. If the skin is exposed to large amounts or a long duration of R-12, the blood circulation at that point ceases and the skin then decays. This is referred to as gangrene, which could require surgery. If R-12 contacts the skin, splash the area with large amounts of water immediately. This increases the temperature of the skin that has been contacted by R-12.

If refrigerant gets in the eye, DO NOT rub it. Wash the eyes with water to increase the temperature, Fig. 6-9. Place a few drops of sterile mineral oil in the eye. Mineral oil provides a protective film over the eyeball to reduce the chance of infection. Seek a physician immediately.

Fig. 6-9. All air conditioner shops should have an emergency eye wash station to remove contamination from the eye. (Lab Safety)

PHOSGENE GAS

When refrigerant is exposed to a flame, *phosgene gas* is produced, Fig. 6-10. Phosgene gas has an unpleasant odor and can have serious effects on the respiratory and neurological systems. The technician is exposed to this danger when using a flame type leak detector to detect A/C leaks. It is for this reason that there must be adequate ventilation to carry away the noxious gas.

SUFFOCATION

Suffocation or asphyxiation is another problem if the technician works with R-12 in an unventilated shop. The R-12 is heavier than air and sinks to the floor. Eventually, this can displace oxygen in the shop. This would lead to suffocation, and could be fatal.

Fig. 6-8. Safety glasses and gloves must be worn when working with refrigerant.

Fig. 6-10. Deadly phosgene gas is produced when refrigerant is exposed to a flame.

EXPLOSIONS

Some technicians place the refrigerant container in hot water to speed up the charging process. Heating the refrigerant in its container causes the pressure inside to increase. This procedure could become dangerous if the refrigerant container is heated above 120°F (48.8°C), Fig. 6-11. This causes internal pressure to exceed the designed container pressure rating, resulting in a possible explosion.

Fig. 6-11. Never heat refrigerant containers above 120°F (48.8°C) or they may explode. (Ford)

ELECTRICAL SHOCK

An *electrical shock* occurs when electricity flows to the ground through the human body. If the voltage and amperage are great enough, death by electrocution will occur. An electrical shock can happen around any electric-powered equipment, especially with wet floors, tools, and hands.

To prevent an electrical shock, all electrical-powered equipment should have a third prong that fits into the ground outlet, Fig. 6-12. This provides maximum protection against shock in case of faulty equipment wiring. Inspection of electrical equipment for proper ground and frayed wiring is recommended before using. Also, route electrical cords away from the hood, doors, hot exhaust manifolds, and rotating fans and pulleys. If the cord becomes pinched or burned, the chance of electrical shock increases.

PHYSICAL INJURIES

Physical injuries such as cuts, burns, muscle strains, and broken bones often occur when improper work techniques are used. Injuries are apt to occur when working with the engine running. This exposes the mechanic to whirling fan blades, rotating drive belts, hot exhaust manifolds, and electric shock from the ignition system.

To prevent injuries, the following are recommended:
1. Think through and decide on the correct procedure before starting work. Be constantly aware of inherent dangers.
2. Use the right tools and equipment for the job.
3. Work at a reasonable pace.
4. Lift with your legs, not your back.

OSHA

OSHA is the Occupational Safety and Health Administration, a branch of the Department of Labor. The purpose of OSHA is to establish and enforce the health and safety guidelines for all types of businesses.

Auto repair shops are subject to inspection by OSHA at any time to be sure they are operating under the prescribed rules and regulations. Auto repair shops are generally safer places to work since OSHA started.

JACKS, JACK STANDS, AND LIFTS

When it becomes necessary to raise the car to work on it, a hoist (hydraulic lift) or floor jack is needed. When using a hoist, the car must be properly positioned to prevent it from slipping off the hoist, Fig. 6-13. This information can be found in the front of every service manual. When a hoist is not available, a floor jack can be used to raise the car, Fig. 6-14. This must also be properly positioned before raising the car.

If a floor jack is used to raise the car, a jack stand must be placed under the car and near the floor jack once the car is raised. The floor jack can then be lowered allowing the weight of the car to rest on the jack stands, Fig. 6-15. Once the car is resting securely on the jack stands, the floor jack may be removed. This is a safety measure

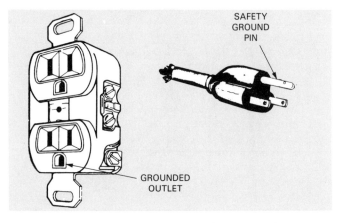

SAFETY GROUND PIN

GROUNDED OUTLET

Fig. 6-12. Electrical connections must be grounded to prevent electric shock.

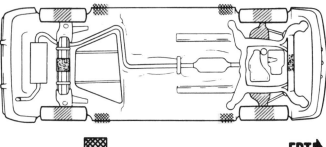

 FRAME CONTACT HOIST   **FRT**

 FLOOR JACK   SUSPENSION CONTACT HOIST

Fig. 6-13. Shown are different hoist and floor jack points. The car must be elevated at the designated points when raising it off the ground. (Oldsmobile)

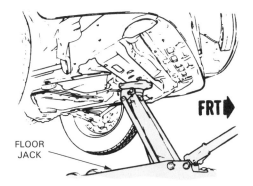

Fig. 6-14. Using a floor jack to elevate the front end of the car. (Oldsmobile)

Fig. 6-15. After raising the car with a floor jack, position a jack stand at the designated point. Then, lower the car onto the jack stand and remove the floor jack.
(Automotive Encyclopedia)

in case the seals in the floor jack were to leak or fail, allowing the car to fall. If a technician was under the car at the time it fell, the outcome could be serious or fatal.

BATTERY SAFETY

When working near the battery, make sure there is no flame or spark near it. A battery contains acid and metal. Any time acid comes in contact with metal, explosive gases are produced. These gases will explode if ignited.

When working on any part of the car's electrical system, always disconnect the negative battery cable from the battery, Fig. 6-16. This breaks the electrical circuit that runs through the entire car. Since the car frame and engine connect directly to the negative side (ground) of the battery, the possibility of an accidental short circuit is prevented. For example, if the ground cable is not disconnected and a "hot wire" should touch the car frame, engine, or any other grounded part, an electrical short could

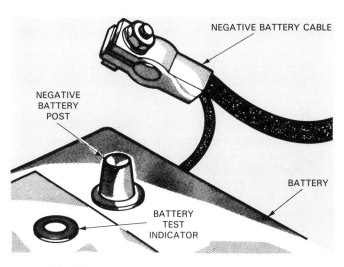

Fig. 6-16. When working on any electrical circuit, always disconnect the negative battery cable from the battery. (Chrysler)

cause a fire or damage expensive electrical and electronic components.

SUMMARY

Safety rules should become a habit. Safety rules are meaningless if not kept in practice at all times. Accidents do occur. Therefore it is necessary to always wear protective devices such as safety glasses, safety shoes and gloves, and to know how to treat minor injuries.

The dangers unique to an air conditioning shop using refrigerant are frostbite and toxic fumes in the presence of an open flame. The danger of frostbite is ever-present when working with refrigerant. R-12 refrigerant, being heavier than air, can accumulate in an unventilated work area and cause suffocation. If R-12 is exposed to open flame, toxic phosgene gas is created. Therefore, adequate ventilation must be maintained in work areas.

KNOW THESE TERMS

Frostbite, Phosgene gas, Suffocation, Electrical shock, Physical injuries, OSHA.

REVIEW QUESTIONS-CHAPTER 6

1. Shop safety is the responsibility of _____.
2. OSHA is a:
   a. Fire extinguisher.
   b. Chemical cleaning solvent.
   c. Government safety organization.
   d. None of the above.
3. All of the following are shop rules, except:
   a. Know your fire exits.
   b. Wear safety glasses at all times.
   c. Respect running engines.
   d. Wearing jewelry.
4. Proper shop ventilation removes dangerous gases, such as:
   a. Phosgene gas.
   b. Carbon monoxide.

   c. Noxious fumes.

   d. All of the above.

5. To speed up charging of an air conditioning system, the refrigerant container can be safely heated by:

   a. Propane torch.

   b. Halide torch.

   c. Cigarette lighter.

   d. Hot water at 120°F or less.

6. Mechanic A says the first aid treatment for R-12 in the eye is to immediately add a few drops of sterile mineral oil.

   Mechanic B says rub the eye.

   Which mechanic is correct?

7. First aid should be followed with a visit to a doctor. True or false?

8. The following should be considered sources of explosion:

   a. Overheated refrigerant containers.

   b. Gasoline tank.

   c. The car battery.

   d. All of the above.

9. Phosgene gas is produced by:

   a. Leaking refrigerant.

   b. Overcharged batteries.

   c. Introducing refrigerant to a flame.

   d. All of the above.

10. The following are sources of electrical shock except:

   a. Frayed electric cord.

   b. Grounded plug.

   c. Wet electrical tools.

   d. Faulty switches.

11. Fire extinguishers are:

   a. Located around the shop.

   b. Not needed.

   c. Graded B for paper fires.

   d. Graded B for electrical fires.

12. When using a floor jack:

   a. Nothing else is needed.

   b. Jack stands are needed.

   c. Seals on a floor jack can leak or fail without warning.

   d. Both b and c.

13. List three hazards involved when working on air conditioning systems with the engine running.

14. When lifting heavy objects, lift with your back. True or false?

15. The hazards of wearing jewelry while working in the shop are:

   a. Burns from electrical shorts.

   b. Snagging on engine parts.

   c. Being caught in rotating mechanisms.

   d. All of the above.

AIR CONDITIONING THEORY, CONSTRUCTION, OPERATION

After studying this chapter, you will be able to:
- Explain the basic A/C principles.
- List the parts of an automotive A/C system.
- Describe each part's function in an automotive A/C system.
- Summarize the different evaporator controls and tell why they are needed.
- Describe what an A/C clutch does and how it works and the types available.
- List the different types of A/C compressors available.
- Explain why high-pressure and low-pressure relief on automotive A/C systems are both needed.

BASIC REVIEW

When liquid refrigerant changes to a vapor, it absorbs heat from the surrounding area. This action is referred to as the latent heat of vaporization, Fig. 7-1.

Liquid refrigerant, like most liquids, boils and changes to a vapor when pressure is reduced, Fig. 7-2. When pressure is applied to the refrigerant vapor, it is condensed to a liquid, Fig. 7-3. During the process of converting a vapor to a liquid by applying pressure, latent heat of condensation is dissipated to the surrounding area, Fig. 7-4.

BASIC REFRIGERATION CYCLE

The *refrigeration cycle,* Fig. 7-5, consists of four phases: compression, condensation, expansion, and evaporation of refrigerant. Consider the starting point at the receiver-drier. At this point, the refrigerant is a hot liquid under high pressure. The liquid refrigerant flows to the expansion valve under high pressure. The expansion valve restricts the flow of the liquid refrigerant, thus reducing its pressure. The low-pressure liquid moves to the evaporator where it expands and changes to a vapor.

During this change of state, large quantities of heat are absorbed from the passenger compartment.

The heat-laden, low-pressure vapor is drawn to the compressor. The compressor changes the low-pressure vapor to a high-pressure vapor and raises its temperature. The high-pressure, high-temperature vapor is pumped to the condenser. The cooler outside air passing over the condenser removes heat from the refrigerant that was picked up from the passenger compartment and condenses it back to a high-pressure liquid. The cycle is then repeated.

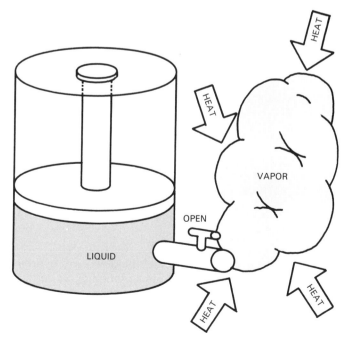

Fig. 7-1. Refrigerant absorbs large amounts of heat when it changes from a liquid to a vapor.

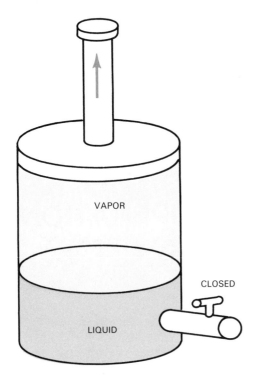

Fig. 7-2. When pressure is reduced, refrigerant boils and changes from a liquid to a gas.

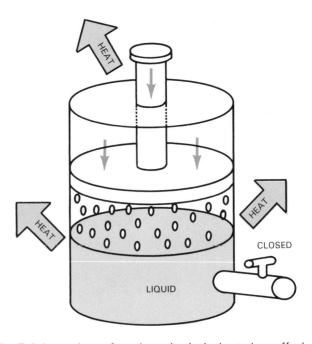

Fig. 7-4. Latent heat of condensation is the heat given off when a vapor changes to a liquid.

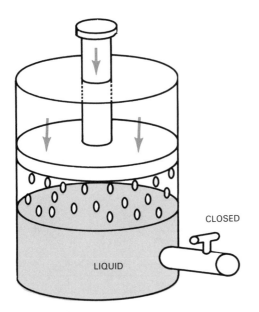

Fig. 7-3. Compressing refrigerant vapor causes it to change to a liquid.

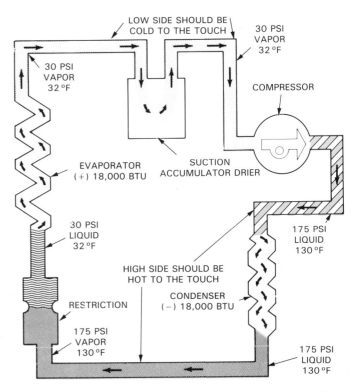

Fig. 7-5. The basic refrigeration or air conditioning cycle.

BASIC AIR CONDITIONING

As a means of better understanding the overall system, consider the following description of air conditioning components in an automobile. A typical automotive air conditioning system, as illustrated in Fig. 7-6, has the following five main components:
1. Receiver-drier or accumulator.
2. Thermostatic expansion valve.
3. Evaporator.
4. Compressor.
5. Condenser.

RECEIVER-DRIER

The receiver-drier removes dirt and moisture from the high-pressure liquid refrigerant. In addition, the receiver tank stores liquid refrigerant. This increases the volume of the system. The extra refrigerant stored in the receiver

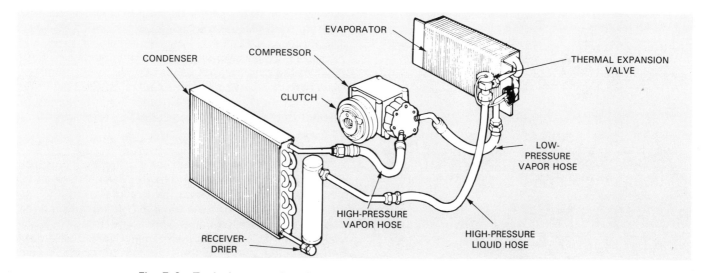

Fig. 7-6. Typical automotive air conditioning system shows major components.

provides for the changes in the quantity demanded by the evaporator under different operating conditions.

One type of receiver-drier used in automotive air conditioning, Fig. 7-7, is a cylindrical metal tank of welded construction. It has inlet and outlet fittings and a sight glass used to observe the level and condition of the refrigerant. The receiver-drier contains a desiccant or drying agent. The receiver-drier also has a filter screen or filter pads. This prevents foreign particles circulating in the system. The receiver-drier is not serviceable and must be replaced if defective, when a major system component is replaced, or if a major leak is repaired.

Sight glass

The *sight glass* provides a window to observe the level and condition of the refrigerant. A sight glass may be found in one of several locations:
1. As part of the receiver-drier.
2. As an integral part of the expansion valve.
3. As a separate unit in the liquid refrigerant line.
4. Valves-in-receiver unit.

A sight glass is a small round window securely sealed in a fitting, Fig. 7-8. Observing the sight glass provides system information as follows:
1. Clear.
2. Foamy.
3. Oil streaks.
4. Cloudy.

THERMOSTATIC EXPANSION VALVES (TXV)

The *expansion valve* provides a restriction or throttles the flow of refrigerant. This restriction reduces the pressure on the liquid refrigerant, thus reducing its boiling point. The expansion valve also meters the amount of refrigerant to the evaporator, by modulating the valve from wide open to closed, which varies with the heat load. The expansion valve separates the high-pressure side from the low-pressure side.

Located at the inlet of the expansion valve, Fig. 7-9, is a screen to trap any particles that break loose in the

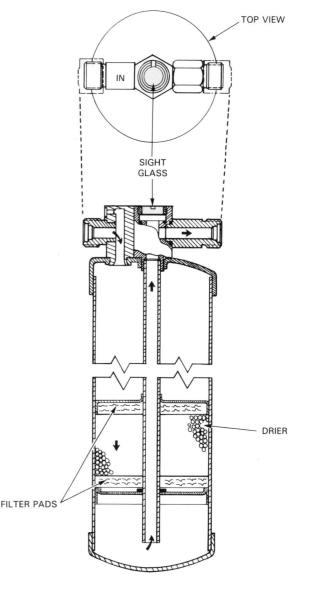

Fig. 7-7. The receiver-drier contains a desiccant that removes water vapor and a filter to strain foreign particles. (Chrysler)

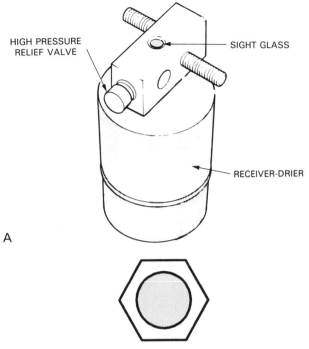

HIGH PRESSURE RELIEF VALVE

SIGHT GLASS

RECEIVER-DRIER

A

CLEAR: CORRECT CHARGE

A clear sight glass indicates the system has the correct charge of refrigerant. It may also indicate that the system has a complete lack of refrigerant, a condition accompanied by a lack of cooling action by the evaporator. Also, the sight glass may be clear and the system might be overcharged (too much refrigerant). This must be verified with test gauge readings.

FOAMY: LOW CHARGE

A foamy or bubbly looking sight glass indicates the system is low on refrigerant, and air has probably entered the system. However, if only occasional bubbles are noticed during clutch cycling or system startup, this may be a normal condition.

OIL STREAKS: COMPRESSOR OIL CIRCULATING

If oil streaks appear on the sight glass, a lack of refrigerant may be indicated, and the system's compressor oil is circulating through the system.

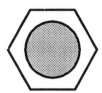

B

CLOUDY: DESICCANT CIRCULATING

A cloudy sight glass indicates that the desiccant contained in the receiver-drier (accumulator) has broken down and is being circulated through the system.

Fig. 7-8. Sight glass. A—Most receiver-driers contain a sight glass at the top. B—The view through the sight glass can determine some problems when ambient temperatures are between 70° and 90°F. (Chrysler and Ford)

receiver-drier. If the screen is plugged, it can be cleaned and the receiver-drier replaced.

An expansion valve is either internally or externally equalized. Equalized means pressure is applied to both sides of the diaphragm. Evaporator inlet pressure is applied to the bottom side of the diaphragm. However, the top side of the diaphragm has evaporator outlet pressure applied through the capillary tube.

Externally equalized

The capillary tube and thermal sensing bulb contains either refrigerant or carbon dioxide (CO_2). The thermal sensing bulb is held against the evaporator outlet. The capillary tube connects the thermal sensing bulb and the top of the expansion valve diaphragm.

The externally equalized expansion valve has an external line that connects the underside of the diaphragm to evaporator inlet pressure. In addition, the capillary tube connects to the top side of the diaphragm, Fig. 7-9. When a large evaporator is used, an externally equalized expansion valve is used to offset the large pressure drop.

Internally equalized

The internally equalized expansion valve has an internal passage that connects the evaporator inlet pressure to the underside of the diaphragm. The capillary tube connects to its top, Fig. 7-9.

TXV Operation

Three forces combine to operate the expansion valve. They are:
1. Spring force below the diaphragm.
2. Evaporator inlet pressure below the diaphragm.
3. Gas pressure inside the thermal bulb and capillary tube that applies pressure to the top of the diaphragm.

An increase or decrease of evaporator outlet temperature causes a corresponding pressure change in the thermal bulb transmitted to the top of the diaphragm through the capillary tube. When the evaporator outlet temperature increases, the pressure at the top of the expansion valve increases overcoming the spring and evaporator pressure under the diaphragm, allowing refrigerant to flow through the restriction. When evaporator outlet temperature decreases, the pressure at the top of diaphragm decreases. Spring pressure and evaporator pressure under the diaphragm are now greater, closing off or reducing the flow of refrigerant through the restriction.

ORIFICE TUBE

The orifice tube is located at the evaporator inlet. The *orifice tube* is similar to the expansion valve in that it provides a pressure drop, reducing pressure on the liquid refrigerant. There are no moving parts with an orifice tube, Fig. 7-10. The orifice tube is constructed of molded plastic around a metal tube (orifice) and a plastic screen at its inlet and outlet. If the screen becomes plugged, it must be replaced with a new orifice tube. In some cases, the accumulator must also be replaced when the system is badly contaminated.

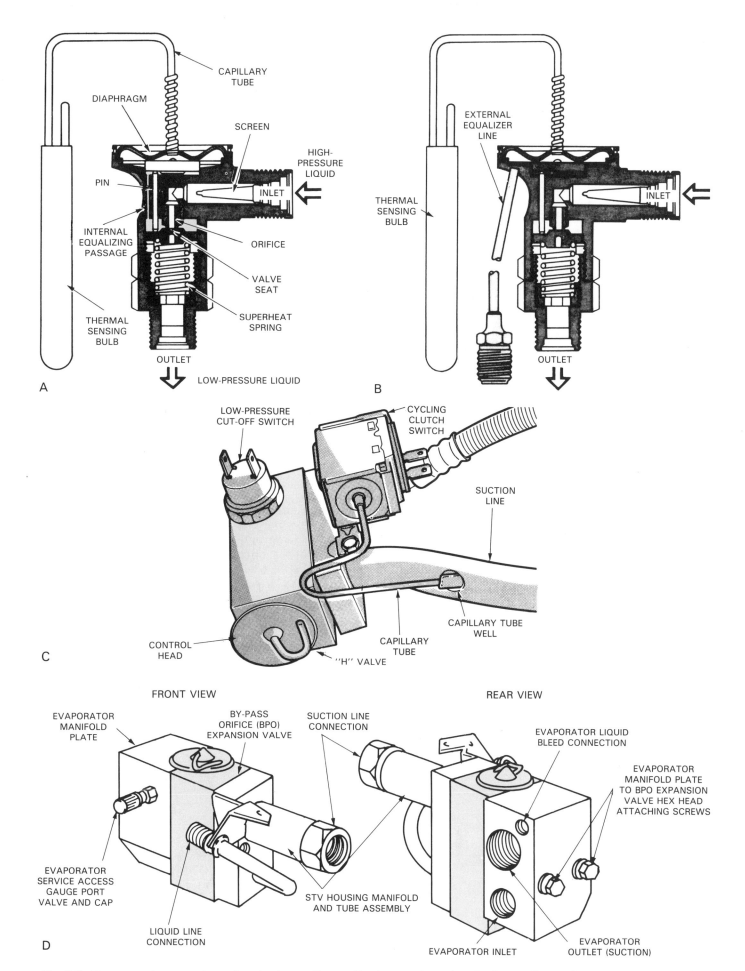

Fig. 7-9. Thermostatic-expansion valve. A—Internally equalized expansion valve. B—Externally equalized expansion valve. C—This is an ''H'' type expansion valve, in color, found on some Chrysler products. It is a rectangular metal block through which the evaporator inlet and outlet attach. The control head is an integral part of the valve. D—Combination valve found on some Ford products. Combination valve combines expansion valve, in color, and STV.

ACCUMULATOR

Systems that use an orifice tube in place of an expansion valve use an accumulator instead of a receiver-drier. Accumulators are located at the evaporator outlet (low-pressure side), as opposed to the receiver-drier which is located in the high-pressure line at the condenser outlet. The *accumulator* incorporates a desiccant (drying agent) to remove moisture from the refrigerant vapor, and separates any liquid which gets through the evaporator. Excessive liquid allowed to reach the compressor would cause severe knocking and damage.

An oil-bleed hole prevents oil from being trapped, thus assuring return of oil to the compressor. There is no sight glass in the accumulator.

EVAPORATOR

The *evaporator* removes heat and moisture from air entering the car. This is achieved as the air flows across the cool surface of the coils and fins of the evaporator.

The evaporator consists of several rows of aluminum tubing which make several passes through closely spaced aluminum fins, Fig. 7-11. The tubing, expanded into the fins, ensures good thermal conductivity.

Low-pressure liquid refrigerant from the expansion valve enters the evaporator. Due to reduced pressure, the refrigerant boils into a vapor absorbing its latent heat necessary for vaporization. Heat from the incoming air is absorbed by the evaporator fins and tubes and, in turn, is absorbed by the refrigerant as it changes state. The air is cooled. As it is cooled, so is water vapor from the air. Some of this water vapor gives up its latent heat, condenses on the fins, and is drained. Thus, the evaporator cools and dehumidifies the air. There are several factors that affect the evaporator's design:
1. Size and length of tubing.
2. Number of fins that surround tubing.
3. Airflow through fins and around tubing.

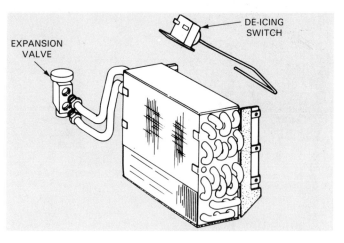

Fig. 7-11. Evaporator core is constructed of aluminum.

Starved/flooded evaporator

An evaporator is said to be starved if the expansion valve does not meter enough refrigerant to the evaporator. There is very little cooling because there is not enough refrigerant changing from a liquid to a vapor. Conversely, an evaporator is said to be flooded if the expansion valve meters too much refrigerant to the evaporator. This also causes very little cooling because there is too much liquid refrigerant to vaporize quickly and therefore heat removal is reduced.

Evaporator controls

The *evaporator controls* provide effective air cooling and at the same time prevent the freezing of moisture that condenses on the evaporator. Evaporator temperature is controlled by maintaining pressure in the evaporator by any one of the following:
1. Cycling clutch switch, Fig. 7-12. The temperature of the evaporator is monitored by this switch through a capillary tube connected at the evaporator outlet. When the temperature of the evaporator outlet is too cold, the switch disengages the com-

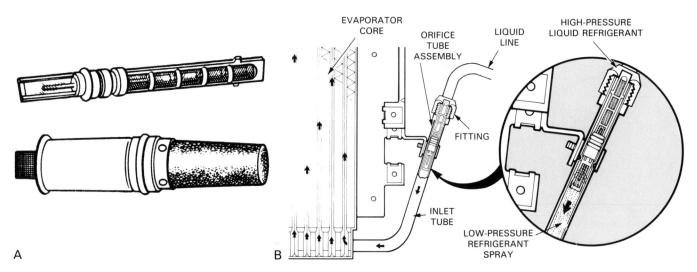

Fig. 7-10. Orifice tube system. A—Top is the new style orifice tube. Bottom is the old style orifice tube. Do not interchange the two. B—The fixed orifice tube is installed at the evaporator inlet. It provides a pressure drop on the liquid refrigerant. (Delco and Ford)

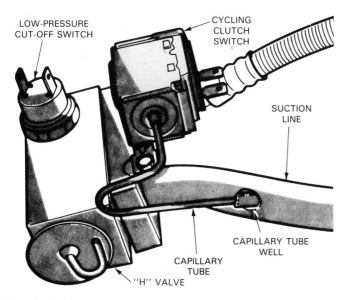

Fig. 7-12. Depending on the evaporator outlet temperature/pressure, cycling clutch switch engages and disengages the a/c clutch electrically. (Chrysler)

pressor clutch by opening a set of contact points, thereby shutting down the A/C system.

2. Suction throttling valve (STV) was used only for a short period in early air conditioning. All STV valves are similar in design except for the operating control mechanism, which is either cable or vacuum diaphragm operated, Fig. 7-13. The STV operates by regulating or throttling the refrigerant outlet flow from the evaporator.

3. Pilot operated absolute (POA) valve located in the evaporator outlet line is shown in Fig. 7-14. The POA valve is a special type with a straight-through refrigerant flow. Control of the POA valve is by an evacuated bellows and needle valve assembly located in the valve capsule. The POA valve is not affected by atmospheric pressure or changes in altitude.

4. The modulator valve, Fig. 7-15, limits and maintains a minimum pressure in the evaporator. It is a suction-relief valve that will allow refrigerant to bypass the evaporator to control the evaporator temperature.

5. Valves-in-receiver (VIR), Fig. 7-16, simply means that the receiver-drier, expansion valve, and the POA valve, including the sight glass, are assembled into one unit. The VIR is serviceable, however, no adjustments or repairs are possible to the individual units; these units must be replaced when malfunctioning. For this reason, the units are sealed by means of O-rings. The external equalizer line between the expansion valve and the outlet of the POA valve, and the expansion valve capillary and thermobulb are all eliminated with the VIR unit. The VIR unit is made up of three separate pressure areas. The upper area is low-pressure gas from the evaporator. The middle area is high-pressure liquid to the evaporator from the expansion valve and low-pressure gas from the POA valve to the compressor. The lower area is high-pressure liquid from the condenser.

6. Evaporator pressure regulator valve (EPR) is shown in Fig. 7-17. The EPR is an internal type of suction

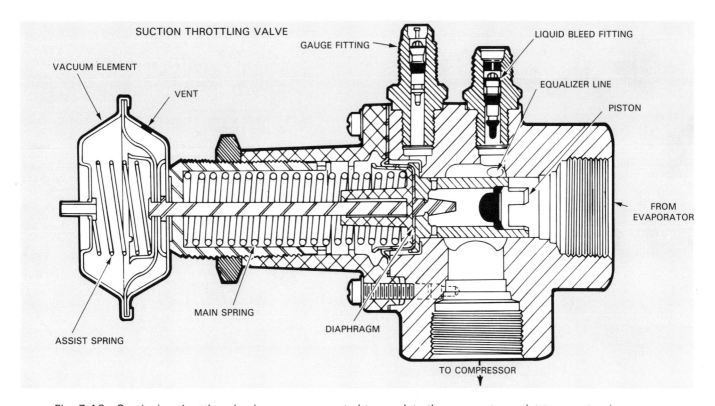

Fig. 7-13. Suctioning throttle valve is vacuum operated to regulate the evaporator outlet temperature/pressure. (Delco Div. of GMC)

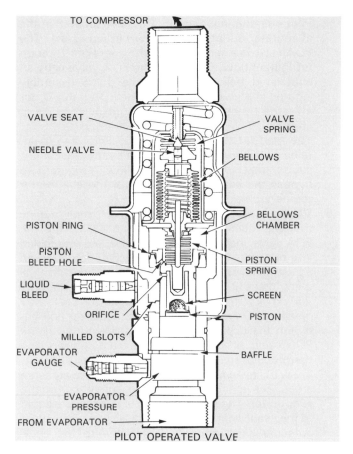

Fig. 7-14. Pilot operated absolute valve regulates evaporator outlet temperature/pressure.

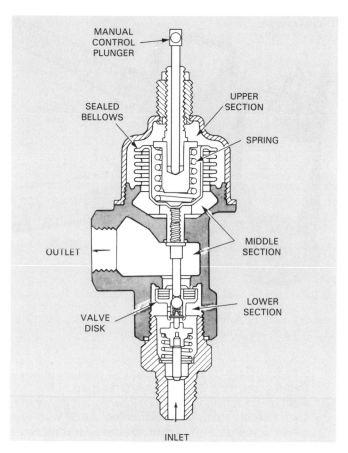

Fig. 7-15. The modulator valve maintains the evaporator outlet temperature and pressure.

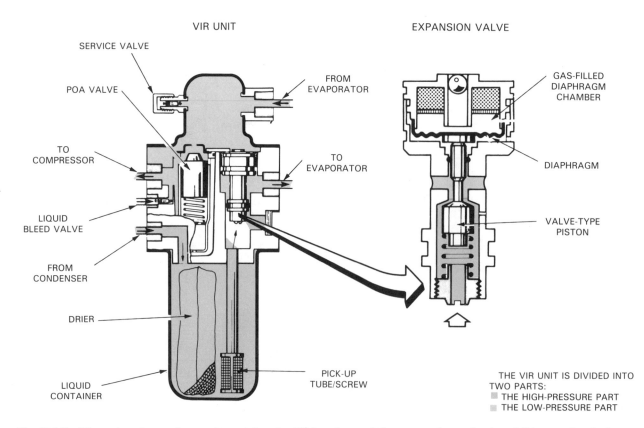

Fig. 7-16. The valves-in-receiver unit contains the POA valve and the expansion valve in addition to the desiccant. (Delco Div. of GMC)

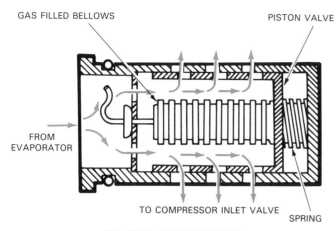

Fig. 7-17. Evaporator pressure regulator valve controls the evaporator outlet temperature/pressure and is located inside the a/c compressor.

throttling valve located in the compressor inlet and designed to prevent evaporator outlet pressure decreasing to the point at which icing of the evaporator core might occur. The EPR operates in the same manner as the POA valve, except the valve piston is controlled by a gas-filled bellows.

7. The pilot operated Evaporator Pressure Regulator valve can be used in place of the previous EPR valve, and is identified by a protrusion at the end of the valve housing. The pilot operated EPR, Fig. 7-18, has a built-in pilot valve, which triggers the main throttling valve providing more precise control of the evaporator outlet pressure. This allows the system to operate at lower temperature without evaporator freeze-up. The valve is not adjustable and is serviced by replacement. If this pilot operated EPR valve is not available for replacement, the standard type EPR valve may be used.

8. Evaporator temperature regulator valve (ETR) is

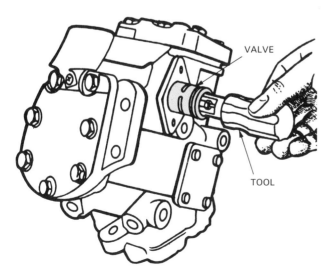

Fig. 7-18. A piloted EPR valve maintains a more precise temperature/pressure of the evaporator outlet and is interchangeable with an EPR valve. (Chrysler)

used with automatic temperature control. The ETR valve, Fig. 7-19, is installed in the same manner as the EPR valve and used in conjunction with an evaporator switch, which is mounted on the evaporator case. The switch senses evaporator coil temperature. At a predetermined point, the switch closes the ETR valve, stopping refrigerant flow completely.

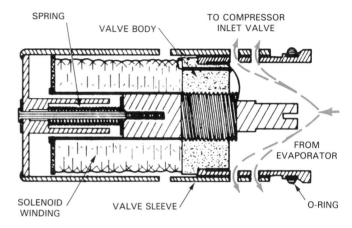

Fig. 7-19. The evaporator temperature regulator valve or solenoid is used in place of an EPR valve. The ETR valve is controlled electrically and is also located inside the compressor. (Chrysler)

COMPRESSOR

The *compressor* is a pump which performs three basic functions:
1. Circulates the refrigerant through the system.
2. Removes low-pressure vapor from the evaporator.
3. Compresses it to a high-pressure, high-temperature vapor.

Types of compressors

There are several different types of A/C compressors. They are:
1. Two-cylinder reciprocating compressors, designed with "in-line" or "V"-type cylinder arrangement. The piston motion is perpendicular to the crankshaft, Fig. 7-20. The reed valve assembly and operation is shown in Fig. 7-21.
2. The four-cylinder radial compressors have cylinders placed around the crankshaft with movement perpendicular to the crankshaft, Fig. 7-22.
3. The axial compressor. Piston motion is parallel to the compressor crankshaft, Fig. 7-23. The pistons are single acting and are moved back and forth in the cylinders by a "wobble" or "swash" plate.
4. The vane rotary compressor has vanes connected to an off-center crankshaft, Fig. 7-24.
5. The variable displacement compressor, Fig. 7-25, varies the angle of the swash plate depending on the heat load placed on the system.
6. The scroll compressor, consisting of a fixed spiral and a moveable spiral that are meshed together.

65

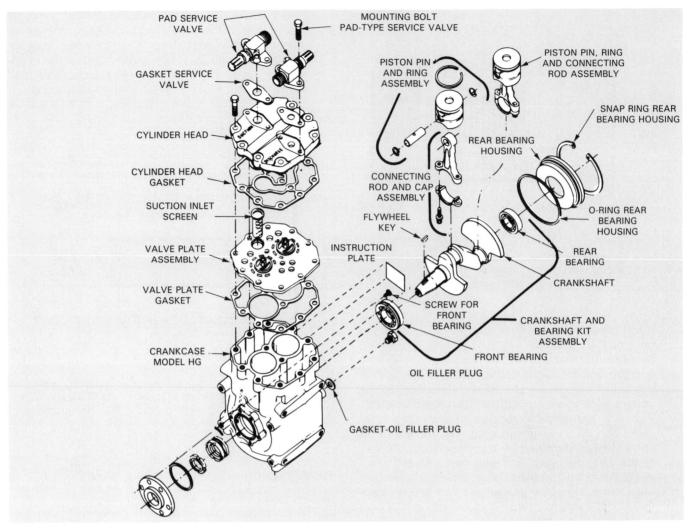

Fig. 7-20. Two-cylinder, reciprocating compressor design.   (Chrysler)

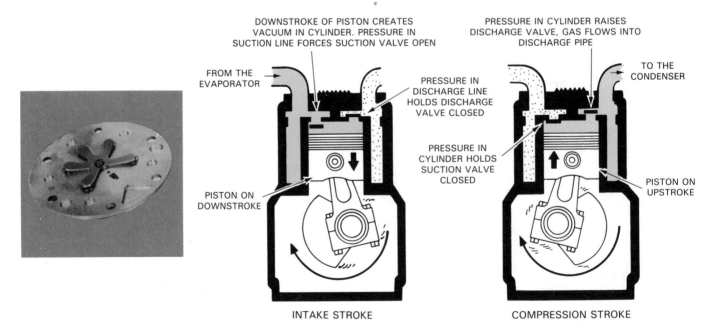

Fig. 7-21. Reed valves. A—Reed valve assembly. B—Reed valve operation. 1—As piston moves upward, pressure causes intake reed valve to flex closed and the exhaust reed valve to flex open. 2—As piston moves downward, a low-pressure area is created. This causes intake reed valve to flex open and exhaust reed valve to flex closed.

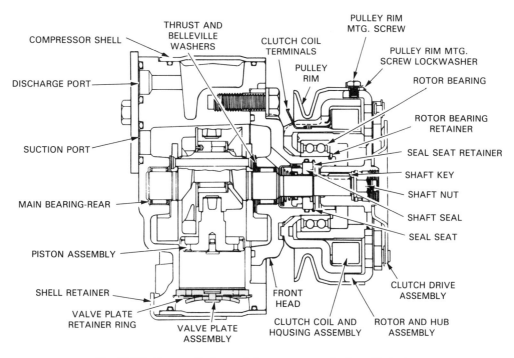

Fig. 7-22. Four-cylinder radial compressor design. (Delco)

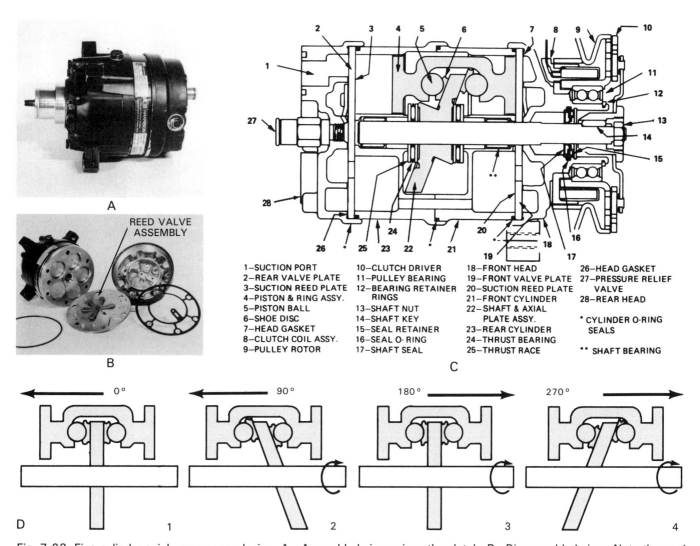

1—SUCTION PORT	10—CLUTCH DRIVER	18—FRONT HEAD	26—HEAD GASKET
2—REAR VALVE PLATE	11—PULLEY BEARING	19—FRONT VALVE PLATE	27—PRESSURE RELIEF
3—SUCTION REED PLATE	12—BEARING RETAINER	20—SUCTION REED PLATE	VALVE
4—PISTON & RING ASSY.	RINGS	21—FRONT CYLINDER	28—REAR HEAD
5—PISTON BALL	13—SHAFT NUT	22—SHAFT & AXIAL	
6—SHOE DISC	14—SHAFT KEY	PLATE ASSY.	* CYLINDER O-RING
7—HEAD GASKET	15—SEAL RETAINER	23—REAR CYLINDER	SEALS
8—CLUTCH COIL ASSY.	16—SEAL O-RING	24—THRUST BEARING	
9—PULLEY ROTOR	17—SHAFT SEAL	25—THRUST RACE	** SHAFT BEARING

Fig. 7-23. Five-cylinder axial compressor design. A—Assembled view minus the clutch. B—Disassembled view. Note the reed plate assembly. C—Cross section view of an axial compressor. D—Rotation of crankshaft causes swash plate to move piston in a linear motion. (Oldsmobile)

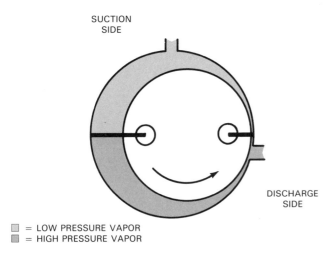

SUCTION
SIDE

DISCHARGE
SIDE

□ = LOW PRESSURE VAPOR
■ = HIGH PRESSURE VAPOR

Fig. 7-24. Vane rotary compressor action.

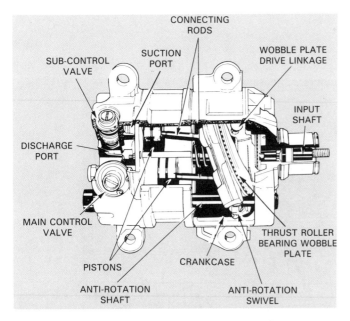

CONNECTING
RODS

SUCTION
PORT

WOBBLE PLATE
DRIVE LINKAGE

SUB-CONTROL
VALVE

INPUT
SHAFT

DISCHARGE
PORT

MAIN CONTROL
VALVE

THRUST ROLLER
BEARING WOBBLE
PLATE

PISTONS

CRANKCASE

ANTI-ROTATION
SHAFT

ANTI-ROTATION
SWIVEL

Fig. 7-25. Variable displacement compressor does not use a clutch that cycles on and off. Instead, the angle of the swash or wobble plate determines compressor displacement and is controlled by a bellows-actuated valve. This eliminates a surging condition that can be felt by the driver when the clutch cycles on and off.   (Cadillac)

Compressor clutch

The *compressor clutch* engages and disengages the compressor. The clutch is an electromagnetic device. When current is applied to the clutch coil, a strong magnetic field is created, pulling the armature inward to engage the crankshaft. There are two basic types of clutches:
1. Rotating.
2. Stationary.

Rotating clutch

This clutch has a magnetic coil which rotates with the pulley. Electric current is supplied to the coil by brushes mounted on the compressor frame that contact the slip ring on the inside of the pulley.

Stationary clutch

This is the most popular type. The magnetic coil mounts on the frame of the compressor and does not rotate, Fig. 7-26. Mounting of the coil is critical for two reasons:
1. Prevents the rotating pulley from contacting the coil.
2. Provides minimum air gap to obtain maximum magnetic force.

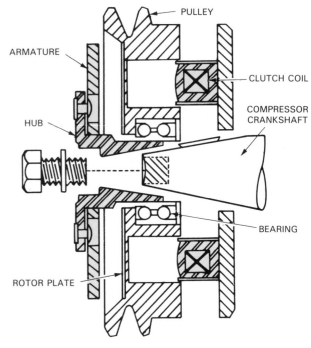

PULLEY

ARMATURE

CLUTCH COIL

COMPRESSOR
CRANKSHAFT

HUB

BEARING

ROTOR PLATE

Fig. 7-26. Cross section view of an electromagnetic clutch. When energized, the armature is locked to the rotor and the A/C compressor is engaged.

Clutch bearing

Both types of clutches incorporate a pulley which rotates on a bearing mounted on the clutch hub, Fig. 7-27. One exception is a compressor which mounts the bearing on the compressor front head assembly.

Clutch operation

In the operation of all clutch designs, when the coil is not energized, the compressor is not operating. The pulley is free to rotate on its bearing without turning the compressor crankshaft. The armature plate is attached to the hub by a spring and is mounted to the compressor crankshaft by means of a keyway and lock nut.

When the clutch coil is energized, the magnetic force draws the armature plate toward the rotor, which is part of the pulley, Fig. 7-26. The pulley is restricted by the bearing from moving laterally, but the armature plate can move against the spring to contact the rotor. The magnetic force locks the armature plate and rotor together. This creates a solid connection between the pulley and the crankshaft, causing the compressor crankshaft to rotate.

When the magnetic coil is de-energized, the spring pressure pushes the armature plate away from the rotor. This allows the pulley to rotate freely on its bearing without rotating the compressor crankshaft. Some

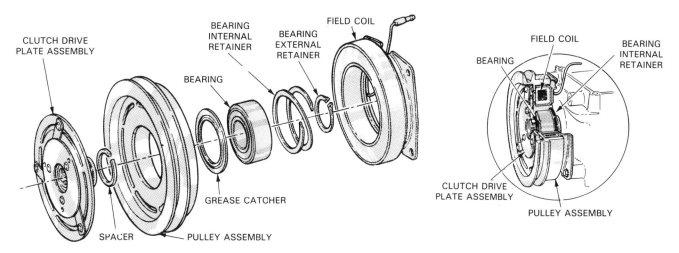

Fig. 7-27. Location of A/C compressor clutch bearing.

designs incorporate slots in both the armature plate and rotor. This concentrates the magnetic field and increases the attraction between the two when the coil is energized.

Several switches control electrical power to the clutch coil: the function-control switch on the instrument panel, ignition switch, and thermostatic switch (if employed). All must be on to energize and engage the clutch. In some applications, an ambient switch is used to prevent the compressor from operating in extremely low temperatures.

CONDENSER

The *condenser* receives the high-temperature, high-pressure gas from the compressor. This gas is converted to a liquid by removing heat.

Automotive air conditioning condensers are usually located behind the grille and in front of the radiator. Air movement at highway speeds is sufficient to obtain adequate heat transfer. At low speeds and idle, airflow across the condenser is provided by the engine fan. In the case of a transversely mounted engine, an electrically-driven fan is used.

Condensers are radiatorlike devices constructed of aluminum tubing to which fins are attached. The tubing is expanded into the fins to provide positive contact for the most efficient heat transfer. Typical condensers are shown in Fig. 7-28.

High-temperature, high-pressure gas from the compressor enters at the top of the condenser. As the gas flows through the condenser, it releases heat to the cooler ambient air flowing over the condenser. Giving up its heat causes the vapor to change to a liquid. Under average heat load, the top two-thirds of the condenser contains refrigerant vapor and the lower third contains liquid refrigerant. The liquid refrigerant in the lower third of the condenser has lost much of its heat. However, the pressure and temperature remain high.

MUFFLER

Mufflers, Figs. 7-29 and 7-30, dampen compressor pumping noises within the system. Mufflers are generally

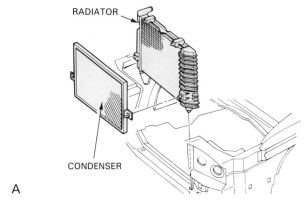

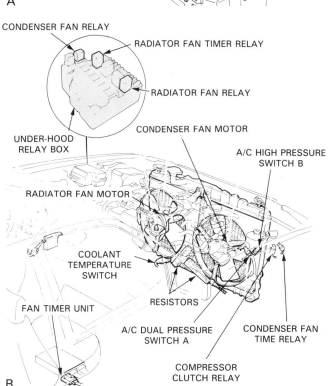

Fig. 7-28. Condenser. A—The condenser is mounted in front of the radiator. B—Some condensers mount adjacent to the radiator, requiring a separate fan and motor. (Honda and Cadillac)

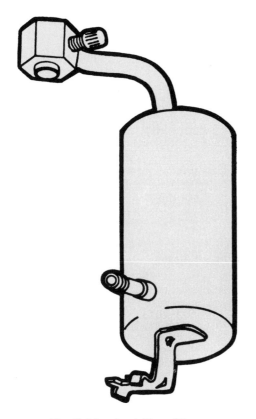

Fig. 7-29. An A/C muffler.

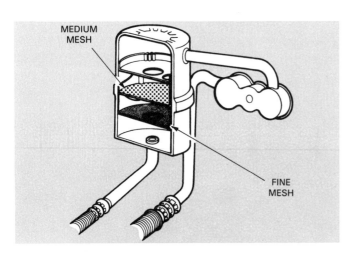

Fig. 7-30. Some A/C mufflers contain two mesh screens to prevent foreign particles from contaminating system if compressor should fail. With this type of muffler in the system, standard flushing procedures are not needed when a compressor fails. (Oldsmobile)

one of two types. One uses the chamber muffling principles. The other is a tuned baffle type and used where extreme noise is a problem.

SERVICE VALVES

Service valves are provided for testing and servicing the air conditioning system. Gauge sets can be attached to the service valves to determine system pressures and to fill or discharge the system refrigerant.

There are two types of service valves, the Schrader valve and a three-position stem-type valve. The Schrader design is similar to that of tire valves.

CAUTION: Do not use a tire valve for replacement, because of the higher pressures.

Connecting test hoses to a Schrader valve is similar to attaching a hand pump to a tire. Some cars are equipped with Schrader valves which will accept a quick-disconnect type hose coupling, as shown in Fig. 7-31.

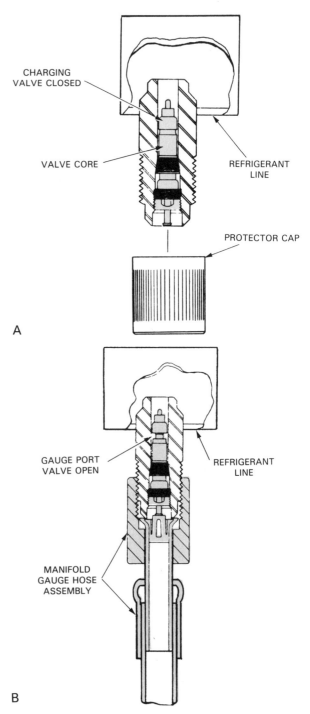

Fig. 7-31. Schrader service valve. A—Similar in design to a tire valve. B—It permits the use of quick disconnect couplings to be used at test ports. (Ford)

Schrader valve

The Schrader valve has only two positions, open or closed. The Schrader valve is automatically opened when a service hose is attached to the valve. A special fitting on the service hose depresses the valve pin, opening the valve. The pin is spring loaded and pops back to a closed position when the service hose is removed.

NOTE: Always remove the gauge hoses from the service valve before removing them from the test gauges. This prevents loss of refrigerant. A service cap protects the valve from contamination.

Three-position service valve

The three-position stem-type service valve is shown in Fig. 7-32. The three-position stem-type valve is generally found on the compressor. One valve is on the high-pressure side and one is on the low-pressure side. The high- and low-side valves are identical. The stem valve has three positions as follows:

1. Refrigerant flow shut off. Rotate the valve clockwise to the front-seated position. Refer to Fig. 7-32A. In this position, the hose to the compressor is blocked off, isolating the compressor for service.

> WARNING: Never operate the compressor with the service valve in the closed position, as compressor damage would result.

2. Normal or system operating position. Turn the stem fully counterclockwise, placing the valve in a back-seated position. Refer to Fig. 7-32B. This position allows refrigerant to flow freely from the compressor through the system. In this position, the

pressure gauge port is blocked off and pressure readings cannot be taken.

3. Service valve in a mid-position. Refer to Fig. 7-32C. This allows the system to operate normally, and pressure readings to be taken. In this position, refrigerant pressure is at all ports.

NOTE: Before removing service hoses, the stem valves must be backseated as shown in Fig. 7-32B. This prevents refrigerant loss.

PRESSURE-RELIEF VALVES

The *pressure-relief valve* prevents excessive refrigerant pressure in the system. The pressure-relief valve is designed to relieve the system pressure at approximately 385 psi (27.1 kg/cm²), which is below the bursting point of any of the components. One of three types of pressure devices is generally used:

1. Spring-loaded valve.
2. Rupture-disc type.
3. Fusible-plug type.

The pressure-relief valve is located in the high-pressure side of the compressor on some units, or at the receiver-drier, Fig. 7-33.

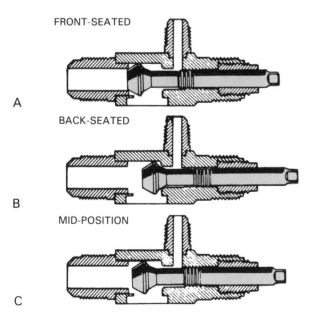

Fig. 7-32. Stem-type service valve must be screwed in or out. A—Service valve screwed all the way in. This blocks flow of refrigerant to compressor. B—Service valve screwed all the way out. This blocks flow of refrigerant to port where test gauge connects. The service valve must be in this position, except during testing, to prevent leakage of the refrigerant. C—Service valve screwed half in to allow refrigerant to also reach the test gauges after they are connected to the test port.

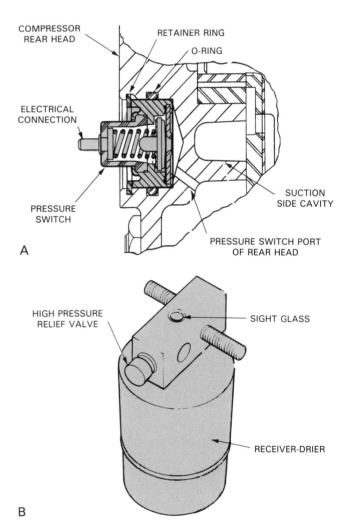

Fig. 7-33. High-pressure relief. A—Pressure-relief switch is at the back side of some compressors. B-Other pressure-relief valves are located at the receiver-drier. (Delco and Chrysler)

The spring-loaded pressure-relief valves most widely used are of tubular construction, housing a spring-loaded poppet valve. A male thread on one end screws into the high-pressure side of the compressor. The opposite end of the valve is open to the atmosphere. Rupture-disc type and fusible-plug type pressure-relief devices have been used. However, when these devices relieve excess pressure, the complete refrigerant charge is lost. The discs or plugs must be replaced after they have failed, and the system evacuated and recharged.

Low-pressure switch

The *low-pressure switch* de-energizes the clutch and stops the compressor. This prevents damage to the compressor due to the lack of lubrication that is normally carried with the refrigerant.

The low-pressure switch, Fig. 7-34, is normally closed and opens when pressure drops below 20 psi (1.41 kg/cm²). The low-pressure switch is located in the high-pressure side of the system, either in the compressor or elsewhere in the line.

Some a/c systems use a *superheat switch* that allows current to flow to a thermal fuse when the refrigerant level is low, Fig. 7-35. When current flows through the heater, the thermal fuse melts, interrupting current to the A/C clutch.

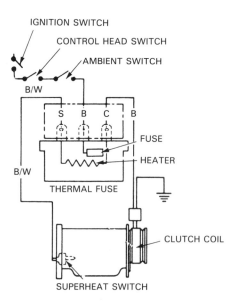

Fig. 7-35. Superheat switch detects hot refrigerant vapors at the compressor inlet. Hot temperature on the low-pressure side may be due to low refrigerant level. Superheat switch completes circuit to thermal limiter when high temperature is detected.

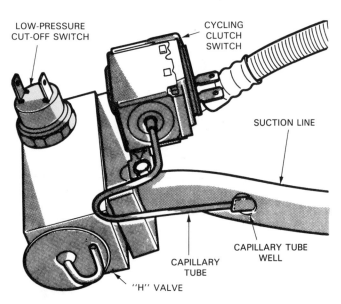

Fig. 7-34. Low-pressure cut-off. Some switches are located at the expansion valve. Another type is a fuse that blows and interrupts current to the clutch when superheat switch, located inside the compressor, detects high temperature in the normally cold, low-pressure side.   (Chrysler)

SUMMARY

Automotive air conditioning maintains the lowest possible evaporator temperature without freezing external moisture. Evaporator temperature controls are used to prevent freeze-up during the operation of the system. It is important to understand the refrigeration cycle in order to diagnose and repair an air conditioning system accurately and safely.

The system is put into operation by starting the compressor. The compressor decreases the pressure in the evaporator, and increases the pressure in the condenser and the refrigerant flow starts. The cold, low-pressure gas from the evaporator is changed to a hot, high-pressure gas by the compressor and pumped into the condenser. In the condenser, heat is removed causing the gas to condense to a high-pressure liquid.

The high-pressure liquid flows through a receiver-drier which removes moisture and foreign material from the liquid refrigerant. The pressure of the liquid is reduced by an expansion valve or orifice tube. Lowering the pressure on the liquid allows it to evaporate and change to a gas. The liquid refrigerant is changed to a gas-absorbing heat at the evaporator. On systems that use an orifice tube, an accumulator is located at the evaporator outlet to trap any liquid refrigerant and moisture before it enters the compressor. A cycling thermostatic switch senses evaporator temperature and cycles the compressor to prevent evaporator freeze-up; other systems maintain backpressure in the suction side. The refrigerant gas returns to the compressor, completing the cycle.

KNOW THESE TERMS

Refrigeration cycle, Receiver-drier, Sight glass, Expansion valve, Orifice tube, Accumulator, Evaporator, Evaporator controls, Compressor, Compressor clutch, Condenser, Muffler, Service valves, Pressure-relief valve, Low-pressure switch, Superheat switch.

REVIEW QUESTIONS—CHAPTER 7

1. The function of a sight glass is to:
    a. Show the oil level.
    b. Show system contamination.

c. Indicate amount of liquid refrigerant.

d. Indicate excessive refrigerant.

2. List the four refrigerant cycles.

3. Name the five major components of an automotive A/C system.

4. Describe and explain the different types of expansion valves.

5. Evaporator pressure control devices are:
   a. POA, EPR, PVC, CCOT.
   b. Modulator, EGR, EPR.
   c. POA, STV, EPR, VIR.
   d. None of the above.

6. The condenser is located in the _____ side of the system, and condenses the _____ to _____ refrigerant.

7. The Schrader valve controls the rate of evaporation. True or false?

8. The compressor compresses refrigerant vapor and:
   a. Vaporizes the refrigerant.
   b. Removes moisture from the system.
   c. Creates a pressure differential to cause refrigerant flow.
   d. None of the above.

9. The POA valve is located:
   a. In the glove compartment.
   b. In the liquid-refrigerant line.
   c. Between the expansion valve and evaporator.
   d. In the evaporator outlet line.

10. Incoming warm air gives up its heat in the evaporator which is absorbed by the:
    a. POA valve.
    b. Compressor.
    c. Refrigerant as it changes state.
    d. Schrader valve.

11. System damage could result because of low refrigerant level if the _____ switch fails to sense the reduction in head pressure.

12. The orifice tube is located:
    a. At the compressor inlet.
    b. In the inlet side of muffler.
    c. In the accumulator drier.
    d. At the evaporator inlet.

13. The in-line reciprocating compressor has:
    a. Six cylinders.
    b. Two cylinders.
    c. Four cylinders.
    d. A swash plate.

14. The VIR assembly combines the POA valve with:
    a. Thermostatic expansion valve.
    b. Desiccant drying agent.
    c. Sight glass.
    d. All of the above.

15. An accumulator is used in place of a receiver-drier when the air conditioning system uses:
    a. An expansion valve.
    b. Silica gel.
    c. Suction throttling valve.
    d. An orifice tube.

16. An expansion valve functions by controlling the amount of liquid refrigerant entering the:
    a. Compressor.   c. Accumulator.
    b. Condenser.   d. Evaporator.

17. Complete the following:
    a. VIR — Valves-in- _____ .
    b. EPR — Evaporator _____ regulator.
    c. POA — Pilot-operated _____ valve.
    d. STV — _____ throttling valve.
    e. ETR — _____ _____ regulator.

18. A _____ clutch is used to engage or disengage the compressor.

19. The muffler is used to suppress:
    a. Blower fan noise.
    b. The sound of bubbles in refrigerant.
    c. Compressor pumping noise.
    d. Fan belt noise.

20. The liquid refrigerant flows to the expansion valve under _____ pressure and from the expansion valve under _____ pressure.

21. The receiver-drier:
    a. Removes moisture from the refrigerant.
    b. Filters contaminants from the refrigerant.
    c. Stores extra refrigerant to cover demand changes.
    d. All of the above.

22. The accumulator is located:
    a. In the high-pressure side of the system.
    b. In the low-pressure side of the system.
    c. Either a or b.
    d. None of the above.

23. The dividing point of an air conditioning system between the high- and low-pressure occurs at:
    a. Compressor.
    b. Evaporator.
    c. Condenser.
    d. Expansion valve.

24. The evaporator:
    a. Keeps the system clean.
    b. Removes heat from the incoming air.
    c. Removes moisture and contaminants from the incoming air.
    d. Both b and c.

25. When the EPR or ETR evaporator control valve is used, it is located in the compressor. True or false?

26. Suction and compression in an air conditioning compressor is controlled by the:
    a. Pilot-operated absolute valve.
    b. Evaporator-pressure regulator valve.
    c. Suction-throttling valve.
    d. Reed valves.

27. Activation of a pressure-relief valve of the rupture-disc type or fusible-plug type results in the complete loss of refrigerant. True or false?

28. The design of the Schrader valve is similar to:
    a. VIR valve.
    b. Reed valve.
    c. Tire valve.
    d. Rotary valve.

29. Airflow across the condenser with a transverse-mounted engine is maintained by a fan that is driven:
    a. By the engine.
    b. By vacuum.
    c. Electrically.
    d. None of the above.

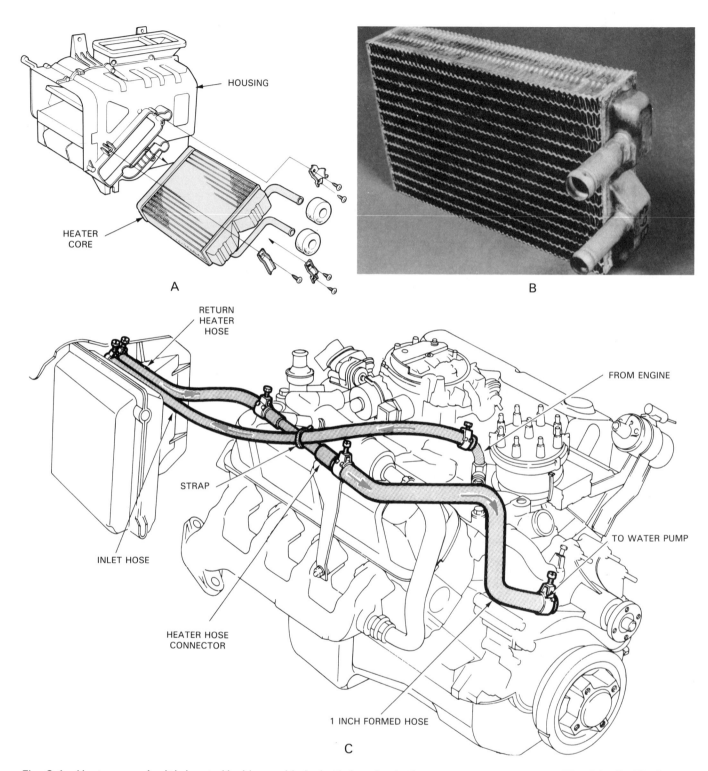

Fig. 8-1. Heater core. A—It is located inside a molded, plastic housing in the passenger compartment. (Honda)   B—The heater core is basically a small radiator. (Everco)   C—Heater hoses connect the engine to the heater core. Hot coolant travels through the heater hoses.   (Ford)

HEATING AND VENTILATION SYSTEMS

8

After studying this chapter, you will be able to:
- *Explain the function of the heating system and how it works.*
- *Describe how the engine cooling system affects heater output.*
- *Summarize the different modes of operation.*

HEATING SYSTEM

The *heating system* keeps the passenger compartment warm during cold weather and the windows (especially the windshield) clear. Glass is a poor conductor of heat. This causes a temperature difference between the inside and the outside of the glass. This is why only the inside of the windows fog up.

The hot, moisture-laden air inside the passenger compartment condenses on the cooler inside surface of the glass. This causes the windows to fog up. It is most noticeable on rainy days due to the high humidity.

Selecting the defroster mode directs heated air to the windshield and gradually forces the condensation to evaporate. This eliminates the fogged windshield.

When the defroster mode is selected on a car equipped with air conditioning, the A/C system is automatically engaged at the same time. The moisture-laden (humid) airflow goes through the evaporator core before passing through the heater core. The moisture then condenses on the evaporator core. This action removes moisture from the incoming airflow, before it is heated by the heater core. The hot, dry airflow to the windshield causes it to rapidly clear.

HEATER CORE

The *heater core* heats the incoming ambient airflow for the heat and defrost modes. It is located in a molded plastic housing in the passenger compartment, Fig. 8-1. A blower motor forces air over the heater core fins. This heats the incoming ambient air. The heated air is distributed through ducts to the passenger compartment.

A leaking heater core is indicated by coolant found on the right front (passenger) floor mat or mist on the inside of the windshield. A clogged evaporator drain has the same effect. This causes a wet spot in the same location.

Water control valve

A *water control valve,* when used, is located in the inlet hose to the heater core, Fig. 8-2. This valve can be controlled by vacuum or a Bowden-type cable. The valve allows hot coolant to the heater core, except when the air conditioning is placed on MAX A/C (vacuum-controlled) or the temperature lever in the full cold position (cable-controlled). This allows maximum cooling in the passenger compartment.

ENGINE COOLING SYSTEM

For the engine to operate at peak efficiency, it must operate at a high temperature within narrow parameters. If the engine operates cooler than desired, not all of the fuel in the combustion chamber burns. This causes spark plug fouling, which reduces fuel economy and performance. The results of below normal engine operating temperatures also causes insufficient heater output.

If the engine runs too hot, the result can be a loss of coolant, resulting in damage to the cylinder walls and heads. If the operation of an overheated engine continues, the engine oil breaks down and the moving metal parts (such as the crankshaft, pistons, and valve train) seize. The engine temperature must be regulated. The engine cooling system consists of the thermostat, water pump, radiator, engine fan, coolant, radiator cap, and hoses.

Thermostat

An *engine thermostat* regulates the engine temperature. It is placed between the coolant outlet and radiator in most cars, Fig. 8-3. A water pump, Fig. 8-4,

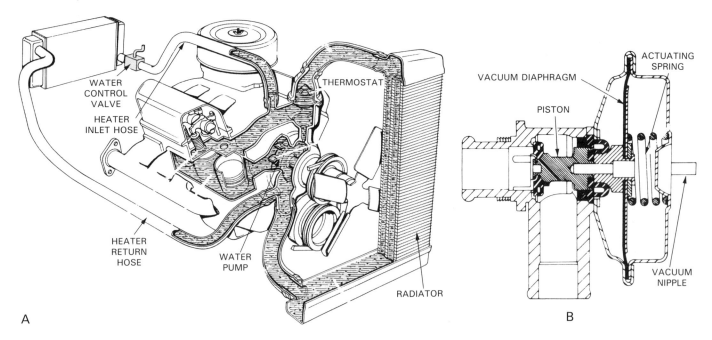

Fig. 8-2. Water control valve. A—The water control valve is located in the inlet heater hose. B—Construction of a vacuum-operated water control valve.

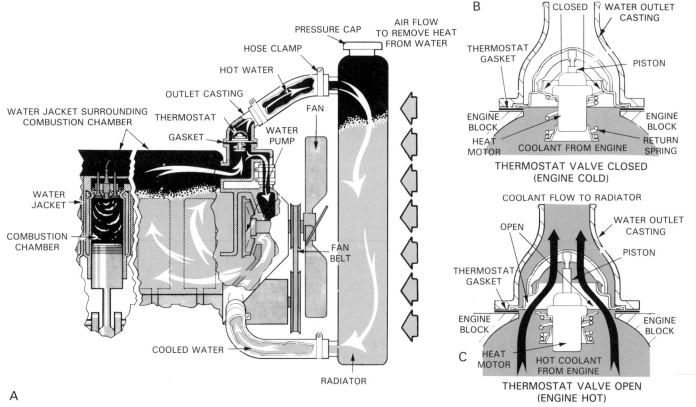

Fig. 8-3. Thermostat. A—It is located between the coolant outlet and radiator inlet on most cars. B—When temperature of the coolant is cold, thermostat is closed. This blocks coolant flow to radiator. This allows engine to reach its operating temperature for peak efficiency. C—When temperature of coolant is hot enough, thermostat opens allowing coolant flow to radiator. (Standard-Thomson)

circulates the cold coolant within the engine block to remove combustion heat from the cylinder walls and other metal parts. After the coolant reaches operating temperature, the thermostat gradually opens.

Thermostats are factory calibrated to open at a specific temperature, which is stamped on the body of the thermostat. Most thermostats are calibrated to open at 195°F (90.5°C) for year round use when a solution of water and ethylene glycol is used. When a thermostat opens, the water pump circulates the hot coolant to the radiator.

Radiator

The *radiator* is made of rows of brass, copper, or aluminum tubing that the coolant travels through, Fig. 8-5. Many metal fins are attached to each row of tub-

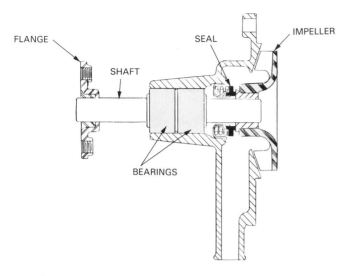

Fig. 8-4. The water pump creates a low-pressure area as it turns, drawing the coolant to its center. The impeller or vanes of the water pump then force the coolant to flow and circulate through entire cooling system.

ing. The coolant-carrying tubes radiate heat. The air flows over these fins and tubes. The radiator dissipates the majority of the engine heat by convection.

A radiator can be a downflow or a crossflow type. A downflow radiator has the coolant circulate from top to bottom. The radiator cap is generally centered on the upper radiator tank, Fig. 8-6. A crossflow radiator has the coolant circulate from side-to-side, with the radiator cap mounted on the side tank, Fig. 8-6.

Engine fans

Rear-wheel-drive cars have the engine fan mounted on the water pump and driven by a belt or belts off the crankshaft pulley, Figs. 8-7 and 8-8. The ribbed belt must be correctly positioned on its pulley, Fig. 8-9. The *engine fan* pulls air through the radiator. The fan is only needed at idle and low speeds. A shroud attached to the radiator prevents incoming air from bypassing the radiator. On front-wheel-drive cars, the fan is driven by an electric motor, Figs. 8-10 and 8-11. At highway speeds, the fan is not needed to pull air through the radiator. This is due to the velocity of the ram airflow.

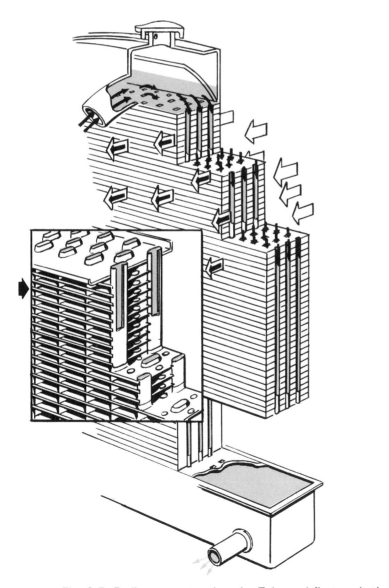

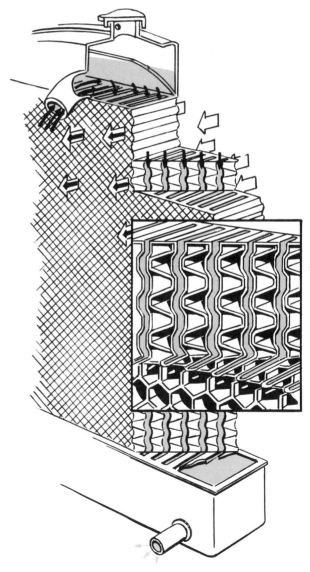

Fig. 8-5. Radiator construction. A—Tube and fin type is the most common. B—Honeycomb design. (DuPont)

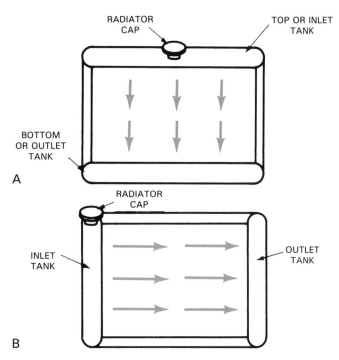

Fig. 8-8. Some newer engines use a V-ribbed belt on a serpentine drive. A serpentine drive requires the use of only one belt to drive all of the various accessories, because both sides of belt transmit power. The belt combines a traditional V-belt with a flat back belt. (Ford)

Fig. 8-6. Coolant flow. A—Downflow radiator has radiator cap centered on top of inlet tank. Arrows indicate direction of coolant flow through radiator. B—Crossflow radiator has radiator cap on side tank. Arrows indicate direction of coolant flow through radiator.

Fan drive clutch

Driving the fan reduces the available horsepower output of the engine. Since a fan is not needed at highway speeds, most car makers use a fan drive clutch, Fig. 8-12, on rear-wheel-drive cars. The *fan drive clutch* is a fluid coupling that contains silicone and is speed and/or

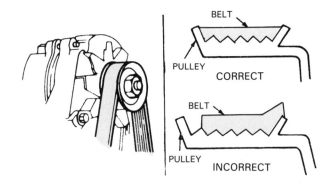

Fig. 8-9. The correct and incorrect positions of a V-ribbed belt on its pulley. (Ford)

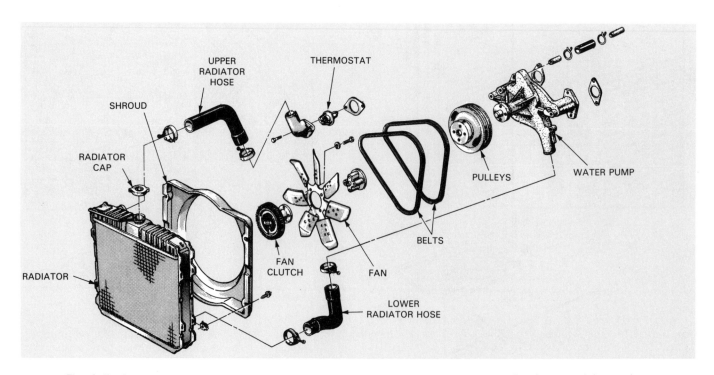

Fig. 8-7. Some engines use two V-belts to drive the fan. The V-belt drives the pulley by a wedging action.

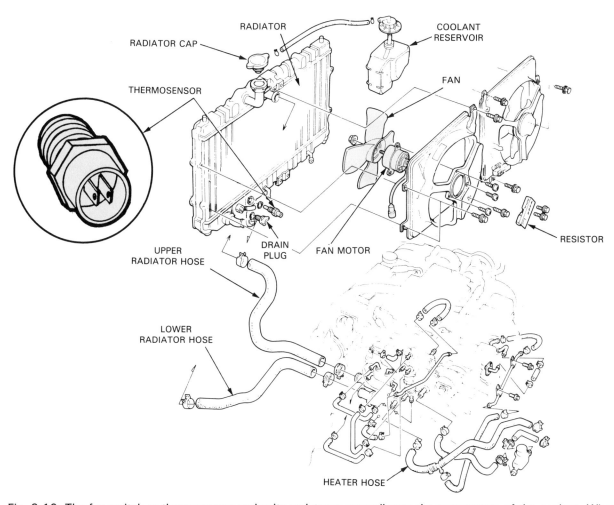

Fig. 8-10. The fan switch or thermosensor varies its resistance according to the temperature of the coolant. When coolant is hot, the fan switch causes the electric fan motor to turn on. When coolant temperature decreases, the fan switch causes the electric fan motor to turn off.   (Honda)

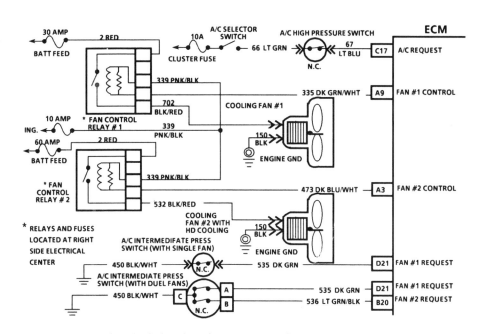

Fig. 8-11. The fan switch sends an electrical signal to the computer. The computer energizes the fan relay when the coolant is hot. The fan motor is energized. However, some cars have the computer turn the fan on directly, eliminating the use of a relay. When the coolant temperature is cooled below a certain point, the sensor signals the computer to de-energize the fan relay.   (Oldsmobile)

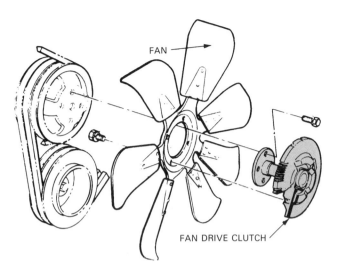

Fig. 8-12. The fan clutch allows the fan to slip at high speeds or low temperatures. This reduces the load on the engine. (Ford)

temperature sensitive. At high temperatures or low speeds, the fan and clutch turn as one unit. At high speeds or cold temperatures, the clutch allows the fan to slip. This reduces the load on the engine. A trace of a black, oily film on the back of the fan clutch indicates a replacement is needed. A defective fan clutch will cause the engine to overheat only at idle and low speeds.

Flexible fan

A flexible fan can be used on rear-wheel-drive cars, Fig. 8-13. It has the same effect as a fan clutch, but is not temperature-sensitive. The fan blades flatten out at high rpms to reduce noise level and drag on the engine.

Electric engine fans

An electric fan motor does not require as much horsepower as a belt-driven fan. The coolant-temperature fan switch, Fig. 8-6, sends a signal to the computer. Most computers, through the use of a fan relay, turn the

electric fan motor "on" during idle after the engine reaches a predetermined temperature, Fig. 8-7. The electric fan operates whenever the air conditioner is turned on, regardless of the engine coolant temperature. Some engine cooling systems have two fan motors or a fan motor with two speeds.

> WARNING: The fan may come on at any time with the ignition on or off. Always disconnect the fan motor electrical connection when working on or near the engine fan.

An engine overheating problem can occur, if the a/c switch fails to turn the radiator fan on. If there is a delay in the thermostatic switch turning the fan on, it may be long enough to allow engine overheating. The failure of a second fan or second fan speed can also cause an engine to overheat.

Electric fan motor bearings are sensitive to dirt. Over a period of time, dirt may accumulate on the shaft and bearings. This produces binding, which could stop or reduce the speed of the fan, resulting in engine overheating. The electric fan motor must then be replaced.

Raising the boiling point

Pure water boils at 212 °F (100 °C) and freezes at 32 °F (0 °). A 50/50 mixture of water and ethylene glycol (antifreeze) forms *engine coolant.* This solution raises the boiling point to 224 °F (106.6 °C). This same concentration of coolant also lowers the freezing point to −34 °F (−36.6 °C), Figs. 8-14 and 8-15. A 100 percent solution of ethylene glycol raises the boiling point to over 300 °F (148.8 °C). However, never use this concentration, as it reduces the heat transfer process and increases the freezing point to −8 °F (−22 °C).

Ethylene glycol contains a water pump seal lubricant. It also contains rust and corrosion inhibitors for the entire cooling system. These additives are destroyed by the engine heat. Therefore, the cooling system should be drained and flushed and new antifreeze installed at least every two years, Fig. 8-16. If antifreeze is never flushed from the system, the weakened inhibitors decrease the corrosion protection of the cooling system.

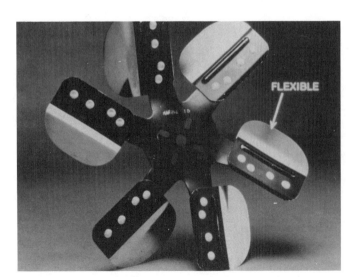

Fig. 8-13. Flexible fan blades flatten out at high rpms to reduce the load on the engine. (Everco)

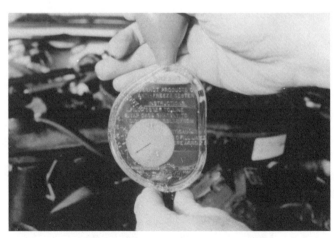

Fig. 8-14. Checking engine coolant with a specially calibrated hydrometer. The coolant should test to at least −20 °F (−28.8 °C). (Everco)

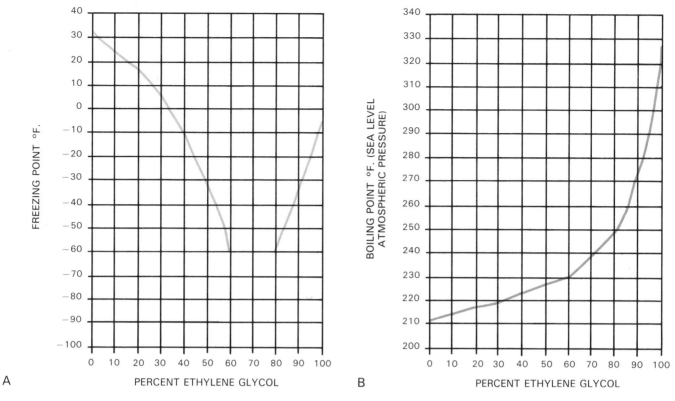

Fig. 8-15. Freezing and boiling points of different strength solutions of ethylene glycol when mixed with water. A—Freezing points. B—Boiling points.

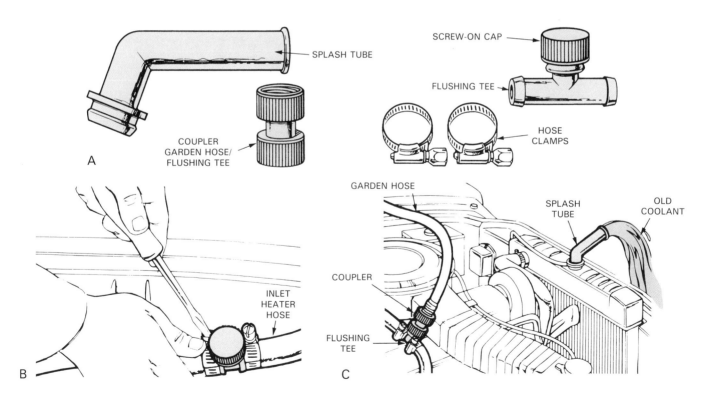

Fig. 8-16. Coolant should be flushed from engine every two years. A—Parts needed to flush the cooling system. B—Cut the inlet heater hose and insert flushing tee. Tighten hose clamps. C—Unscrew the flushing-tee cap. Screw on one end of coupler to flushing tee. Then, screw on other end of coupler to garden hose. Remove radiator cap and install splash tube. Turn garden hose on until clear water is running out of splash tube. Remove splash tube and install proper amount of antifreeze solution. Install radiator cap. Unscrew garden hose from coupler and coupler from flushing tee. Finally, screw on flushing tee cap. (Prestone)

Radiator pressure cap

Increasing pressure on a liquid (coolant in this case), raises its boiling point. A *radiator pressure cap* is used to increase pressure on the coolant, Fig. 8-17. Most radiator pressure caps are rated at 15 psi. This increases the boiling point to 265°F (129.4°C) when using a 50/50 mixture of water and ethylene glycol.

The radiator pressure cap also relieves excess pressure to prevent the radiator hose or tank from bursting. It also vents vacuum, formed inside the radiator tank during cool down, to prevent the tank or hoses from collapsing, Fig. 8-18.

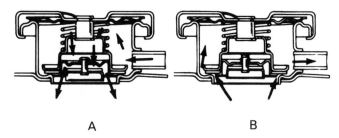

A   B

Fig. 8-18. Pressure and vacuum relief. A—Vacuum tends to form as radiator cools down after engine has been shut off. Vacuum, inside radiator, pulls vacuum valve down allowing atmospheric pressure into radiator. B—Pressure-relief valve is held closed by spring pressure. When excessive pressure develops inside radiator, the pressure-relief valve is raised off its seat. This vents excess pressure to the atmosphere or coolant reservoir.   (Oldsmobile)

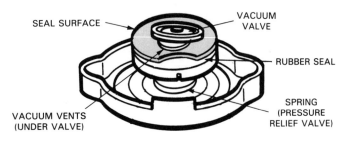

Fig. 8-17. Construction of a modern radiator pressure cap. (Ford)

Coolant overflow

Overflow of coolant from the radiator goes through a small rubber hose that connects to a plastic reservoir, Fig. 8-19. The coolant is siphoned from the reservoir back into the radiator as the radiator cools down. This is referred to as a *closed system.*

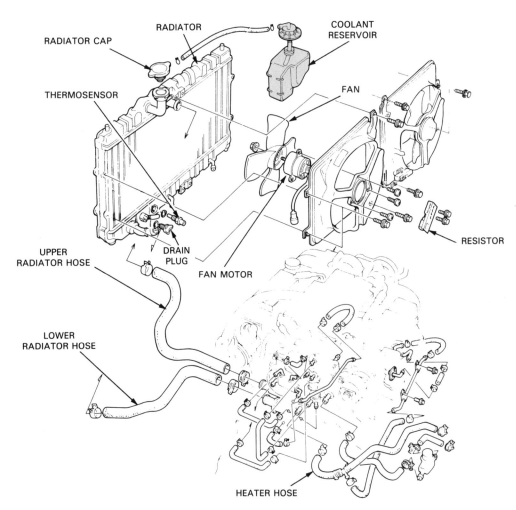

Fig. 8-19. Coolant overflows into the plastic reservoir. As radiator cools down, after engine has been shut off, coolant is siphoned back into the radiator.   (Honda)

VENTILATION SYSTEMS

The *driver controlled ventilation system* is one that the driver of the car has full control over the temperature, amount, and direction of airflow. A *full-time constant ventilation system* is when the blower operates continually at a very low speed, except when the mode selector is in the off position. A *separate ventilating system* involves air ducts that are separate of the heating and air conditioning system. A heating and ventilation system has the airflow enter at one common point, Fig. 8-20.

Ram/forced air

Ram air is the airflow due to vehicle speed. The amount of ram air that enters the passenger compartment is controlled by the position of a door, in the evaporator/heater housing, and the speed of the car. *Forced air* is caused by a blower fan, Fig. 8-21, and is independent of vehicle speed.

Passenger compartment pressure

A positive pressure, above atmospheric pressure, in the passenger compartment is preferred to assure that all air leakage is outward. Ram air, forced air, or a combination of both provides the higher pressure. With the windows rolled up, the excess pressure vents to the atmosphere through pressure release grilles in the door pillars, Fig. 8-22.

Ducts and hoses

Early model automobiles used cloth and rubber around a wire frame for air circulation hoses. Modern cars use molded plastic ducts for airflow distribution. The *ducts* direct the heated or cooled airflow from the heater/evaporator case to the passenger compartment.

Registers

The *registers* direct and regulate the flow of air from the air ducts inside the passenger compartment, Fig. 8-23A. There are two types of air registers, the ball and the louver design.

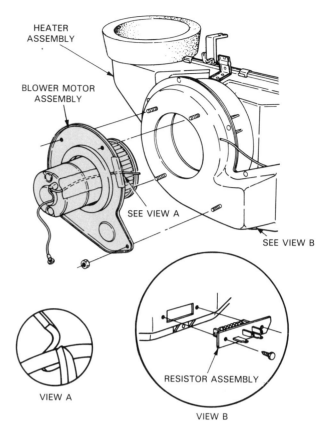

Fig. 8-21. Blower motor attaches to the heater/evaporator housing. (Ford)

The louver-type register is the most common, Fig. 8-23B. It directs and regulates the airflow to selected areas of the passenger compartment. The louvers can be positioned to direct the airflow to a selected area of the passenger compartment or completely shut off the airflow.

The ball type, which is seldom used, is a sphere with a through hole that directs and regulates the airflow by rotating the ball in its socket, Fig. 8-24. The airflow can

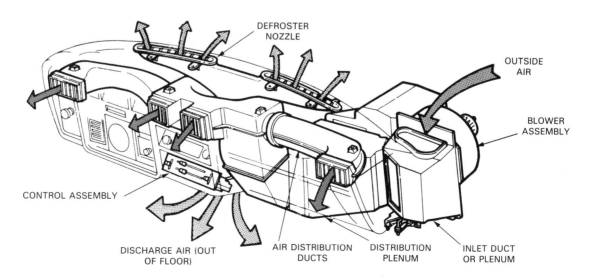

Fig. 8-20. Incoming air from the outside can be heated or cooled. Airflow for air conditioning comes out of dash registers. The heated airflow comes out of defroster and floor outlets. (Ford)

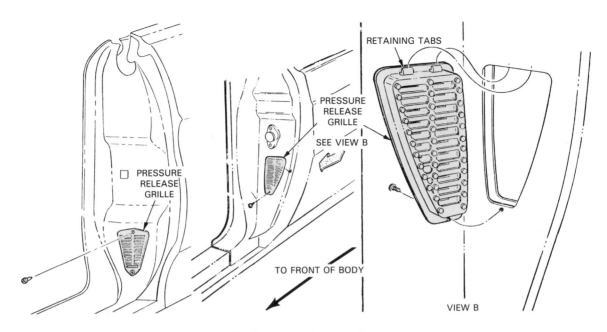

Fig. 8-22. Pressure-release grille location.

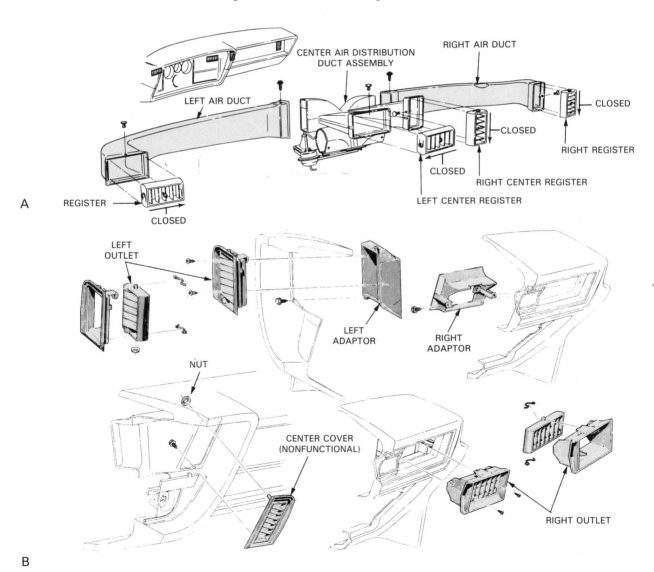

Fig. 8-23. The registers are located in the dash panel at air duct outlets. A—The registers can be individually closed to block airflow. The registers can also be individually positioned to direct airflow. B—Louvered type register.   (Ford)

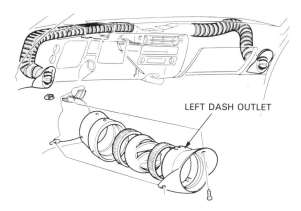

Fig. 8-24. Ball-type register.

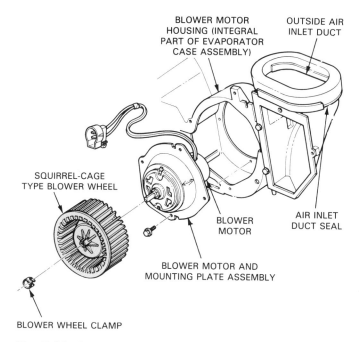

Fig. 8-26. Squirrel-cage type blower is the most common. (Ford)

be directed by turning the ball. The airflow can also be shut off by rotating the ball until the hole disappears.

Screens, filters, and water traps

Outside air enters the plenum chamber at the base of the windshield. The plenum chamber is a cavity designed into the firewall area or a molded plastic housing attached to the underdash or firewall area. Inlet protection of the plenum chamber is in the form of louvers in the cowl, Fig. 8-25A. Plastic screens, which are the most common, can also be fastened over the plenum chamber opening, Fig. 8-25B. The screen or louvers keep out debris. The plenum chamber separates the rain water from incoming air by using sharp bends that provide a rapid change in the direction of airflow.

Blower

Fan blade or squirrel-cage blowers are the two types found on cars. Current ventilating system blowers are of the squirrel-cage type, Fig. 8-26. This design is quieter, more efficient, and consumes less space than the fan-blade type.

The blower assembly is located in the heater/evaporator housing. The blower provides forced air for ventilation, heating, and air conditioning. When the car is in motion, additional airflow is provided by ram air.

Blower electrical circuit

The speed of the blower motor is determined by the position of the fan switch. The switch selects which resistor(s) will be used to determine current flow to the motor, Fig. 8-27. The amount of resistance determines the fan speed. The lower blower speeds have current directed through resistors of high value, restricting current flow.

The blower motor is designed using permanent magnets or a series-wound field. The blower motor is protected from a current overload by a fuse. The fuse, generally 25 amps, is located in the fuse panel with the other fuses. Typical blower motor current draw ranges from approximately 6 amps at low fan speed to 20 amps at high fan speed. If the blower motor fuse blows (interrupts the electrical circuit), the blower motor may be drawing too much current and may be at fault.

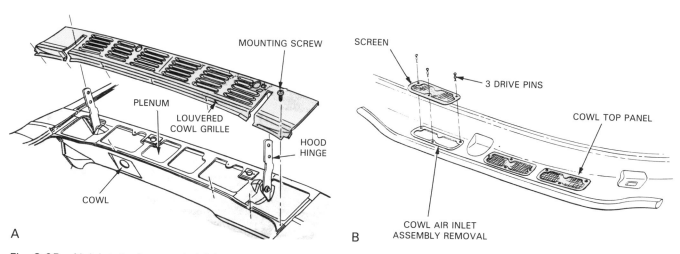

Fig. 8-25. Air inlet. A—Louvered air inlet prevents debris from entering plenum chamber. B—Screen at air inlet prevents debris from entering plunum chamber.

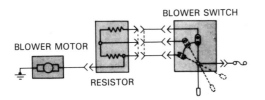

Fig. 8-27. Blower or fan switch determine which resistor current travels through before going to blower motor. The amount of resistance determines fan speed. (Ford)

AIR DISTRIBUTION CONTROL

The mode, temperature, and fan speed are selected at the control head, Fig. 8-28. *Manually-controlled heating and air conditioning systems* use a temperature-control lever that operates a Bowden cable, Fig. 8-29. It positions the temperature blend-air door in the evaporator/heater housing. While most heat, defrost, and recirc mode doors are operated by vacuum motors, some are controlled by Bowden cables, Fig. 8-29.

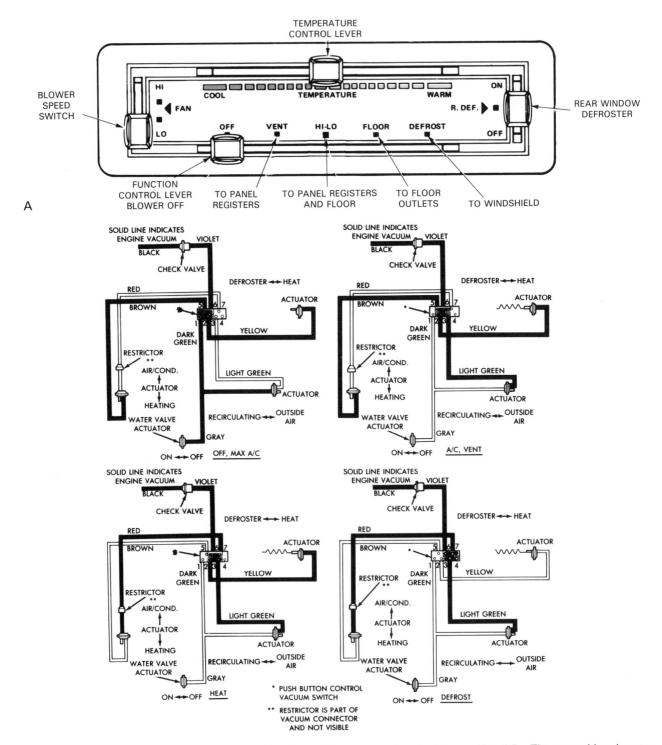

Fig. 8-28. Temperature control head. A—Lever position determines temperature inside car. (Ford) B—The control head routes vacuum, in solid black, to different vacuum motors, depending on the mode selected. (Chrysler)

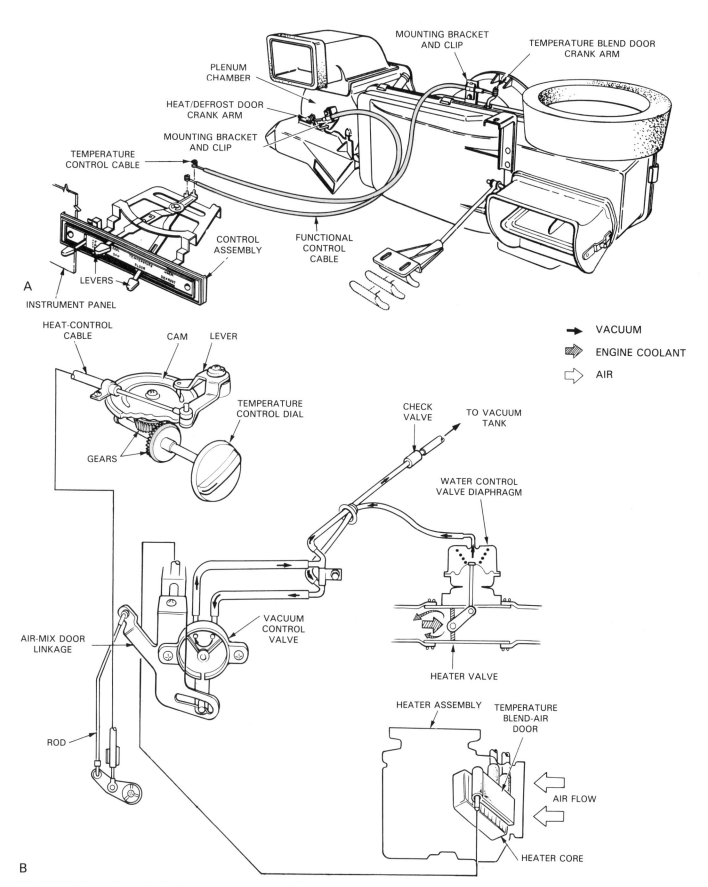

Fig. 8-29. Manually-controlled heating and air conditioning systems use a Bowden cable. A—The cable is attached to a lever at the control head. The position of lever and cable regulates the position of the temperature blend-air door. Some mode doors are controlled by a cable instead of vacuum motors. (Ford) B—Some cars use a gear to drive a lever. The gear at the back of the dial meshes with another gear. It is attached to a rotating cam. A lever attached to the cam moves the cable. This regulates the position of the temperature blend-air door and vacuum to the water control valve. (Honda)

MODES OF OPERATION

There are different paths the airflow can take, once inside the heater/evaporator housing. This is dependent on the position of the temperature blend-air door and the mode doors in the evaporator/heater housing. While all of the airflow must first go through the evaporator core, the airflow is only cooled when the air conditioner is turned on.

Air conditioning mode

When the air conditioner is turned on, the air flows through the evaporator core and is cooled and dehumidified. The position of the temperature blend-air door prevents the cooled, dehumidified airflow from going through the heater core, Fig. 8-30. It can be adjusted, using the temperature control, to achieve a comfortable level. The cooled, dehumidified airflow is then directed to the dash outlets by the floor-panel and panel-defrost

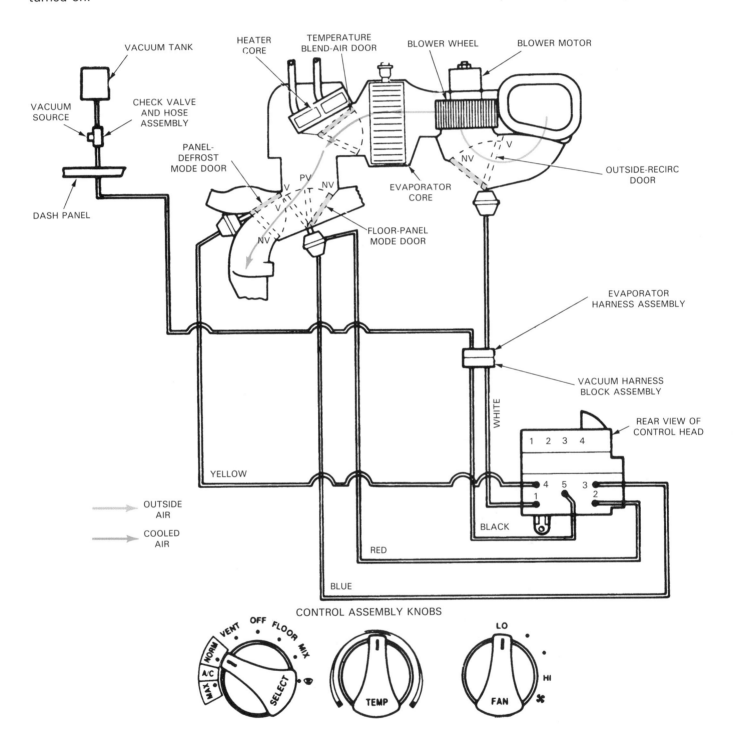

Fig. 8-30. The temperature-control cable positions the temperature blend-air door. It blocks the cool, dehumidified airflow from going through heater core. The vacuum motor for the floor-panel mode door has no vacuum applied to it. The vacuum motor for the panel-defrost mode door has vacuum applied to it. This causes it to block the airflow from going to floor outlets. The panel-defrost mode door blocks the airflow from going to defroster outlets, while directing it to the dash outlets only. (Ford)

mode doors. The position of the floor-panel mode door prevents the cooled airflow from going to the floor outlets. The position of the panel-defrost mode door prevents the cooled airflow from going to the defroster outlets.

Max A/C mode

The only difference between the selection of air conditioning and maximum air conditioning is the position of the outside-recirc mode door, Fig. 8-31. The position of the outside-recirc mode door prevents any outside air from entering the heater/evaporator case. The recirc

mode door redirects the air that has been previously cooled and dehumidified, in the passenger compartment, back through the evaporator for further cooling. This makes it easier and faster to cool and dehumidify the airflow. This is critical on hot, humid days.

Heat mode

When the heat is turned on, the position of the temperature blend-air door directs the airflow through the heater core, Fig. 8-32. The position of the floor-panel mode door directs most of the heated airflow to the floor outlets, with a small amount of the heated airflow

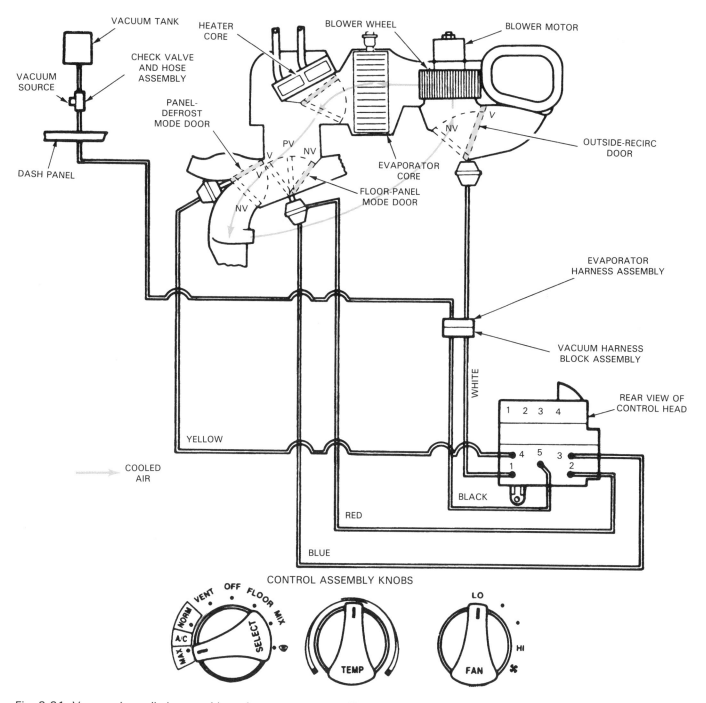

Fig. 8-31. Vacuum is applied to outside-recirc vacuum motor. This positions outside-recirc mode door to block outside airflow from entering the heater/evaporator case. The passenger compartment airflow is recirculated through the evaporator. (Ford)

directed to the defroster outlets. The position of the panel-defrost mode door prevents the heated airflow from going to the dash outlets.

Defroster mode

When the defroster is selected, the air conditioner is also turned on. This dehumidifies and cools the airflow before it is heated. This action provides rapid clearing of a fogged windshield. The position of the temperature blend-air door directs the cool, dehumidified airflow through the heater core. The airflow now becomes heated, Fig. 8-33. The position of the floor-panel mode door directs most of the airflow to the defroster outlets, while some of the airflow goes to the floor outlets. The position of the panel-defrost mode door prevents the airflow from going to the dash outlets.

Bi-level mode

Some cars have a "bi-level" position at the control head. Airflow comes out the dash register as well as the

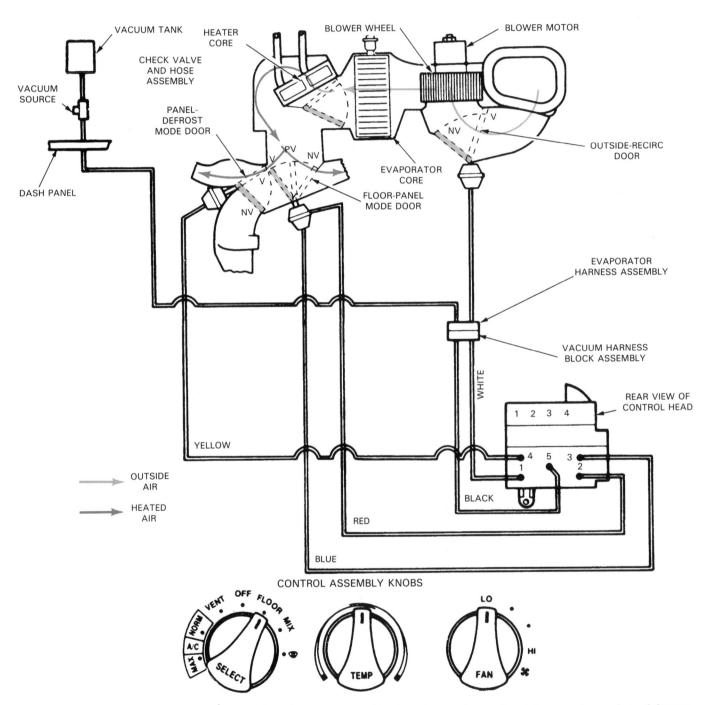

Fig. 8-32. The temperature-control cable positions the temperature blend-air door so that entire airflow must pass through heater core. Vacuum motor for floor-panel mode door has vacuum applied to it. This allows most of heated airflow to floor outlets and some to defroster outlets. Vacuum motor for panel-defrost mode door has no vacuum applied to it. This blocks the heated airflow from the dash outlets. (Ford)

floor outlets at the same time, Fig. 8-34. This feature can be used to blow hot or cold air.

FLUIDIC DEFROSTER

This system is currently used on some GM all-purpose vehicles (APV). It is used instead of the standard duct-type system because of the large windshield that must be heated. The *fluidic defroster* directs the heated airflow from the heater/evaporator case to the windshield

without any moving parts or ducts. The heated airflow continually moves in an oscillating motion across the windshield. The fluidic defroster requires less space than a system using ducts.

Fluidic defroster operation

When the defroster is first turned on, the heated airflow is discharged out of one nozzle only. This is due to the nozzle's design. The fluidic defroster has two nozzles, control ports, and an inertance tube. The

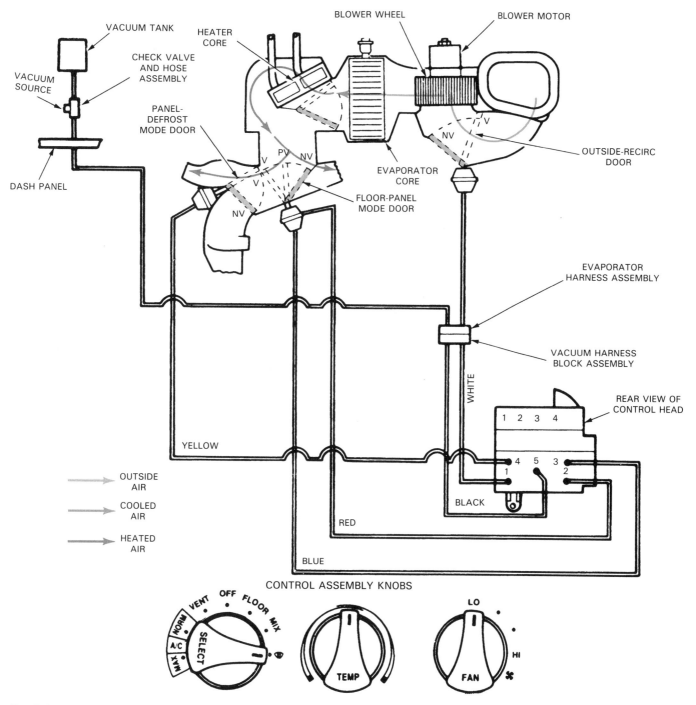

Fig. 8-33. Since air conditioner is also on, airflow is dehumidified before it passes through heater core. Vacuum motor for floor-panel mode door has no vacuum applied to it. This allows most of heated airflow to defroster outlets and some to the floor outlets. Vacuum motor for panel-defrost mode door also has no vacuum applied to it. This blocks the heated airflow from going to the dash outlets. (Ford)

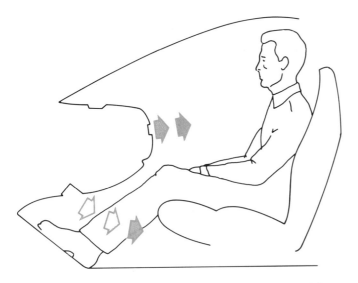

Fig. 8-34. Bi-level position allows airflow from dash and floor outlets at the same time. (Cadillac)

pressure in the *inertance tube* deflects the direction of the defrost air stream.

The heated air flows past the two control ports. An inertance tube connects the control ports, Fig. 8-35. Air also flows inside the inertance tube. A slight vacuum or negative pressure (—) exists at one control port and positive pressure (+) at the opposite port. The pressure difference between the control ports directs the heated airflow through a nozzle.

As pressure changes at the control ports, the heated airflow switches directions. The heated airflow is now discharged out the other nozzle, Fig. 8-35. The cycle continually and automatically repeats. The sweeping motion of the heated airflow, Fig. 8-36, reduces the thin insulating layer of air against the windshield. This increases the heat transfer process.

SUMMARY

Heating and ventilation systems used by the major auto manufacturers are similar in function. The heater

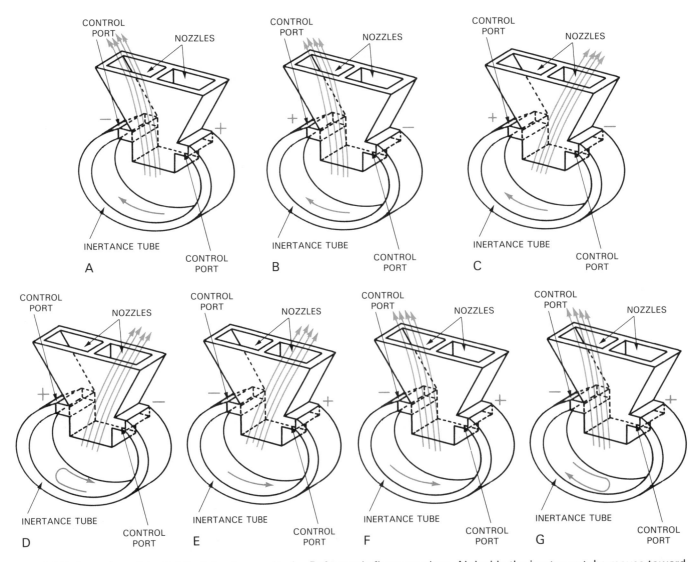

Fig. 8-35. Operation of the fluidic defroster nozzle. A—Defroster is first turned on. Air inside the inertance tube moves toward the control port with negative pressure. Heated airflow is directed past the control port with negative pressure. B—Positive and negative pressure change at the control ports. C—Direction of heated airflow changes. Heated airflow is discharged past the control port with negative pressure. D—Airflow inside inertance tube switches direction. E—Positive and negative pressure switch control ports. F—Heated airflow switches direction. Heated airflow is discharged past the control port with negative pressure. G—Airflow inside inertance tube changes direction. Cycle is now complete and starts over. (Bowles Fluidic Corp.)

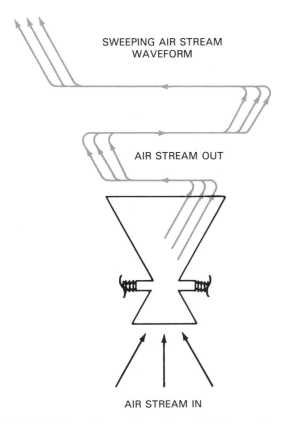

SWEEPING AIR STREAM
WAVEFORM

AIR STREAM OUT

AIR STREAM IN

Fig. 8-36. Sweeping motion of heated airflow as it continually changes directions. (Bowles Fluidic Corp.)

core heats the ambient airflow to warm the passenger compartment and clear the windshield.

The engine must operate at high temperatures within narrow parameters. The temperature at which the thermostat opens, the boiling point of the coolant, and the pressure rating of the radiator cap all affect engine operating temperature. Engine fans pull air through the radiator at idle and low speeds. Engine fans are belt driven on rear-wheel-drive cars and driven by an electric motor on front-wheel-drive cars. An engine fan is not needed at highway speeds.

The ambient airflow passes through the evaporator core first. However, the airflow is not cooled unless the air conditioner is turned on. The temperature blend-air door position determines the airflow through or around the heater core. When the MAX A/C mode is selected, the recirc door blocks the ambient airflow from entering the heater/evaporator case. The passenger compartment airflow is recirculated through the evaporator core. When the heat or defrost mode is selected, the temperature blend-air door directs all or a portion of the airflow through the heater core.

KNOW THESE TERMS

Heating system, Heater core, Water control valve, Engine thermostat, Radiator, Engine fan, Fan drive clutch, Engine coolant, Radiator pressure cap, Closed system, Driver controlled ventilation system, Full-time constant ventilation system, Separate ventilating system, Ram air, Forced air, Ducts, Registers, Manually-controlled heating and air conditioning system, Fluidic defroster, Inertance tube.

REVIEW QUESTIONS—CHAPTER 8

1. Define ram air.
2. Define forced air.
3. What is the purpose of the heating system?
4. Briefly explain how windows fog up.
5. List the components of the engine cooling system.
6. Describe how the passenger compartment is heated.
7. Name three things that affect engine operating temperature and heater output.
8. What is the purpose of the radiator?
9. Everything is fine on a front-wheel-drive car during highway driving. However, the engine overheats during city (stop and go) driving.
   Mechanic A states the fan clutch may be defective.
   Mechanic B states the electric engine fan relay may be defective.
   Who is right?
   a. Mechanic A.
   b. Mechanic B.
   c. Both Mechanics A and B.
   d. Neither Mechanic A nor B.
10. The customer complains about a wet spot on the passenger's front floor mat.
    Mechanic A states the evaporator drain may be clogged.
    Mechanic B states the heater core may be leaking.
    Who is right?
    a. Mechanic A.
    b. Mechanic B.
    c. Both Mechanics A and B.
    d. Neither Mechanic A nor B.
11. When the bi-level mode is selected, heated or cooled air flows from the:
    a. Dash registers.
    b. Floor registers.
    c. Both a and b.
    d. None of the above.
12. All ambient air flows through the evaporator core first. True or false?
13. The position of the temperature blend-air door determines how much air flows through the evaporator core. True or false?
14. When the high blower motor speed is selected, how much current is flowing through its circuit?
15. What is the purpose of the water control valve?
16. A car is equipped with air conditioning. The defrost mode is selected. Air flows through only the heater core. True or false?
17. Why is the fluidic defroster system used?
18. A car is equipped with air conditioning. The heat mode is selected. The air conditioner is also automatically engaged at the same time. True or false?

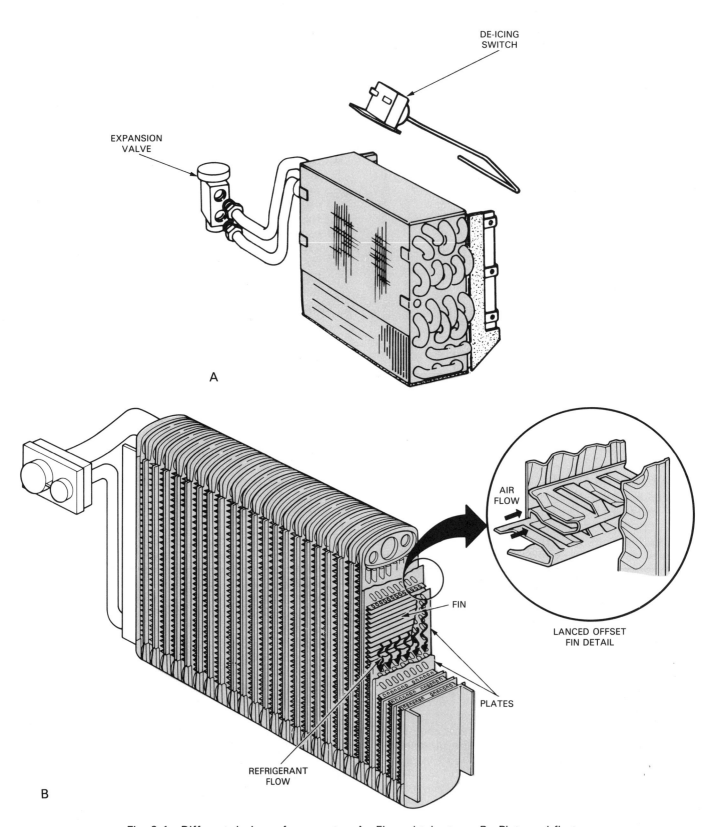

Fig. 9-1. Different designs of evaporator. A—Fin and tube type. B—Plate and fin type.

EVAPORATORS, CONDENSERS, AND HEATER CORES

After studying this chapter, you will be able to:
- Explain the operation of evaporators, condensers, and heater cores.
- Describe how evaporators, condensers, and heater cores are constructed.
- Relate the design and construction of condensers, evaporators, and heater cores to their operating characteristics.
- Compare the similarities and differences of evaporators, condensers, and heater cores.
- Summarize the reasons for specific locations and mounting techniques for evaporators, condensers, and heater cores.

INTRODUCTION

The evaporator, condenser, and heater core are all similar to the radiator in construction and design; they are all heat-exchange devices. While the evaporator removes heat from the airflow, the condenser and heater core, like the radiator, give off heat to the airflow.

Comparing the three radiatorlike devices:
1. The condenser and evaporator both transfer greater amounts of heat than the heater core. This is because engine coolant in the heater does not change state.
2. The method of heat transfer is the same for the condenser and the heater core. This means heat radiates from these sources. However, heat inside the car moves toward the cooler evaporator core.
3. The operating pressures differ in these radiatorlike devices. The heater core, along with the radiator itself, operates from 13 to 18 psi. The evaporator operates at pressures ranging from 13 to 30 psi. The condenser operates at pressures ranging from 150 to 300 psi.

EVAPORATORS

The *evaporator core* removes both heat and moisture from the air entering the car. The evaporator may be plate and fin or the fin and tube type as illustrated in Fig. 9-1. The fin and tube type is the most common.

The location of the evaporator is generally under the dash on the front passenger side. Construction of the evaporator consists of several rows of aluminum tubing that make several passes through closely spaced aluminum fins.

The tubing is hydraulically expanded into the aluminum fins to ensure good thermal conductivity/transfer. The evaporator is enclosed in a thermoplastic case assembly which is mounted on the firewall. In the case assembly, provisions are made for the blower fan mounting and a condensate trough with a one-way rubber drain valve.

Operation of evaporator

In operation, liquid refrigerant enters the evaporator. Due to the reduced pressure on the refrigerant, it boils into a vapor absorbing the latent heat of vaporization. The heat in the incoming air is absorbed by the evaporator coils and fins. The refrigerant absorbs the heat during its change of state.

The air, and the water vapor in the air, are cooled below the dew point. Some of this water vapor cools (gives up its latent heat) and condenses on the evaporator fins. Thus, the evaporator cools and dehumidifies the air within the passenger compartment. The incoming air is also cleaned, as dust and pollen are trapped by moisture on the fins and coils of the evaporator.

Heat load removed by evaporator

Heat load is the amount of heat to be removed from the incoming air to obtain a comfortable temperature and humidity level inside the car. Heat load is affected by ambient temperature and humidity. High temperature and humidity levels increase the heat load on the air conditioning system. High incoming air temperatures require more refrigerant flow in the evaporator to absorb the additional amount of heat. High humidity results in excessive moisture accumulation on the evaporator fins, restricting heat transfer which adds to the heat load.

The latent heat of vaporization of R-12 is 38.6 calories/gram (69.5 BTU/lb.) in the evaporator at normal operating pressure of 1.06 kg/cm to 2.12 kg/cm (13 psi to 30 psi). Evaporator pressure is affected by the heat load; the higher the heat load, the higher the evaporator pressure.

There is a definite relationship between temperature and pressure for a refrigerant. When heat is added to the refrigerant, the pressure increases; when heat is removed, the pressure decreases. The relationship of pressure and temperature of R-12 for a wide operating range is illustrated in Fig. 9-2.

Evaporator freeze-up

Evaporator freeze-up is the result of the moisture in the air condensing and then freezing on the evaporator core. The ice on the fins blocks the airflow through the evaporator and stops the cooling until the ice melts. If the components that control temperature and pressure in the evaporator malfunction and allow the evaporator's temperature to drop to 32 °F (0 °C), freeze-up of the evaporator core will occur.

Flooded evaporator

A *flooded evaporator* occurs when there is too much refrigerant flowing into the evaporator. Flooding can be the result of the sensing bulb of the expansion valve being misplaced, improperly insulated, in poor contact with the evaporator tail pipe, or a defective expansion valve.

Starved evaporator

A *starved evaporator* occurs when there is not enough refrigerant flowing into the evaporator. Starvation can be caused by a defective expansion valve, a plugged orifice tube, clogged strainers, or corroded internal parts. Damaged internal and/or wrong parts installed could be the cause of either flooding or starvation.

Inspection of evaporator

The evaporator is the most difficult of all components to inspect visually because of its enclosed location. Airflow blockage through the evaporator, due to debris, bent fins, and/or refrigerant leaks (oil smudges), necessitate removal of the evaporator housing for visual inspection.

Evaporator drain tube

The evaporator drain tube, Fig. 9-3, can be checked with a probe to be certain it is not plugged. A plugged drain tube causes the condensed water vapor to be trapped inside the evaporator/heater housing. This results in fogged windows and stagnant water inside the housing that produces bacteria-caused odors. If a musty smell is present, spray a disinfectant, such as Lysol® , through the drain tube. This kills the odor-producing bacteria inside the evaporator/heater housing. If the water level is high enough inside the evaporator/heater housing, water will leak onto the front passenger side carpet.

CONDENSERS

The *condenser* receives the high-temperature, high-pressure gas from the compressor and converts it to a

PRESSURE-TEMPERATURE RELATIONSHIP OF REFRIGERANT R-12

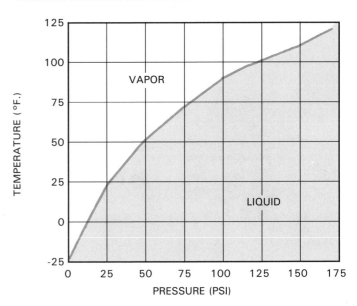

Temp. F.	Press. PSI	Temp. F.	Press. PSI	Temp. F.	Press. PSI
0	9.1	43	39.7	76	78.3
2	10.1	44	40.7	77	79.2
4	11.2	45	41.7	78	81.1
6	12.3	46	42.6	79	82.5
8	13.4	47	43.6	80	84.0
10	14.6	48	44.6	82	87.0
12	15.8	49	45.6	84	90.1
14	17.1	50	46.6	86	93.2
16	18.3	51	47.8	88	96.4
18	19.7	52	48.7	90	99.6
20	21.0	53	49.8	92	103.0
21	21.7	54	50.9	94	106.3
22	22.4	55	52.0	96	109.8
23	23.1	56	53.1	98	113.3
24	23.8	57	55.4	100	116.9
25	24.6	58	56.6	102	120.6
26	25.3	59	57.1	104	124.3
27	26.1	60	57.7	106	128.1
28	26.8	61	58.9	108	132.1
29	27.6	62	60.0	110	136.0
30	28.4	63	61.3	112	140.1
31	29.2	64	62.5	114	144.2
32	30.0	65	63.7	116	148.4
33	30.9	66	64.9	118	152.7
34	31.7	67	66.2	120	157.1
35	32.5	68	67.5	122	161.5
36	33.4	69	68.8	124	166.1
37	34.3	70	70.1	126	170.7
38	35.1	71	71.4	128	175.4
39	36.0	72	72.8	130	182.2
40	36.9	73	74.2	132	185.1
41	37.9	74	75.5	134	190.1
42	38.8	75	76.9		

Fig. 9-2. Top—Curve shows the pressure-temperature relationship of R-12 from data on chart at bottom.   (Ford)

slightly cooler, high-pressure liquid. The operation of the condenser is opposite to the operation of the evaporator. High-temperature, high-pressure gas from the compressor enters at the top of the condenser. As the gas flows through the condenser, it releases the heat to the cooler ambient air flowing through the condenser.

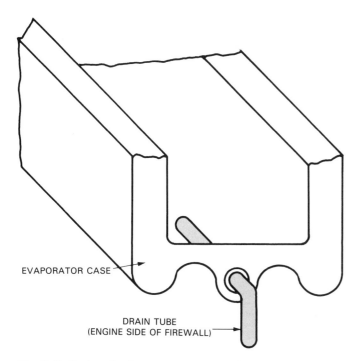

Fig. 9-3. Drain tube in evaporator case allows condensation to drain. A probe can check if it is blocked and not allowing the water to drain.

Change of state within condenser

Giving up its heat causes the gas to change to a liquid. This release of heat is known as latent heat of condensation (the large amount of heat released during a change of state). Under average heat load, the top two-thirds of the condenser contains a hot refrigerant vapor and the lower-third contains a hot, liquid refrigerant. The liquid refrigerant in the lower-third of the condenser has lost much of its heat, but it is still hot and under high pressure.

Condenser location

The condenser is usually located in front of the radiator. Both are heat exchangers, but a change of state does not take place inside the radiator as it does in the condenser. Since the heated airflow from the condenser goes through the radiator, the radiator must be of a larger size and capacity to handle the extra heat load. Also, it is the function of the radiator to dissipate heat from the engine and the condenser.

Heat transfer from condenser

Air movement at highway speeds is sufficient to obtain adequate heat transfer from the condenser to the airflow. At low speeds and idle, airflow through the condenser and radiator is provided by the engine fan. The ambient air temperature is always lower than the high-pressure refrigerant gas temperature. Therefore, heat is transferred from the hot condenser to the cooler, ambient airflow.

The condenser is constructed of aluminum serpentine tubing to which fins are attached. The tubing is expanded into the fins to provide positive contact for the most efficient heat transfer. A typical condenser is shown in Fig. 9-4. The high-temperature, high-pressure gas enters

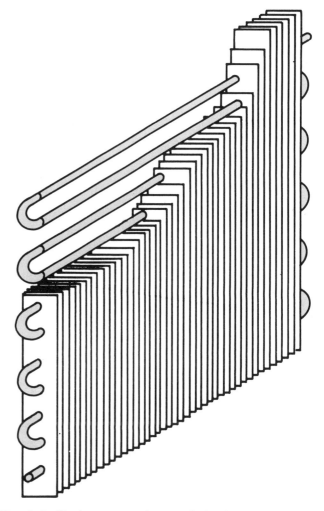

Fig. 9-4. Single-pass condenser of the fin and tube construction.

the condenser at the top and exits the condenser at the bottom as a somewhat cooler, high-pressure liquid. Condensers must be able to withstand pressures of 400 to 500 psi at all times.

Condenser temperature

Condenser temperature is defined as the temperature of the hot refrigerant gases entering the condenser. Condenser pressure/temperature must be high enough to create a wide temperature differential between the hot-refrigerant vapor and the ambient airflow passing over the condenser fins and coils.

Condenser designs

The prime objective in condenser design is to expose the maximum amount of refrigerant possible to the cool, ambient airflow. Generally, a single-pass condenser design (one row of tubing) is used. However, if the width and height are restricted, a double or triple-pass design (two or three rows of tubing) would provide more exposure to the cooler airflow through a relatively smaller condenser configuration, Fig. 9-5.

A variation of the tube-fin condenser is the parallel-flow condenser. It is smaller and thinner than the tube-fin type condenser, Fig. 9-6. Also, it requires less

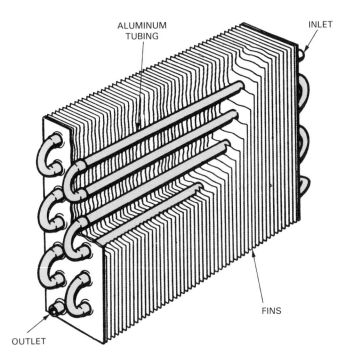

Fig. 9-5. Double-pass fin and tube type condenser showing the two rows of tubing.

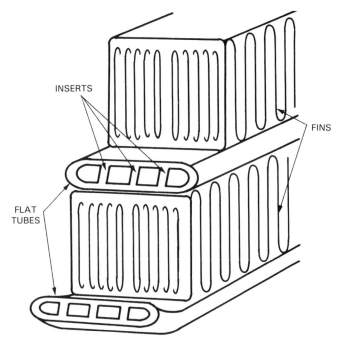

Fig. 9-7. The flat-tube design increases heat transfer to the airflow. The inserts are an integral part of the flat tube and assist in the heat transfer process. (Modine)

Fig. 9-6. Condenser size difference. A—Tube and fin condenser. B—Parallel-flow condenser. Note the parallel-flow design has side inlet and outlet tanks.   (Modine)

refrigerant while maintaining the same level of cooling performance inside the passenger compartment. The flat-profile tube has significantly more area exposed to the airflow than the round-tube design, Fig. 9-7. This provides a greater heat transfer.

HEATER CORES

The *heater core* gives off its heat to the incoming ambient airflow and directs it into the passenger compartment. The difference between the heater core and the condenser is that the heater core has hot engine coolant flowing through it compared to the hot, high-pressure refrigerant gases flowing through the condenser.

The heater core is located in the evaporator/heater housing. In most cars, the housing is located at the firewall, Fig. 9-8. The heater core design can be either the fin and tube type or the cellular (honeycomb) design. Both designs provide a large amount of surface area for optimum heat transfer. However, the honeycomb design heater core is the most popular type used in passenger cars, Fig. 9-9. The heater core is constructed of copper or brass because of its ability to conduct and transfer heat.

SUMMARY

The three radiatorlike devices, the evaporator, condenser, and heater core, all function as heat exchangers. The radiator, heater core, and condenser dissipate heat to the airflow. However, the evaporator absorbs heat from the airflow. The heater core dissipates heat to the incoming air to heat the car interior.

The pressures in the evaporator and the condenser are significant to their function which is the change of state of the refrigerant. The pressure in the heater core is insignificant to its function because the coolant always remains a liquid.

The heater core and the evaporator are both located in the evaporator/heater housing, under the dash. They both can change the temperature of the incoming airflow that is directed to the passenger compartment. The condenser is usually located in front of the radiator where it can dissipate heat to the cooler, ambient airflow. The heated air flows through the radiator which must be of adequate size to dissipate the added heat.

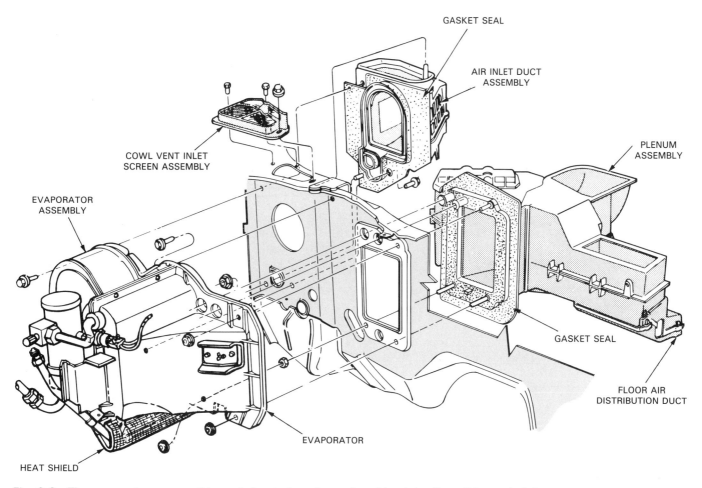

Fig. 9-8. The evaporator core on this car is located on the engine side of the firewall instead of the passenger compartment. (Ford)

KNOW THESE TERMS

Evaporator core, Heat load, Evaporator freeze-up, Flooded evaporator, Starved evaporator, Condenser, Condenser temperature, Heater core.

Fig. 9-9. Heater cores found in passenger cars are usually of the honeycomb design. (Everco and Automotive Encyclopedia)

REVIEW QUESTIONS—CHAPTER 9

1. The evaporator radiates heat it has picked up. True or false?
2. Condensation of the refrigerant is done inside the:
   a. Evaporator.   c. Radiator.
   b. Condenser.   d. Heater core.
3. The operating pressure of the evaporator is:
   a. 150 to 300 psi.   c. 12 to 14 psi.
   b. 13 to 30 psi.   d. None of the above.
4. The condenser is located:
   a. Under the dash panel.
   b. In the evaporator/heater housing.
   c. Passenger compartment.
   d. In front of the radiator.
5. Explain the purpose of the condenser.
6. Explain how the evaporator cools the passenger compartment.
7. Why is the condenser mounted in front of the radiator?
8. Ram air affects the performance of all three radiatorlike devices. True or false?
9. What change of state occurs in the:
   a. Heater core?
   b. Condenser?
   c. Evaporator?
10. What two design types are used for heater cores?

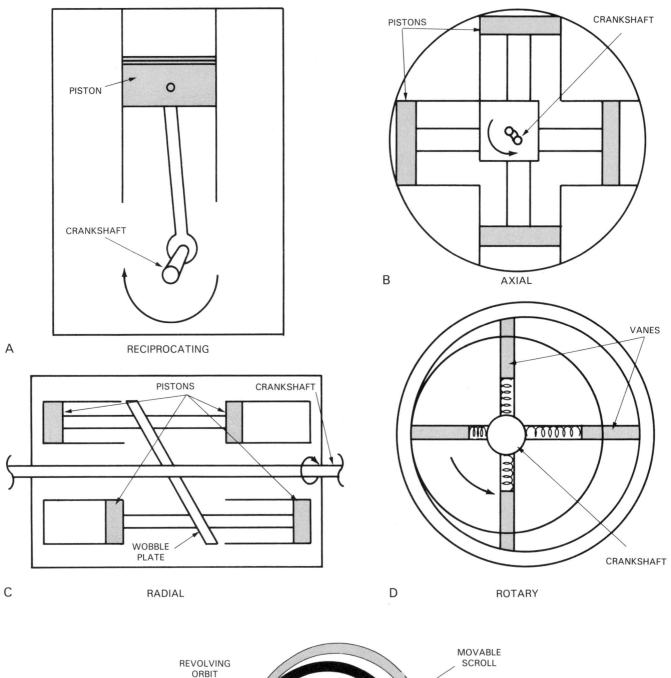

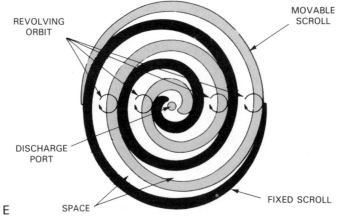

Fig. 10-1. The five basic compressor designs. A—Reciprocating. B—Radial. C—Axial. D—Rotary vane. E—Scroll. (Mitsubishi)

AIR CONDITIONING COMPRESSORS

10

After studying this chapter, you will be able to:
* *List and compare the different compressor designs.*
* *Explain how the different compressors operate.*
* *Summarize the operation of an a/c compressor clutch.*

INTRODUCTION

An *air conditioning compressor* is the "heart" of an air conditioning system. Like a human heart, it is a pump. It is important for you to understand the types and construction of compressors. The function of an air conditioning compressor is to:

1. Circulate refrigerant through the lines and components.
2. Remove low-pressure vapor from the evaporator by creating a suction.
3. Compress the low-pressure vapor, from the evaporator, to a high pressure, high-temperature vapor.
4. Operate quietly and dependably.
5. Consume a minimum amount of engine horsepower.

COMPRESSOR CLASSIFICATIONS

There are several types of compressors that can be found on a modern car. The compressor is usually classified by cylinder arrangement. The major classifications of compressors are the:

1. *RECIPROCATING.* The cylinders are arranged perpendicular to the crankshaft, Fig. 10-1A.
2. *RADIAL.* The cylinders are located in a circle around the crankshaft, Fig. 10-1B.
3. *AXIAL.* The cylinders are located parallel to the compressor crankshaft, Fig. 10-1C.
4. *ROTARY VANE.* Spinning rotor and sliding vanes produce suction and pressure, Fig. 10-1D.
5. *SCROLL.* The scroll compressor consists of two scrolls. One scroll remains stationary while the other scroll moves in an orbiting motion. The

refrigerant is compressed between the two scrolls, Fig. 10-1E.

RECIPROCATING COMPRESSOR

Reciprocating compressors are designed with both in-line and V-type cylinder arrangements. Piston movement is perpendicular to the crankshaft in either type. An in-line, two-cylinder, reciprocating compressor is shown in Figs. 10-2 and 10-3. A reciprocating V-type air conditioning compressor is shown in Fig. 10-4. The cylinders are offset approximately 90 degrees, Fig. 10-5.

Reciprocating compressor construction

The main body or crankcase of the reciprocating compressor serves as the envelope for the rotating parts. The crankcase material can be either cast iron or die-cast aluminum, depending on the manufacturer. The crankcase is drilled and tapped so the cylinder head, baseplate, clutch coil, sump, and mounting brackets can be attached, Fig. 10-6.

The crankshaft is of cast-iron construction and machined to accept antifriction-type bearings, Fig. 10-7. The connecting rod uses friction-type bearings and connects the piston to the crankshaft, Fig. 10-8. The connecting rod is cast aluminum. The connecting rod attaches to the piston with a steel wrist pin. The pistons are also aluminum and grooved to accept cast-iron piston rings.

VALVE PLATE/REED VALVES

The *valve plate* supports the reed valves and seals the top of cylinders. The cylinder head holds the valve plate in place. A *reed valve* is a thin, flat piece of spring steel that covers a suction or discharge port. It controls the flow of refrigerant gas in or out of the compressor, Fig. 10-9.

101

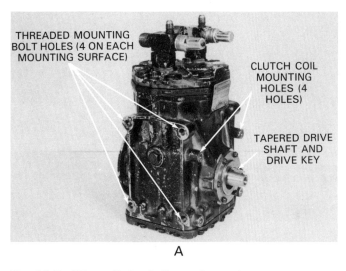

Fig. 10-2. Two-cylinder, in-line reciprocating compressor. A—Compressor minus the clutch coil and pulley. B—The shaft seal prevents compressor oil from leaking.

Reed valve operation

The suction or discharge gas pressure overcomes the spring tension of the reed valve. This causes it to lift off the port allowing the refrigerant vapor to flow, Fig. 10-10. The suction reed valve opens when the piston

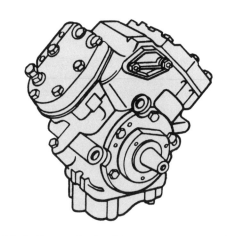

Fig. 10-4. Two-cylinder, V-type compressor. (Ford)

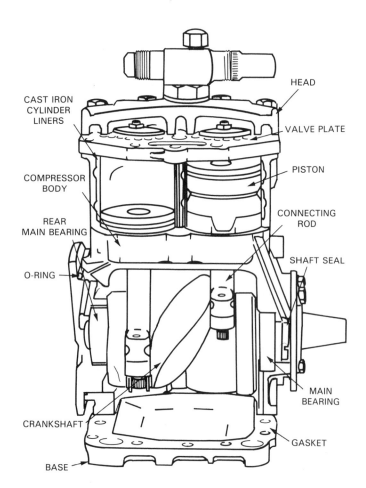

Fig. 10-3. Note the position of the crankshaft in relation to the pistons.

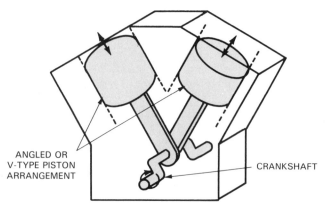

Fig. 10-5. Cutaway view of a V-type compressor.

moves down on the intake stroke and closes when the piston is on the compression stroke, Fig. 10-11. The discharge reed valve opens when the piston moves up on the compression stroke and remains closed on the intake stroke, Fig. 10-11. There is one set of reed valves, discharge and suction, for each cylinder.

Fig. 10-6. Two-cylinder, in-line compressor block. It has tapped holes for bolting items to it.

Fig. 10-7. The cast-iron crankshaft fits at the bottom of the block.

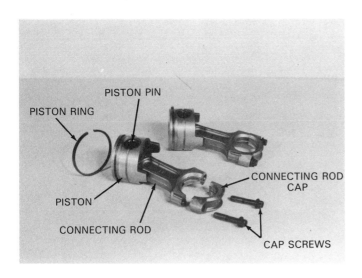

Fig. 10-8. Cast aluminum connecting rod connects the piston. The connecting rod cap fits around the crankshaft and is then bolted in place.

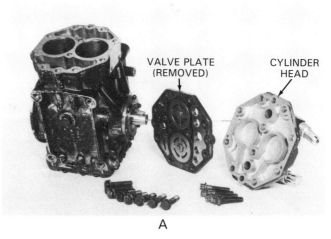

A

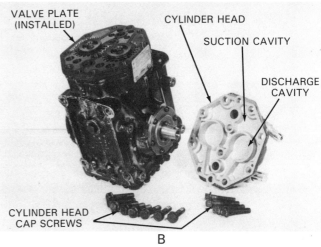

B

Fig. 10-9. Valve plate. A—Valve plate removed from compressor. B—Valve plate installed on compressor.

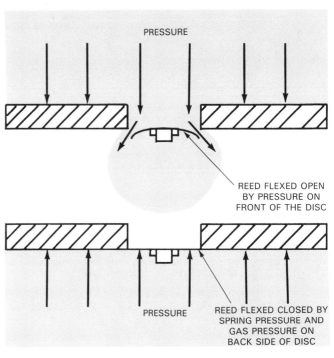

Fig. 10-10. Reed valve action.

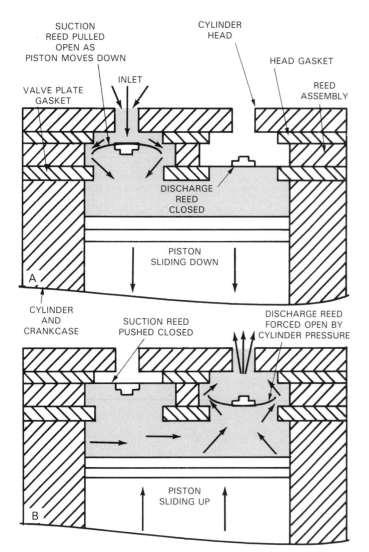

Fig. 10-11. Reed valve operation in relation to piston move-ment. A—Inlet reed valve is open and discharge reed valve is closed while piston moves downward. B—Inlet reed valve is closed and discharge reed valve is open while piston moves upward.

Fig. 10-12. Radial compressor minus clutch coil and pulley.

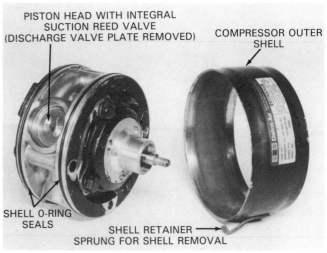

Fig. 10-13. Radial compressor with steel shell removed. The intake reed valve is located on top of the piston.

Fig. 10-14. Discharge reed valve mounts at top of cylinder.

RADIAL COMPRESSOR

The four-cylinder radial (R4) compressor is used on smaller engines because of its light weight, low horse-power consumption, and small space requirement, Fig. 10-12. The pistons reciprocate perpendicular to the crankshaft.

Radial compressor construction

The cylinder block is cast aluminum, Figs. 10-13 through 10-15. It provides a housing for the rotating group consisting of aluminum pistons, aluminum yoke, steel crankshaft, and a steel slider block.

The eccentric drive consists of a slider block on the crankshaft throw, Fig. 10-16. The slider block is ma-chined on all four sides and provides a bearing surface for the two yokes. Two pistons are pressed into each yoke, Figs. 10-17 and 10-18. The pistons are pressed into the yokes after the rotating group is in place.

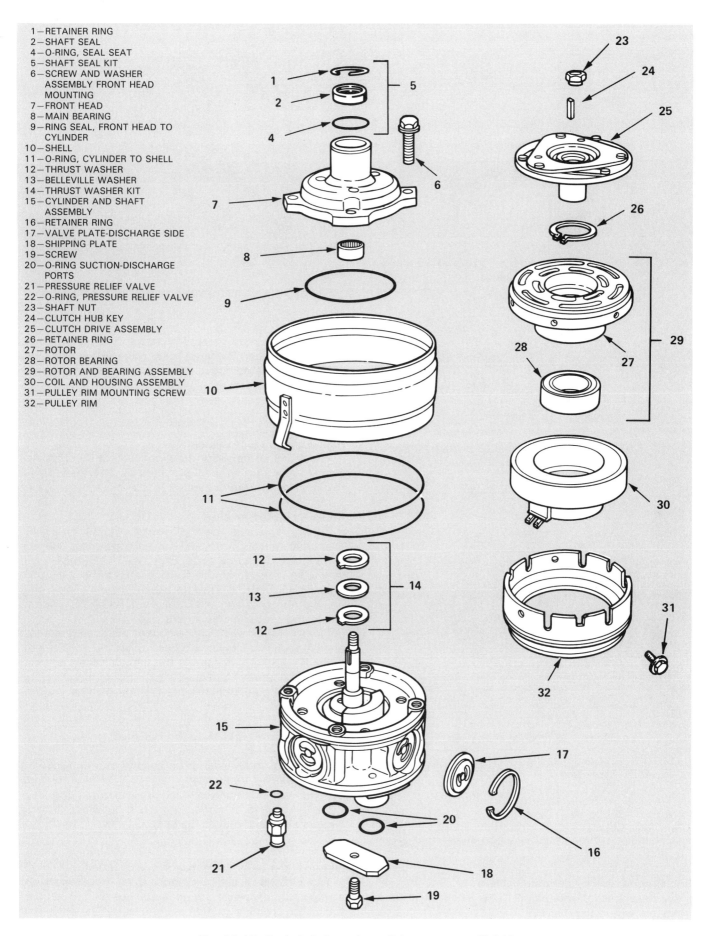

1—RETAINER RING
2—SHAFT SEAL
4—O-RING, SEAL SEAT
5—SHAFT SEAL KIT
6—SCREW AND WASHER
ASSEMBLY FRONT HEAD
MOUNTING
7—FRONT HEAD
8—MAIN BEARING
9—RING SEAL, FRONT HEAD TO
CYLINDER
10—SHELL
11—O-RING, CYLINDER TO SHELL
12—THRUST WASHER
13—BELLEVILLE WASHER
14—THRUST WASHER KIT
15—CYLINDER AND SHAFT
ASSEMBLY
16—RETAINER RING
17—VALVE PLATE-DISCHARGE SIDE
18—SHIPPING PLATE
19—SCREW
20—O-RING SUCTION-DISCHARGE
PORTS
21—PRESSURE RELIEF VALVE
22—O-RING, PRESSURE RELIEF VALVE
23—SHAFT NUT
24—CLUTCH HUB KEY
25—CLUTCH DRIVE ASSEMBLY
26—RETAINER RING
27—ROTOR
28—ROTOR BEARING
29—ROTOR AND BEARING ASSEMBLY
30—COIL AND HOUSING ASSEMBLY
31—PULLEY RIM MOUNTING SCREW
32—PULLEY RIM

Fig. 10-15. Exploded view of a radial compressor. (Buick)

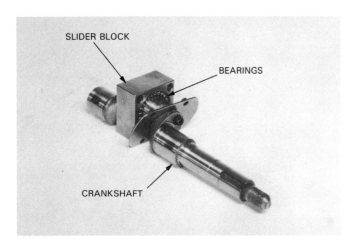

Fig. 10-16. Slider block mounted on crankshaft rotates on anti-friction bearings.

Fig. 10-18. Assembled yoke connected to slider block.

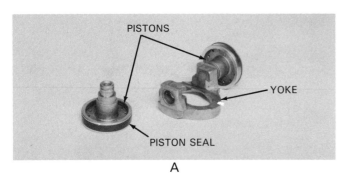

A

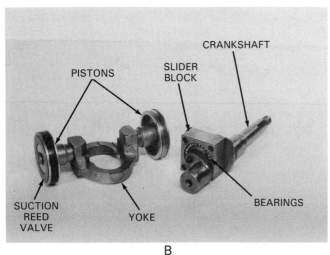

B

Fig. 10-17. Yoke and pistons. A—Pistons are pressed into yoke. B—Assembled yoke connects to slider block.

Therefore, the housing and rotating group cannot be disassembled for repair and must be replaced as an entire unit.

Radial compressor operation/valving

As the crankshaft rotates, the slider block causes each yoke and piston to reciprocate, Fig. 10-19. The valves in the radial compressor differ from other reciprocating compressors.

The suction reed valve attaches to the piston head, Fig. 10-13. The discharge reed valve attaches to the valve plate located above the cylinder bore, Figs. 10-14 and 10-15, and acts as a cylinder head. A snap ring holds the discharge reed valve in place without a gasket or seal.

Radial compressor lubrication

The radial compressor does not require an oil pump. Compressor lubrication is provided by oil splashed as a result of piston movement.

Radial compressor shell

Two O-rings seal the shell to the cylinder and shaft assembly housing, Fig. 10-13. O-rings also seal the suction and discharge ports, Fig. 10-20. A D-ring is used in sealing the aluminum front head to the assembly housing, Fig. 10-21. The shaft seal consists of an O-ring (inside the front head and inner diameter of the graphite seal), and a ceramic seal seat, Fig. 10-22.

The assembly and disassembly of the shell requires a special tool. It is similar to a gear puller. When the compressor needs replacement, the old shell may be used with a new assembly, Fig. 10-23. Prior to installing the shell, you should lubricate the O-rings with new refrigerant oil.

FIVE-CYLINDER AXIAL COMPRESSOR

The five-cylinder axial compressor was introduced for use on smaller engines in the late 1970s. The five-cylinder compressor uses reciprocating pistons, Fig. 10-24. A swash or *wobble plate* is a flat piece of thick circular steel that moves the pistons back and forth, Fig. 10-25.

Five-cylinder axial compressor construction

The pistons in a five-cylinder axial compressor are single acting. A *single-acting piston* has only one end of the piston produce suction and pressure. The bottom or back of the piston is fastened to the connecting rod. The connecting rod fastens to the wobble plate.

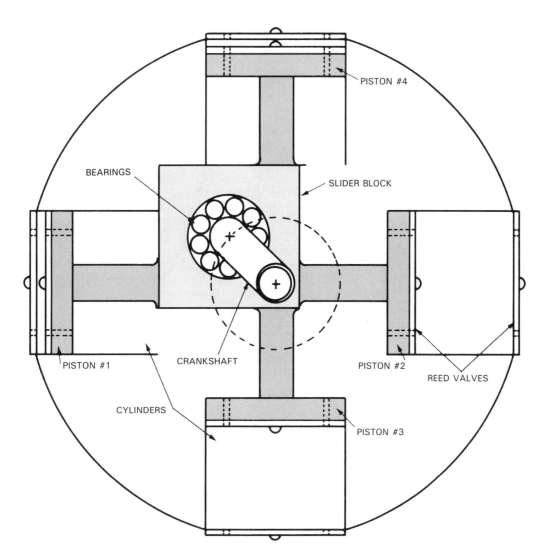

Fig. 10-19. The slider block revolves with the crankshaft. This converts the rotary motion of the crankshaft to reciprocating action of the pistons. The pistons move perpendicular to the crankshaft.

VARIABLE DISPLACEMENT COMPRESSOR

The *variable displacement compressor,* a five-cylinder axial compressor, changes the angle of the wobble plate, Figs. 10-26 and 10-27. The angle of the wobble plate depends on the cooling load. The wobble-plate angle controls evaporator temperature without cycling the clutch on and off.

Variable displacement compressor construction

The cylinder block is made of aluminum. Five separate cylinders are bored in the block, parallel to the crankshaft. The front and rear cylinder heads are bolted to the cylinder block. The aluminum pistons are machined to accept two piston rings and a connecting rod. The valve plate is installed between the head and the cylinder block.

Variable displacement compressor operation

When there is very little demand for cooling, the angle of the wobble plate is reduced, Fig. 10-28A. The greater the cooling load placed on the A/C system, the greater the angle of the wobble plate, Fig. 10-28B. The pivot

pin allows the wobble plate to change angles, Fig. 10-29. The bellows-actuated control valve determines the position or angle of the wobble plate, Fig. 10-30. When the A/C system is turned off, the horseshoe spring, Fig. 10-27B, returns the wobble plate to the start-up angle. This ensures almost instant pressure when the A/C system is turned on.

Variable displacement compressor lubrication

No oil pump is required for compressor lubrication. A pressure differential between the low-pressure side and the crankcase oil sump forces the circulation of compressor oil.

SIX-CYLINDER AXIAL COMPRESSOR

The six-cylinder axial compressor, Fig. 10-31, is used on cars with large engines. Six-cylinder compressors have the same reciprocating action as the five-cylinder compressor, but have double-acting pistons, Fig. 10-32. *Double-acting pistons* use both ends of the piston during one stroke, Fig. 10-33. Actually, a six-cylinder compressor uses only three double-acting pistons, Fig.

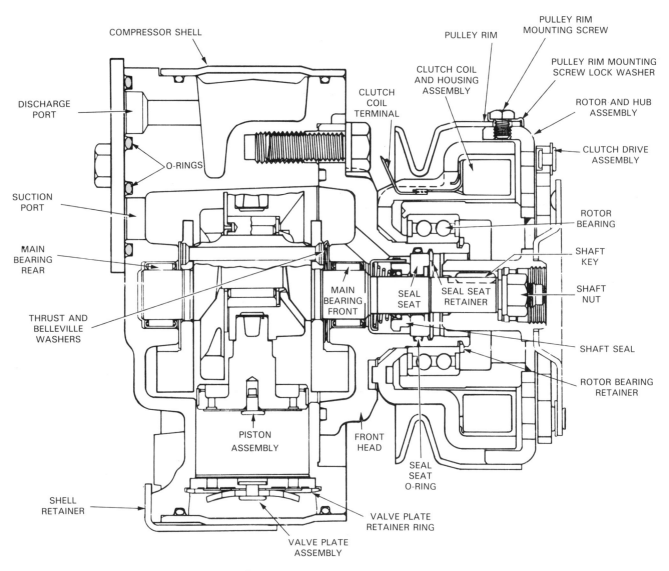

Fig. 10-20. O-rings seal suction and discharge ports.

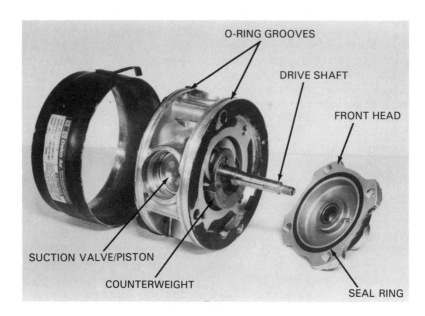

Fig. 10-21. Outer shell and front head removed from assembly. Discharge reed valve assembly has also been removed to view piston and cylinder.

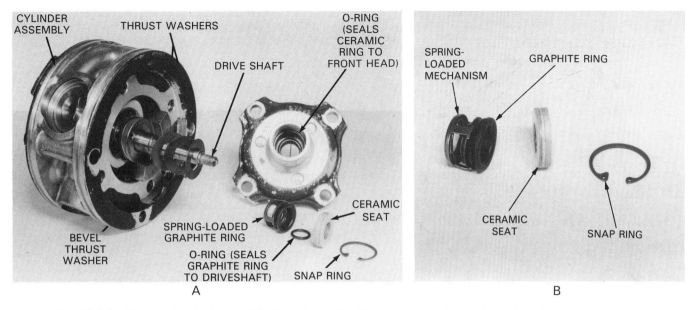

Fig. 10-22. Front seals. A—Located in front head. B—Close-up view of graphite seal and ceramic-seal seat.

Fig. 10-23. The shipping bar maintains alignment of the internal parts and must be removed prior to installation.

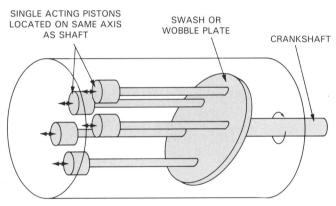

Fig. 10-25. The pistons of a five-cylinder, axial compressor are attached to a wobble plate. As the crankshaft turns, the wobble plate causes the pistons to reciprocate.

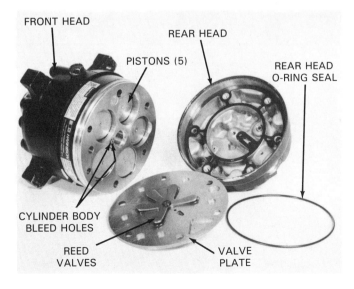

Fig. 10-24. Partially disassembled view of a five-cylinder, axial compressor. The reed valves are located in the rear cylinder head.

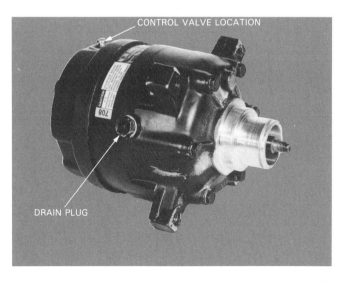

Fig. 10-26. The variable displacement compressor, minus the clutch coil and pulley, has a control valve that determines the wobble-plate angle.

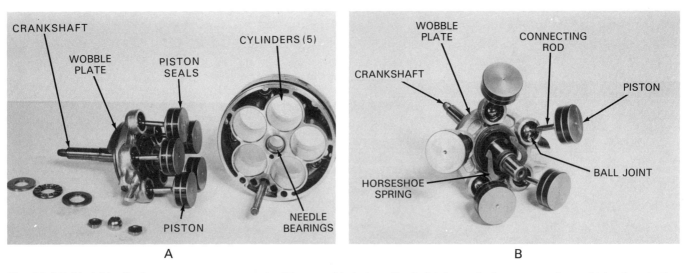

Fig. 10-27. Variable displacement compressor. A—Disassembled view. B—Ball-joint swivel connects the wobble plate to the connecting rod. Horseshoe spring returns wobble plate to start-up angle after air conditioner has been turned off.

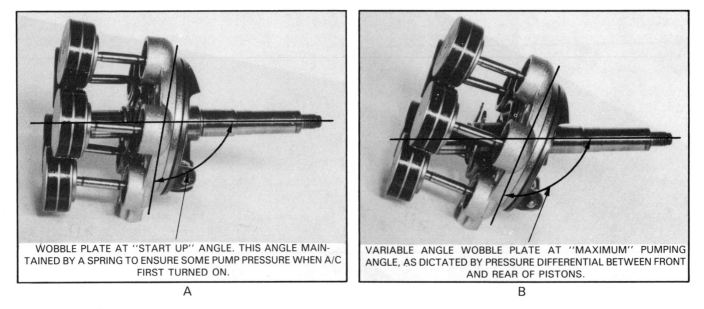

WOBBLE PLATE AT "START UP" ANGLE. THIS ANGLE MAINTAINED BY A SPRING TO ENSURE SOME PUMP PRESSURE WHEN A/C FIRST TURNED ON.

A

VARIABLE ANGLE WOBBLE PLATE AT "MAXIMUM" PUMPING ANGLE, AS DICTATED BY PRESSURE DIFFERENTIAL BETWEEN FRONT AND REAR OF PISTONS.

B

Fig. 10-28. Angle-changing wobble plate. A—Start-up angle. B—Maximum-pumping angle.

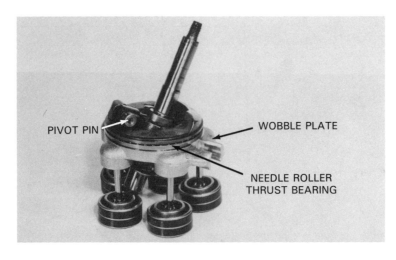

Fig. 10-29. Wobble plate is mounted on a needle-roller thrust bearing.

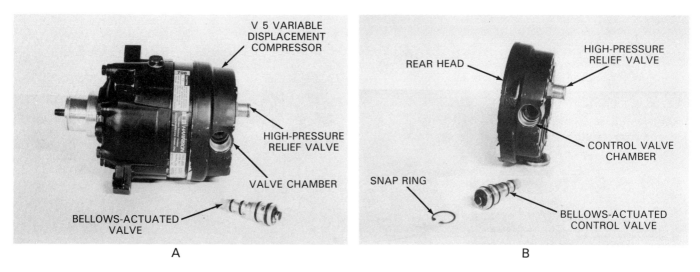

Fig. 10-30. Bellows-actuated control valve. A—Valve monitors A/C system low-side pressure. Pressure difference, between front and rear of pistons, determines wobble-plate angle. B—The valve is located in the rear cylinder head.

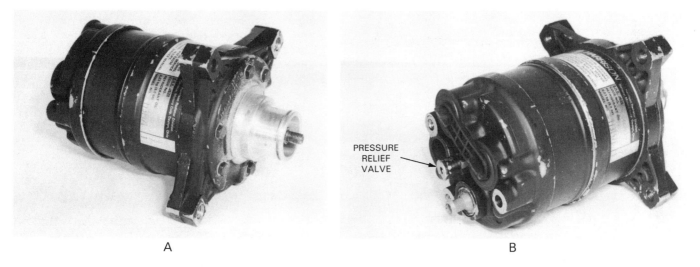

Fig. 10-31. Six-cylinder axial compressor. A—Compressor minus the clutch coil and pulley assembly. B—Rear view shows location of pressure-relief valve.

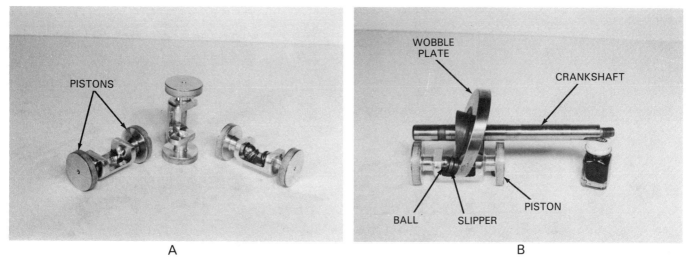

Fig. 10-32. Dual-acting pistons. A—One-piece construction has pistons at each end. B—View shows how piston assembly connects to wobble plate.

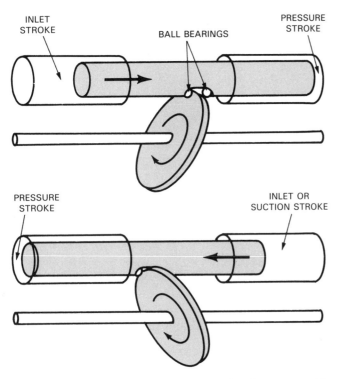

Fig. 10-33. As the wobble plate moves, the piston assembly reciprocates. While one piston is on the suction or intake stroke, the opposing piston is on the compression stroke.

10-34. Since both ends of each double-acting piston pump refrigerant, Fig. 10-35, it is termed a six-cylinder compressor.

Six-cylinder axial compressor construction

The earlier six-cylinder compressors used cast-iron cylinder heads bolted onto a steel shell. Current models use aluminum cylinder blocks and heads. Also, the length of the aluminum-cylinder compressor was shortened three and one-half inches. The combination of shortening its length and using aluminum resulted in a weight reduction of approximately 20 pounds.

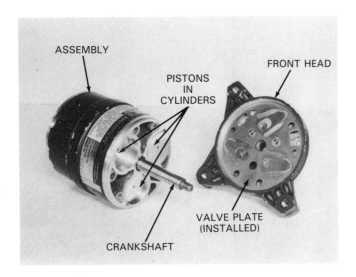

Fig. 10-34. Front head removed, showing one end of a six-cylinder axial compressor.

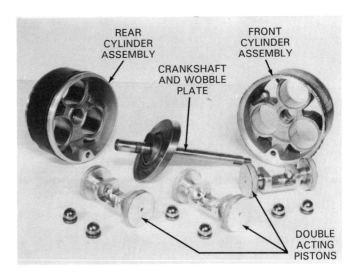

Fig. 10-35. Six-cylinder axial compressor completely disassembled.

The pistons are machined to fit around the outside diameter of the swash plate. An aluminum compressor requires the use of Teflon® piston rings, Fig. 10-36. The cast-iron compressor requires the use of cast-iron piston rings.

Six-cylinder axial compressor lubrication

The earlier cast-iron six-cylinder compressor used a gear-type oil pump located in the rear head, Fig. 10-37. It provided positive oil pressure to all moving parts. The newer aluminum six-cylinder compressor has no oil sump or pump. Its lubrication system features baffles, dams, and grooves to collect and direct oil to the bearings and swash plate.

ROTARY-VANE COMPRESSOR

A rotary-vane compressor does not use reciprocating pistons. This design has a spinning rotor with vanes inserted in rotor slots, Fig. 10-38. The rotary-vane compressor is a relatively new design.

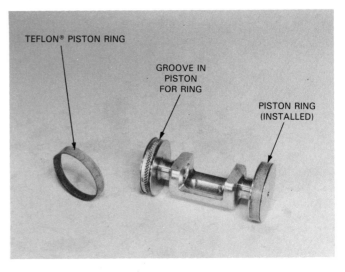

Fig. 10-36. A Teflon® piston ring is used on each piston.

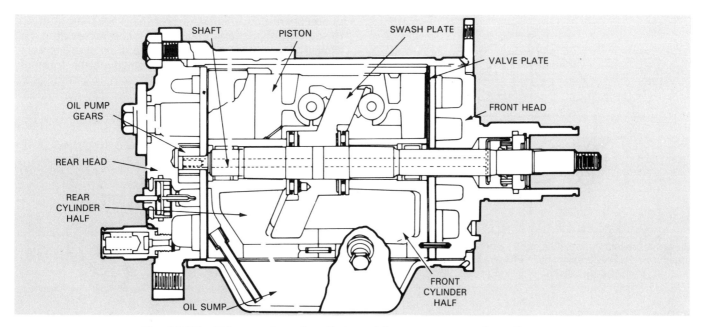

Fig. 10-37. Older cast-iron six-cylinder axial compressors used an oil pump.

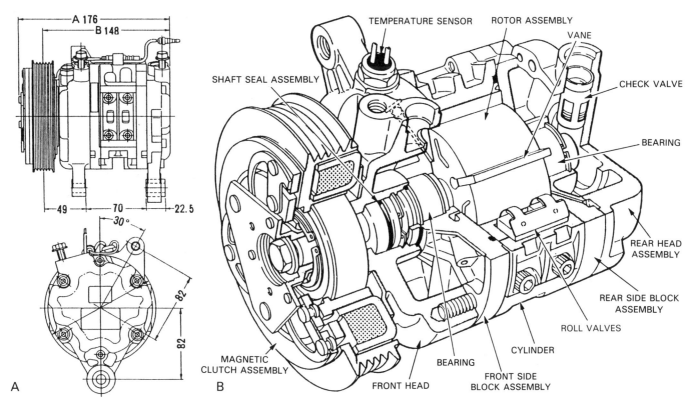

Fig. 10-38. Rotary vane compressor. A—Cross section. B—Cutaway view.   (Zexel Illinois, Inc.)

Rotary vane compressor operation

As the rotor turns, refrigerant gas from the evaporator flows into the compressor through a check valve. The gas is drawn into the low-pressure chamber inside the rear head.

The gas then is pulled through two suction ports into the cylinder chamber. The rotor turned by the drive shaft has five vanes mounted on it. As it rotates, the vanes press tightly against the walls of the chamber, with a film of oil providing a gas-tight seal. The elliptical shape of the chamber provides a decreasing volume, compressing the refrigerant, Fig. 10-39. The compressed gas flows into the discharge chamber, where a baffle is used to separate refrigerant oil from the gas. Finally, the liquid refrigerant flows from the compressor to the condenser.

Each complete rotation of the 5-vane rotor performs ten intake, compression, and discharge cycles.

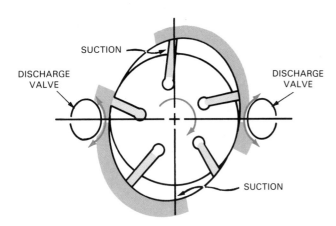

Fig. 10-39. As the rotor turns, the vanes force the refrigerant to an increasingly smaller area where the refrigerant is pressurized. The pressurized refrigerant is forced out the discharge valves.   (Zexel Illinois, Inc.)

SCROLL COMPRESSOR

The scroll compressor is an unusual design, Fig. 10-40. However, the concept is old and was first patented in the early 1900s. Current use is limited to a few car models.

Scroll compressor construction

The stationary scroll is fitted to the inner diameter of the housing. The internal space of the housing is now divided into the front (low-pressure area) and rear (high-pressure area). A reed valve is located at the center or discharge port. Intake valves are not needed on this design.

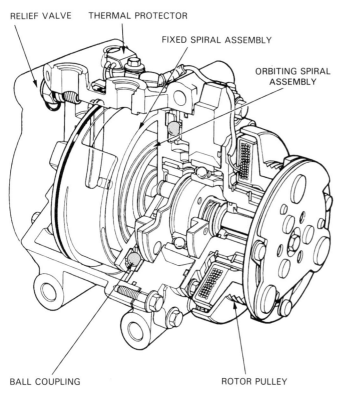

Fig. 10-40. A cutaway view of the scroll compressor. (Honda)

An eccentric bushing connects the crankshaft stud pin to the movable scroll, Fig. 10-41. The offset stud pin allows the orbiting radius of the movable scroll to vary within limits. The counterweight balances the force of the orbiting parts.

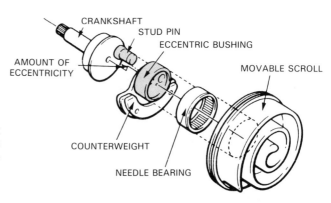

Fig. 10-41. The movable scroll is mounted on an eccentric bushing. (Mitsubishi)

The ball coupling maintains the relationship between the two scrolls, Figs. 10-40 and 10-42. The ball coupling receives the axial force of the movable scroll and, therefore, also acts as an orbiting thrust bearing.

Scroll compressor operation

The scroll compressor contains two scrolls, Fig. 10-43. One scroll remains stationary (fixed). The other scroll orbits the fixed scroll. The relationship of the two scroll varies as the movable scroll orbits and compresses the refrigerant. The volume of refrigerant is gradually reduced as it moves toward the center or discharge port. The suction-compression-suction cycle takes approximately two crankshaft revolutions.

Scroll compressor bypass valve operation

A bypass valve is located in the high-pressure side of the compressor, Fig. 10-42. The bypass valve moves between the 50 and 30 percent bypass ports, Fig. 10-42. The position of the bypass valve regulates how much refrigerant vapor is routed back to the low-pressure side. Refrigerant flow is based on cooling demand.

Upon engaging the compressor, the pressurized refrigerant is directed to the front of the bypass valve only. This forces the bypass valve back and uncovers the 50 percent bypass port. This means 50 percent of the refrigerant flow is redirected to the low-pressure side.

Immediately after the compressor is engaged, refrigerant pressure increases on the back side of the bypass valve. This causes the bypass valve to move forward. It now covers both the 30 and 50 percent bypass ports. Zero percent refrigerant is now bypassed. When cooling demands are low, the bypass valve moves slightly forward and uncovers the 30 percent bypass port.

A/C COMPRESSOR CLUTCH

The *compressor clutch* provides a means of electrically engaging and disengaging the a/c compressor from the

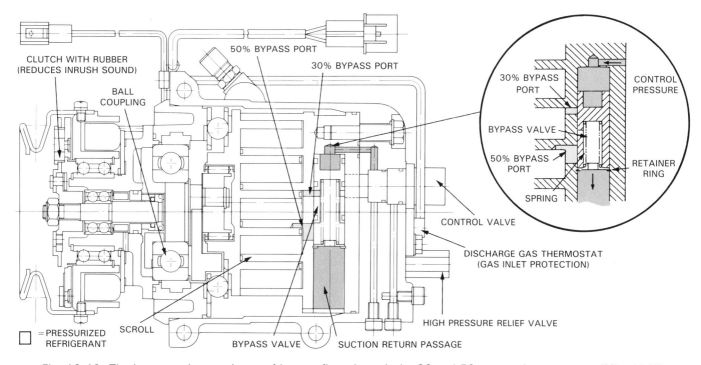

Fig. 10-42. The bypass valve regulates refrigerant flow through the 30 and 50 percent bypass ports. (Mitsubishi)

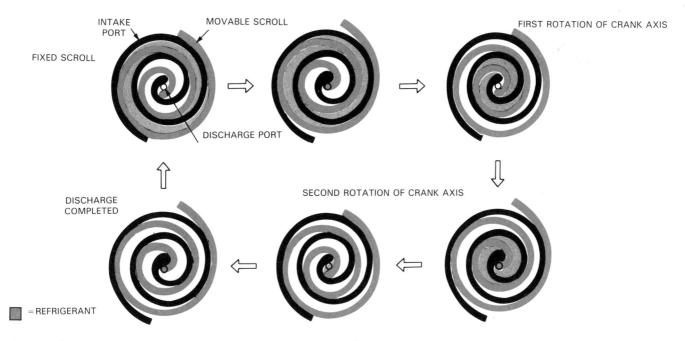

Fig. 10-43. The scroll compressor requires two complete crankshaft revolutions to complete one cycle. (Mitsubishi)

engine. The basic parts of a typical a/c compressor clutch include the:

1. *CLUTCH PLATE.* A flat steel friction surface splined to the compressor shaft.
2. *CLUTCH PULLEY.* A drive pulley, mounted on an antifriction bearing, located between the clutch plate and compressor housing.
3. *CLUTCH BEARING.* An antifriction bearing mounted inside the clutch pulley.
4. *CLUTCH COIL ASSEMBLY.* An electromagnet, consisting of many windings encapsulated in a hous-

ing, used to pull the clutch plate into contact with the compressor pulley, Fig. 10-44.

Clutch operation

When the coil is energized, the magnetic field attracts the clutch plate. This engages it to the clutch pulley and the compressor shaft now rotates. When the coil is de-energized, the magnetic field is broken. Springs force the clutch plate away from the pulley. The clutch plate disengages and the compressor crankshaft does not rotate, Fig. 10-45.

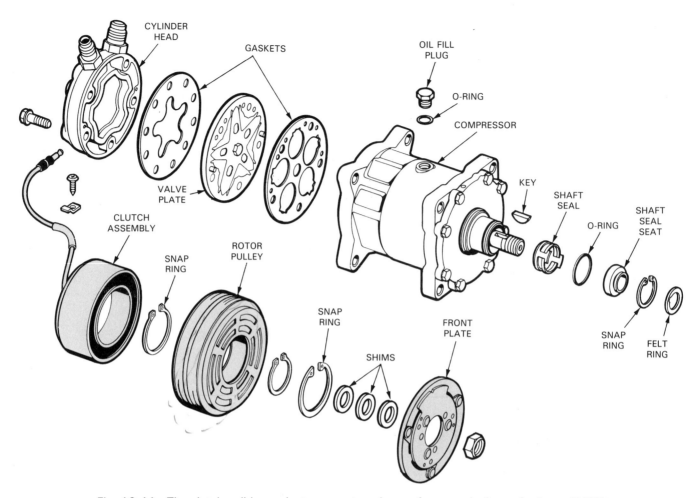

Fig. 10-44. The clutch coil is an electromagnet made up of many windings of wire. (AMC)

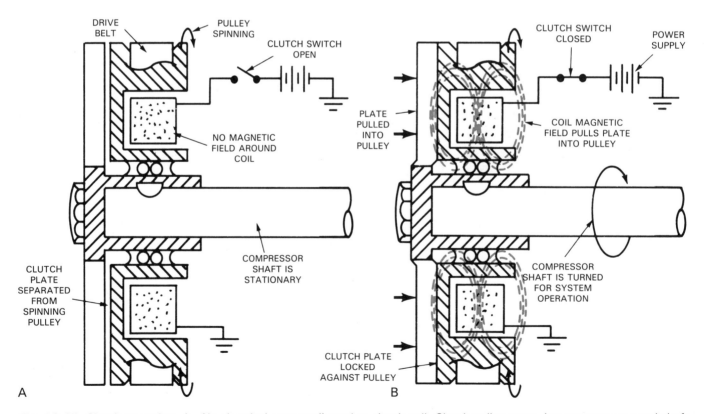

Fig. 10-45. Clutch operation. A—No electrical current allowed to clutch coil. Clutch pulley turns, but compressor crankshaft is disengaged and does not turn. B—Electrical current flows to the clutch coil and magnetic force pulls the plate into the pulley, causing the compressor crankshaft to turn.

Cycling the clutch

Once the air conditioner is turned on, some A/C systems automatically cycle the clutch off and on. This occurs as long as the air conditioner or defrost mode remains selected. This prevents evaporator freeze-up while maintaining maximum cooling.

A thermal-sensing device (clutch cycling switch), connects to the evaporator outlet by a capillary tube, Fig. 10-46. The switch interrupts electrical current to the clutch and de-energizes it when the temperature of the evaporator core approaches freezing. Once evaporator temperature increases, electrical current flows from the thermal-sensing device (clutch cycling switch) and energizes the clutch coil.

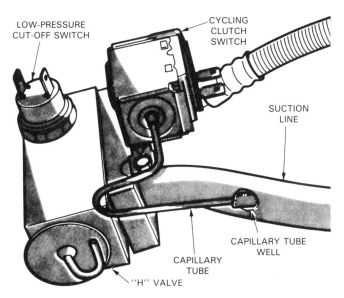

Fig. 10-46. Clutch cycling switch senses evaporator outlet temperature. It interrupts electrical current to the clutch coil when the air conditioner is on as the evaporator nears freezing.

REPAIRS

Repairs that can be made to an air conditioning compressor in the field are limited. Replacement of the front compressor seal, clutch coil/assembly, and clutch bearing are the repairs made in the field. If parts within the compressor fail, the entire unit is replaced. The compressor is NOT repaired or rebuilt in the field. If a new compressor is needed, the clutch assembly from the old compressor is transferred to the new compressor.

SUMMARY

The compressor, often referred to as the ''heart'' of the air conditioning system, performs five functions. It:
1. Circulates refrigerant through the system.
2. Removes low-pressure vapor from the evaporator.
3. Compresses refrigerant to a high-pressure, high-temperature vapor.
4. Operates quietly and dependably.
5. Consumes minimal engine horsepower.

Automotive air conditioning compressors vary in design and construction. Most are of the reciprocating-piston type, the exception being the scroll and rotary-vane design.

The reciprocating and radial type has pistons move perpendicular to the crankshaft. The axial-type compressor has pistons move parallel to the rotating crankshaft. A five-cylinder axial compressor uses a wobble plate to move the single-acting pistons. A variable displacement compressor is a five-cylinder axial compressor with an angle-changing wobble plate. It changes the angle depending on the cooling load placed on the A/C system. A six-cylinder axial compressor is basically the same as the five-cylinder axial compressor, except for the double-acting pistons.

A rotary-vane compressor uses sliding vanes in an offset rotor. As the rotor turns, the vanes force the refrigerant to an increasingly smaller area. This pressurizes the refrigerant. Neither the rotary-vane nor scroll compressor use an intake valve.

The scroll compressor has a movable and stationary scroll. As the movable scroll orbits, the refrigerant is pressurized between the two scrolls. The bypass valve regulates refrigerant flow based on the cooling demand.

An air conditioning compressor clutch electrically connects and disconnects the compressor from the engine. Energizing the electromagnet engages the compressor clutch; de-energizing the electromagnet disengages the clutch. Some systems automatically cycle the clutch off and on once the air conditioner is turned on. This prevents evaporator freeze-up, which maintains maximum cooling.

KNOW THESE TERMS

Air conditioning compressor, Reciprocating, Radial, Axial, Rotary vane, Scroll, Valve plate, Reed valve, Wobble plate, Single-acting piston, Variable displacement compressor, Double-acting piston, Compressor clutch, Clutch plate, Clutch pulley, Clutch bearing, Clutch coil assembly.

REVIEW QUESTIONS—CHAPTER 10

1. An in-line, reciprocating compressor has how many cylinders?
   a. Five.
   b. Four.
   c. Three.
   d. Two.
2. The sliding yoke drive is used in which of the following compressors?
   a. Axial.
   b. In-line.
   c. Rotary.
   d. Radial.
3. All reciprocating compressors have either an in-line or V-type cylinder arrangements. True or false?
4. A four-cylinder radial compressor is used on smaller engines because of its:
   a. Light weight.
   b. Low horsepower consumption.
   c. Both of the above.
   d. None of the above.

5. The swash or wobble plate drive is used in the following compressor designs:
   a. In-line.
   b. Radial.
   c. Rotary.
   d. Axial.
6. List the basic functions of a compressor.
7. The reed valves control refrigerant flow entering and leaving most compressors. True or false?
8. The weight reduction of the aluminum six-cylinder compressor, compared to the cast-iron six-cylinder compressor, is about:
   a. 5 lbs.
   b. 9.85 lbs.
   c. 15 lbs.
   d. 20 lbs.
9. A reed valve is a:
   a. Poppet valve operated by a wobble plate.
   b. Spring-loaded ball check valve.
   c. Piece of flat spring steel.
   d. Solenoid-operated one-way valve.
10. Explain the purpose of the a/c clutch coil.
11. Piston motion, of the in-line and V-type compressors, is:
    a. Parallel to the crankshaft.
    b. Perpendicular to the crankshaft.
    c. Both a and b.
    d. None of the above.
12. Describe a single-acting and double-acting piston.
13. When the clutch field coil is energized, the:
    a. Compressor is disengaged.
    b. Clutch plate is drawn into the pulley.
    c. Magnetic field collapses.
    d. None of the above.
14. An air conditioning compressor:
    a. Increases refrigerant temperature and lowers pressure.
    b. Decreases refrigerant temperature and increases pressure.
    c. Increases refrigerant temperature and pressure.
    d. Decreases refrigerant temperature and pressure.
15. Briefly explain how a scroll compressor operates.

RECEIVER-DRIERS AND ACCUMULATORS

11

After studying this chapter, you will be able to:
* List the functions of a receiver-drier or accumulator.
* Explain the construction of a receiver-drier or accumulator.
* Describe construction of a valves-in-receiver unit.
* Identify when to change the receiver-drier or accumulator.

INTRODUCTION

The receiver-drier or accumulator protects the system from moisture and foreign particles by filtering the refrigerant as it circulates. It also acts as a reservoir for extra refrigerant and separates the vaporized refrigerant from its liquid state. An understanding of construction and operation will help when troubleshooting problems caused by these components.

EFFECTS OF MOISTURE

A refrigerant is a fluorocarbon compound. When it combines with moisture in the air conditioning system, hydrochloric and hydrofluoric acids form. These acids cause corrosion, creating pinhole-size leaks in the evaporator and condenser. The moisture also combines with the refrigerant oil to form sludge which can plug the system and prevent the A/C compressor valves from sealing. The moisture can also freeze in the suction hose, evaporator, or expansion valve. This blocks the flow of refrigerant and results in a loss of cooling until the ice thaws.

DETECTING MOISTURE

Detecting moisture in the A/C system may not be easy. This is because it takes time for the moisture to condense and then freeze, so the test gauges generally register normal pressures. However, a clue from the driver of the car may help.

The driver states the A/C system will work for about 10 minutes and then stops cooling. Approximately 5 to 10 minutes later the air conditioning starts cooling again. The A/C system then works normal for another 10 minutes until it stops cooling again. The problem cause is moisture inside the A/C system freezing and blocking the flow of refrigerant. The ice melts and the refrigerant flows until the moisture in the system freezes again.

A defective evaporator temperature control device or a long clutch cycling operation may cause ice to form on the outside of the evaporator core instead of internally. This blocks the airflow through the evaporator fins. This condition can be detected by system pressure.

RECEIVER-DRIER ASSEMBLY

The receiver-drier is located in the high-pressure liquid line between the condenser and expansion valve, Fig. 11-1. A receiver-drier is found on systems that use an expansion valve. A receiver-drier assembly cannot be repaired and must be replaced when defective or any time the system is opened to replace a component.

The *receiver-drier* provides a reservoir to receive the liquid refrigerant from the condenser, remove moisture, and filter out foreign particles, Fig. 11-2. The receiver-drier stores extra liquid refrigerant and thereby increases the volume of the system. The extra refrigerant provides for changes in demand under high temperature and humidity conditions. High-temperature, high-humidity conditions require a greater amount of refrigerant to flow to maintain the same level of cooling. The extra refrigerant also compensates for minor refrigerant losses.

Receiver-drier filter

The receiver-drier contains a *filter screen* or *filter pads* to trap and retain foreign particles, preventing them from moving through the system and plugging small orifices, Fig. 11-2. To reduce or eliminate the amount of moisture

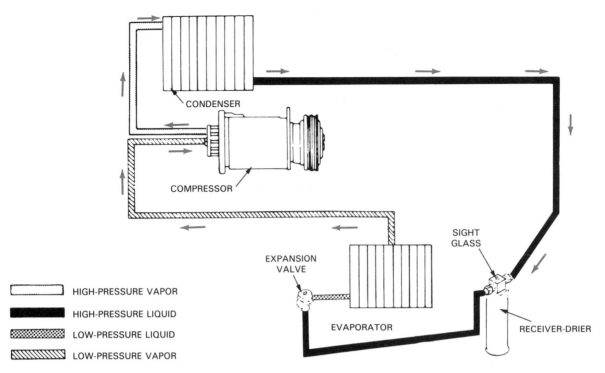

HIGH-PRESSURE VAPOR

HIGH-PRESSURE LIQUID

LOW-PRESSURE LIQUID

LOW-PRESSURE VAPOR

Fig. 11-1. The receiver-drier is located in the high-pressure liquid line. It is found on systems that use an expansion valve.   (Isuzu)

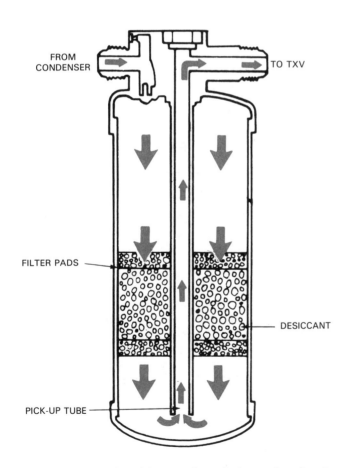

Fig. 11-2. The receiver-drier contains a desiccant that absorbs moisture in the system. The filter pads trap particles to prevent them from circulating through the system. The pick-up tube is positioned near the bottom so that only the heavier liquid refrigerant can enter. (Ford)

that has entered the air conditioning system, a desiccant is placed inside the receiver-drier, Fig. 11-2.

DESICCANT

Desiccant is a moisture absorbing material contained within the receiver-drier. Its function is to absorb small amounts of moisture within the A/C system. The amount of moisture it can hold depends on the type of desiccant and its volume. Desiccants can be made of:

1. Activated silica alumina.
2. Silica gel.
3. Alumina gel.
4. Calcium sulfate.
5. Calcium chloride.
6. Molecular sieve (a porous sintered metal).
7. Mobil-gel®.

Five cubic inches of silica gel has the capacity of absorbing and holding about 100 drops of water at 150 °F (65.5 °C). Moisture exceeding 100 drops of water is released into the system.

Characteristics of desiccants

The desiccant must be kept cool or it will release the moisture it has absorbed. The receiver-drier is usually located near the radiator and condenser where it is in the path of the cooler, incoming airflow. The desiccant must meet several requirements:

1. Not react with the refrigerant or its oil.
2. Must be stable and not decompose. If it decomposes, the fine particles of decomposed desiccant plug the small orifices in the A/C system.
3. Have high moisture retention. Some desiccants absorb 16 percent of their weight in moisture.
4. Have minimum restriction on the flow of refrigerant.

RECEIVER-DRIER CONSTRUCTION

The receiver-drier used in automotive air conditioning, Fig. 11-2, consists of a small steel tank with a welded top and bottom. The inlet and outlet fittings, welded to the top cover, connect lines from the condenser and expansion valve. The top cover contains a *pick-up tube* that extends close to the bottom of the receiver-drier. Liquid refrigerant is heavier than in its vaporized state. The liquid refrigerant sinks to the bottom of the receiver-drier. The position of the pick-up tube allows only liquid refrigerant to leave the receiver-drier.

The desiccant, sealed in the receiver drier when it is assembled, is held in place by different methods. One method contains the desiccant in a mesh bag while another method places it between two screens. The mesh or screens not only hold the desiccant in place, but act as a strainer to prevent foreign particles from circulating through the system.

Receiver-drier sight glass

The *sight glass,* when used, is generally located at the top of the receiver-drier or somewhere in the high-pressure liquid line, Fig. 11-1. It is used to check the level and condition of the refrigerant charge, Fig. 11-3. A clear sight glass indicates the system has either absolutely no charge or an adequate charge of refrigerant. If the air conditioner is cooling and the sight glass is clear, the refrigerant charge is adequate. However, if the air conditioner is not cooling and the sight glass is clear or has

oil streaks, the system is completely empty of refrigerant.

If the refrigerant charge in the system decreases, vaporized refrigerant enters the liquid line and bubbles appear in the sight glass, Fig. 11-3. Occasional bubbles, at the sight glass, indicate the system is slightly low on refrigerant or the desiccant is saturated and releasing some moisture. Foam or a heavy stream of bubbles indicates the system has a very low refrigerant level. Using the sight glass to determine the refrigerant level is only reliable when ambient temperature is at least 70 °F (21 °C).

Many later systems do not include a sight glass in the receiver-drier design or anywhere in the high-pressure liquid line. In these cases, it is necessary to use pressure gauges to determine the amount of refrigerant in the system.

VALVES-IN-RECEIVER

The *valves-in-receiver* (VIR) contains an expansion valve and a POA valve (pilot operated absolute) combined with a receiver-drier and sight glass, Fig. 11-4. The POA valve controls the temperature of the evaporator to prevent it from freezing. The expansion valve meters refrigerant to the evaporator. The VIR unit is bolted together and is serviceable. This allows replacement of the desiccant bag, expansion valve capsule, and POA valve capsules. The VIR assembly makes for a more responsive system by placing both valves in one location, thus eliminating connecting lines.

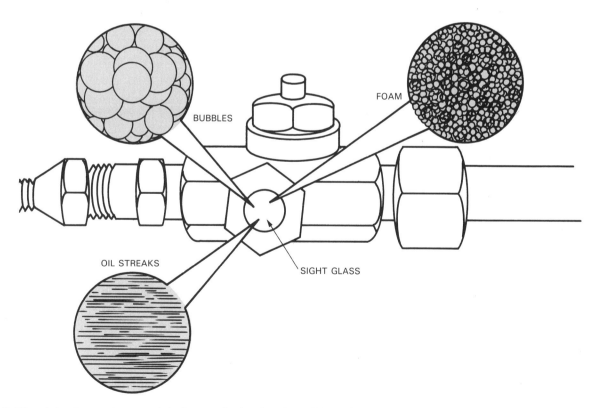

Fig. 11-3. The sight glass, when used, indicates the level and condition of refrigerant. A clear sight glass can mean the system is completely full or completely empty. Oil streaks indicate the system is completely empty. Bubbles indicate the system is low on refrigerant. Foam indicates the system is very low on refrigerant. A cloudy condition indicates the desiccant, in the receiver-drier, is circulating in the system.

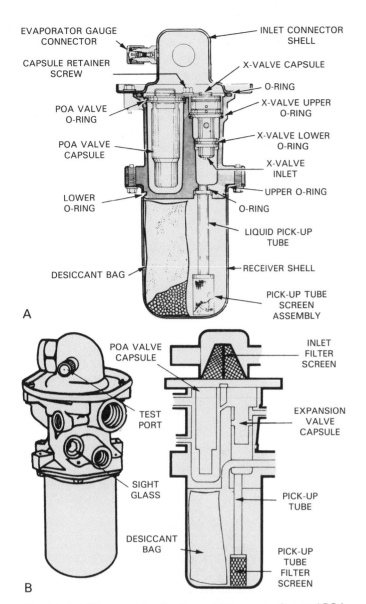

A

B

Fig. 11-4. VIR assembly. A—It combines expansion and POA valve in receiver-drier. B—Location of sight glass and test port on VIR.

ACCUMULATOR

Air conditioning systems that use an orifice tube require an accumulator instead of a receiver-drier. The accumulator is placed on the low-pressure vapor side at the evaporator outlet, Fig. 11-5. The *accumulator* contains a desiccant and acts as a reservoir for refrigerant vapor, but does not contain a sight glass, Fig. 11-6. The accumulator prevents any liquid refrigerant, that is not vaporized in the evaporator, from going to the compressor. The accumulator is not serviceable. It is replaced when defective, when the orifice tube is clogged, or any time the system is opened for repairs.

The refrigerant enters the accumulator and the heavier liquid refrigerant falls to the bottom of the housing where it accumulates. The vaporized refrigerant is light and rises to the top of the housing. The pick-up tube inlet is positioned near the top of the housing so that only vaporized refrigerant leaves the accumulator, Figs. 11-7 and 11-8. Since liquid does not compress, significant amounts of liquid refrigerant leaving the accumulator would damage the compressor.

A *liquid-bleed hole* at the bottom of the housing, Fig. 11-6, allows compressor oil and some liquid refrigerant to flow to the compressor at a controlled rate. A fine mesh filter screen prevents contaminants from plugging the bleed hole.

A simple check of the refrigerant level in this system is comparing the temperature of the evaporator inlet pipe to its outlet pipe. The outlet pipe should feel as cold as the evaporator inlet pipe. If the inlet pipe is colder than the outlet, low refrigerant level is a possibility. A pressure gauge should be used to make a more accurate check of the refrigerant level. Operate the system with all car windows open and the blower on "high."

A/C FLUSHING

Flushing is done when the A/C compressor fails and needs replacement or the desiccant breaks loose and collects in the evaporator, condenser, and lines. A *flushing agent* is a refrigerant with a boiling point higher than that

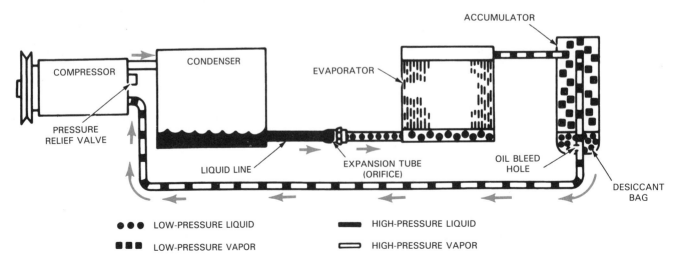

Fig. 11-5. An accumulator is found on systems that use an orifice tube. The accumulator is located on the low-pressure vapor side of evaporator outlet. (Oldsmobile)

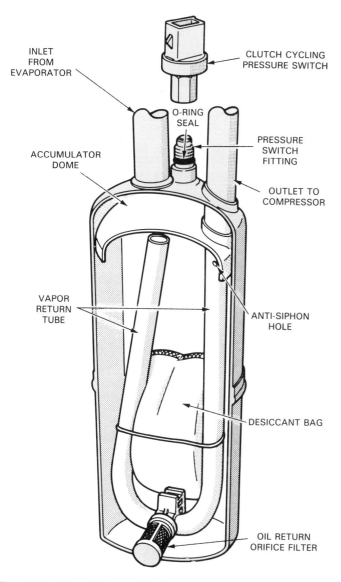

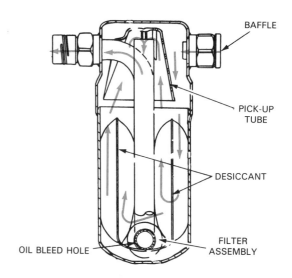

Fig. 11-8. Accumulators have an umbrella-shaped diverter. This prevents liquid refrigerant from entering pick-up tube in accumulator. (Oldsmobile)

of R-12, Fig. 11-9. This allows the refrigerant to remain in a liquid state for effective flushing. Each component of the A/C system is separated from the system and individually flushed.

After flushing the system, install a new receiver-drier or accumulator. The fixed-orifice tube must also be replaced, when used, because it cannot be cleaned. The a/c system is then evacuated for at least one-half hour before recharging it with refrigernat. Evacuation time should be longer at high altitudes.

SUMMARY

The receiver-drier or the accumulator are similar in that they both contain desiccants to absorb moisture in the system. The receiver-drier allows only liquid refrigerant to leave. The accumulator allows only vaporized refrigerant to leave. Also, the receiver-drier is in the high-

Fig. 11-6. The pick-up tube is positioned high in the accumulator so that only vaporized refrigerant enters. Dome prevents liquid refrigerant from entering pick-up tube. The accumulator also contains a desiccant. The oil return orifice allows oil inside the accumulator back to the compressor. (Ford)

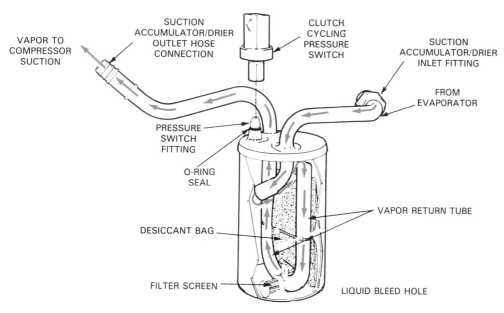

Fig. 11-7. The vaporized refrigerant from evaporator enters the pick-up or vapor return tube. Vaporized refrigerant then goes to the compressor.

Refrigerant	Vaporizes °C (°F)[1]	Approximate Closed Container Pressure[1] kPa (psi)[2]					Adaptability
		15.57 °C (60 °F)	21.13 °C (70 °F)	26.69 °C (80 °F)	32.25 °C (90 °F)	37.81 °C (100 °F)	
R-12	−29.80 (−21.6)	393 (57)	483 (70)	579 (84)	689 (100)	807 (117)	Self Propelling
R-114	3.56 (38.4)	55.16 (8)	89.63 (13)	131 (19)	172 (25)	221 (32)	
R-11[3]	23.74 (74.7)	27 (8 in. Hg)	10 (3 in. Hg)	7 (1)	34 (5)	62 (9)	
R-113	47.59 (117.6)	74 (22 in. Hg)	64 (19 in. Hg)	54 (16 in. Hg)	44 (13 in. Hg)	27 (8 in. Hg)	Pump Required

[1] At sea level atmospheric pressure.
[2] kPa (psi) unless otherwise noted.
[3] R-11 is also available in pressurized containers. This makes it suitable for usage when special flushing equipment is not available. However, it is more toxic than R-12 and R-114.

Fig. 11-9. Due to the characteristics of R-11, it is used as a flushing agent for automotive air conditioning systems. (Ford)

pressure liquid side of the system, and the accumulator is on the low-pressure vapor side of the system. Neither the receiver-drier nor accumulator are serviceable and must be replaced when defective or any time the system is opened for repairs.

Some systems use a design which includes in one unit the receiver-drier, pilot operated absolute (POA) valve, expansion valve, and sight glass. This assembly is known as the valves-in-receiver (VIR).

KNOW THESE TERMS

R-12, Receiver-drier, Filter screen, Filter pads, Desiccant, Pick-up tube, Sight glass, Accumulator, Liquid-bleed hole, Flushing agent.

REVIEW QUESTIONS—CHAPTER 11

1. The following are included in the VIR assembly:
   a. Muffler.
   b. Evaporator.
   c. POA valve.
   d. None of the above.
2. The accumulator can be disassembled for service. True or false?
3. The accumulator uses an umbrella-shaped diverter to:
   a. Absorb moisture.
   b. Filter out particles.
   c. Separate the liquid from vapor.
   d. None of the above.
4. The receiver-drier is located in the low-pressure side of the system. True or false?
5. How does temperature influence the moisture retention of the desiccant?
6. Oil streaking in the sight glass indicates:
   a. Excessive refrigerant.
   b. Excessive compressor oil in the system.
   c. System low on desiccant.
   d. Complete lack of refrigerant.
7. Desiccant in the receiver-drier or accumulator is used to:
   a. Increase the refrigerant pressure.
   b. Control refrigerant flow in the system.
   c. Maintain a constant temperature of the refrigerant oil.
   d. Remove and retain moisture.
8. The pick-up tube in the accumulator is:
   a. Positioned to pick up only liquid refrigerant.
   b. Used to muffle noises.
   c. Positioned to pick up only vaporized refrigerant.
   d. Positioned to pick up and retain contaminants.
9. The pick-up tube in the receiver-drier is positioned to pick up only liquid refrigerant. True or false?
10. Explain why moisture is considered the most troublesome factor in an air conditioning system.
11. What are the similarities and differences of a receiver-drier and an accumulator?
12. What are the functions of an accumulator and receiver-drier?

AIR CONDITIONING CONTROL DEVICES

12

After studying this chapter, you will be able to:
* Explain the construction and operation of refrigerant flow control devices.
* Describe the construction and operation of compressor control devices.
* List the different devices that maintain needed engine power under load and promote smooth engine idle.

INTRODUCTION

This chapter will discuss control devices which improve system efficiency, provide system safeguards, and maintain the best possible driveability. To improve system efficiency, devices are used to control the flow of refrigerant to obtain maximum cooling without evaporator freeze-up. Devices are also used to control compressor operation preventing system damage due to excessive pressure or loss of refrigerant. Devices are also used to temporarily relieve the air conditioning load on the engine while maintaining needed horsepower and smooth engine operation.

REFRIGERANT FLOW CONTROL DEVICES

Devices that control the refrigerant flow are necessary to prevent evaporator freezing which results in a loss of cooling. The objective of these devices is to maintain a constant evaporator temperature during changes in ambient temperature and humidity.

Suction throttling valve (STV)

The suction throttling valve (STV) determines the evaporator core temperature by limiting the minimum evaporator pressure. This valve maintains a minimum pressure of 28 psi in the evaporator. This action provides maximum cooling while protecting the evaporator against freeze-up. The STV is located in the evaporator outlet line, Fig. 12-1. It operates on spring pressure opposing evaporator pressure.

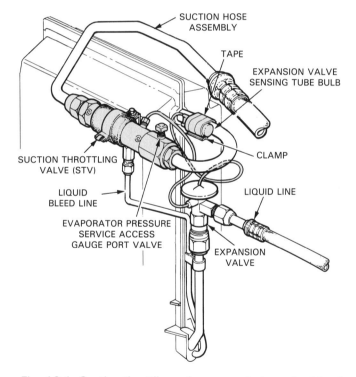

Fig. 12-1. Suction throttling valve connects to underside of externally equalized expansion valve. (Ford)

Operation of the STV

The refrigerant vapor flow is controlled by the piston inside the valve body piston. Fig. 12-2. The bellows inside the valve body determines the position of the piston. The refrigerant vapor flows through the valve inlet through three openings in the lower skirt of the piston. The refrigerant then flows through the valve outlet to the compressor. A small portion of the vapor flow is diverted to the interior of the piston through a hole in its wall. This pressure is transmitted to the bellows.

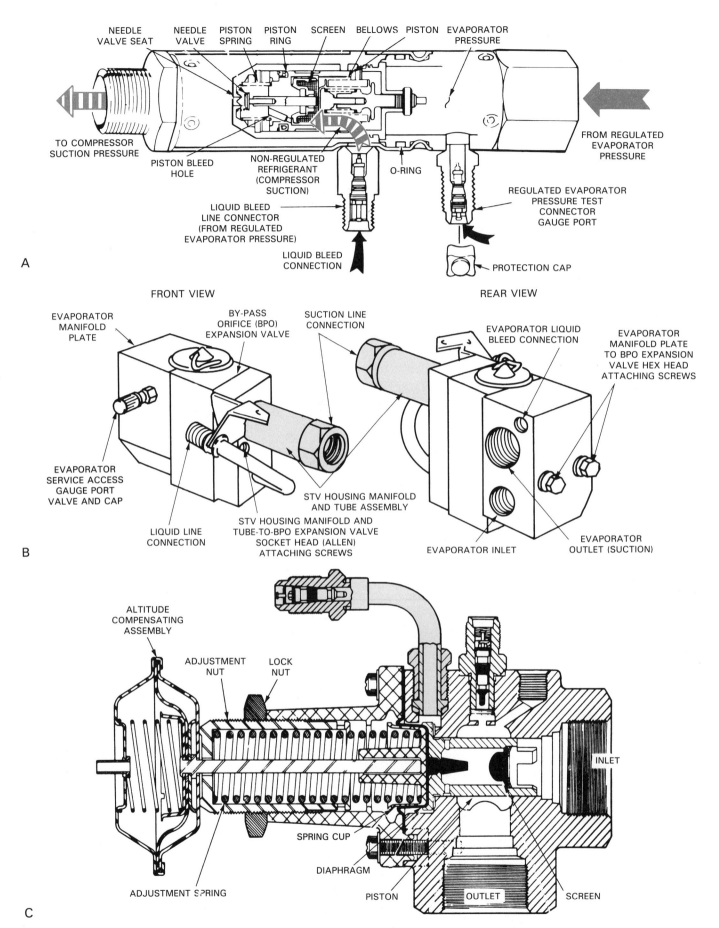

Fig. 12-2. Two different designs of suction throttling valves. Both are located at the evaporator outlet. A—This design is the straight-through type. B—Combination valve, used on some Ford products, combines STV and expansion valve. Refrigerant exits through needle valve. C—This design has the inlet 90° apart from the outlet. Note that valve is vacuum-operated. (Ford and Delco)

Evaporator pressure is applied to the inside of the bellows. It is opposed by spring and atmospheric pressure. An increase of evaporator pressure causes the piston to move against spring pressure, opening the valve. Vapor now flows to the compressor. This decreases evaporator pressure. Spring and atmospheric pressure forces the piston closed and the cycle repeats.

Pilot operated absolute (POA)

The *pilot operated absolute* (POA) *valve* is located in the evaporator outlet and regulates evaporator temperature, Fig. 12-3. It contains an evacuated bellows referenced to almost a perfect vacuum rather than atmospheric pressure as in the case of the STV. A pilot valve sits on top of the bellows.

Operation of the POA valve

Evaporator pressure acts on one side of the piston and spring pressure on the opposite end, Fig. 12-6. Evaporator pressure increases until it is greater than spring pressure. This unseats the piston, allowing refrigerant to flow through the system.

As refrigerant flows through the piston bleed hole, evaporator pressure combined with spring pressure acts on the back side of the piston, forcing it closed, Fig. 12-4. Evaporator pressure can now build up in the area surrounding the evacuated bellows. The pressure collapses the bellows, pulling the pilot valve or needle from its seat.

Pressure is reduced as the refrigerant flows through the needle's seat to the compressor. This reduces evaporator pressure acting against the bellows and it begins to expand. This forces the needle against its seat

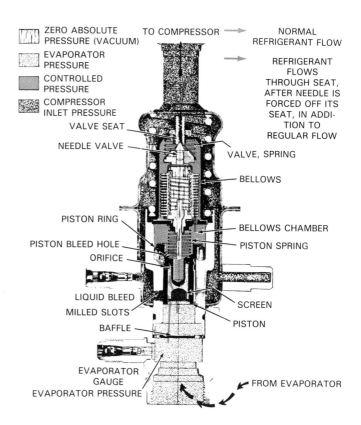

Fig. 12-4. Refrigerant flows through the POA valve. As pressure builds around evacuated bellows, it collapses and the needle valve is pulled from its seat. This allows additional flow through the needle-valve seat, which reduces pressure around the bellows. It expands, forcing the needle valve against its seat and blocking refrigerant flow.   (GMC)

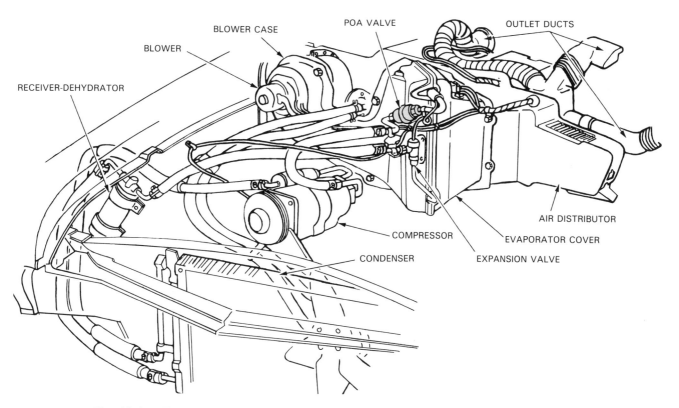

Fig. 12-3. Pilot operated absolute valve is also located at the evaporator outlet.   (GMC)

stopping refrigerant flow to the compressor. Evaporator pressure now builds at the front side of the piston and overcomes spring pressure. This forces the piston open and the cycle is repeated.

Valves-in-receiver (VIR)

The *valves-in-receiver* (VIR) combines the POA and expansion valve in the receiver-drier, Fig. 12-5. Later versions are evaporator equalized and called EEVIR or VIR-EE, Fig. 12-6. The POA and expansion valve operate the same as when installed in separate locations. Placing both valves in one unit eliminates the external equalizer tube (to the expansion valve), thermal bulb, and capillary tube (from thermal bulb to expansion valve). Also included in the assembly are the drying agent (desiccant) and sight glass.

The VIR or EEVIR is located in the engine compartment near the evaporator case. The evaporator outlet and inlet lines are connected to this assembly as well as the line from the condenser and compressor, Fig. 12-7. All components of the VIR/EEVIR are serviceable.

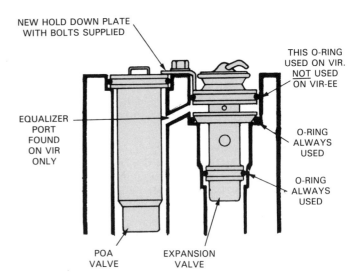

Fig. 12-6. Detailed view of POA valve and expansion valve in their respective chambers. (Murray Corp.)

Evaporator pressure regulator (EPR)

The *evaporator pressure regulator* (EPR) *valve* is another method of controlling evaporator pressure. The EPR valve is located in the compressor at the suction inlet. It is essentially an automatic suction throttling device. It is not adjustable and must be replaced if it fails. An oil-return passage inside the valve permits oil-laden refrigerant to be returned to the compressor crankcase. Another function of this oil-return passage allows the compressor crankcase to be pressurized. This prevents moisture from entering through the compressor shaft seals.

There are two types of EPR valves. The bellows is one type and the pilot operated is another type, Fig. 12-8. Both designs operate using evaporator pressure and spring pressure.

Operation of the EPR valve

When the evaporator begins to warm, evaporator pressure increases and overcomes spring pressure. This causes the piston valve to open, Fig. 12-8. As the refrigerant vapor now flows to the compressor, evaporator pressure gradually decreases. The spring forces the piston valve closed.

The piston valve eventually reaches a balance between spring and evaporator pressure. The balance is maintained until either the load on the evaporator or the compressor speed changes. Then, the piston valve establishes a new balanced position. The EPR valve is designed to maintain a minimum of 22 to 26 psig back pressure in the evaporator. The effect ensures maximum cooling without evaporator freeze-up.

Evaporator temperature regulator (ETR)

The *evaporator temperature regulator* (ETR) *valve* is located in the same place as the EPR valve. It is a solenoid valve, Fig. 12-9, that is normally open and actuated by a thermal switch. The switch, mounted on the evaporator housing, has a temperature sensing capillary extending through the coil fins of the evaporator. The ETR valve regulates by temperature, not pressure, and is strictly an on and off valve.

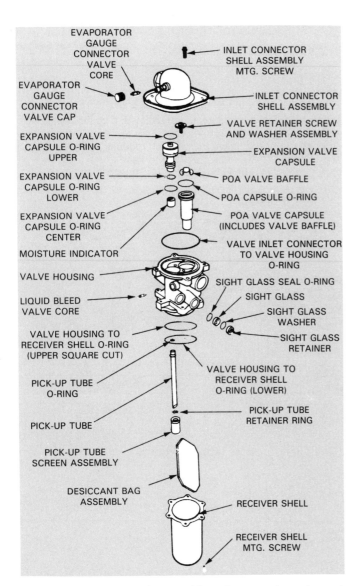

Fig. 12-5. Valves-in-receiver combines the expansion valve and POA valve in one unit. All items are serviceable.

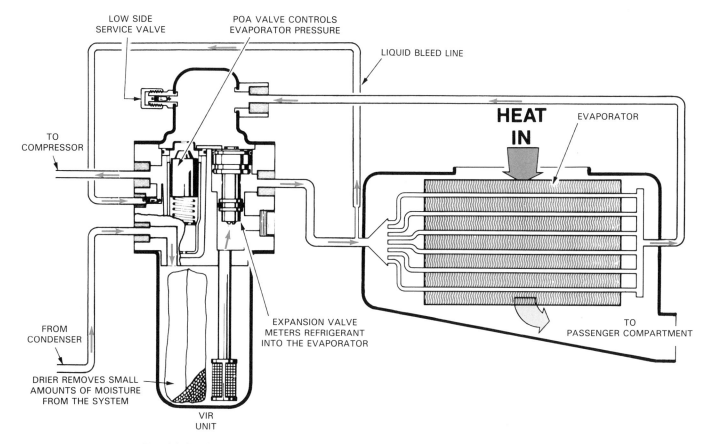

Fig. 12-7. All air conditioning lines connect to the VIR assembly.   (GMC)

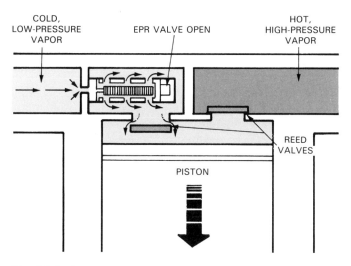

Fig. 12-8. Cross section of an EPR valve. Piston valve is normally closed. As evaporator pressure builds, the piston valve opens. This allows refrigerant vapor to the compressor.

Operation of the ETR valve

When evaporator temperature nears the freezing point, the switch closes the electrical circuit to the solenoid, energizing it. The valve closes and blocks the refrigerant vapor flow to the compressor until evaporator temperature increases. When evaporator temperature increases, the thermal switch opens the electrical circuit to the solenoid, de-energizing it. The valve opens and allows refrigerant to flow.

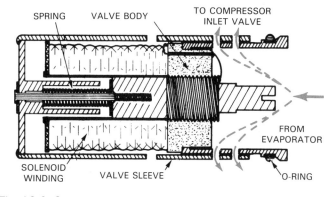

Fig. 12-9. Cross section of an ETR valve. It is a solenoid located in the compressor suction inlet. (Chrysler)

Robotrol

This device is used in some aftermarket a/c systems. The *robotrol valve* is located in the compressor suction inlet. It automatically controls evaporator pressure by regulating the flow of refrigerant vapor to the compressor. Its function and location are similar to the EPR valve. However, it has an adjustment screw, Fig. 12-10, which allows compensation for different areas (altitudes) of the country to maintain 26 psig in the evaporator.

Selectrol

This device, used in some aftermarket A/C systems, is similar to the robotrol valve, but is driver-adjustable. The *selectrol valve* is located in the evaporator outlet and

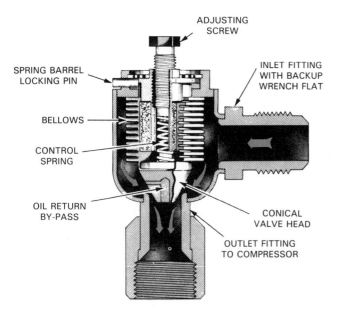

Fig. 12-10. Cross section of a robotrol valve. Note the adjustment screw at its top. Arrows indicate refrigerant flow. (Mark IV)

controls evaporator pressure by regulating the flow of refrigerant vapor to the compressor, Fig. 12-11. The driver controls evaporator pressure by turning a knob on the dash.

COMPRESSOR CONTROL DEVICES

Compressor control devices interrupt the electrical circuit to the a/c clutch when pressures are low. This action causes the clutch to disengage from the compressor. This either prevents the evaporator from freezing or protects the compressor from seizing due to an insufficient supply of oil. A low refrigerant level decreases pressure, along with the supply of oil. Other devices protect the system from excessively high pressures.

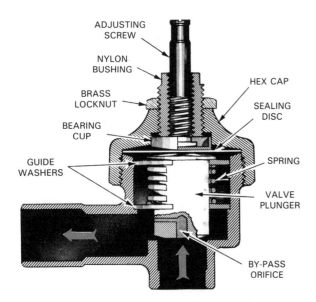

Fig. 12-11. Cross section of a selectrol valve. Arrows indicate refrigerant flow. (Mark IV)

Thermostatic clutch cycling switch

The most common type of compressor control is the *thermostatic clutch cycling switch,* Fig. 12-12, which turns the compressor clutch on and off. A capillary tube connects from the evaporator outlet to the switch. The capillary tube is filled with a gas. The gas expands and contracts as the temperature in the evaporator changes, causing the switch to cycle the clutch on and off.

When evaporator temperature approaches freezing, the thermostatic switch opens the electrical circuit, disengaging the compressor clutch. The compressor clutch will not engage until temperature in the evaporator reaches the predetermined level. Once the temperature reaches the specified level, the switch closes the electrical circuit to the clutch, engaging it to the compressor. Some switches can be adjusted by service personnel to change the temperature range at which the clutch cycles on and off.

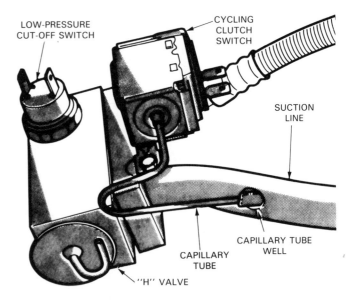

Fig. 12-12. Thermostatic clutch cycling switch senses evaporator outlet temperature through capillary tube. Switch interrupts electrical current to the clutch when evaporator temperature approaches freezing. (Chrysler)

Ambient temperature switch

At low temperatures, oil is very thick and resists flowing. Compressor oil is no exception. Operation of the a/c compressor at low temperatures could cause internal damage due to inadequate lubrication. An *ambient temperature switch* in the air inlet duct or in front of the radiator, Fig. 12-13, opens the electrical circuit to the clutch at temperatures below 40°F (4.4°C). This prevents the clutch from engaging the compressor. Sometimes a temperature range may be given from 32° to 50°F (0° to 10°C) for the setting. The switch must be replaced if defective.

Low-pressure cut-off switch

As the refrigerant circulates, it carries compressor oil to lubricate the internal parts of the compressor. A *low-pressure cut-off switch,* Fig. 12-14, protects the compressor from internal damage in the event of a large loss

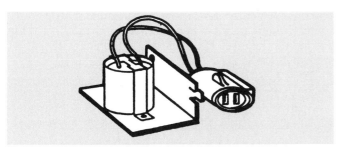

Fig. 12-13. Ambient temperature switch interrupts electrical current to the clutch during cold weather. This protects the compressor from inadequate lubrication. (Murray Corp.)

of oil-laden refrigerant. The switch opens when high-side pressure falls below 40 psi. This switch can be located in the high-pressure liquid line, compressor outlet, or receiver-drier. This switch is not repairable and must be replaced if defective.

Pressure cycling switch

The pressure cycling switch is electrically connected to the A/C compressor clutch. The *pressure cycling switch*, Fig. 12-15, combines the function of clutch cycling switch, low-pressure cut-off switch, and ambient temperature switch.

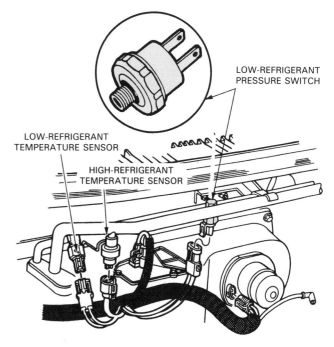

Fig. 12-14. Low-pressure cut-off switch also protects the compressor from inadequate lubrication due to a loss of oil-laden refrigerant. (Murray Corp.)

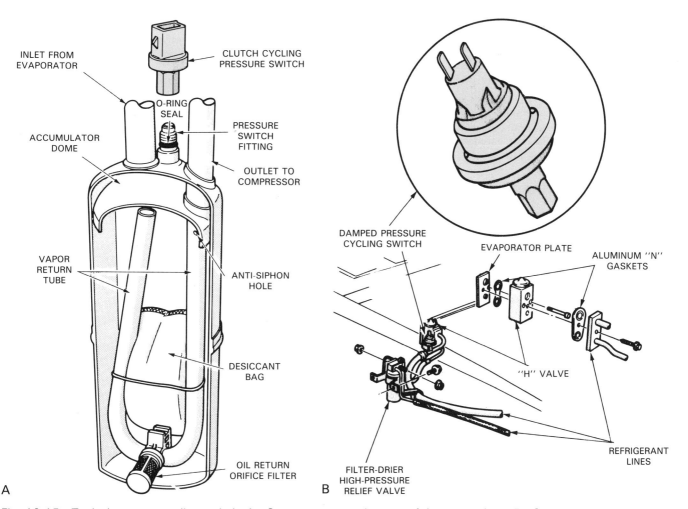

Fig. 12-15. Typical pressure cycling switch. A—Some are mounted on top of the accumulator. B—Some are mounted in line. (Ford and Chrysler)

If pressure decreases to 24.5 psi, the pressure cycling switch opens the electrical circuit to the clutch, disengaging it from the compressor. This prevents evaporator freeze-up or internal damage to the a/c compressor. If pressure increases to 47 psi, the switch closes the electrical circuit to the clutch. This causes the clutch to engage the compressor. Due to the pressure-temperature relationship of refrigerant, the switch also remains open during cold weather, preventing the clutch from engaging the compressor.

Thermal limiter/superheat switch

The superheat switch, located on the back side of the compressor, contains a set of contact points, Fig. 12-16. It connects electrically to the thermal limiter, Fig. 12-17.

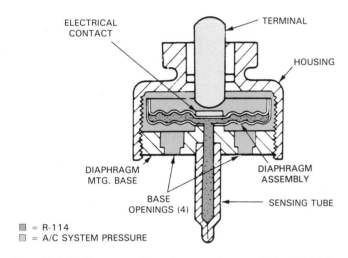

Fig. 12-16. Cross section of a superheat switch. R-114 in sensing tube expands when exposed to a high temperature vapor. This causes diaphragm to flex upward. Since electrical contact is mounted on top of diaphragm, the circuit to the resistor-type heater is complete.

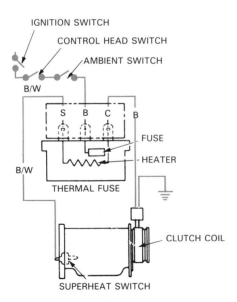

Fig. 12-17 Wiring diagram from superheat switch to resistor-type heater inside thermal limiter. When circuit is complete, heat causes the fuse inside thermal limiter to blow and interrupt electrical current to the clutch.

The *thermal limiter* is basically a fuse connecting the A/C switch from the control panel to the clutch coil. The thermal limiter, Fig. 12-18, is usually attached to the compressor bracket.

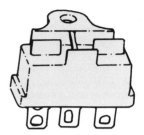

Fig. 12-18. Thermal limiter removed from electrical system.

The superheat switch is normally exposed to a low temperature vapor at the compressor suction inlet. When the *superheat switch* senses a high temperature vapor (due to a low refrigerant level), the contact points close. Current now flows to a resistor-type heater in the thermal limiter. Heat melts the fuse, which opens the electrical circuit to the clutch coil, disengaging it from the compressor. This protects the compressor against internal damage due to the loss of oil-laden refrigerant needed to lubricate its enclosed moving parts. Prior to replacing the thermal fuse, the cause of refrigerant loss must be corrected. The system must be evacuated and then recharged.

HIGHER-THAN-NORMAL PRESSURE

On extremely hot, humid days or when airflow through the condenser is restricted, it can cause higher-than-normal pressure in the A/C system. This can cause inadequate A/C cooling.

If spraying the condenser with water decreases the pressure, the problem can be a restriction of airflow (debris in front of the condenser), or an internal restriction in the condenser (an accumulation of oil). In an aftermarket A/C system, the condenser could be too small and cause the same problem.

Higher-than-normal pressures during city driving

The air conditioner provides adequate cooling (normal system pressure) during highway driving. While city driving, the cooling is inadequate (high-system pressure). This problem is insufficient airflow through the condenser at low speeds. This may be a slipping fan clutch on rear-wheel-drive cars. The radiator fan electric motor bearing, found on front-wheel-drive cars, may bind and reduce fan speed. Low alternator output can also reduce the electric fan speed. Most systems have devices to control excessively high pressure.

Pressure-relief valve

A *pressure-relief valve* is a spring-loaded, poppet valve that screws into the high-pressure side of the compressor, Fig. 12-19. The pressure-relief valve vents excess pressure to the atmosphere at approximately 385 psi. This is well below the bursting point of A/C hoses.

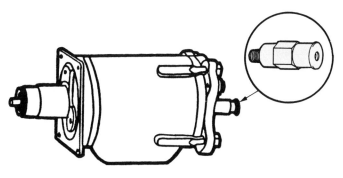

Fig. 12-19. Pressure-relief valve is located on the back of compressor. (Murray Corp.)

High-pressure cut-off switch

The *high-pressure cut-off switch,* Fig. 12-20, opens the electrical circuit to the clutch, disengaging it from the compressor, when high-side pressure reaches 375 psi. This prevents refrigerant from venting to the atmosphere through the pressure-relief valve. However, the pressure-relief valve opens at 385 psi should there be a problem with the high-pressure cut-off switch. When pressure returns to normal, the switch closes and and the clutch is energized again.

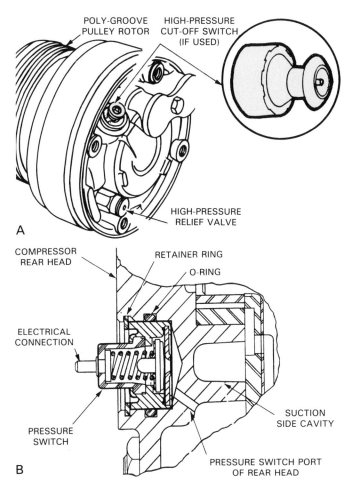

Fig. 12-20. High-pressure cut-off switch. A—Close-up view of switch. B—Cross section of switch installed in back side of compressor. (Murray Corp.)

DRIVEABILITY/POWER MAINTENANCE CONTROLS

Driveability is the smooth and sustained operation of the engine during idle, acceleration, and cruising speeds. Controls are designed to maintain these qualities during all phases of engine operation. When a passenger car has a four-cylinder or a small six-cylinder engine and comes equipped with air conditioning, problems are encountered that do not usually occur with the larger engines.

The problem is usually maintaining adequate horsepower with the air conditioner engaged during acceleration. Different controls are needed to disengage the A/C compressor under specific circumstances to maintain driveability.

A/C cut-out relay/switch

The *A/C cut-out relay* electrically disengages the compressor clutch during wide open throttle (WOT), such as when passing or hill climbing, and when entering the expressway. The air conditioner can "absorb" as much as two horsepower from the total amount available. On a four-cylinder engine, this can reduce performance enough to be a problem. To resolve this problem, the air conditioning clutch is disengaged during wide open throttle (WOT) on small engines.

The throttle positioner sensor signals the computer there is a WOT condition. The computer, then, de-energizes the A/C cut-out relay, Fig. 12-21, and the A/C clutch disengages. When the throttle opening is reduced, the computer senses this through the throttle positioner sensor. The computer, then, energizes the a/c cut-out relay. This allows current flow to the a/c clutch and engages the compressor.

A mechanical switch is used on some cars equipped with automatic transmissions, Fig. 12-22. Its function is similar to the a/c cut-out relay during full-throttle operation.

Low-vacuum switch

During wide open throttle, vacuum is extremely low. Some systems use a *low-vacuum switch* that senses manifold pressure and interrupts electrical current to the A/C clutch under low vacuum (high-manifold pressure). This s.vitch performs the same function as an A/C cut-out relay.

Power steering pressure switch

The *power steering pressure switch* is located on the rack and pinion housing, Fig. 12-23, and monitors the hydraulic pressure. Its function is to electrically disengage the A/C clutch from the compressor when power steering pump creates a load on the engine. sure is high (usually during parking maneuvers), the power steering pump creates a load on the engine. Reducing the load on the engine maintains a smooth idle or low-speed operation.

Power brake time-delay relay

A *power brake time-delay relay* is used on some cars with automatic transmission and power-assist brakes. The function of the relay is to interrupt compressor operation for three to five seconds when the brake pedal is depressed. This reduces the load on the engine and,

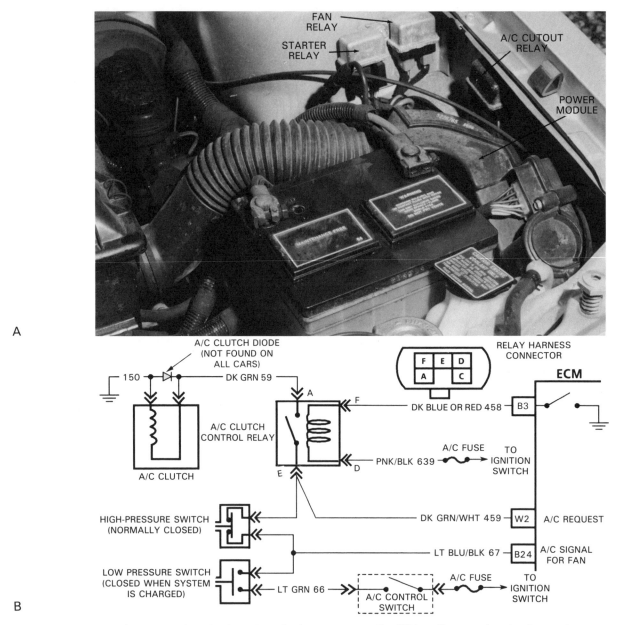

Fig. 12-21. The A/C cut-out relay. A—Location of relay on one car. B—Wiring diagram showing how relay connects computer to clutch coil. Note that pressure switches are wired in series to the relay. (Automotive Encyclopedia and Oldsmobile)

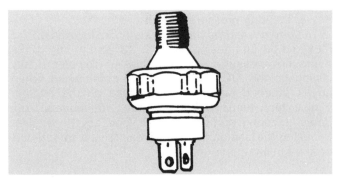

Fig. 12-22. Some cars use a switch which senses hydraulic pressure in the automatic transmission. High hydraulic pressure usually indicates a wide open throttle condition, causing transmission to downshift into passing gear. High pressure also closes contacts in the switch, sending a signal to computer to interrupt electrical circuit to the clutch. (JETAIR, INC.)

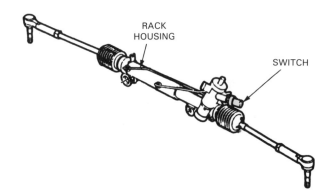

Fig. 12-23. Location of power steering pressure cut-out switch on one application. Voltage signal sent to computer causes it to de-energize A/C cut-out relay when hydraulic pressure is high. The A/C clutch then disengages from the compressor until hydraulic pressure is reduced. (Oldsmobile)

thus, increases the engine vacuum needed for the power-brake booster. The relay, located under the dash, can be serviced through the glove box opening, Fig. 12-24.

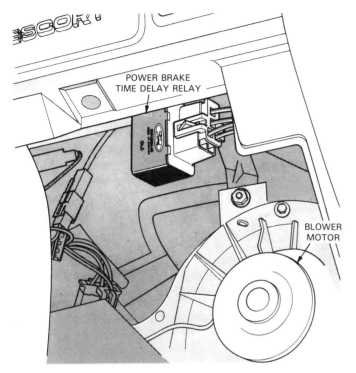

Fig. 12-24. Location of power brake time-delay relay on one car. (Ford)

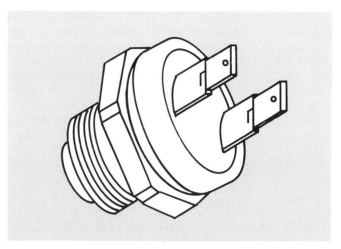

Fig. 12-25. When high-coolant-temperature switch sends a signal to computer, A/C cut-out relay is de-energized. This causes A/C clutch to disengage from compressor when coolant becomes too hot. Engine load is removed to reduce chance of overheating. (Murray Corp.)

High-coolant-temperature switch

The *high-coolant-temperature switch,* used on some models, Fig. 12-25, interrupts the electrical circuit to the A/C clutch when engine-coolant temperature becomes excessively high. This reduces the load on the engine and thereby decreases the probability of overheating.

Electronic control module delay timer

The electronic control module (ECM) or computer is used on some cars to control the A/C clutch operation. The *ECM delay timer* inside the computer comes into operation at idle and speeds below 1400 rpm when the air conditioner is turned on. The timer delays energizing the A/C clutch for several seconds while the computer increases the idle speed to prevent the engine from stalling.

Large engine driveability controls

While the previous mentioned controls are needed for small engines to maintain smooth operation, some controls are needed on larger engines. One device is a solenoid mounted to the carburetor, Fig. 12-26. Whenever the air conditioner is turned on, the solenoid is energized and the plunger extends, increasing the idle speed. This prevents engine stalling due to the increased load. When the air conditioner or the engine is turned off, the solenoid is de-energized, decreasing the idle speed to prevent dieseling.

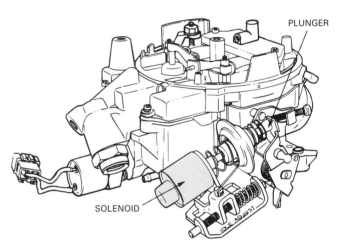

Fig. 12-26. When the air conditioner is turned on, the solenoid is energized and extends its plunger, causing the idle speed to increase. This prevents engine stalling while air conditioner is on during idle. When engine or air conditioner is turned off, solenoid is de-energized, reducing the idle speed. This prevents engine run-on or dieseling. (Ford)

SUMMARY

The clutch cycling switch, suction throttling valve (STV), pilot operated absolute valve (POA), valves-in-receiver (VIR), evaporator pressure regulator (EPR), and evaporator temperature regulator (ETR) all provide the same function. The purpose of these valves is to maintain maximum cooling without evaporator freeze-up by controlling refrigerant flow through the system.

The clutch cycling switch, ambient temperature switch, high-pressure cut-out switch, low-pressure cut-out switch, pressure-relief valve, pressure-sensing switch, and thermal limiter/superheat switch all provide the same function. The purpose of these devices protect the compressor from damage due to excessive pressures and/or temperatures.

The energy required to drive an A/C compressor is significant. A greater percentage of available horsepower is used on small engines than large engines. Manufacturers have devised a number of controls to disengage the A/C clutch from the compressor to maintain the needed power of small engines. Controls such as the power steering pressure switch, A/C cut-out relay, power brake time-delay relay, and low-vacuum switch all function to open the electrical circuit to the compressor clutch. These controls for driving and idle quality improvement are not used on every car. Check the specific car service manual to determine the controls used.

KNOW THESE TERMS

Suctioning throttle valve, Pilot operated absolute valve, Valves-in-receiver, Evaporator pressure regulator valve, Evaporator temperature regulator valve, Robotrol valve, Selectrol valve, Thermostatic clutch cycling switch, Ambient temperature switch, Low-pressure cut-off switch, Pressure cycling switch, Thermal limiter, Superheat switch, Pressure-relief valve, High-pressure cut-off switch, A/C cut-out relay. Low-vacuum switch, Power steering pressure switch, Power brake time-delay relay, High-coolant-temperature switch, ECM delay timer.

REVIEW QUESTIONS—CHAPTER 12

1. Valves in receiver contain:
   a. POA and ETR. c. POA and STV.
   b. EPR and ETR. d. POA and expansion valve.

2. The clutch cycling switch turns the compressor on and off. It is operated by the:
   a. Wide open throttle switch.
   b. Orifice tube.
   c. Antidieseling relay.
   d. Capillary tube.

3. The low-vacuum switch interrupts the electrical circuit to the compressor clutch when engine vacuum is low. This occurs:
   a. When braking to stop the car.
   b. During period of downhill deceleration.
   c. During extended period of idle.
   d. During hill climbing.

4. Electronic control module delay timer is used to:
   a. Delay A/C operation during parking maneuvers.
   b. Delay A/C operation until idle stabilizes after start-up.
   c. Stops the compressor during wide open throttle operation.
   d. Delays fan operation during cold weather.

5. What is a refrigerant flow control device?

6. Explain the differences and similarities between the pressure cycling switch and the thermostatic clutch cycling switch.

7. Explain how the POA valve operates.

8. What is the purpose of the A/C cut-out relay and why is it needed?

9. What function does the EPR and ETR valve perform?

10. What is the purpose of the ambient temperature switch and why is it needed?

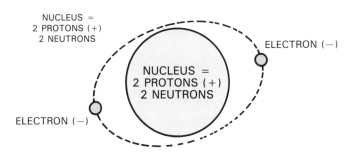

13

ELECTRICITY, ELECTRONICS, AND VACUUM CIRCUITS/COMPONENTS

After studying this chapter, you will be able to:
- *Explain the theory of basic electricity.*
- *Give examples of solid state electronics.*
- *Troubleshoot electrical problems using test equipment and wiring diagrams.*
- *Identify and explain the operation of vacuum components.*

ELECTRICITY

Electric comes from the Greek word meaning amber, since the Greeks discovered that rubbing amber with a silk cloth attracted feathers. Static electricity refers to an electrical charge at rest, as opposed to current flow (amperage). When this static charge is released, electrons flow from the charged body.

STATIC ELECTRICITY

A familiar example is the static charge acquired while walking across a carpet on a dry day. Friction causes the free electrons to leave the carpet and are stored on the human body. Dry air is an insulator and prevents the electrons from going back to the carpet. When a charged object approaches, for example, the excess electrons flow fast enough to jump the gap and produce a spark. While amperage is minute, static electricity produces approximately 25,000 V. This amount of voltage is enough to cause a noticeable shock. However, since amperage is minute, the shock is a nondamaging sensation.

BASIC ELECTRICAL CONCEPTS

A basic knowledge of electricity is essential to "troubleshoot" problems in the heating and air conditioning system's electrical circuits. *Matter* (solid, liquid, or gas) is made up of molecules. A *molecule* is made up of atoms. The size of a single atom is very small. To illustrate this point, 250,000,000 hydrogen atoms placed side by side equal only one inch.

Atoms

An *atom* is composed of electrons, protons, and neutrons. *Electrons* are negatively charged. *Protons* are positively charged. A *neutron* is neither negatively nor positively charged. The electrons balance or neutralize the effect of the protons. The protons and neutrons are at the center or nucleus of the atom. The electrons orbit the nucleus, Fig. 13-1. The number of electrons, protons, and neutrons, as well as their arrangement, determine the element. An *element* contains only atoms of the same kind. Elements differ in their electrical properties.

Electrons

Electrons loosely attracted to the nucleus (free to move from one atom to the next) are called *free electrons.* Electrons held closely to the nucleus (not free to move from one atom to the next) are called *bound electrons,* Fig. 13-2.

Conductors/insulators

Elements that have free electrons are called *conductors.* Elements such as copper, silver, or gold are excellent conductors of electricity. A metal wire which has

Fig. 13-1. The helium atom is shown. Its nucleus is composed of two protons and two neutrons. The two electrons orbit the nucleus.

voltage applied to it causes the orbiting electrons of the wire to flow from one end of the wire to the opposite end, Fig. 13-3. Matter that has bound electrons is an *insulator.* Insulators do not conduct electricity and prevent current flow.

LIKE AND UNLIKE

Electrical

Unlike electrical charges (a positive and a negative charge) attract each other. However, like electrical charges (two positive or two negative charges) repel each other, Fig. 13-4A.

Magnetic

A magnet has *North and South poles.* The magnetic lines of force leave the North pole and enter its South pole, Fig. 13-4B. A North magnetic pole attracts a South magnetic pole. However, a North magnetic pole repels another North magnetic pole. Also, a South magnetic pole repels another South magnetic pole.

ELECTROMAGNETISM

A magnetic field always surrounds a current-carrying wire, Fig. 13-5A. Current flowing through a wire coil in-

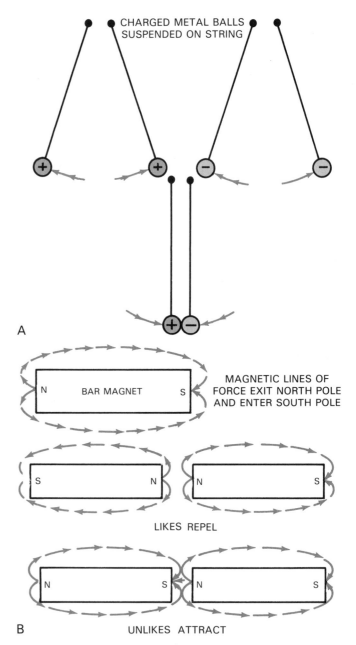

A

B

Fig. 13-4. Like and unlike charges and magnetic fields. A— Top. Like charges repel each other. Bottom. Opposite charges attract each other. B—Magnetic field leaves the magnet's North pole and enters at its South pole. A magnet's North pole is attracted to a South pole. However, two North poles repel each other and the same is true for two South pole magnets.

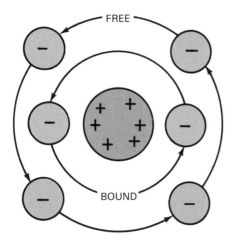

Fig. 13-2. The carbon atom has six electrons. Two of the electrons are in the inner orbit and bound to the nucleus. Four of the electrons are in the outer orbit. They are free to travel from one atom to the next. Therefore, carbon is a conductor of electricity.

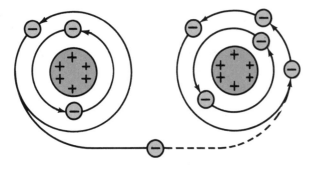

Fig. 13-3. Unbalanced atom attracts free electrons from another atom. Imbalance that causes free electrons to move is the principle of current flow.

creases the magnetic force, Fig. 13-5B. This principle is used in relays and solenoids. When a metal conductor passes through a magnetic field created by North and South poles, voltage is produced in the conductor, Fig. 13-6.

ELECTRICAL MEASUREMENT

Electricity is measured in volts and amps. *Voltage* is the amount of electrical pressure or push. *Amperage* is the amount of current flowing through an electrical circuit. Voltage is necessary to cause a flow of electrons

MAGNETIC FIELDS

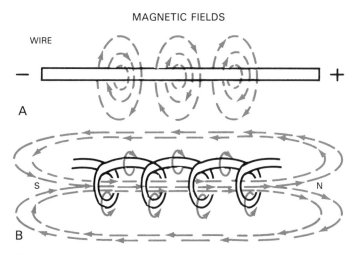

Fig. 13-5. Magnetic fields. A—Magnetic field surrounds a current-carrying wire. B—Magnetic field of coiled wire is stronger than wire that runs straight.

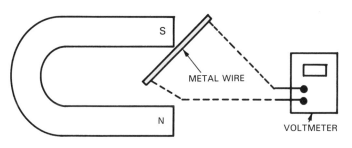

Fig. 13-6. Voltage is induced in metal wire as it passes between a magnet's North and South poles.

through a conductor. Examples of "electrical pumps" that cause current flow are batteries, alternators, and generators. An electrical circuit must have some type of resistance (motor, light bulb, or resistor) in it. An *ohm* is the amount of resistance of an electrical device or component. One volt pushed through one ohm equals one amp flowing through an electrical circuit. Voltage and amperage are independent of each other. Voltage can be high while amperage is low.

OHM'S LAW

The relationship between *electromotive force* (voltage), current flow (amperage), and resistance to current flow (ohms) is known as *Ohm's Law.* Ohm's Law is expressed mathematically as follows:

$$\text{(Amperage) Intensity} = \frac{\text{Electromotive force}}{\text{Resistance}}$$

$$\text{or} \quad I = \frac{E}{R}$$

When amperage and resistance are known and voltage is not, the formula is $E = I \times R$. When resistance is not known and voltage and amperage are known, the formula is:

$$R = \frac{E}{I}$$

ELECTRON THEORY/CIRCUITS

The conventional theory states electrons flow from the positive to the negative. However, the electron theory states just the opposite, that current flows from negative to positive, Fig. 13-7. Most scientists believe the electron theory is more accurate. The path electrons take can be in a series, parallel, or series-parallel circuit.

In a *series circuit,* current flow through a resistor or resistors has only one path, Fig. 13-7. However, in a *parallel circuit,* current flow through the resistors has more than one path, Fig. 13-8. In a *series-parallel circuit,* current flow through the resistors has one path for a portion and, then, more than one path for another portion of the circuit, Fig. 13-9.

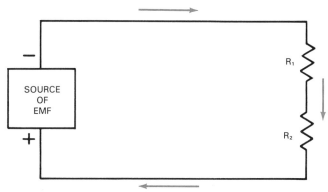

Fig. 13-7. Current flow has only one path in a series circuit. Resistance is in line with current flow.

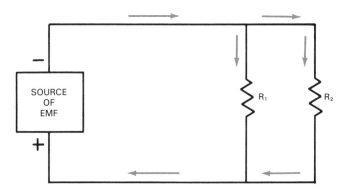

Fig. 13-8. Current flow has two paths in a parallel circuit. Each unit of resistance is parallel to the other.

ELECTRONIC COMPONENTS

Solid state/semiconductors

Solid state means an electrical device that has no moving parts. The only thing that moves through a solid state device is the electrons. Diodes and transistors are examples of solid state devices. Solid state devices start, stop, amplify, or regulate current flow. Semiconductor elements are used in the construction of solid state devices. *Semiconductor* elements are neither good insulators nor good conductors. However, semiconductor elements can be made into conductors.

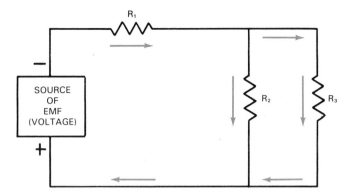

Fig. 13-9. Current flow has one path and then two paths, or vice versa, in a series-parallel circuit.

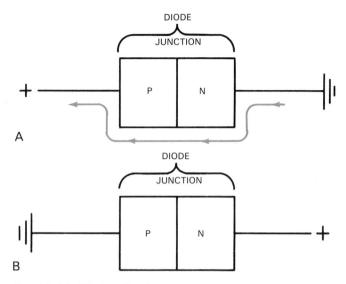

Fig. 13-10. Diodes. A—Current flows through diode when N type material is to the negative side of circuit and P type material is to positive side. B—No current flows through diode when leads are switched.

Semiconductor construction

Silicon and germanium are the most common used semiconductor elements. Silicon and germanium are prepared in a special way. This preparation is accomplished by adding specific kinds and amounts of other elements to change its atomic structure. This is called "doping." Some of the elements used for doping are arsenic, boron, antimony, and aluminum. Adding these elements provide free electrons available for current flow. This now makes the semiconductor a conductor. A semiconductor element having free electrons is called "N" (negative) type material.

Conversely, when other elements are added to a semiconductor, the atomic structure can be changed to provide room for more electrons. Vacancies for electrons are called "holes." Electrons pass relatively easy through these holes. A semiconductor material having holes is called "P" (positive) type.

Solid state sensors

A sensor that is solid state contains no mechanical moving parts. The only thing that moves through a solid state sensor is the electrons. One example of a solid state sensor is a thermistor. A thermistor varies its resistance according to the temperature change of a substance (liquid or gas). Measuring the temperature of the passenger compartment for an automatic temperature control (ATC) system is an example.

A photoelectric sensor (transistor) is sensitive to light. Light applied to the base of the transistor turns it on and current flows through the circuit. A sunlight load sensor for an automatic temperature control (ATC) systems is one use.

Diodes/rectifiers

Diodes or rectifiers are basically the same device. A *diode* is an electrical check valve that allows current flow in one direction and blocks current flow in the opposite direction. In other words it rectifies the current. A diode is composed of a "P" type material bonded to "N" type material. This provides material having free electrons bonded to a material having holes for the electrons. Electrons flow from the "N" material to the "P" material, Fig. 13-10. Diodes conduct electricity when voltage is applied in one direction and prevents current flow when

voltage is applied from the opposite direction. Diodes can also act as an electrical circuit protection device.

A/C clutch diode

An A/C clutch diode is installed in an auto electrical system when a computerized fuel/ignition system is used. The A/C clutch diode is wired in parallel with the A/C compressor clutch, Fig. 13-11.

When the air conditioner is turned on, the A/C clutch is energized and a magnetic field is produced. Then, when the air conditioner is turned off, the A/C clutch is de-energized and the magnetic field collapses. When the magnetic field collapses, high voltage is produced and introduced into the electrical circuit. This action is similar to that of the ignition coil.

The *A/C clutch diode* provides an electrical path to ground for electrical spikes (high voltage) to prevent damage to the computer. Should the A/C clutch diode become defective, the computer will be destroyed by electrical spikes.

Checking diodes

A diode has high resistance in one direction and low resistance in the opposite direction. Checking a diode requires the use of an ohmmeter. The diode must be removed from its circuit. Connect one test lead from the ohmmeter to the top of the diode. Connect the other test lead to the bottom of the diode. The reading will show either high or low resistance. Then, switch the leads. This reading should be opposite the first reading. An example follows:

The first reading indicates low resistance and, then, the test leads are switched. The second reading indicates high resistance. This indicates the diode is good. It does not matter if the first reading indicates high or low resistance, just that one is high and the other is low. Readings that are both high or low resistance indicates a defective diode that must be replaced.

TYPICAL CONTROL INPUTS TO A/C CLUTCH

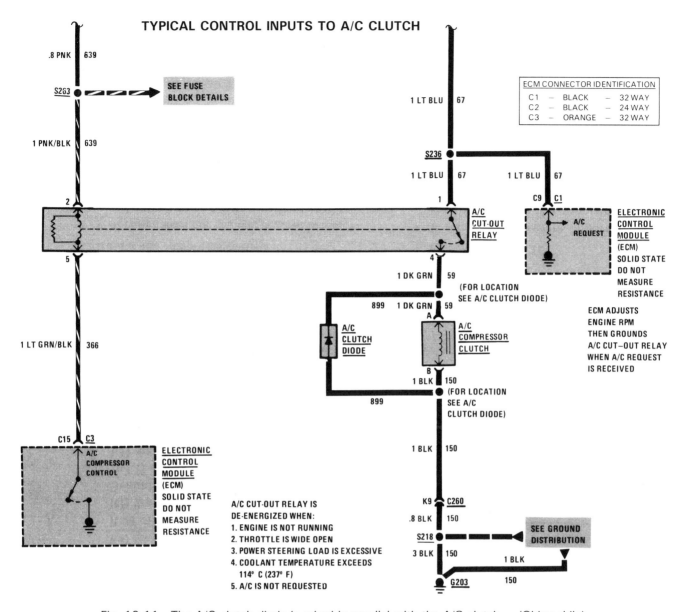

Fig. 13-11. The A/C clutch diode is wired in parallel with the A/C clutch. (Oldsmobile)

Transistors

Like diodes and rectifiers, transistors are composed of ''P'' and ''N'' material. The *transistor* is composed of three parts called the emitter, collector, and base, Fig. 13-12. Transistors are of two types. One type is the PNP and the other type is NPN, Fig. 13-12. A transistor acts as a switch and/or amplifies the voltage signal.

Resistors

A *resistor* is a component containing a specific amount of resistance. Some resistors are constructed of resistance wire wound in a coil. Some are of the fixed-carbon construction providing a range of sizes and values. In operation, the resistor reduces current flow by transforming part of the electrical energy into heat that dissipates to the atmosphere.

Capacitor/condenser

A *capacitor* or *condenser* is the same thing. It is a component that stores excess or unwanted voltage. A

capacitor consists of metal plates separated by insulating material encased in a cylindrical steel shell. Some uses for capacitors include suppression of electrical noise from the ignition and charging system. Electrical noise interferes with radio reception and computer operation.

Integrated circuit

An *integrated circuit* (IC) is composed of miniature resistors, transistors, diodes, and capacitors on a wafer-thin piece of silicon. Computers are made of many integrated circuits. Without this miniaturization process, a computer found on today's car could approach the size of a room to perform the same calculations.

ELECTROMECHANICAL DEVICES

Relays

A *relay* is a magnetic switch. A relay controls high-amperage current using a low-amperage control circuit, Fig. 13-13. Relays save long lengths of large diameter

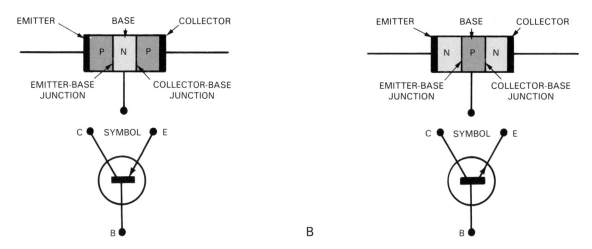

Fig. 13-12. Transistors. A—PNP transistor. Note position of arrow of emitter on symbol. B—N—N transistor. Note position of arrow of emitter on symbol.

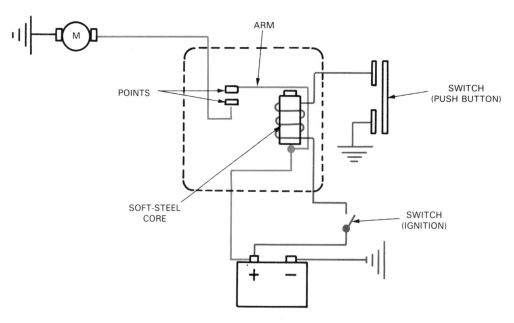

Fig. 13-13. Relay control circuit, low amperage, is in gray. When both switches are closed in control circuit, electromagnetic field concentrating on steel core pulls arm down and both points close. High amperage current, in color, shows flow to motor.

wire. This prevents an unwanted voltage drop.

The relay contains a coil of small-diameter wire wrapped around a soft-iron core, Fig. 13-13. When both switches are closed, voltage is applied to the windings around the steel core. This creates a strong electromagnetic field that pulls the steel arm down. The contacts now close and high-amperage current flows to the motor causing it to run.

Solenoids

Electrical energy can be changed to mechanical energy through the use of a solenoid. When energized, the solenoid develops a magnetic field and, in turn, draws a plunger or plate into the current-carrying coil. This creates mechanical movement. An A/C compressor clutch is one type of solenoid,m Fig. 13-14.

TROUBLESHOOTING ELECTRICAL SYSTEMS

Hot and ground wire

A *hot wire* connects an electrical component to the battery positive terminal. Most electrical components share a common ground through the car body that starts at the negative terminal of the battery. However, many cars today have much plastic throughout the car that makes a common ground impossible. It then becomes necessary to also have a ground wire, as well as a hot wire, to an electrical component.

Open circuit

An *open circuit* prevents the current from returning to the battery. It is a broken or discontinued circuit due to

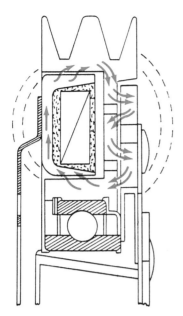

Fig. 13-14. The A/C compressor clutch is a solenoid. The electromagnet pulls the plate in contact with the pulley. The compressor is now engaged.

cut wires, blown fuse, defective switch, or an unplugged connector. An open circuit can exist in a hot wire or ground circuit.

Short between circuits

A *short between circuits* occurs when two current-carrying conductors (of the same polarity) come into contact. Insulation around the wires can wear, allowing the metal wires to contact each other. For example, when the hot wire going to the brake stop-light switch shorts to the hot wire from the headlights, the headlights and brake lights are both turned on whenever the brake pedal is applied.

Short circuit to ground

A *short circuit to ground* is when a hot wire connects directly to ground without first going through a unit of resistance (light bulb, motor, resistor). As an example, a sheet metal screw may pierce insulation of a hot wire as it is screwed in. The screw makes contact with both the hot wire and ground circuit, increasing the amperage enough to blow a fuse or trip a circuit breaker.

Ground check

The ground circuit is just as important as the hot wire to an electrical component's operation. Connect one lead of the test light to a known hot wire connection. With the other lead, connect it to the electrical component's ground. If the test light glows, the ground circuit is okay. If the test light is dim, the ground connection is probably loose or corroded. If the test light does not glow, the component is not grounded.

ELECTRICAL CIRCUIT PROTECTION

Fuses

An electrical circuit is designed to carry a specified amperage. Current exceeding specifications will destroy

electrical and/or electronic components and/or melt the wiring. A *fuse* is used to protect the electrical circuit.

Fuses are rated according to their amperage-carrying capacity. This rating can be found on the fuse, Fig. 13-15. The fuse consists of a soft metal conductor. It melts when amperage in the circuit exceeds the fuse's rating, Fig. 13-16. The fuse must be replaced when it "blows" (fails).

A blown fuse may be due to a short circuit to ground. However, a fuse can blow due to a one-time electrical surge. If no electrical problems are detected, it is safe to assume that an electrical surge caused the fuse to blow and no corrective action is needed. Repairs are needed if a short circuit to ground is the cause, otherwise the replacement fuse will also blow.

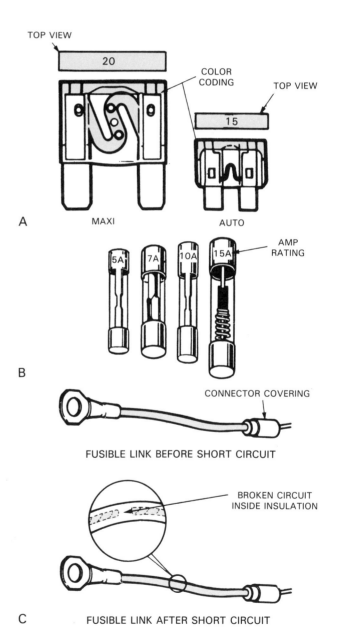

Fig. 13-15. Fuses. A—Blade-type fuse. Amperage rating is numbered at its top and color coded. B—Older glass-type fuse has its amperage rating imprinted at one end of metal conductor. C—Fusible link is an insulated wire with its conductor having a low-melting point. (Oldsmobile)

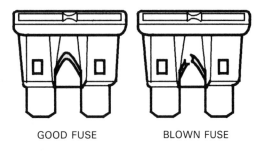

GOOD FUSE   BLOWN FUSE

Fig. 13-16. Blown fuse center conductor melts and interrupts electrical current. (Oldsmobile)

Fuse boxes are generally of a molded plastic construction. The location of the fuse box is generally under the instrument panel. Other components found in the fuse box are turn-signal flashers, relays, and circuit breakers, Fig. 13-17. Circuit breakers also protect the electrical circuit.

Circuit breakers

The difference between a circuit breaker and a fuse is that a circuit breaker resets itself automatically as soon as the amperage returns within its limits. Circuit breakers are normally used in circuits that have an electrical motor. An electric motor that binds can also cause excess amperage.

The *circuit breaker* is a bimetallic switch. When subjected to excessive current flow (heat), the contacts open. This is referred to as a "tripped" circuit breaker. The circuit breaker trips (opens) as a result of the different expansion rates of the dissimilar metals, Fig. 13-18. A circuit breaker does not require replacement when it trips.

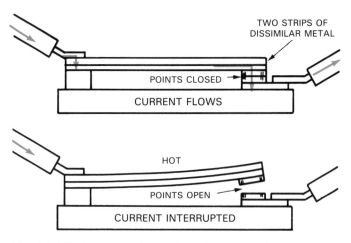

TWO STRIPS OF DISSIMILAR METAL

POINTS CLOSED

CURRENT FLOWS

HOT

POINTS OPEN

CURRENT INTERRUPTED

Fig. 13-18. Contact points open when excessive amperage flows through circuit breaker. When amperage returns to normal, circuit breaker contact points close automatically.

TEST EQUIPMENT

Voltmeter

To diagnose an electrical problem, special equipment and meters are needed. A *voltmeter* measures the voltage of a circuit. It is connected in parallel with the voltage source, Fig. 13-19. A voltmeter can also measure a voltage drop, Fig. 13-20. The circuit must remain operational when checking the voltage drop.

Voltage lower than specified indicates corroded or loose connections, weak battery, or defective charging system. A voltage drop greater than specified indicates an internal short of a motor, light bulb, or resistor. It may also indicate a loose or corroded electrical connection.

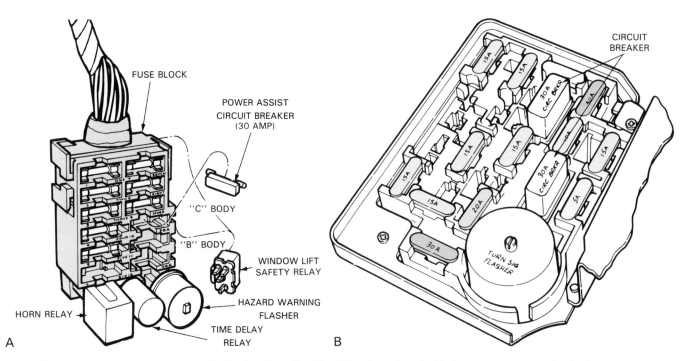

A — FUSE BLOCK

POWER ASSIST CIRCUIT BREAKER (30 AMP)

"C" BODY

"B" BODY

WINDOW LIFT SAFETY RELAY

HAZARD WARNING FLASHER

HORN RELAY

TIME DELAY RELAY

B — CIRCUIT BREAKER

TURN SIG FLASHER

Fig. 13-17. Fuse box. A—Relays installed in fuse box. B—Circuit breakers installed in fuse box. note number indicating amperage rating on fuses. (Chrysler and Ford)

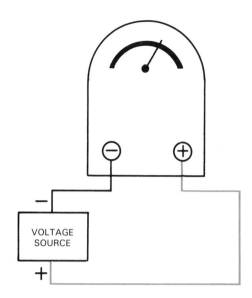

Fig. 13-19. Measuring voltage requires positive terminal of meter connected to hot source. Negative terminal connects to negative side of voltage source.

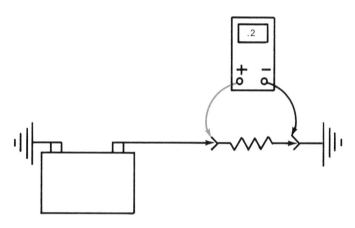

Fig. 13-20. Measuring voltage drop requires positive terminal connected to battery side of electrical component and negative terminal connected at opposite end of resistance unit. Voltage drop automatically determines difference of voltage across resistance unit.

Ammeter

An *ammeter* is needed to read the amperage in a circuit. It is hooked in series with the voltage source, Fig. 13-21. This means the circuit must first be disconnected at one point. Measure amperage in a circuit, other than starter current draw, by removing the fuse and inserting the ammeter leads (in series). Amperage draw higher than specified indicates a short circuit to ground or a binding motor.

Ohmmeter

An *ohmmeter* measures the resistance of a circuit. It is also connected in series, but only to a "dead circuit" (no voltage or current flow), Fig. 13-22. This means the wire or component is disconnected from the circuit to measure its resistance. The ohmmeter has its own voltage source. Connecting an ohmmeter to a "live circuit" could destroy the ohmmeter. Excessive resistance

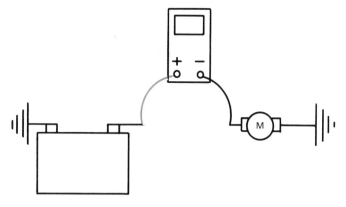

Fig. 13-21. Circuit must be broken and ammeter connected to measure amperage. Positive terminal of ammeter connects to battery hot side and negative terminal to the electrical-load side.

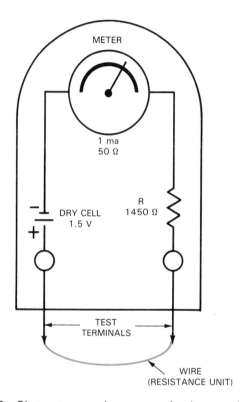

Fig. 13-22. Ohmmeter uses its source of voltage as input. Amount of resistance is determined by output voltage. It does not matter which terminal is connected from meter to either end of wire, since circuit must be dead.

indicates corroded or loose connections. Infinite resistance indicates an open circuit.

Multimeter

A *multimeter,* Fig. 13-23, combines the function of an ohmmeter, voltmeter, and ammeter. The multimeter can be of an analog or digital type. Currently, the digital type, Fig. 13-23, is used due to the inherent high internal impedance (10 megohms) needed to diagnose computerized systems. Using an analog multimeter on a computerized systems can give false readings and/or destroy the computer.

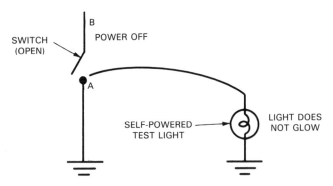

Fig. 13-24. Test light lead to ground and hot wire circuit. Test light will not glow at point A since switch is open. However, test light will glow if it is moved to point B.

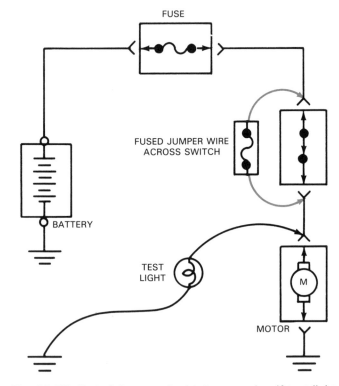

Fig. 13-25. Switch bypassed with jumper wire. If test light glows and motor now works, the switch is defective. However, if test light glows and motor does not operate, the motor is defective.

Fig. 13-23. Digital multimeter. (TIF Instruments)

WARNING: Never connect an ohmmeter directly to the on-board computer. This will damage the computer. Refer to individual car manuals for test procedures.

Test light

A test light is a valuable tool to check a circuit for voltage, Fig. 13-24. It consists of a 12 V bulb in a socket connected by test leads. Connect one test lead from ground to a point in the hot wire circuit. If the test light glows, voltage is present at that point. If the test light does not glow, there is an opening or break in the circuit between the two points, Fig. 13-24.

WARNING: Never use a test light when checking the components or wiring of a computerized system. This will destroy the computer.

Fused jumper wire

Bypassing a switch, electrical connection, or any length of wire determines which is at fault. The switch or electrical connection is disconnected and a fused jumper wire inserted in its place, Fig. 13-25. A motor that now runs indicates the switch is defective and must be replaced. The fuse, attached to the jumper wire,

should be of the same rating of the circuit it protects. The fused jumper wire protects the circuit should it accidentally be grounded.

WARNING: Never use a jumper wire across sensors, actuators, or a computer, as this will destroy the computer.

Short locator

A fuse that repeatedly blows can be caused by a short circuit to ground. A test light can be used to help locate a short circuit to ground. The test light acts as a substitute for a blown fuse. Disconnect all components (motor, bulbs, etc.) the individual fuse protects. A test light that now glows, Fig. 13-26, indicates a grounded

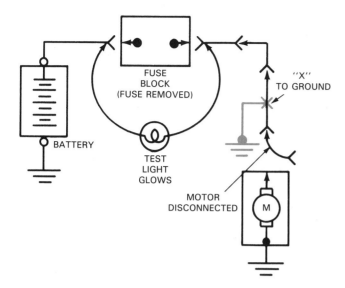

Fig. 13-26. If test light glows when connected in series across fuse, a grounded circuit is indicated. Disconnect all electrical components that fuse protects one at a time. If test light continues to glow, wire is grounded. However, if test light does not glow after disconnecting an electrical component, that component is internally grounded and must be replaced.

wire in the circuit. If the test light did not glow, reconnect the electrical components one at a time. Should the test light now glow, the electrical component (motor, bulbs, etc.) connected last is internally grounded and must be replaced.

NOTE: A turn-signal flasher can also be used as a substitute fuse while locating a short circuit to ground.

The flasher makes an audible "clicking" while tracing the short. This is more desirable method if the technician is outside the passenger compartment. Once the short circuit to ground has been located and repaired, the turn-signal flasher will not make an audible click.

SERVICE MANUALS

Service manuals are a "necessary tool" when troubleshooting the electrical circuit. Service manuals include information on electrical test procedures, electrical specifications, electrical component and wiring location, Fig. 13-27, warnings, Fig. 13-28, and wiring diagrams, Fig. 13-29.

Fig. 13-28. Symbol indicates a component that can be destroyed by static electricity or electrostatic discharge. (Oldsmobile)

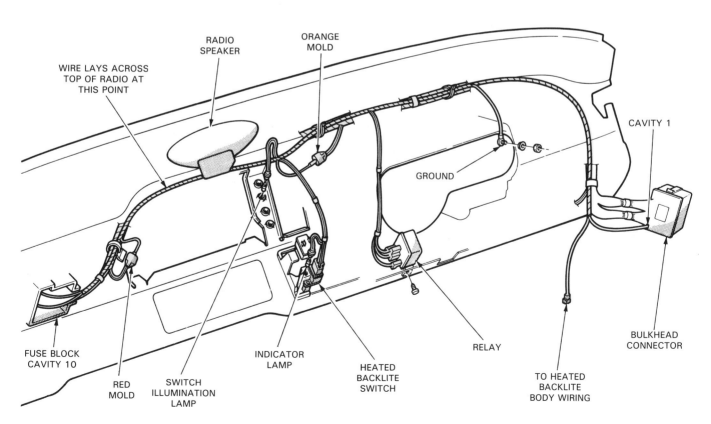

Fig. 13-27. Location of wiring harness for a specific circuit and its components can be found in service manual.　(Chrysler)

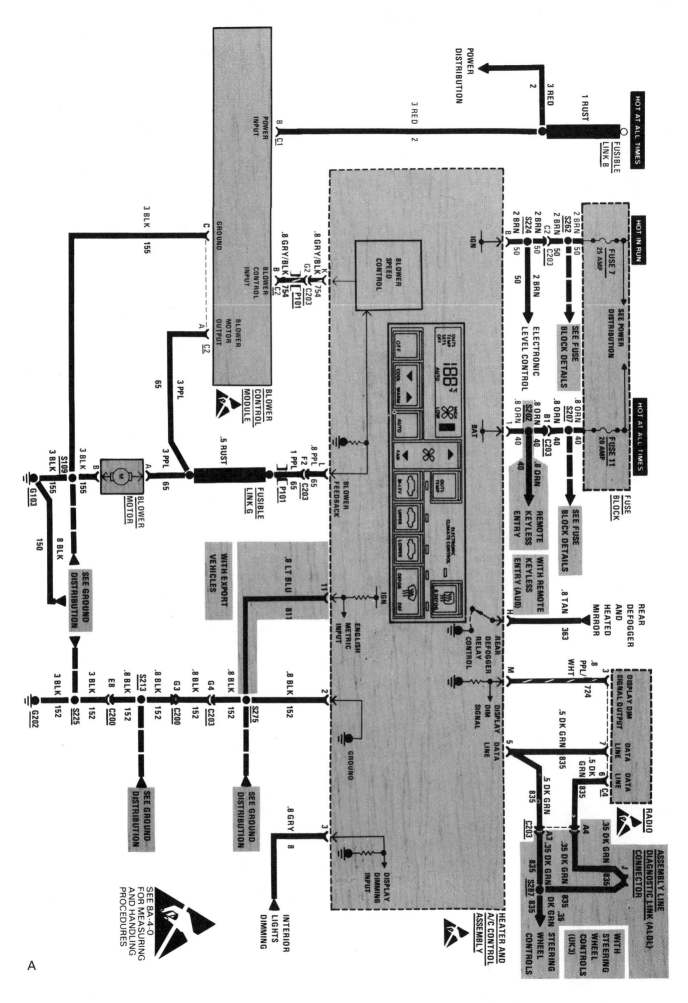

Fig. 13-29. A—Wiring diagram shows hot wire routing to electrical components and ground locations. (Chrysler)

A

LEGEND OF SYMBOLS USED ON WIRING DIAGRAMS			
+	POSITIVE		CONNECTOR
–	NEGATIVE		MALE CONNECTOR
	GROUND		FEMALE CONNECTOR
	FUSE		MULTIPLE CONNECTOR
	CIRCUIT BREAKER		DENOTES WIRE CONTINUES ELSEWHERE
	CAPACITOR		SPLICE
Ω	OHMS	J2 2	SPLICE IDENTIFICATION
	RESISTOR		OPTIONAL WIRING WITH / WIRING WITHOUT
	VARIABLE RESISTOR		THERMAL ELEMENT (BI-METAL STRIP)
	SERIES RESISTOR		"Y" WINDINGS
	COIL	88:88	DIGITAL READOUT
	STEP UP COIL		SINGLE FILAMENT LAMP
	OPEN CONTACT		DUAL FILAMENT LAMP
	CLOSED CONTACT		L.E.D.-LIGHT EMITTING DIODE
	CLOSED SWITCH		THERMISTOR
	OPEN SWITCH		GAUGE
	CLOSED GANGED SWITCH	TIMER	TIMER
	OPEN GANGED SWITCH		MOTOR
	TWO POLE SINGLE THROW SWITCH		ARMATURE AND BRUSHES
	PRESSURE SWITCH		DENOTES WIRE GOES THROUGH GROMMET
	SOLENOID SWITCH	#36	DENOTES WIRE GOES THROUGH 40 WAY DISCONNECT
	MERCURY SWITCH	#19 STRG COLUMN	DENOTES WIRE GOES THROUGH 25 WAY STEERING COLUMN CONNECTOR
	DIODE OR RECTIFIER	INST PANEL #14	DENOTES WIRE GOES THROUGH 25 WAY INSTRUMENT PANEL CONNECTOR
	BI-DIRECTIONAL ZENER DIODE		

B

Fig. 13-29. B—Symbols used on wiring diagrams.   (Oldsmobile)

ELECTRICAL WIRE SIZES/MARKINGS

Various wire sizes are used throughout the car. The wire size is its diameter and is assigned a gauge number. The American Wire Gauge (AWG) is normally used as the standard. It ranges from 0000 (.460 in.) to 30 gauge (.010 in.).

The required wire size is directly related to the electrical load. The greater the amperage demand, the larger the wire diameter must be to handle the load, Fig. 13-30. The wire diameter and length affect resistance. The larger the wire diameter and shorter its length, the less resistance it offers.

WARNING: Never mix the gauge of wire when splicing for needed repairs. This could have an adverse effect on the operation of the electrical circuit.

The electrical insulation of automotive wiring is color-coded. Many different colored wires run throughout the car. Some wires have a color "tracer" to distinguish them from the other wires. The tracer is a very thin stripe that runs the length of the wire, Fig. 13-31.

READING A WIRING DIAGRAM

Wiring diagrams, Fig. 13-29, provide a schematic of the hot wire path to each electrical component. The wiring diagram also shows where each component picks up its ground. Each wire on the diagram is numbered with its size and color. This aids in tracing the individual wire on the diagram to its destination. Sometimes a wire may travel across many pages of a wiring diagram. Wiring diagrams also show junctions, splices, and numbered cavities of multiple connectors.

NOTE: Manufacturers differ in the method of numbering the wiring on the diagram. Therefore, it is essential to read and understand the individual service manual's symbols and numbering system first.

Wiring Color Code Chart					
COLOR CODE	COLOR	STANDARD TRACER	COLOR CODE	COLOR	STANDARD TRACER
BK	BLACK	WT	PK	PINK	BK OR WH
BR	BROWN	WT	RD	RED	WT
DB	DARK BLUE	WT	TN	TAN	WT
DG	DARK GREEN	WT	VT	VIOLET	WT
GY	GRAY	BK	WT	WHITE	BK
LB	LIGHT BLUE	BK	YL	YELLOW	BK
LG	LIGHT GREEN	BK	*	WITH TRACER	
OR	ORANGE	BK			

Fig. 13-31. Color coding of electrical insulation. (Chrysler)

VACUUM CIRCUITS AND COMPONENTS

Vacuum

Vacuum is a pressure less than atmospheric pressure. Vacuum is measured in inches of mercury (Hg). A perfect vacuum is 29.92 in. Hg at sea level. Most car engines produce only a partial vacuum of about 18 in. Hg at sea level during idle. However, some engines do not produce enough vacuum and must use a vacuum pump. Some pumps are driven by a separate electric motor and others are belt-driven by the engine.

Total Approx. Circuit Amperes		Total Circuit Watts		Total Candle Power		Wire Gauge (For Length in Feet)											
6V	12V	6V	12V	6V	12V	3'	5'	7'	10'	15'	20'	25'	30'	40'	50'	75'	100'
0.5	1.0	3	6	3	6	18	18	18	18	18	18	18	18	18	18	18	18
0.75	1.5			5	10	18	18	18	18	18	18	18	18	18	18	18	18
1.0	2	6	12	8	16	18	18	18	18	18	18	18	18	18	18	16	16
1.5	3			12	24	18	18	18	18	18	18	18	18	18	18	14	14
2.0	4	12	24	15	30	18	18	18	18	18	18	18	18	16	16	12	12
2.5	5			20	40	18	18	18	18	18	18	18	18	16	14	12	12
3.0	6	18	36	25	50	18	18	18	18	18	18	16	16	16	14	12	10
3.5	7			30	60	18	18	18	18	18	18	16	16	14	14	10	10
4.0	8	24	48	35	70	18	18	18	18	18	16	16	16	14	12	10	10
5.0	10	30	60	40	80	18	18	18	18	16	16	16	14	12	12	10	10
5.5	11			45	90	18	18	18	18	16	16	14	14	12	12	10	8
6.0	12	36	72	50	100	18	18	18	18	16	16	14	14	12	12	10	8
7.5	15			60	120	18	18	18	18	14	14	12	12	12	10	8	8
9.0	18	54	108	70	140	18	18	16	16	14	14	12	12	10	10	8	8
10	20	60	120	80	160	18	18	16	16	14	12	10	10	10	10	8	6
11	22	66	132	90	180	18	18	16	16	12	12	10	10	10	8	6	6
12	24	72	144	100	200	*18	18	16	16	12	12	10	10	10	8	6	6
15	30					18	16	16	14	10	10	10	10	10	6	4	4
20	40					18	16	14	12	10	10	8	8	6	6	4	2
25	50					16	14	12	12	10	10	8	8	6	6	2	2
50	100					12	12	10	10	6	6	4	4	4	2	1	0
75	150					10	10	8	8	4	4	2	2	2	1	00	00
100	200					10	8	8	6	4	4	2	2	1	0	4/0	4/0

Fig. 13-30. Chart shows gauge size needed, depending on circuit amperage and length of wire.   (Belden Mfg. Co.)

Vacuum circuit

A *vacuum circuit,* Fig. 13-32, is similar to an electrical circuit, except it routes vacuum instead of electricity. The vacuum source on most engines is at the intake manifold. Plastic or rubber tubing connects the vacuum actuators to the source of vacuum, Fig. 13-32.

Vacuum motors

A *vacuum actuator* or *motor* converts vacuum into mechanical energy. The diaphragm is spring loaded and encased in a plastic or metal housing, Fig. 13-33. The diaphragm separates vacuum from atmospheric

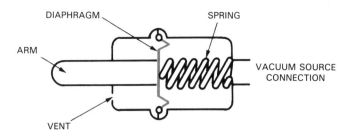

Fig. 13-33. Vacuum motor is separated by a diaphragm. Atmospheric pressure enters through vent. Vacuum is applied to opposite side of diaphragm against spring pressure.

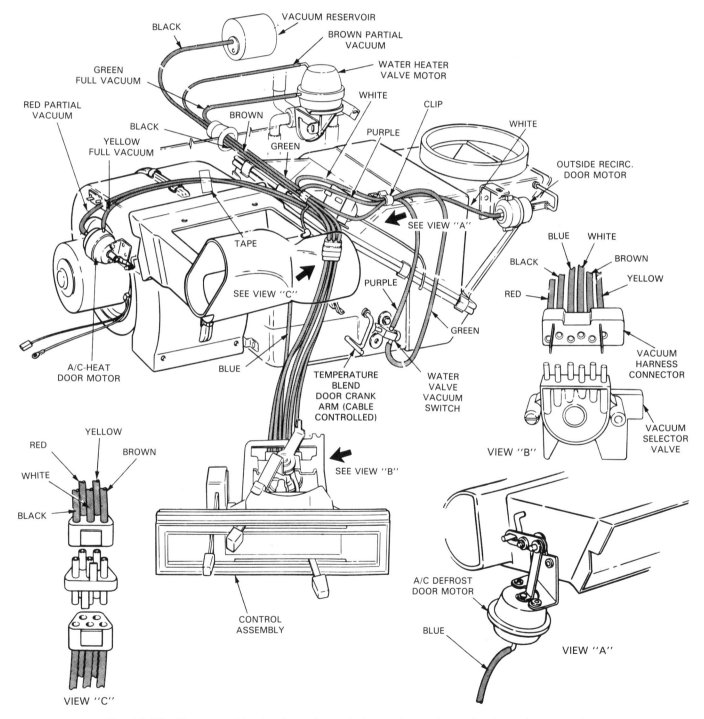

Fig. 13-32. Vacuum tubing is also color-coded to make tracing a circuit on the car easier.

151

pressure. Vacuum applied to one side of the diaphragm allows atmospheric pressure to push the diaphragm, against spring pressure, in the direction of the vacuum, Fig. 13-34.

Vacuum reservoir

Vacuum reservoirs store vacuum during idle and deceleration, Fig. 13-35. During wide open throttle (WOT), vacuum drops off to almost zero or atmospheric pressure. This would normally cause the vacuum motor to return to its closed position. However, vacuum from the reservoir provides a smooth and continuous operation of the vacuum-operated devices.

Vacuum restrictions

Restrictions are used in some vacuum lines to provide a very short delay time in energizing a vacuum motor, Fig. 13-36. This provides a smooth and gradual application of the vacuum motor and devices it operates.

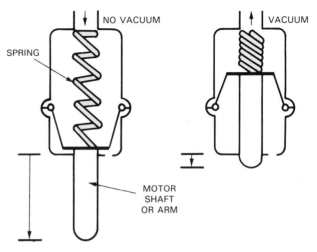

Fig. 13-34. When vacuum is applied at motor, arm moves inward. When vacuum is removed, spring pushes diaphragm forward.

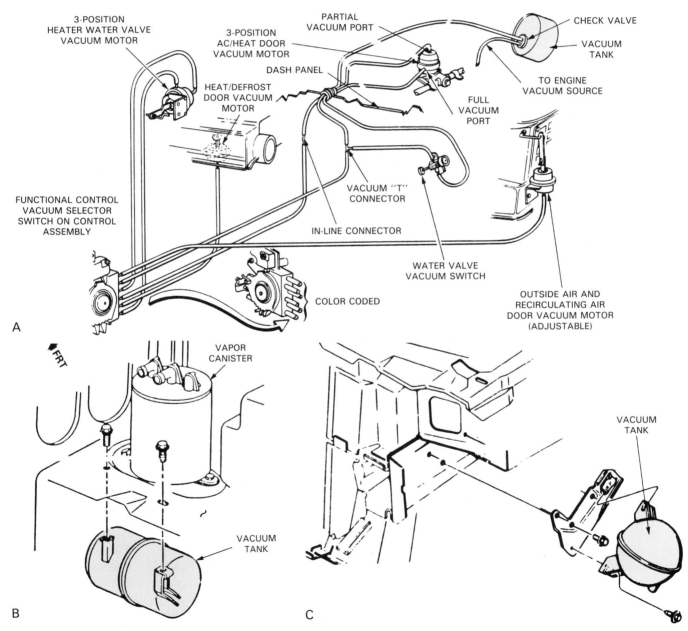

Fig. 13-35. Vacuum reservoir. A—Coffee-can shaped vacuum reservoir. Check valve maintains vacuum inside reservoir until needed. B—Cylindrical vacuum reservoir. C—Spherical vacuum reservoir. (Ford and Oldsmobile)

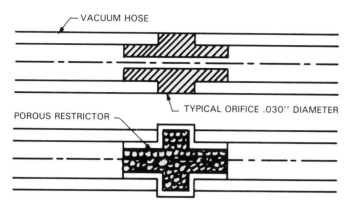

Fig. 13-36. Restriction in vacuum line delays action of vacuum motor. Restrictor can be an orifice or porous type.

VACUUM PROBLEMS

When a vacuum-operated device fails to work properly, problems fall into one of three causes:
1. A vacuum leak is one cause. The vacuum hose can be disconnected or cracked. A vacuum motor diaphragm may be ruptured which also allows vacuum to leak.
2. A pinched vacuum hose is another cause. A pinched vacuum line prevents vacuum from going to the vacuum-operated device. A hand-held vacuum pump can be used for testing either of these causes.
3. An insufficient supply of vacuum is the final cause. This may be due to the engine's inability to produce enough vacuum. An unintended restriction in the line or at the source of vacuum may not allow an adequate supply of vacuum to the vacuum-operated device. This problem may be more noticeable in cold weather. While it is not a vacuum problem, binding linkage to a vacuum-operated device has the same effect.

VACUUM DIAGRAM

A vacuum diagram is needed to track down vacuum leaks and pinched vacuum hoses, Fig. 13-37. The vacuum diagram shows the color code of each vacuum hose, where it connects, and location of the vacuum-controlled components. This diagram shows the routing of vacuum hoses for the heating and air-conditioning system.

SUMMARY

Matter is composed of molecules, which is made up of atoms. Protons, neutrons, and electrons make up the atom. Elements are composed of like atoms. Elements with free electrons are conductors of electricity. Matter with bound electrons is an insulator.

When voltage is applied to a wire, the wire has a magnetic field surrounding it. A magnetic field exits the magnet's North pole and enters its South pole. When a wire passes through a magnetic field, voltage is induced in the wire. The relationship between voltage, amperage, and resistance is expressed in Ohm's Law. Current can travel in a series, parallel, or series-parallel circuit.

Solid state devices have no moving parts and are made of semiconductor elements. A semiconductor element is neither a good conductor nor insulator. However, a semiconductor can be made to conduct electricity. Diodes and transistors are solid state devices. Transistors are of the NPN or PNP type. A transistor is made of a collector, emitter, and base. When the proper voltage signal is applied to its base, current flows through the transistor and the circuit. An A/C clutch diode protects the computer from electrical spikes when the air conditioner is turned off.

A relay and solenoid are electromechanical devices. When voltage is applied to a coiled wire, a strong magnetic field is created. It is strong enough to pull a set of contacts, plate, or plunger towards the magnetic field. A resistor reduces current flow and is of the coil or fixed-carbon construction. A capacitor stores excess voltage to prevent electrical noise that may interfere with radio reception and computer operation.

An open circuit is when current flow is interrupted in either the hot wire or ground circuit. A short between circuits is when two current-carrying conductors of the same polarity connect that otherwise are insulated from each other. A short circuit to ground is when no unit of resistance (motor, bulb, resistor) is between the positive and negative side of the circuit. A short circuit to ground causes amperage to increase enough to damage electrical components and wiring.

A fuse or circuit breaker protects the electrical circuit from damage due to excess amperage. A fuse and circuit breaker are rated according to its amperage capacity. A multimeter, made up of a voltmeter, ohmmeter, and ammeter, is needed to troubleshoot problems in an electrical circuit. A digital multimeter is needed to diagnose computerized systems due to its high internal impedance or the computer will be destroyed. Never connect a jumper wire across sensors, actuators, or a computer, as this will destroy the computer. Never connect an ohmmeter or test light directly to a computer, as this will destroy the computer.

Vacuum is a pressure less than atmospheric pressure. A perfect vacuum is 29.92 in. Hg at sea level. Most engines only produce a partial vacuum of 18 in. Hg at sea level during idle. A vacuum hose connects its source to each vacuum motor. Vacuum motors work on a pressure differential. A vacuum reservoir stores vacuum to maintain continuous operation of vacuum-controlled devices when engine vacuum momentarily decreases. A restriction in a vacuum line provides smooth and gradual application of the vacuum motor.

KNOW THESE TERMS

Electric, Matter, Molecule, Atom, Electrons, Protons, Neutrons, Element, Free electrons, Bound electrons, Conductor, Insulator, North and South poles, Voltage, Amperage, Ohm, Electromotive force, Ohm's Law, Series circuit, Parallel circuit, Series-parallel circuit, Solid state, Semiconductor, Diode, A/C clutch diode, Transistor, Resistor, Capacitor, condenser, Integrated circuit, Relay, Solenoid, Hot wire, Open circuit, Short between circuits, Short circuit to ground, Fuse, Circuit breaker, Voltmeter, Ammeter, Ohmmeter, Multimeter, Vacuum, Vacuum motor, Vacuum reservoir.

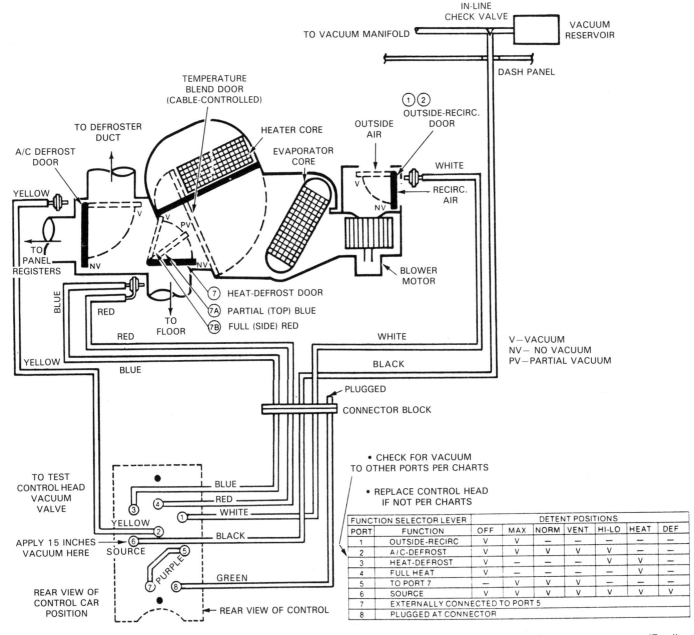

FUNCTION SELECTOR LEVER		DETENT POSITIONS						
PORT	FUNCTION	OFF	MAX	NORM	VENT	HI-LO	HEAT	DEF
1	OUTSIDE-RECIRC	V	V	—	—	—	—	—
2	A/C-DEFROST	V	V	V	V	V	—	—
3	HEAT-DEFROST	V	—	—	—	V	V	V
4	FULL HEAT	V	—	—	—	—	V	—
5	TO PORT 7	—	V	V	V	—	—	—
6	SOURCE	V	V	V	V	V	V	V
7	EXTERNALLY CONNECTED TO PORT 5							
8	PLUGGED AT CONNECTOR							

Fig. 13-37. Vacuum diagram indicates color of individual vacuum hoses and its routing to each vacuum motor. (Ford)

CHAPTER 13—REVIEW QUESTIONS

Write your answers on a separate sheet of paper. Do not write in this book.

1. A necessary reference to aid in correcting an electrical or vacuum problem is called a _____ _____.

2. Two electrical power sources in a car are the battery and an alternator. True or false?

3. When electricity cannot return to the battery, it is a/an:
   a. Closed circuit.
   b. Series circuit.
   c. Series-parallel circuit.
   d. Open circuit.

4. A circuit breaker:
   a. Can be manually reset.
   b. Automatically resets itself.
   c. Melts when overloaded.
   d. Both a an b.

5. When a hot wire's conductor comes in contact with another hot wire's conductor, it is a/an:
   a. Open circuit.
   b. Short between circuits.
   c. Series circuit.
   d. Parallel circuit

6. A fuse is a:
   a. Glass tube encapsulating a soft-metal conductor.
   b. Metal conductor in plastic.
   c. None of the above.
   d. Both a and b.

7. A resistor reduces current flow by transforming electrical energy into _____.

8. What two basic tools are used to check for voltage?
   a. Test light.
   b. Digital multimeter.
   c. Both a and b.
   d. None of the above.
9. Define vacuum.
10. A solid state device is a/an:
    a. Semiconductor.
    b. Diode.
    c. Battery.
    d. None of the above.
11. An atom is made of neutrons, protons, and electrons. True or false?
12. Which of the following does not exhibit resistance?
    a. Resistor.
    b. Light bulb.
    c. Motor.
    d. None of the above.
13. A relay is a magnetic switch used to control high amperage with a low-amperage circuit. True or false?
14. A current-carrying wire always has a _____ _____ around it.
15. A device that protects the electrical circuit and components is a/an:
    a. Fuse.
    b. Circuit breaker.
    c. Diode.
    d. All of the above.
16. The purpose of the vacuum reservoir is to:
    a. Store vacuum when engine is not operating.
    b. Dissipate vacuum during WOT.
    c. Regulate vacuum pressure.
    d. Contain a desiccant.
17. The result of a corroded connection is:
    a. Excessive resistance.
    b. Grounded circuit.
    c. Excessive voltage.
    d. Blown fuse.
18. Electrons loosely attracted to the nucleus are insulators. True or false?
19. The relationship between voltage, amperage, and resistance is expressed mathematically in a formula known as:
    a. Gumperson's Law.
    b. Newton's Law.
    c. Ohm's Law.
    d. Electron Law.
20. A semiconductor is:
    a. Not a good conductor.
    b. Not a good insulator.
    c. Both a and b.
    d. None of the above.
21. Two semiconducting elements are _____ and _____.
22. Adding "impurities" to a semiconducting element is called doping. True or false?
23. A solenoid is an electrical device which:
    a. Regulates vacuum.
    b. Turns mechanical motion into electrical energy.
    c. Turns electrical energy into mechanical motion.
    d. All of the above.
24. An AWG wire size 30 is:
    a. Larger than a number 16.
    b. 17 times larger than an AWG number one.
    c. Larger in diameter than a number 20.
    d. .010 in. diameter.
25. Which of the following can cause an open circuit:
    a. Closed switch.
    b. Blown fuse.
    c. Spliced wire.
    d. Connected terminal.
26. Always remove power from the circuit before testing when using a 12 V test light. True or false?
27. Why is a restriction used in a vacuum line?
28. An AWG wire size 17 will carry higher amperage than an AWG wire size 19. True or false?
29. What "tool" is common to troubleshooting a vacuum or electrical circuit problem?
30. When testing a computerized system, a _____ multimeter MUST be used.
31. Jumper wires must never be used across computers, sensors, or actuators. True or false?
32. An ohmmeter or test light is used to check the on-board computer. True or false?

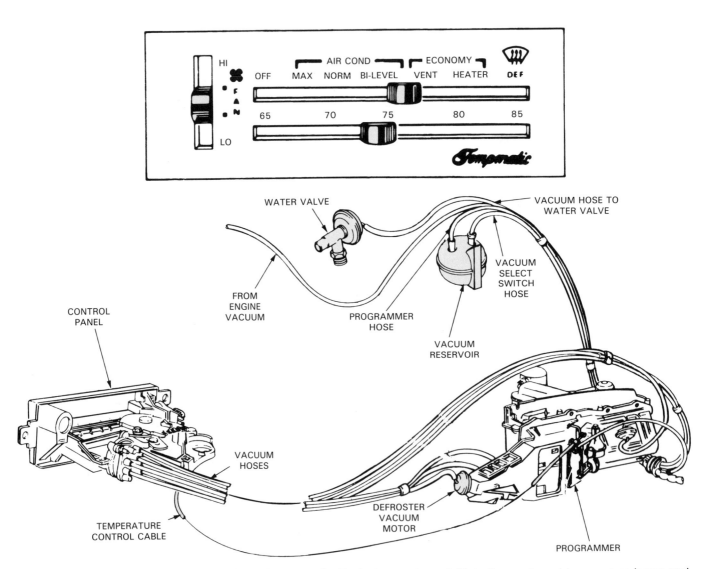

Fig. 14-1. Semiautomatic temperature control system. A—Typical control panel. Note the mode and temperature levers and fan switch. B—Note the vacuum motors, vacuum hoses, vacuum reservoir, vacuum-operated water valve, temperature control cable, and programmer. (Oldsmobile)

14

AUTOMATIC TEMPERATURE CONTROL: COMPUTER AND NONCOMPUTER

After studying this chapter, you will be able to:
- *Explain the differences and similarities between a manual, semiautomatic, and a fully-automatic temperature control system.*
- *Summarize the operation of a semiautomatic and fully-automatic temperature control system.*
- *List the different parts used for the semiautomatic and fully-automatic temperature control system.*

INTRODUCTION

A *manually-controlled heating and air conditioning system* requires constant adjustment of the temperature control lever to maintain the desired temperature inside the car. The *semi- or fully-automatic temperature control system* automatically heats or cools by constantly positioning the temperature blend-air door. This maintains the selected temperature inside the passenger compartment.

Early versions of the fully-automatic temperature control system used electromechanical devices to control all mode functions. Since the mid-1980s, the fully-automatic temperature control system uses a computer to control most mode functions.

SEMIAUTOMATIC TEMPERATURE CONTROL SYSTEM

The semiautomatic temperature control (SATC) system is noncomputerized. The temperature and mode are manually selected. No other adjustments are needed to maintain a constant temperature inside the passenger compartment. The blower motor speed is controlled independently of the temperature and mode selection. The semiautomatic temperature control system consists of a control panel, vacuum hoses, vacuum motors, compensator, and a programmer, Fig. 14-1.

SATC programmer

The *programmer* controls the position of the temperature blend-air door. The programmer consists of a vacuum motor, vacuum checking relay, and linkage, Fig. 14-2. Engine vacuum, compensator, and sliding resistor (attached to the temperature control cable) all provide input to the programmer. The compensator (aspirator) contains an in-car temperature sensor. Data from the in-car temperature sensor and the temperature selected by the driver determines where the programmer positions the temperature blend-air door.

The vacuum motor in the programmer constantly positions the temperature blend-air door, Fig. 14-3. This maintains the desired temperature inside the passenger compartment.

SATC compensator

The *compensator* regulates the amount of vacuum to the vacuum motor in the programmer, based on passenger compartment temperature. There is a restriction at the top of the compensator. The airflow past the restriction causes a pressure drop at this point. This venturi effect forces passenger compartment air through the compensator. The airflow is routed past the in-car temperature sensor.

SATC vacuum checking relay

The *vacuum checking relay* prevents the programmer from positioning the temperature blend-air door in the full cold position during low vacuum (WOT) conditions. This is accomplished by a spring-loaded diaphragm inside the relay. The spring forces the diaphragm against the vacuum port when vacuum drops off. The vacuum supply is then blocked to the vacuum motor inside the programmer. This prevents the vacuum-operated temperature blend-air door from moving to the "cold" position.

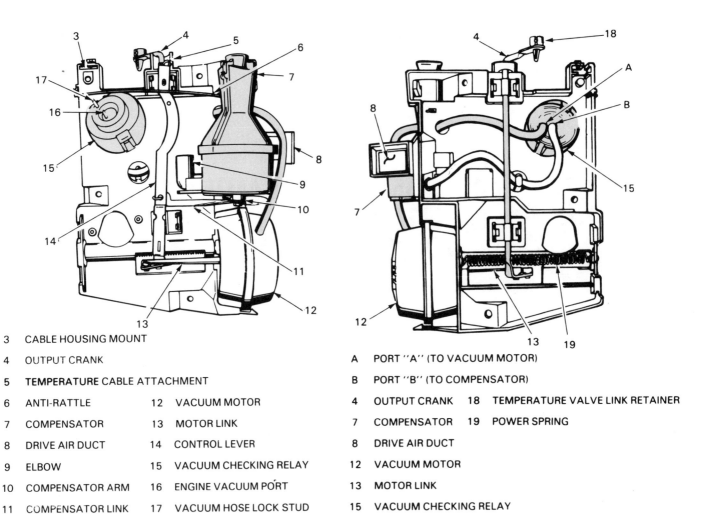

3	CABLE HOUSING MOUNT		
4	OUTPUT CRANK		
5	**TEMPERATURE** CABLE ATTACHMENT		
6	ANTI-RATTLE	12	VACUUM MOTOR
7	COMPENSATOR	13	MOTOR LINK
8	DRIVE AIR DUCT	14	CONTROL LEVER
9	ELBOW	15	VACUUM CHECKING RELAY
10	COMPENSATOR ARM	16	ENGINE VACUUM PORT
11	COMPENSATOR LINK	17	VACUUM HOSE LOCK STUD

A	PORT "A" (TO VACUUM MOTOR)		
B	PORT "B" (TO COMPENSATOR)		
4	OUTPUT CRANK	18	TEMPERATURE VALVE LINK RETAINER
7	COMPENSATOR	19	POWER SPRING
8	DRIVE AIR DUCT		
12	VACUUM MOTOR		
13	MOTOR LINK		
15	VACUUM CHECKING RELAY		

Fig. 14-2. Programmer used on the semiautomatic temperature control system. A—Front view. B—Rear view.

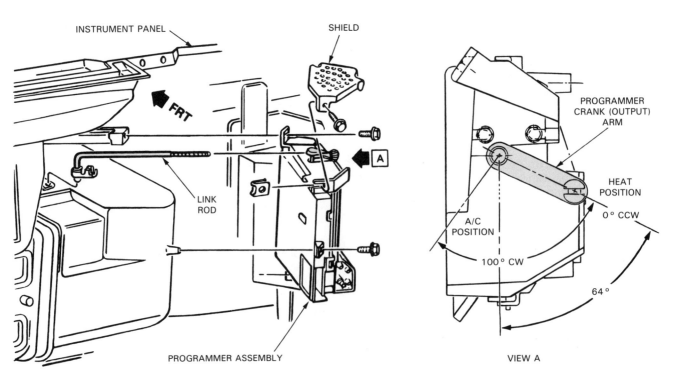

Fig. 14-3. The output crank connects to the link rod. The other end of the link rod connects to the temperature blend-air door. (Oldsmobile)

TYPICAL COMPUTER CONTROLLED SYSTEM

There are many different computer control designs. This depends on the manufacturer. It is extremely important to have the specific service manual when diagnosing or making the needed repairs.

The computer controls the A/C clutch, blower speed, temperature blend-air door position, and the mode doors. A computerized automatic temperature control system has an infinite number of temperature blend-air door positions and blower speeds. The computer program includes a delay function that gradually increases or decreases the blower speed.

The computer constantly draws a low standby current (less than 10 mA). This enables the computer to retain in its memory the last temperature selected by the driver of the car. Service to the electronic control head is limited to light bulb replacement. If the control head is defective, it cannot be serviced and must be replaced.

COMPUTERIZED AUTOMATIC TEMPERATURE CONTROL (ATC)

The current fully-automatic temperature control systems are computerized. This requires the driver to program only the temperature and mode, the rest is automatic. A fully-automatic temperature control system has a:

1. *Digital microprocessor* that compares data from the many sensors to an internally stored program. The microprocessor then activates the different devices it controls to maintain the desired temperature selected by the driver.
2. Self-diagnostic feature.
3. Digital vacuum-fluorescent display. It displays passenger compartment temperature, ambient temperature, and error codes. Most displays have English-metric conversion capability at the push of a button.
4. Flat membrane faceplate with pressure-sensitive switches for mode, temperature and fan speed selection.

Computerized ATC system controls

The fully-automatic temperature control system is similar to the semiautomatic temperature control system, Fig. 14-4. However, the fully-automatic temperature control system contains a microprocessor that controls the heating, cooling, and blower speed functions, Fig. 14-5. A microprocessor compares the data from the many sensors to predetermined values stored in its memory. The microprocessor then adjusts the various actuators. The fully-automatic temperature control system has:

1. A programmer that contains a bi-directional electric motor instead of a vacuum motor, Fig. 14-6. The electric motor positions the temperature blend-air door to maintain the desired temperature inside the car.
2. A programmer with solenoids, Fig. 14-6. Each solenoid controls vacuum to a specific vacuum motor that operates a mode door, Fig. 14-7. The push buttons at the control panel operate the solenoids. However, some systems have an electric motor for each mode door instead of a vacuum-operated motor, Fig. 14-8.
3. An ambient (outside) temperature sensor, Fig. 14-9. It can be positioned in front of the radiator and/or in the plenum chamber. The sensor located in the plenum chamber provides more accurate temperature data during idle and low speed driving. The sensor located in front of the radiator provides

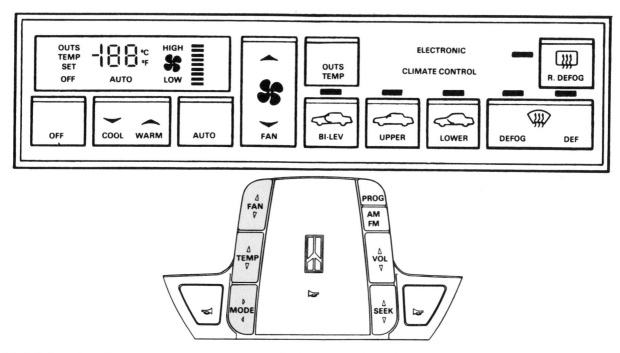

Fig. 14-4. Fully-automatic temperature control system. A—Most control panels are similar to this. B—Some have the controls mounted in the center of the steering wheel.

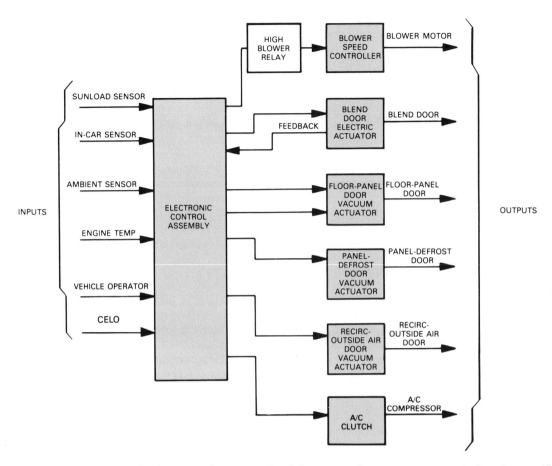

Fig. 14-5. Diagram shows the inputs and outputs of a fully-automatic temperature control system. (Ford)

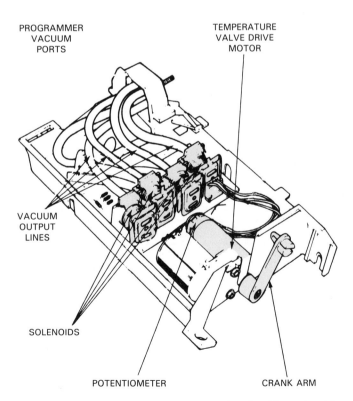

Fig. 14-6. This programmer contains solenoids. The solenoids regulate vacuum to each vacuum-operated mode door. The programmer also contains an electric motor that positions the temperature blend-air door. (Oldsmobile)

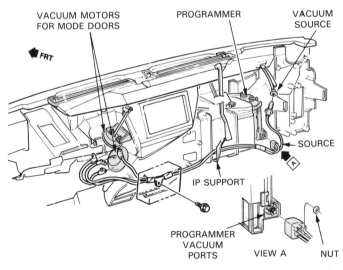

Fig. 14-7. Note the vacuum connection at the programmer. The programmer directs the vacuum to the specific vacuum motor based on the mode selected.

more accurate temperature data during highway driving.

4. An engine coolant temperature sensor (also used for the computerized fuel/ignition system), in-car temperature sensor/aspirator, Fig. 14-10, and sunload sensor, Fig. 14-11.

5. A *blower motor control module* includes a resistor

160

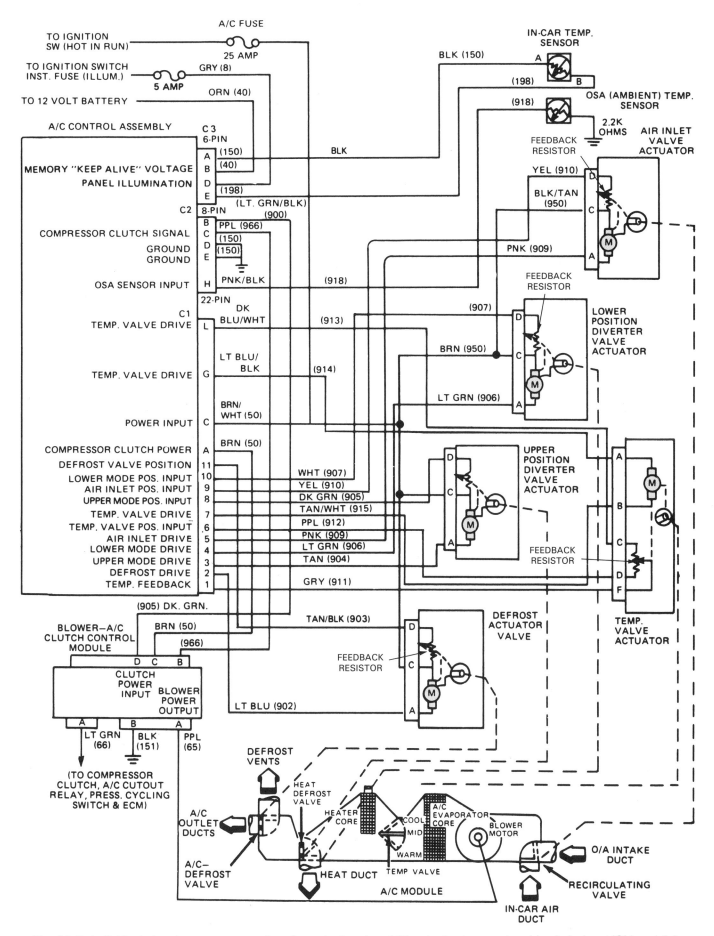

Fig. 14-8. Individual electric motors control each mode door in addition to the temperature blend-air door. (Oldsmobile)

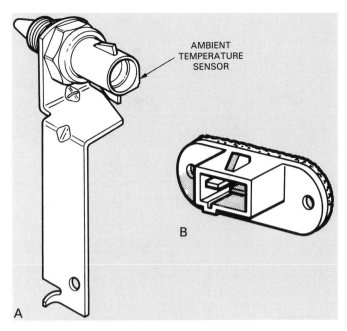

Fig. 14-9. Ambient temperature sensors. A—Located in front of the condenser. B—Located in the plenum chamber. (Ford)

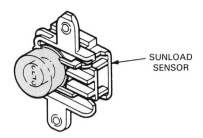

Fig. 14-11. Sunload sensor. It is positioned in the instrument panel just below the windshield or in the headliner above the windshield. (Ford)

6. A pressure reducer valve, on some models, instead of a water valve at the heater core inlet.
7. A *cold engine lockout* (CELO) feature on some models. This delays the blower motor from operating until the engine reaches operating temperature when the heat mode is selected. This usually takes three to five minutes. The blower motor operates immediately when the defrost mode is selected.

NOTE: Never operate the system with the blower motor disconnected from the control module. This will destroy the control module. A shorted A/C clutch diode will also cause blower control module failure. Check the A/C clutch diode before replacing a failed blower control module.

Computerized ATC sensors

The fully-automatic system contains different sensors. The *ambient temperature sensor* provides outside air

circuit to automatically vary the blower speed, depending on the cooling/heating demand, Fig. 14-12. The temperature blend-air door position and temperature inside the car determines the blower speed. However, the blower speed can be manually overridden. The blower control module may also control the A/C compressor clutch operation.

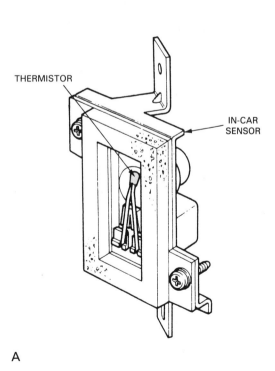

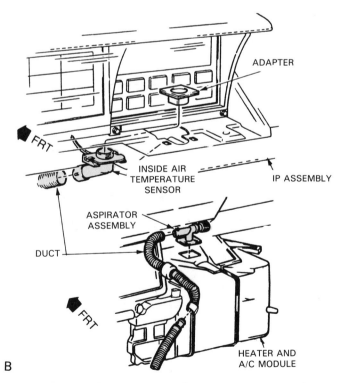

Fig. 14-10. In-car temperature sensor is a thermistor. A—This type mounts under the dash. (Ford) B—This system uses an aspirator to direct airflow from passenger compartment past the in-car temperature sensor. Aspirator's inlet is restricted and creates a pressure drop. Atmospheric pressure forces the airflow to low-pressure area at aspirator and through its ducts to in-car temperature sensor. (Oldsmobile)

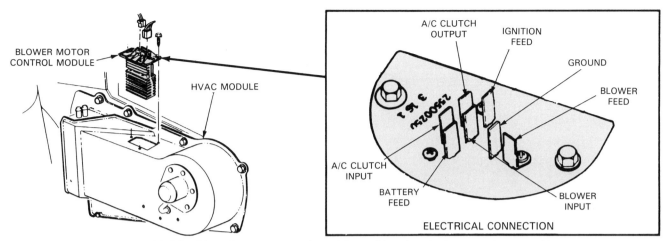

Fig. 14-12. Blower motor control module and its electrical connections. (Oldsmobile)

temperature data to the microprocessor, Fig. 14-9. The microprocessor compares the outside temperature to the temperature inside the passenger compartment. The *in-car temperature sensor* provides passenger compartment air temperature input to the microprocessor, Fig. 14-10. An *aspirator* directs a small amount of passenger compartment airflow, through a duct, past the in-car temperature sensor. The *sunload sensor,* Fig. 14-11, compensates for the greenhouse effect of the glass windows and can override the signal from the in-car temperature sensor.

Computerized ATC programmer

One type of programmer contains four solenoids, potentiometer (variable resistor), electric motor, and linkage, Fig. 14-6. The solenoid energized depends on the mode selected. An energized solenoid allows vacuum to a specific vacuum-operated motor, Fig. 14-7. The mode doors direct the airflow from the heater/evaporator case.

The programmer also contains a bi-directional electric motor, Fig. 14-6. It controls the position of the temperature blend-air door. Its position determines the desired temperature inside the passenger compartment. The position of the temperature blend-air door is automatically and constantly adjusted. This maintains the desired temperature inside the car based on data from the ambient, in-car temperature, and sunload sensors.

Another type of programmer used on some fully-automatic temperature control systems does not contain any solenoids, since there are no vacuum motors. Instead, each mode door has its own electric motor, Fig. 14-8. A variable feedback resistor is attached to an actuator arm. When the actuator arm changes position, current travels through the resistor and feeds back to the microprocessor. The current that flows through the resistor informs the microprocessor of the position of the door. The amount of current available depends on the variable resistor position and inputs from the ambient temperature, in-car temperature, and sunload sensors.

ERROR CODES

The fully-automatic temperature control system contains a microprocessor that can diagnose certain prob-

lems with its system. The display may flash an F° or a C°. This indicates to the driver a problem exists with the system. On the other hand, some systems illuminate a CHECK ENGINE light that informs the driver of a problem. The error code must be obtained or accessed from its memory for display.

The microprocessor (computer) retains error codes in its memory. An *error code* informs the technician which area and components to check to find the problem, Fig. 14-13. The error code does not pinpoint a problem with the system. Error codes will not detect a problem with the A/C system refrigerant flow control devices, compressor, evaporator, condenser, or refrigerant level. See Fig. 14-14. Accessing error codes is different for each car model. Consult the individual service manual. The following is a typical method of initiating a computer self-test feature:

1. Run engine until coolant temperature is 120 °F (48.9 °C).
2. Press the OFF and DEFROST buttons at the same time. Then, push the AUTO button within two seconds to display the error codes. Write down each error code as it appears. Then, refer to the appropriate service manual for the error code chart to determine the malfunctioning component or circuit.
3. If the screen display remains blank for more than 20 seconds, the self-test feature is not detecting the malfunction. The technician must proceed with diagnostics using the appropriate car service manual.
4. Normal operation of the automatic temperature control system is terminated until the self-test is exited. Exit the self-test feature by depressing the COOLER button.

SUMMARY

The automatic temperature control system automatically heats or cools the passenger compartment to maintain the selected temperature. The position of the temperature blend-air door determines the temperature inside the passenger compartment. The programmer constantly adjusts the temperature blend-air door to maintain the desired temperature.

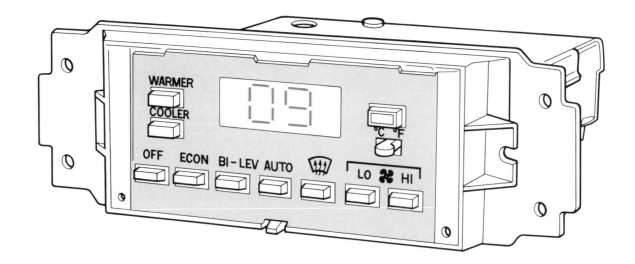

ERROR CODE KEY

ERROR CODE	DETECTED CONDITION	TROUBLESHOOTING/REPAIR PROCEDURES
01	Blend actuator out of position[3]	• Refer to "Blend Door Actuator Diagnosis"
02	Floor/Panel actuator out of position	• Refer to "Floor/Panel Door Actuator Diagnosis"
03	Pan/Def actuator out of position	• Refer to "Panel/Defrost Door Actuator Diagnosis"
04	Outside Air/Recirc actuator out of position	• Refer to "Outside Air/Recirc Door Actuator Diagnosis"
05	Blend actuator over current[3]	• Refer to "Blend Door Actuator Diagnosis"
06	Floor/Panel actuator over current	• Refer to "Floor/Panel Door Actuator Diagnosis"
07	Pan/Def actuator over current	• Refer to "Panel/Defrost Door Actuator Diagnosis"
08	Outside Air/Recirc actuator over current	• Refer to "Outside Air/Recirc Door Actuator Diagnosis"
09	No failures found in Self-Test. See "Diagnosis When Self-Test Indicates No Errors Found"	
10	If it appears with any other code, ignore it. If it appears alone, it is the same as 88.	
11	Clutch signal low	• Refer to "Clutch Signal Low Diagnosis"
12	Sensor string open[1]	• Refer to "Sensor Diagnosis"
13	Sensor string shorted[2]	• Refer to "Sensor Diagnosis"
14	Control head defective	• Replace control head
15	Blower signal shorted to B+	• Refer to "Blower Always Off Diagnosis"
88	No failures found in Self-Test. See "Diagnosis When Self-Test Indicates No Errors Found"	

[1] If car interior is very cold this error code (12) may appear in Self-Test.
[2] If car interior is very hot this error code (13) may appear in Self-Test.
[3] If a 1 or 5 appears in conjunction with any other codes, follow troubleshooting for 1 or 5 codes first.

Fig. 14-13. Error codes. A—Error codes are displayed after performing access sequence. B—Look up error codes in service manual. This gives the technician a starting point of the area that should be checked to find the problem. (Ford)

DIAGNOSIS WHEN SELF-TEST AND FUNCTIONAL TEST DO NOT IDENTIFY A PROBLEM AND ITS POSSIBLE SOURCE

Refer to the chart which follows for symptoms, their possible cause, and the test or repair procedures required.

DIAGNOSIS WHEN SELF-TEST INDICATES NO ERRORS FOUND

CONDITION	POSSIBLE SOURCE	ACTION
Cool discharge air when system is set to Auto 90° F.	Heater system malfunction	▶ Check coolant level.
	Blend door not in max heat	▶ Check thermostat.
		▶ Test per Blend Door Actuator Diagnosis (Assume that 2 was displayed in the Self-test.)
Warm discharge air in Auto 60° F.	Clutch circuit malfunction	▶ Test clutch circuit per No Clutch Operation Diagnosis
	Check refrigerant	▶ Refer to Section 2.
	Blend door not in max. A/C position	▶ Check position of blend door
		Check shaft attachment
		▶ Test per Blend Door Actuator Diagnosis (Assume 2 was displayed in the Self-Test).
	Outside Recirc door not in recirc	▶ Test per Vacuum System Diagnosis
Cool air in 85° F. max. heat in 90° F.	Sensor shorted	▶ Troubleshoot according to Sensor Diagnosis
Heat in 65° F. max. cool in 60° F.	Sensor open	▶ Troubleshoot according to Sensor Diagnosis
No blower	Faulty CELO switch wiring	▶ Test per No Blower Section of Bloweer Speed Controller and Heat Blower Relay Diagnosis
	Faulty blower controller	
	Faulty high blower relay	
	Faulty control assembly	
	Faulty blower motor	
	Faulty wiring	
High blower only	Faulty control assembly	▶ Test per High Blower Only Section of Blower Speed Controller and High Blower Relay Diagnosis
	Faulty high blower relay	
	Faulty blower controller	
	Faulty wiring	
Clutch is on in off function	Faulty control assembly	▶ Test according to Clutch does not Disengage when in off function
	Faulty wiring or interface components	

Fig. 14-14. Self-test feature does not detect problems with all areas affecting temperature control. Procedure gives possible problem areas to check when a problem exists and no error codes are flashed.

DIAGNOSIS WHEN SELF-TEST INDICATES NO ERRORS FOUND (Continued)

CONDITION	POSSIBLE SOURCE		ACTION
Control assembly digits and LCD do not light up.	Fuse	▶	Replace fuse
	Ignition Circuit No. 298 open Ignition Circuit No. 797 open	▶	Check Circuit No. 298 Check Circuit No. 797
	Ground Circuit No. 57A open		Check Circuit No. 57A
	Faulty control assembly		Change control assembly
Cold air is delivered during heating when engine is cold	Damaged wiring	▶	Place system at 90° F. Auto With ignition OFF. (ignition must be OFF when grounding Circuit No. 244 for valid results) ground Circuit No. 244 at engine temp. switch. Start vehicle if blower is off, replace cold engine lockout (CELO). If blower is on, check wiring. If OK, replace control assembly.
	Damaged or inoperative engine temp. switch	▶	Replace engine temperature switch
Temp set point does not repeat after turning OFF ignition	Circuit No. 797 not connected to control assembly	▶	Remove control assembly connector. With ignition OFF, check for 12 volts at Pin 12 (Driver's side connector VA)
	Damaged or inoperative control assembly	▶	If no voltage, check fuse wiring. If voltage, replace control assembly
The control assembly temperature display will not switch from Fahrenheit to Centigrade when the EM trip computer button is pushed.	Damaged or inoperative wiring, trip minder, or control assembly	▶	CAUTION: ACCIDENTAL SHORTING OF THE WRONG PIN COULD DESTROY THE CONTROL ASSEMBLY. Short Pin 20 of connector VA (Circuit No. 506) to ground. Turn ON ignition. If display does not switch, from F to C, Circuit No. 506 is open at the control assembly and the control assembly is damaged. Otherwise check the wiring and the trip minder.
System does not control temperature	Sensor hose not connected to aspirator or sensor	▶	Inspect and service
	Aspirator not secured to evaporator case	▶	Inspect and service
	Sensor seal(s) missing or not installed properly	▶	Inspect and service
	Aspirator or sensor hose blocked with foreign material or kinked	▶	Inspect and service
	Damaged aspirator hose	▶	Inspect and service

Fig. 14-14. Continued.

The similarities between the manual and semiautomatic system are that both systems must have the mode, blower fan speed, and initial temperature selection manually adjusted. When the temperature is set on the semiautomatic temperature control system, the programmer automatically and constantly adjusts the position of the temperature blend-air door. The programmer contains a compensator, vacuum motor, vacuum checking relay, and linkage.

The fully and semiautomatic temperature control systems have programmers that automatically adjust the position of the temperature blend-air door. The programmer on the semiautomatic temperature control system uses a vacuum motor to position the temperature blend-air door. A fully-automatic temperature control system uses a computer that controls the programmer based on data from the various sensors. The programmer contains an electric motor to adjust the temperature blend-air door position and solenoids that regulate vacuum to the vacuum-operated mode doors. In addition, the computer has a self-diagnostic feature to analyze some of its system problems.

Programmers found on some computerized automatic temperature control systems do not have solenoids regulating vacuum to the vacuum-operated mode doors. The programmer contains only an electric motor that controls the position of the temperature blend-air door. These systems use a separate electric motor, controlled by the computer, for each mode door.

KNOW THESE TERMS

Manually-controlled heating and air conditioning system, Semiautomatic temperature control system, Fully-automatic temperature control system, Programmer, Compensator, Vacuum checking relay, Digital microprocessor, Blower motor control module. Cold engine lockout, Ambient temperature sensor, In-car temperature sensor, Aspirator, Sunload sensor, Error code.

REVIEW QUESTIONS—CHAPTER 14

1. The sunload sensor:
   a. Displays ambient temperature.
   b. Cycles the compressor clutch.
   c. Compensates for the greenhouse effect.
   d. All of the above.
2. The self-test feature, found on computerized automatic temperature control systems, pinpoints the specific problem. True or false?
3. The aspirator:
   a. Directs airflow past the in-car temperature sensor.
   b. Cycles the compressor clutch.
   c. Controls the evaporator pressure.
   d. Both a and b.
4. What are the similarities and differences between a fully and semiautomatic temperature control system?
5. Explain the operation of a fully-automatic temperature control system.
6. Explain the operation of a semiautomatic temperature control system.
7. Explain the differences between the two programmers that can be found on a fully-automatic temperature control system.
8. What is the relationship between the compensator and the in-car temperature sensor?
9. Current fully-automatic temperature control systems are noncomputerized. True or false?

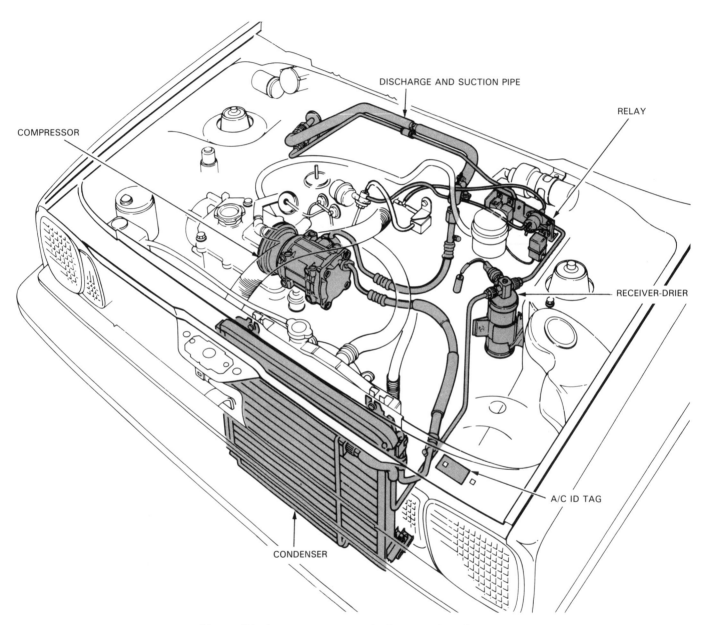

DISCHARGE AND SUCTION PIPE

RELAY

COMPRESSOR

RECEIVER-DRIER

A/C ID TAG

CONDENSER

Air conditioning components to be inspected.   (Subaru)

15 SYSTEM INSPECTION

After studying this chapter, you will be able to:
- *Describe the causes for insufficient cooling.*
- *Troubleshoot the A/C vacuum circuit.*
- *List the causes for insufficient heater output.*
- *Give examples of A/C electrical problems.*

INSPECTION

Inspection is an important first step in determining and defining the problem. Causes of many air conditioning problems can be seen or felt by the mechanic.

Start by listening to the owner explain the problem, to obtain clues on where to begin. Start the car and attempt to operate the air conditioning through all modes to evaluate system performance.

INITIAL INSPECTION

Feel the airflow temperature at the outlets while switching between heat and air conditioning modes,

Fig. 15-1. The passenger compartment should be at least 20 °F (11.1 °C) cooler than the ambient temperature when the MAX A/C mode is selected. If hot air blows out of the A/C registers, the compressor may not be engaged, the refrigerant level is low, or the temperature blend-air door is not working properly.

If the A/C mode is selected and hot air blows, check that the A/C clutch is engaged. If it is, check the refrigerant level at the sight glass. If the A/C system does not use a sight glass, feel the A/C lines for a temperature differential or attach manifold gauges.

INSUFFICIENT COOLING

Since some A/C systems do not have a sight glass to check the refrigerant level, feel the A/C lines. The high-pressure side should feel hot to the touch, while the low-pressure side should feel cold, Fig. 15-2. If the temperature differential of the A/C lines does not exist, it may be due to a low refrigerant level or a defective part.

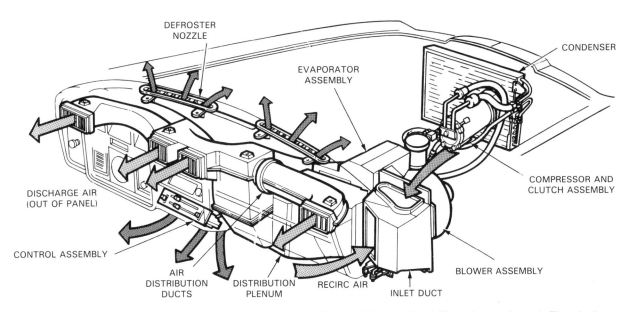

Fig. 15-1. The air that comes out the dash registers should be cold when the A/C mode is selected. The air that comes out the floor and defroster registers should be hot when the heater or defrost mode is selected. (Ford)

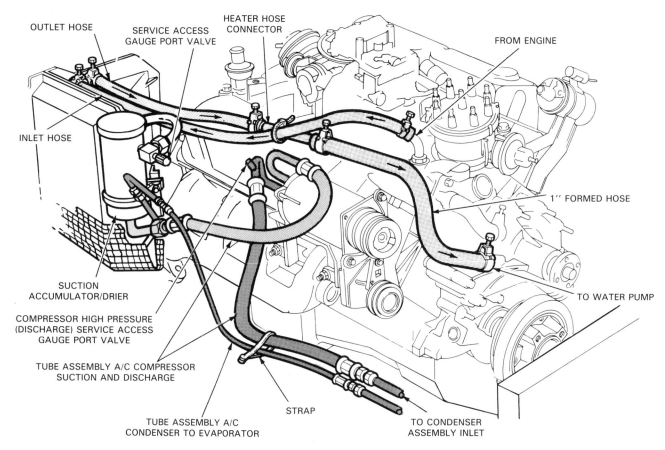

Fig. 15-2. The high-pressure side should be hot to the touch. The low-pressure side should be cold to the touch. (Ford)

Condenser

Visually inspect the condenser for debris in the fins (for example, bugs and/or leaves) or if any fins are bent. This restricts the airflow through the condenser (and radiator) and prevents the heat from dissipating. This causes A/C system pressures to increase. The cooling effect inside the passenger compartment is reduced. Engine overheating may also result. Remove all debris from between the fins. Straighten any bent fins. If the condenser is okay, attach the manifold-gauge set. See Chapter 16, Performance Testing.

A/C leak

A low refrigerant level indicates a leak. Visually inspect the refrigerant hoses, lines, compressor, and condenser for oil smudges. Oil often leaks out with the refrigerant. After a period of time, dirt accumulates and combines with the refrigerant oil. This forms the oil smudge, a mudlike substance.

If the A/C system is completely empty of refrigerant, it is necessary to add refrigerant first. Then, leak test the A/C system. Leakage of one-half ounce of refrigerant per year from the A/C system is considered normal.

Leak testing

Verification of refrigerant leaks requires the use of a leak detector, preferably an electronic one, Fig. 15-3. This type of leak detector is the most accurate. Move the probe under the line connections, Fig. 15-4, since refrigerant is heavier than air. To check the evaporator, turn on the A/C and blower. Insert the probe in the

register. When a leak is detected, this device will increase its rate of clicking, emit a loud sound, or flash a light.

All air conditioning leak testing must be done with the engine turned off. Leak test the high-pressure side immediately after turning the engine off, while pressure remains high. Check the low-pressure side for leaks after the engine has been shut off for several minutes. This allows a pressure build up in the low-pressure side making leak detection easier. If A/C pressures are normal, the problem may be the temperature blend-air door is not working.

Temperature blend-air door

The *temperature blend-air door,* Fig. 15-5, directs all, none, or a portion of the airflow through the heater core. The *temperature blend-air door position* determines the portion of airflow that is heated. The temperature blend-air door can be controlled by an electric motor, vacuum motor, or a cable. Manual systems use a cable. If the cable breaks or binds, the passenger compartment temperature cannot be controlled. A broken cable prevents the temperature blend-air door position from changing when the temperature control lever is readjusted. Replace the broken or binding cable.

Water control valve

The *water control valve* (when used), Fig. 15-6, prevents hot coolant from entering the heater core when the MAX A/C mode is selected. This helps reduce the heat load inside the passenger compartment when max-

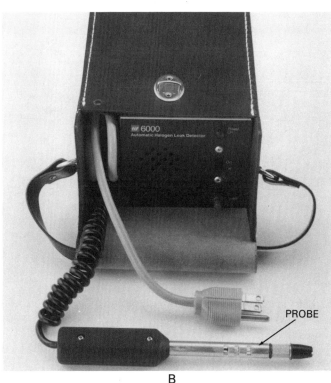

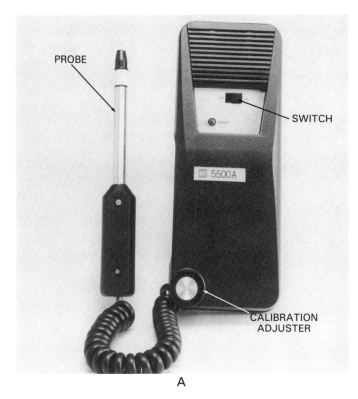

Fig. 15-3. Electronic leak detectors. A—Battery powered unit. B—Household or 115 V AC powered unit (TIF)

imum cooling is needed. Observe the opening and closing of the water control valve if it has external linkage. If the water control valve is suspect, squeeze closed the inlet heater hose. Insert a thermometer in the center dash

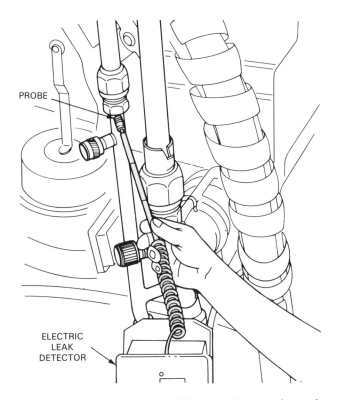

Fig. 15-4. Place probe under A/C lines and connections when checking for leaks. (Ford)

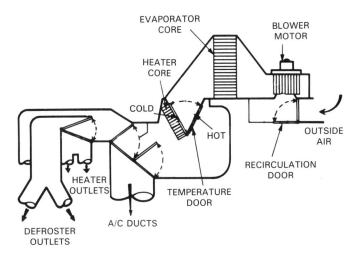

Fig. 15-5. The temperature blend-air door directs the airflow through the heater core. The recirculation door blocks outside air from entering heater/evaporator case when the MAX A/C mode is selected. (Oldsmobile)

register. With the MAX A/C mode selected, roll up all windows and place the blower on high speed. If the temperature at the center dash register decreases about 5 °F (2.8 °C) after five minutes, the water control valve is defective.

Recirculation door

The *recirculation door* blocks ambient airflow from entering the heater/evaporator case when the MAX A/C mode is selected, Fig. 15-5. The air from the passenger compartment is recirculated through the evaporator core.

171

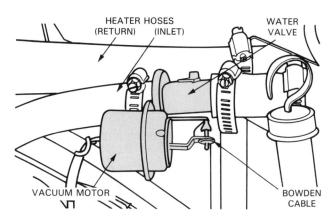

Fig. 15-6. Water control valve. If it is defective, hot coolant can enter heater core during MAX A/C. A defective valve may also prevent the hot coolant from entering heater core when the heat or defrost mode is selected. (Buick)

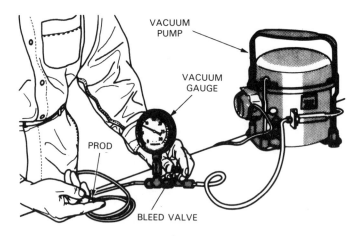

Fig. 15-8. Turn vacuum pump on. Place finger over vacuum hose end or prod. Adjust bleed valve to obtain desired vacuum gauge reading. (Chrysler)

Check that the recirculation door closes or blocks outside air when in the MAX A/C mode. The recirculation door can bind or its motor may be defective.

A/C VACUUM CIRCUITS

Airflow that is discharged out of the incorrect register may indicate a problem with the vacuum circuit. Inspect the routing of vacuum hoses to make sure they are away from light bulbs and other sources of heat. The heat may melt the vacuum hoses, causing them to leak, Fig. 15-7.

Listen for a ''whistling'' or ''hissing'' noise, which indicates a vacuum leak. *Vacuum* is less than atmospheric pressure. Therefore, a *vacuum leak* allows atmospheric pressure into the vacuum circuit. This reduces or eliminates the vacuum. Without a pressure differential, vacuum-operated devices do not work.

A/C vacuum circuit testing

Checking the vacuum circuit for leaks requires use of a vacuum pump and an in-line gauge, Fig. 15-8. Remove vacuum hose connector plug from the control head and insert vacuum prod into each line at the plug, Fig. 15-9.

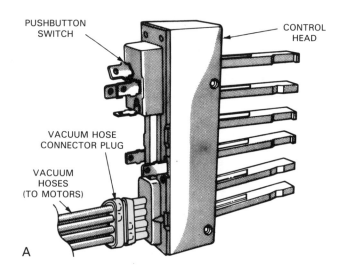

A

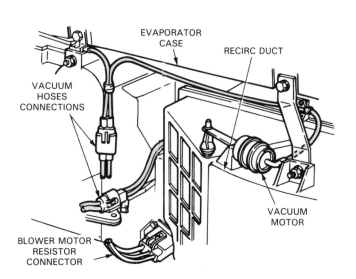

Fig. 15-7. Vacuum hoses and connections can be a source of vacuum leaks. (Ford)

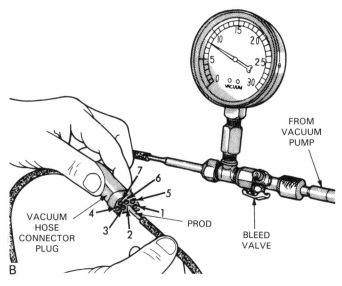

B

Fig. 15-9. Troubleshootoing A/C vacuum circuits. A—Remove the vacuum hose connector plug from control head. B—Insert prod into each vacuum hose, one at a time, at connector plug end. Note vacuum gauge reading after inserting prod into each line. Vacuum should hold. If not, a leak exists in the line or its motor is defective. (Chrysler)

Note amount vacuum drops after inserting prod into each line. If vacuum drops more than specified, a leak exists in the vacuum line, its connections, or vacuum motor.

To determine if a vacuum motor or the lines are at fault, remove the vacuum line from its motor. Connect the vacuum line from vacuum pump to each vacuum motor, one at a time, Fig. 15-10. If the vacuum motors hold a steady vacuum, the leak is in the vacuum line or its connections. If vacuum leaks are not found and the mode doors still do not respond, the vacuum valve in the control head is probably at fault. Replace or repair the control head. A binding mode door has the same effect.

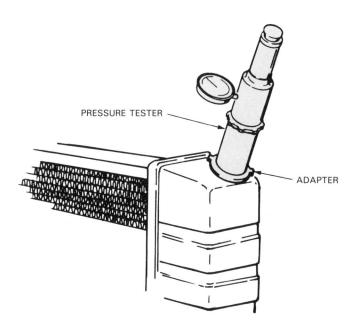

Fig. 15-11. Pressure test the cooling system to locate leaks. Do not overpressurize the cooling system. (Harrison Radiator)

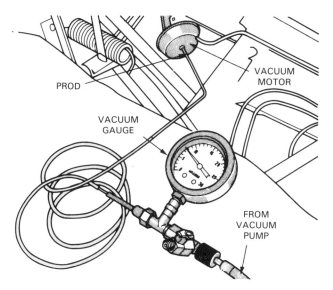

Fig. 15-10. If vacuum did not hold, remove vacuum line from its motor. Insert prod in vacuum motor fitting. If vacuum still does not hold, the vacuum motor is leaking. Replace the vacuum motor. However, if vacuum holds, the vacuum line from the control head is leaking. Trace the individual vacuum line until leak is found, Make the needed repairs. (Chrysler)

Thermostat

The thermostat, Fig. 15-12, may be the cause of no passenger compartment heat. An upper radiator hose that is not hot to the touch indicates a:
1. Thermostat stuck open.
2. Thermostat removed.
3. Low temperature thermostat.

Heater core

If the thermostat is not the cause, the problem may be an internally plugged heater core or a defective water

INSUFFICIENT HEATER OUTPUT

The heater is needed to heat the ambient airflow to the passenger compartment. Insert a thermometer in the floor register. The temperature at this register should be at least 144 °F (62.2 °C) at an ambient temperature of 60 °F (15.5 °C). Always check the temperature reference chart in the appropriate service manual. Insufficient heater output can be caused by many things.

Coolant mixture/level

The recommended coolant mixture is 50 percent ethylene glycol and 50 percent water. Excessive ethylene glycol solutions contribute to insufficient heater output, because of the reduced heat transfer characteristics.

A low coolant level also can cause insufficient heater output. A low coolant level allows air in the cooling system. Air cannot retain and transfer heat as effectively as a liquid. A low coolant level may indicate the cooling system is leaking. Check the cooling system for leaks with a pressure tester, Fig. 15-11.

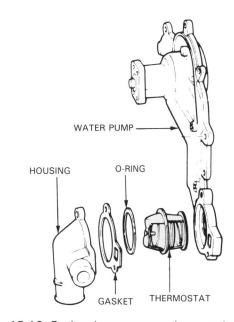

Fig. 15-12. Engine thermostat regulates coolant flow to the radiator. An engine thermostat is rated according to its opening temperature. If it sticks in the open position, overcooling will result. If it sticks in the closed position, the engine will overheat. (Harrison Radiator)

control valve. If the heater inlet hose (between the water control valve and heater core) is hot and the heater return hose is cooler, the heater core is internally plugged, Fig. 15-13. The heater core may have leaves and other debris collect against or in its fins. This is an external restriction that prevents the airflow from going through the heater core, Fig. 15-14.

Water control valve

The heater inlet hose after the water valve should be hot, except during the MAX A/C mode. If the heater inlet hose (between the water control valve and the heater core) is not hot, the water control valve is not opening, Fig. 15-6. This prevents the hot coolant from entering the heater core.

Temperature blend-air door cable

The cable may break, kink, or become disconnected. As a result, the temperature blend-air door position cannot be adjusted. Control of heat output is lost. Replace the broken or binding (kinked) cable. Reattach a disconnected cable.

A/C ELECTRICAL SYSTEM

This section deals with the testing of the electrical systems as it applies to the A/C clutch. The *compressor*

Fig. 15-14. Digital display multimeter. (TIF)

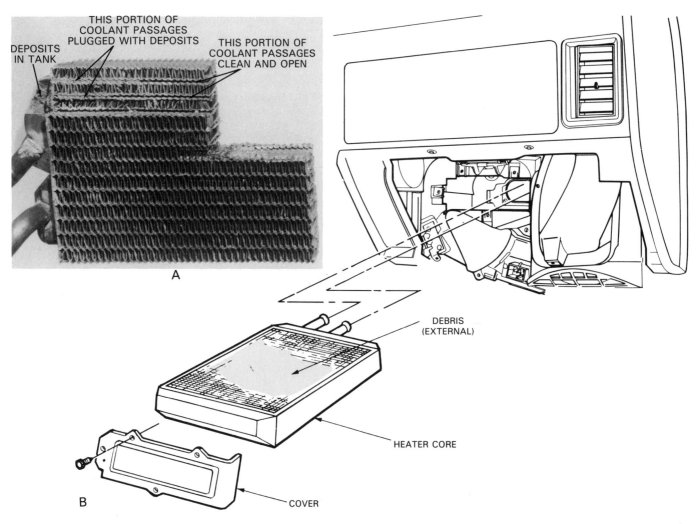

Fig. 15-13. Plugged heat core. A—Cutaway view of an internally plugged heater core. Deposits restrict coolant flow through its tubes. B—Externally plugged heat core. Leaves and debris restrict the airflow through its fins.   (Ford)

clutch is an electrically-controlled device. When the air conditioner is turned on and the clutch does not engage, the problem could be:

1. An open circuit.
   a. Blown thermal limiter/fuse.
   b. Electrical connection disconnected.
   c. Pressure cut-out switch open.
   d. A/C clutch relay defect.
2. A defective control head.
3. A short circuit.
4. An open or shorted clutch coil.

A/C electrical testing

A *multimeter,* Fig. 15-14, combines the function of a voltmeter, ammeter, and ohmmeter. It is used to measure resistance, voltage or current flow. Some displays have digital readings, while others have an analog. A multimeter with 10 megohms impedance must be used to prevent possible damage to the computer.

Check that battery voltage is present at the electrical leads to the clutch coil. If not, track down the circuit until the cause (an open or short circuit) is found. If battery voltage is present and clutch remains inoperative, disconnect the electrical leads from the clutch coil. Check the continuity against specifications in the service manual, Fig. 15-15.

OTHER INSPECTIONS

The following checks may or may not directly affect the passenger compartment temperature. However, they are suggestions that can prevent other problems that have a negative effect on the heating and A/C system.

Check the tension of the fan drive belts. In the example shown, Fig. 15-16, the belts deflect one-half inch

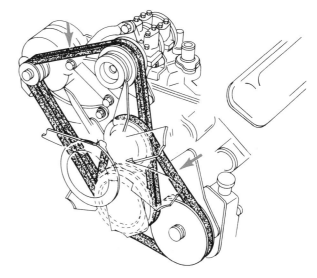

Fig. 15-16. Arrows indicate where to depress belt when checking its tension. Belt should have some play, but not more than one-half inch.   (Chrysler)

midpoint between the top two pulleys. If the fan belts are not tight enough, the belts will slip and the engine fan speed will be too slow at idle. This could cause the engine to overheat and raise A/C pressures. The drive belts should also be checked for unusual wear, Fig. 15-17. Pulley misalignment also causes premature belt wear. Any defect should be corrected.

Check the radiator and heater hose condition, Fig. 15-18. Rubber hoses used on automotive applications are generally constructed of oil, chemical, and heat resistant material. Excessive amounts of these substances can speed deterioration of the hoses. Replacement of

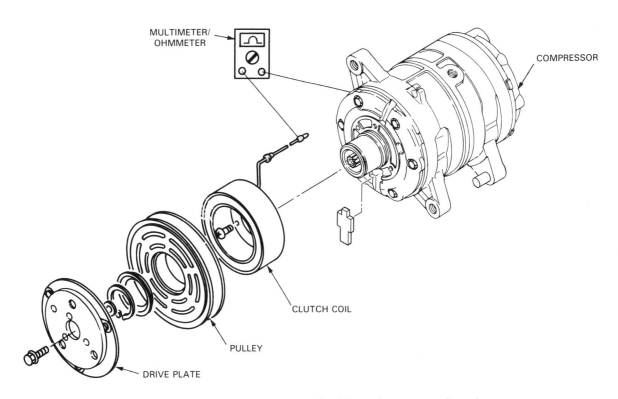

Fig. 15-15. Check resistance of clutch coil with an ohmmeter.   (Isuzu)

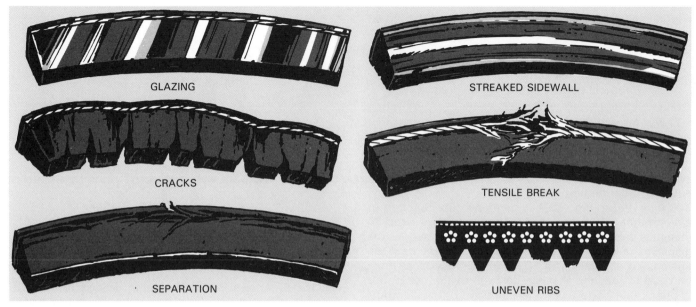

Fig. 15-17. Abnormal belt conditions. Glazing is caused by a slipping belt. Small cracks at irregular intervals indicate belt replacement. Deep cracks at regular intervals indicate a pulley that is too small. Belt separation is caused by oil or grease contamination. Streaked sidewall is caused by sand or other abrasives between the belt and pulley. Tensile break can be due to forcing the belt over the pulley. Uneven rib wear is due to foreign objects in the sprocket. (Gates Rubber Co.)

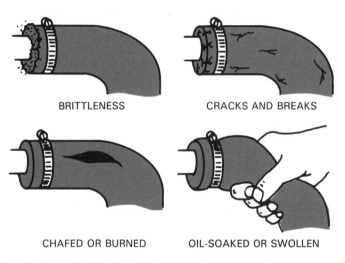

Fig. 15-18. Check all coolant-carrying hoses for abnormal conditions.

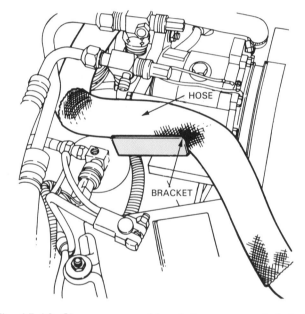

Fig. 15-19. Sharp corners of bracket can wear a hole in the hose. (American Motors)

damaged hoses prevents the possible loss of coolant. Prevent the hoses from contacting hot manifolds and sharp edges, Fig. 15-19.

SUMMARY

Inspection and basic testing of an air conditioning system requires the technicians natural senses (visual, hearing, and touch). Less than a 20 °F (11.1 °C) difference between ambient and passenger compartment temperature may indicate a problem with the A/C system. Check the clutch operation, refrigerant level, A/C system pressures, and vacuum circuit operation.

The high-pressure side should feel hot. The low-pressure side should feel cooler. Check that the condenser fins are not restricting the airflow. If the condenser is not a problem and temperature differential between the low and high-pressure side is not evident, connect the manifold-gauge set. If the A/C system pressure are fine, the temperature blend-air door may not be working. A defective water control valve or recirculation mode door causes insufficient cooling when the MAX A/C mode is selected.

Insufficient heater output can be caused by a low coolant level. This may be due to a leak. Insufficient heater output can also be caused by the incorrect solution of ethylene glycol. A defective thermostat may also cause low heater output. An internally plugged heater core or defective water control valve prevents the hot engine coolant from heating the heater core. An externally plugged heater core reduces or could prevent airflow through the heater core, resulting in little or no heat.

The compressor clutch is an electrically-controlled device. It should engage the compressor when the air conditioner is turned on. If it does not, the coil may be defective or an open circuit in one of its controls.

The tension of the fan belt should be checked and corrected. The condition of the fan belt, radiator hoses, and heater hoses should be inspected for unusual wear. These items can affect the engine cooling and passenger compartment heating operation. Replace any worn belts, hoses, or pulleys.

KNOW THESE TERMS

Temperature blend-air door, Temperature blend-air door position, Water control valve, Recirculation door, Vacuum, Vacuum leak, Compressor clutch, Multimeter.

REVIEW QUESTIONS—CHAPTER 15

1. Briefly explain how to leak-test the A/C system.
2. The clutch does not engage the compressor when the A/C mode is selected.
   Mechanic A states the control head may be defective.
   Mechanic B states the thermal limiter may be blown or the low-pressure cut-out switch is open.
   Who is right?
   a. Mechanic A.
   b. Mechanic B.
   c. Both Mechanics A and B.
   d. Neither Mechanic A nor B.
3. What amount of refrigerant leakage is considered normal?
4. Briefly explain how to troubleshoot the vacuum circuit.
5. The MAX A/C mode is selected. However, the passenger compartment remains warm. The A/C system pressures are normal.
   Mechanic A states the temperature blend-air door cable may be broken.
   Mechanic B states the recirculation mode door is not working.
   Who is right?
   a. Mechanic A.
   b. Mechanic B.
   c. Both Mechanics A and B.
   d. Neither Mechanic A nor B.
6. List five causes for insufficient heater output.
7. Mechanic A states that bugs caught between the condenser's fins can cause reduced A/C performance.
   Mechanic B states that bent condenser fins reduce A/C performance.
   Who is right?
   a. Mechanic A.
   b. Mechanic B.
   c. Both Mechanics A and B.
   d. Neither Mechanic A nor B.
8. Where does an inspection start?
   a. Under the hood.
   b. Feeling the temperature of the A/C hoses.
   c. Checking the temperature at the A/C outlets.
   d. Listening to the owner's explanation of the problem.
9. If hot air blows when the A/C mode is selected, the technician should:
   a. Check that the A/C clutch is engaged.
   b. Check the refrigerant level.
   c. Check the temperature blend-air door operation.
   d. All of the above until problem is found.
10. Define what is meant by vacuum leak and how it affects vacuum-operated devices.

RELATIVE HUMIDITY (%)	AMBIENT AIR TEMP		LOW SIDE PSIG	ENGINE SPEED (rpm)	CENTER DUCT AIR TEMPERATURE		HIGH SIDE PSIG
	°F	°C			°F	°C	
20	70	21	29	2000	40	4	150
	80	27	29		44	7	190
	90	32	30		48	9	245
	100	38	31		57	14	305
30	70	21	29	2000	42	6	150
	80	27	30		47	8	205
	90	32	31		51	11	265
	100	38	32		61	16	325
40	70	21	29	2000	45	7	165
	80	27	30		49	9	215
	90	32	32		55	13	280
	100	38	39		65	18	345
50	70	21	30	2000	47	8	180
	80	27	32		53	12	235
	90	32	34		59	15	295
	100	38	40		69	21	350
60	70	21	30	2000	48	9	180
	80	27	33		56	13	240
	90	32	36		63	17	300
	100	38	43		73	23	360
70	70	21	30	2000	50	10	185
	80	27	34		58	14	245
	90	32	38		65	18	305
	100	38	44		75	24	365
80	70	21	30	2000	50	10	190
	80	27	34		59	15	250
	90	32	39		67	19	310
90	70	21	30	2000	50	10	200
	80	27	36		62	17	265
	90	32	42		71	22	330

Fig. 16-1. Temperature at center register varies, depending on humidity. Should ambient temperature be 90 °F (32.2 °C), discharge air temperature will vary from 48 °F (8.9 °C) to 71 °F (21.7 °C), depending on humidity. Note that humidity also affects high- and low-side pressures. (Ford)

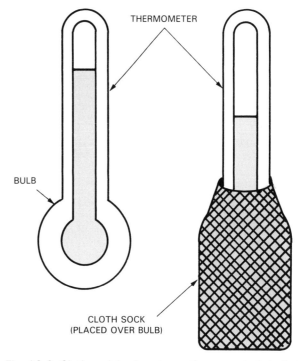

16 PERFORMANCE TESTING

After studying this chapter, you will be able to:
- Explain the purpose of an A/C system performance test.
- Describe the basic parts of a manifold-gauge set.
- Troubleshoot A/C system problems with pressure gauge readings.

PERFORMANCE TESTING

A *performance test* determines if the discharge air temperature (center register of dash) is correct based on the humidity and ambient temperature. A performance test also includes checking the low- and high-side pressures of the A/C system. An air conditioning system requires a performance test to determine if and where a problem exists. Specifications, which can be found in the appropriate service manual, vary depending on the year, make, and model.

PRELIMINARY INSPECTION

Always confirm the customer's complaint of no or insufficient cooling. The customer may feel that a problem exists when it is a normal condition. The first check should determine the discharge air temperature at the center register with the windows rolled up. Once the complaint is found to be valid, make a visual inspection under the hood. Do this before connecting any gauges. This eliminates wasted time. Problems such as a loose A/C drive belt can be corrected in the amount of time it takes to connect the manifold-gauge set and take the readings.

HUMIDITY

Humidity is the amount of moisture in the air. It is an important factor when determining if the A/C system is working properly. A customer may complain the passenger compartment is not cool enough on a hot, humid day. The technician, after checking the discharge air temperature at the center register, determines the A/C system is working properly. Explain to the customer how temperature and humidity affects the performance of the A/C system, Fig. 16-1.

Measuring humidity

Determining relative humidity requires the use of a psychrometer, which uses a cloth sock placed over the thermometer's bulb, Fig. 16-2. The evaporation causes

THERMOMETER

BULB

CLOTH SOCK
(PLACED OVER BULB)

Fig. 16-2. Cloth sock is placed over thermometer's bulb. Cloth sock is then moistened with water. Swing thermometer back and forth for several minutes. The wet bulb reading should be less than the dry bulb reading, unless humidity is 100 percent.

a temperature reduction. The reduction depends on the humidity. Observe the wet bulb reading. Unless humidity is at 100 percent, the wet bulb reading will be lower than the dry bulb reading. The less humidity, the greater the temperature reduction.

Reading humidity

To find the approximate relative humidity, a special graph is needed, Fig. 16-3. Interpreting the dry and wet bulb reading requires very little plotting on the graph. From the wet bulb reading, make a horizontal dashed line. The curved lines represent the percent of relative humidity.

The curved line nearest the point of intersection of the dashed line and the dry bulb reading determines the relative humidity. For example, a wet bulb reading is taken and it is 70°F (21°C). A horizontal dashed line is placed on the graph from the wet bulb mark at 70. Suppose the ambient temperature (dry bulb reading) is

105°F (40.5°C). The closest curved line to where the dashed line and dry bulb reading intersect is 30 percent, which is the relative humidity, Fig. 16-3. However, if the wet bulb reading is 70°F (21°C) and the dry bulb reading is 80°F (26.6°C), the curved line nearest the point of intersection is 70 percent.

NOTE: Direct-reading humidity gauges are available. However, they lack the accuracy of a psychrometer.

MANIFOLD GAUGES

Air conditioning or *manifold gauges* usually consist of a high-pressure gauge (right side), and a low-pressure gauge (left side), connected to a manifold, Fig. 16-4. The *high-pressure gauge* is read clockwise and registers from 0 to 500 psi. The *low-pressure gauge,* a compound gauge, measures both pressure and vacuum. The low-pressure gauge is read clockwise from 0 to 250 psi. The vacuum scale is read counterclockwise from 0 to 30 in. Hg. Service hoses connect the manifold gauges to the A/C service valves of the car.

> CAUTION: The A/C system contains refrigerant under high pressure. Refrigerant can cause frostbite. Make sure you take preventive measures when testing the A/C system. Also, take the necessary precautions when the engine is running.

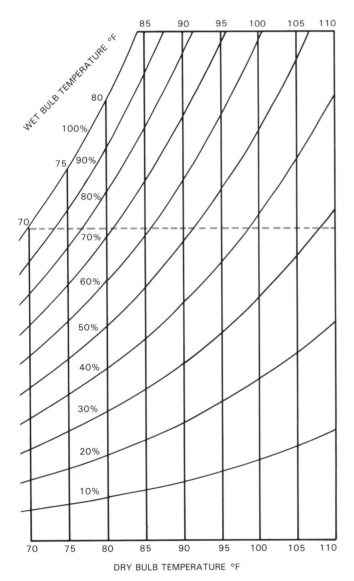

Fig. 16-3. Place a horizontal dashed line on graph from wet bulb reading. Where horizontal dashed line intersects with vertical line of dry bulb or ambient temperature determines the relative humidity.

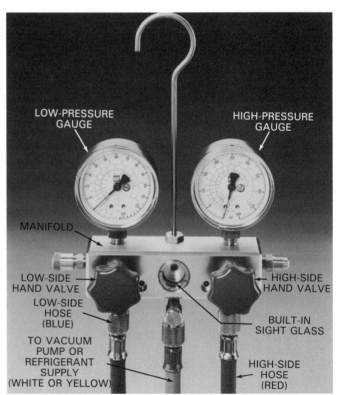

Fig. 16-4. Manifold connects high- and low-pressure gauges. Each gauge has its own service hose that connects at the manifold. The center service hose is used to discharge, charge, and evacuate the A/C system. Note the three inner scales, R-12, R-22, R-502, of both gauges. These scales determine the temperature, in Fahrenheit, of the refrigerant used at a specific pressure.   (TIF Instruments)

Service hoses

The blue service hose connects the manifold gauge to the accumulator or another point on the low-pressure side of the A/C system, Fig. 16-5A. The red service hose connects the manifold gauge to the compressor outlet line or another point on the high-pressure side of the A/C system, Fig. 16-5A. The coupler at the end of each A/C service hose screws on the service valve. When a Schrader valve is used, the depressor pin pushes on the valve, Fig. 16-5B. This allows pressurized refrigerant from the A/C system to the gauges, Fig. 16-6. The center (white or yellow) service hose attached to the manifold assembly is used during the discharging, evacuation, and charging process.

Discharging is the removal of refrigerant from the A/C system. *Evacuation* is the removal of air and moisture from the A/C system with the use of a vacuum pump. *Charging* is the addition of refrigerant to the A/C system. The center service hose connects to a supply of refrigerant when charging or a vacuum pump during evacuation. When discharging the A/C system, refrigerant exits through the center service hose. This hose serves no purpose in performance testing.

Purging

When connecting the gauges, a small amount of air can be trapped within the service hoses. This can cause false gauge readings. *Purging* is the process of removing the air from the service hoses. This is a necessary step. Use the following sequence:

1. Loosen the low-side service hose at the Schrader valve.
2. Open the high-pressure hand valve one turn.
3. Crack open the low-pressure hand valve for three seconds (until refrigerant "hisses" from the low-

pressure hose).
4. Then, close both high- and low-pressure hand valves and retighten the low-pressure service hose at the Schrader valve.

Manifold hand valves

The *manifold hand valves* control the flow of refrigerant (or vacuum) in and out of the auto A/C system. The hand valves, when closed, isolate the center service hose. The low-side hand valve is opened when the A/C system is discharged, charged, or evacuated, Fig. 16-7. The low-side hand valve remains closed when performance testing the system. The high-side hand valve usually remains closed, regardless of the function.

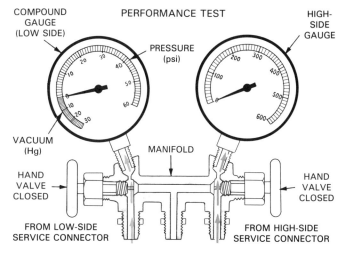

Fig. 16-6. When the hand valves are closed, the pressurized refrigerant is routed to only the gauges. (John Deere)

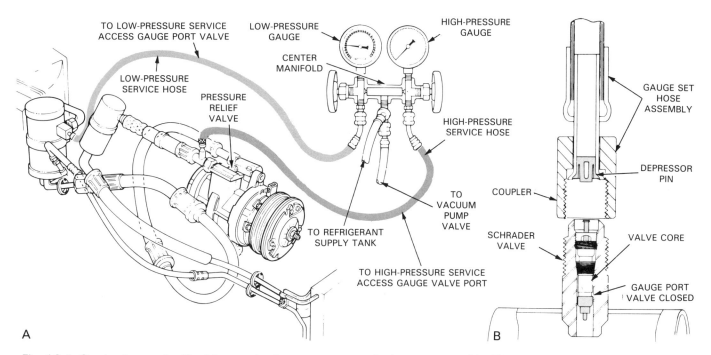

Fig. 16-5. Service hoses. A—The blue service hose connects to the low-pressure side. The red service hose connects to the high-pressure side. B—The depressor pin, inside the coupler, depresses the valve core once the coupler is tightly screwed on the Schrader valve. This allows some of the pressurized refrigerant to its gauge. (Ford)

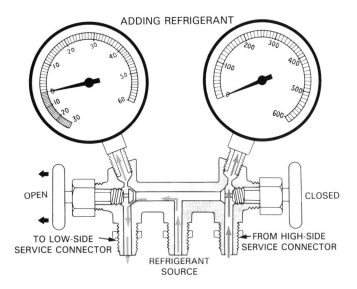

Fig. 16-7. Charging the A/C system. Open the low-side hand valve. Pressurized refrigerant is routed through manifold to A/C system and gauges.

Third gauge

An extra low-pressure gauge, Fig. 16-8, is required for testing Chrysler systems that use an evaporator pressure regulator (EPR) or evaporator temperature regulator (ETR) valve. This gauge measures the pressure drop across the evaporator control valve. The auxiliary low-pressure gauge is connected by a service hose to the compressor inlet fitting. This gauge does not have a hand valve since it is not connected to the manifold.

STATIC PRESSURE

A *static pressure check* determines if the A/C system contains enough refrigerant for a performance test. This check is performed before starting the engine. The high-

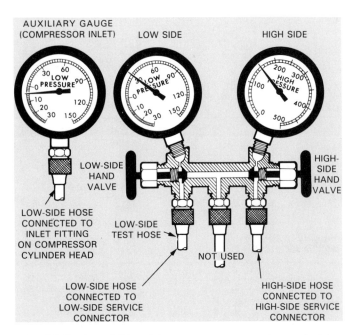

Fig. 16-8. An additional low-pressure gauge is needed for diagnosis on cars that use an EPR or ETR valve.

and low-side pressure gauges will read about the same.

Generally, static pressure below 50 psi at an ambient temperature of 70 °F (21.1 °C) indicates the system is probably very low in refrigerant. Add refrigerant to the A/C system before proceeding with the performance test. However, if static pressure is above 50 psi under these conditions, refrigerant supply is adequate for a performance test.

NOTE: Static pressure check does not mean the A/C system contains the correct refrigerant charge. It only means the A/C system has an adequate amount of refrigerant needed for testing.

OVERCHARGED SYSTEM

Some manifold-gauge sets also have a built-in sight glass, Fig. 16-4. This is handy if the A/C system does not have a sight glass. Disconnecting the A/C clutch, once it has been engaged, can show if the system has an excessive or proper refrigerant charge.

Foaming that appears in the sight glass in less than 45 seconds after disconnecting the A/C clutch indicates the system is properly charged. However, if foaming appears after 45 seconds, the A/C system is overcharged with refrigerant.

STABILIZING THE SYSTEM

The system must be stabilized before accurate pressure tests can be made. To stabilize the system, proceed as follows:

1. Set parking brake.
2. Start engine. Operate at fast idle (2000 rpm).
3. Keep hood open and close all car windows.
4. Operate A/C system at maximum cooling with blower on high.
5. Run engine approximately 10 minutes before taking gauge readings. For best results, place a high-volume fan in front of radiator grille. This ensures an adequate supply of airflow across the condenser and substitutes for ram air.
6. Read high- and low-pressure gauges. Compare readings to the normal range of operating pressures in the service manual, Fig. 16-1. Pressure readings that fall outside the normal operating range indicate a malfunction in the A/C system.

PRESSURE GAUGE READINGS

This section explains the use of a manifold-gauge set as a diagnostic instrument. When an A/C system will not pass a performance test, further testing is required for an accurate diagnosis.

The pressure gauge readings vary with A/C system design. This is best shown in the chart in Fig. 16-9. It shows approximate test pressure ranges for a variety of A/C system designs. Always use the appropriate service manual.

Interpreting gauge readings

The majority of air conditioning complaints are complete lack of cooling, insufficient cooling, or intermittent cooling. Diagnosis of a problem relies on a correct interpretation of the manifold gauge readings.

NOTE: Gauge readings can indicate any one of several different malfunctions. One example of an abnormal

			AT LOW PRESSURE TEST FITTING (P.S.I.)			
Ambient (Outside Air) Temperature	***At High Pressure Test Fitting (P.S.I.)**	**S.T.V., P.O.A. or V.I.R. Systems**	****Cycling Clutch System with T.X.V. and Rec.-Dehyd.**	****Cycling Clutch System with Expansion (Orifice) Tubes and Accumulator (C.C.O.T.)**	**CCOT System with Pressure Cycling Switch**	**Chrysler Corp. with Evaporator Pressure Regulator Valve**
60°F.	120-170	28-31	7-15	—	—	—
70°F.	150-250	28-31	7-15	24-31	24-31	22-30
80°F.	180-275	28-31	7-15	24-31	24-31	22-37
90°F.	200-310	28-31	7-15	24-32	24-31	25-37
100°F.	230-330	28-35	10-30	24-32	24-36	—
110°F.	270-360	28-38	10-35	24-32	—	—

APPROXIMATE TEST PRESSURE RANGES FOR NORMAL FUNCTIONING SYSTEMS

*Pressures may be slightly higher on very humid days or lower on very dry days.

**Pressure just before clutch disengages (cycles off).

Fig. 16-9. Air conditioning system pressures vary. Look in the specific service manual. (GMC)

pressure gauge reading is when the high side is higher than specified and the low side is also higher than specified (high side "high" and low side "high"). In this example, 10 different possible malfunctions are listed. Therefore, the gauge reading by itself does not always pinpoint the problem. Further testing and checks must be done to isolate the cause for many problems.

High side "normal" and low side "normal"

The pointer falls within the normal (colored) range on the high- and low-side pressure gauges, Fig. 16-10. When pressures are normal and cooling is insufficient, check for:

1. Defective water control valve.
2. Malfunctioning temperature blend-air door.
3. Air in refrigerant system.
4. Moisture in refrigerant system. This will cycle between both gauges reading normal and both gauges reading low.
5. Recirculation door not closed when MAX A/C mode is selected.

High side "high" and low side "high"

The pointer is above the normal (colored) range on the high- and low-pressure gauges, Fig. 16-11A. This indicates the following should be checked:

1. Engine cooling system overheating.
2. Restrictions in condenser airflow.
3. Internal restriction in condenser.
4. Refrigerant overcharge.
5. A/C drive belts slipping.

NOTE: Problems 1 through 5 may create excessively high pressures between 300-400 psi on the high side.

6. Expansion valve thermostatic bulb not properly insulated or incorrectly mounted.

7. Large amounts of air in system.
8. Oil overcharge.
9. Expansion valve stuck open.
10. POA valve defective.

NOTE: Determine if the expansion valve is at fault first. Remove the expansion valve capillary tube from the evaporator outlet line. Place the capillary tube in ice water, Fig. 16-11B. On Chrysler products that use the expansion "H" valve, spray the control head with refrigerant, Fig. 16-11C. Pressure should now drop to between 21-25 psi on the low-side gauge. Should

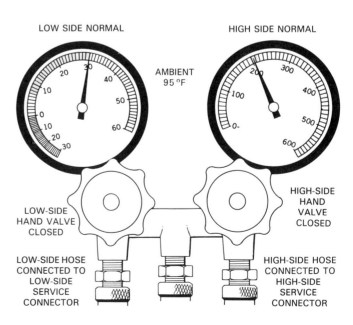

Fig. 16-10. Low- and high-side gauges show normal pressure.

183

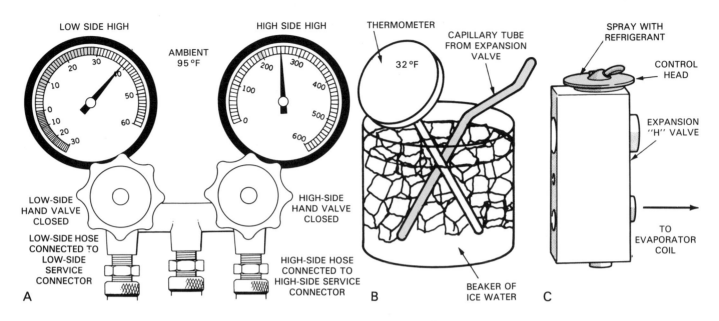

Fig. 16-11. A—High- and low-side gauges are both higher than normal. B—Close the expansion valve by placing its capillary tube in ice water. Pressure should drop on the low side, indicating expansion valve has closed. C—On Chrysler products that use the expansion "H" valve, spray refrigerant on the control head.

pressure fail to drop to at least 25 psi, the expansion valve is stuck open.

High side "low" and low side "low"

The pointer on the high- and low-pressure gauges drops below the normal (colored) pressure range, Fig. 16-12A. This indicates:

1. Low refrigerant charge.
2. Moisture in system.
3. Expansion valve inlet screen clogged.

NOTE: Heavy sweating or frost on expansion valve inlet indicates a plugged inlet screen (restriction). Make the needed repairs.

4. Expansion valve stuck closed.
5. Capillary tube damaged.
6. Orifice tube in Clutch Cycling Orifice Tube (CCOT) system plugged. Outlet side of orifice tube warmer than normal. Replace the orifice tube.
7. POA valve defective.
8. Defective compressor cycling switch causes short "on" time of clutch engagement, Fig. 16-12B.
9. Refrigerant flow through receiver-drier obstructed.

NOTE: Check the operation of the expansion valve first. Remove capillary tube from evaporator outlet. Place capillary tube in ice water, Fig. 16-11B. On Chrysler products with the expansion "H" valve, spray the control head with refrigerant for 15 seconds, Fig. 16-11C. Pressure should decrease on the low-side gauge.

Remove capillary tube from ice water or stop spraying "H" valve with refrigerant. Low-side pressure should increase as the cooling effect wears off. Should low-side pressure fail to increase, the expansion valve is stuck closed and must be replaced.

A/C systems that cycle the clutch can experience rapid cycling (on and off) of the clutch. This can be another cause of high side "low" and low side "low" gauge readings. The conditions that cause rapid clutch cycling are shown in Fig. 16-12C.

High side "low" and low side "high"

The pointer on the high-side gauge is below the normal (colored) range. The pointer on the low-side gauge is above the normal (colored) range, Fig. 16-13. This indicates:

1. An internal compressor leak.
2. Compressor reed valves broken.
3. A blown compressor head gasket.
4. Excessively worn pistons, cylinders, and/or rings.

NOTE: This reading could also be caused by an improperly adjusted thermostatic switch or poor contact between sensing bulb and evaporator. Correcting the adjustment and/or improving the bulb contact could bring gauge readings back to normal. This should be checked and corrected before proceeding with any work on the compressor.

Rule of thumb

Many experienced technicians use the following general guidelines for diagnosis. Low side "low" usually means low refrigerant charge, plugged expansion valve, or a restriction in the high side. Low side "high" usually means an open expansion valve, poor contact between sensing bulb and evaporator line, or evaporator valve (EPR, ETR, POA, or STV valve) stuck closed. High side "low" usually means low refrigerant or a compressor related problem. High side "high" usually means a refrigerant overcharge, restricted airflow through condenser, internal restriction in condenser, or overheated engine cooling system.

THE CHRYSLER EPR SYSTEM

Checking the operation of the EPR valve requires an additional low-pressure gauge. Connect this third gauge to the compressor inlet Schrader valve, Fig. 16-14. Pressure should register 17 psi or less, but not a vacuum, Fig. 16-15. Engine rpm should be 1750 during testing. The low-side gauge should register between 21-25 psi.

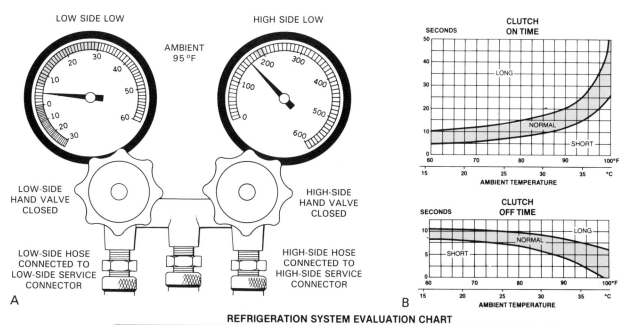

REFRIGERATION SYSTEM EVALUATION CHART

Clutch Cycle Frequency			Gauge Pressures		Probable Causes
Rate	On Time	Off Time	High Side	Low Side	
—	—	Always OFF	—	—	• Clutch circuit OPEN or switch or relay malfunction • Blown fuse (short) • Clutch malfunction • Refrigerant charge very low
—	Always ON①	—	Normal to High	Normal to High	• Ambient temperature/humidity very high
—	Always ON①	—	Normal	Normal	• Compressor clutch seized
—	Always ON①	—	Normal to Low	Low	• Cycling switch—sticking closed
—	Always ON①	—	Low	High	• Suction line—restricted
Slow	Long	Short	High	Normal to High	• Condenser—Inadequate airflow
			High	Normal	• Air in refrigerant • Refrigerant overcharge
			Normal to High	Normal to High	• Humidity very high
			Normal	Normal	• Moisture in refrigerant • Excessive compressor oil in system
			Low	High	• Compressor performance subnormal
Slow	Short	Long	Normal to Low	Normal	• Evaporator airflow subnormal
Normal to Slow	Long	Short	Low	High	• Orifice tube not installed or O-ring seal leaking
Normal to Slow	Normal to Long	Normal	Normal	Low	• Clutch cycling switch-low setting
Normal to Slow	Normal	Normal to Long	Normal	High	• Clutch cycling switch-high setting
Fast	Short	Normal	Normal	Normal	• Liquid line or orifice tube partially restricted • Condenser partically restricted
Fast	Short	Normal to Short	Normal to Low	Normal	• Evaporator core—partically restricted • Suction line—partially restricted
Fast	Short to Very Short	Short to Very Short	Normal to Low	Normal	• Refrigerant charge low
Fast	Very Short	Long	Normal to Low	Normal	• Liquid line or orifice tube serverely restricted
			Normal to Low	Normal	• Condenser severely restricted
			Low	Normal	• Evaporator core severely restricted
Very Fast	Very Short	Very Short	Low	Normal	• Clutch cycling switch—range to close
	ERRATIC		—	—	• Clutch cycling switch—dirty contacts or sticking open

①SYSTEM MAY RUN CONTINUOUSLY AT AMBIENT TEMPERATURES ABOVE 95°F

ADDITIONAL POSSIBLE CAUSE COMPONENTS
ASSOCIATED WITH INADEQUATE COMPRESSOR OPERATION

• COMPRESSOR CLUTCH Slipping • LOOSE DRIVE BELT
• CLUTCH COIL Open—Shorted, or Loose Mounting
• CONTROL ASSEMBLY SWITCH—Dirty Contacts or Sticking Open
• CLUTCH WIRING CIRCUIT—High Resistance, Open or Blown Fuse

ADDITIONAL POSSIBLE CAUSE COMPONENTS
ASSOCIATED WITH A DAMAGED COMPRESSOR

• CLUTCH CYCLING SWITCH—Sticking Closed or Compressor Clutch Seized
• SUCTION ACCUMULATOR/DRIER—Refrigerant Oil Bleed Hole Plugged
• REFRIGERANT LEAKS

Fig. 16-12. A—High- and low-side gauges are both lower than normal. B—Graphs show normal amount of time clutch remains on and off for specific ambient temperatures. C—Chart shows causes for slow and faster than normal clutch cycling time. (Ford)

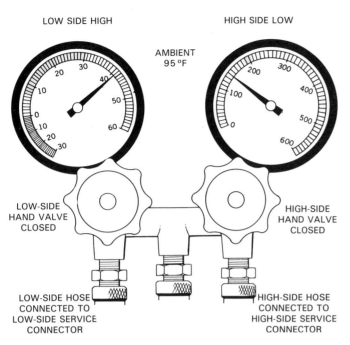

Fig. 16-13. Low-side gauge registers higher than normal pressure. High-side gauge registers lower than normal pressure.

VARIABLE DISPLACEMENT COMPRESSOR PERFORMANCE TEST

A performance test on an A/C system with a variable displacement compressor requires the use of a graph, Fig. 16-16. The high- and low-side pressure readings should intersect within the white area of the graph.

High- and low-side pressures that intersect in the gray area indicate a refrigerant overcharge or a restriction in the high side. A refrigerant overcharge is indicated if the liquid line between the condenser and orifice tube is

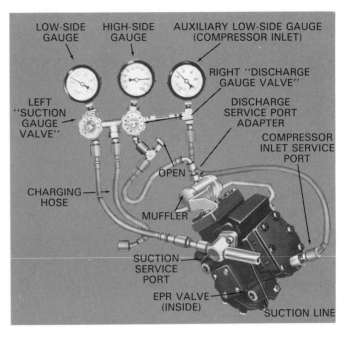

Fig. 16-14. On Chrysler products that use an EPR or ETR valve, the low-side service hose connects to Schrader valve at compressor inlet line. High-side service hose connects to Schrader valve on muffler. Additional low-pressure service hose connects to Schrader valve on compressor's cylinder head. (Chrysler)

warm to the touch. However, a restriction in the high side is indicated if the same line is cold.

Low- and high-side pressures within 30 psi that intersect in the striped area of the graph indicate a defective compressor, compressor stuck in low mode, plugged orifice tube, insufficient refrigerant charge, or a defective control valve. First, determine if the compressor is only stuck in the low mode by trying to free it up. This

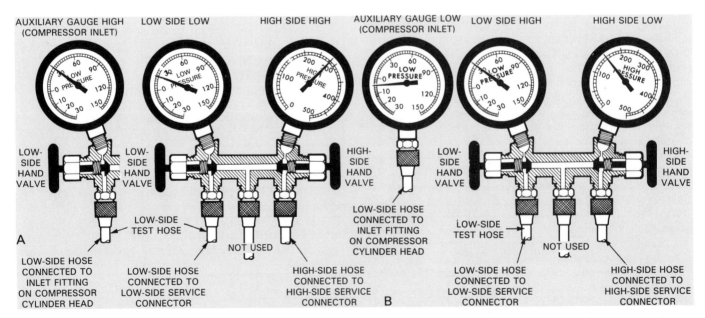

Fig. 16-15. A—When high-side and additional low-side gauges register higher than normal and low-pressure gauge registers lower than normal, the EPR valve is stuck open. B—When high-side and additional low-side gauges register lower than normal and low-side gauge registers higher than normal, EPR valve is stuck closed. When EPR valve is stuck open or closed, discharge the A/C system. Remove EPR valve from the compressor inlet and replace it with a new one.

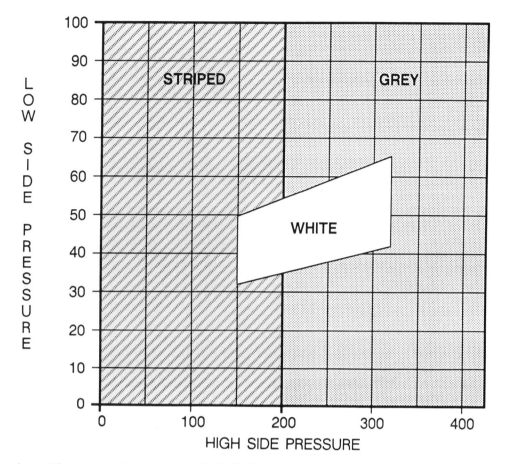

Fig. 16-16. Graph used for systems that employ variable displacement compressor. High- and low-side pressures that intersect in white area of graph indicate normal pressures. (Oldsmobile)

requires all car windows closed, temperature lever at full cold, blower motor on high speed, hood raised, and engine running at 3000 rpm. Cycle the mode lever from vent to air conditioning every 20 seconds for three minutes.

High- and low-side pressures remaining the same after three minutes of cycling the mode lever may indicate another problem. Turn the engine and A/C system off. Make sure the clutch is disengaged. Attempt to turn the A/C clutch plate, not the pulley, by hand (no wrench). A clutch plate that can be easily turned, by hand, indicates a defective compressor. Discharge the A/C system and replace the compressor.

Low-side pressure between 25-35 psi that intersects a high-side pressure in the striped area of the graph, Fig. 16-16, indicates another problem. This condition usually points to an insufficient refrigerant charge or a plugged orifice tube. Should inadequate cooling remain a problem after adding 14 oz. (.396 kg) of refrigerant, discharge A/C system and replace the orifice tube.

Low-side pressure outside of the 25-35 psi range may indicate a defective control valve. Stabilize the engine for five minutes at 3000 rpm. Turn the MAX A/C on at full cold with low blower speed. Make sure all windows are rolled up and the hood raised. Low-side pressure now outside the 25-35 psi range indicates the control valve is defective. Discharge the A/C system. Remove and replace the defective control valve from the compressor.

SUMMARY

There is not a uniform or standard diagnosis procedure that applies to all A/C systems. This is due to a variety of system designs and methods of operation. A/C systems operate satisfactorily when air outlet temperatures and pressure readings are within the ranges indicated on the performance charts. Discharge air temperatures that are not satisfactory indicate further testing and inspection is needed. Prior to conducting a performance test, a visual inspection should be made to save time.

A performance test requires the manifold gauges are connected to the auto A/C system and the hand valves properly adjusted. Pressure readings will vary with ambient air temperature and humidity. Stabilize the system prior to conducting the performance test. This ensures accurate pressure readings. Use diagnostic charts provided by shop manuals in conjunction with pressure gauge readings. This will determine if the system is within specifications and a malfunction exists.

KNOW THESE TERMS

Performance test, Humidity, Manifold gauges, High-pressure gauge, Low-pressure gauge, Discharging, Evacuation, Charging, Purging, Manifold hand valves, Static pressure check.

REVIEW QUESTIONS—CHAPTER 16

1. The high-side service hose is connected to the:
   a. Compressor inlet line.
   b. Accumulator.
   c. Psychrometer.
   d. Compressor outlet line.
2. Cooling the temperature sensing bulb is done to:
   a. Open the expansion valve.
   b. Start the compressor.
   c. Close the expansion valve.
   d. Lower the temperature in accumulator.
3. What is the purpose of a performance test?
4. A large fan is placed in front of the radiator during performance testing. This:
   a. Stabilizes the gauge readings.
   b. Substitutes ram air.
   c. Provides ventilation in the testing area.
   d. Removes the exhaust fumes.
5. A compressor related problem is indicated by:
   a. High side "high" and low side "high."
   b. High side "low" and low side "low."
   c. High side "normal" and low side "low."
   d. High side "low" and low side "high."
6. During performance testing, the:
   a. High-side hand valve is opened; low-side hand valve closed.
   b. High- and low-side hand valves remain closed.
   c. Low-side hand valve is opened; high-side hand valve closed.
   d. High- and low-side hand valves are opened.
7. During the charging process, the:
   a. Hand valves are both closed.
   b. Hand valves are both opened.
   c. High-side hand valve is opened; low-side hand valve closed.
   d. Low-side hand valve is opened; high-side hand valve closed.
8. After installation of the manifold-gauge set and prior to testing the A/C system, it is necessary to _____ the service hose of _____.
9. A third manifold gauge is used when testing systems incorporating a/an:
   a. EPR valve.
   b. Expansion valve.
   c. Orifice tube.
   d. Variable displacement compressor.
10. An expansion valve stuck open generally causes:
    a. Noise in the compressor.
    b. High, low-side pressure.
    c. Low, low-side pressure.
    d. Bubbles in the sight glass.
11. Sweating/frosting of the high-pressure line is caused by:
    a. A restriction in the line.
    b. No cooling fan in front of radiator.
    c. Blocked airflow through condenser.
    d. System overcharged with refrigerant.
12. The manifold gauge center hose is used when:
    a. Evacuating the system.
    b. Discharging the system.
    c. Charging the system.
    d. All the above.

Match the following.

GAUGE READING	PROBLEM
13. Low-side gauge reads LOW.	a. Compressor malfunction.
14. Low-side gauge reads HIGH.	b. Overcharged system.
15. High-side gauge reads LOW.	c. Low refrigerant charge.
16. High-side gauge reads HIGH.	d. Expansion valve.

17. Which problem or problems cause insufficient cooling with normal gauge pressure readings:
    a. Faulty water control valve.
    b. Temperature blend-air door malfunction.
    c. Both a and b.
    d. Neither a nor b.
18. An internal or external condenser restriction would cause:
    a. Both gauges registering higher than normal pressures.
    b. Both gauges registering lower than normal pressures.
    c. Low-side, "high" and high-side "low."
    d. Low-side "low" and high-side "high."
19. The third gauge, when used, should register:
    a. 24 psi.
    b. 29 psi.
    c. 17 psi.
    d. 18 psi.
20. A variable displacement compressor A/C system is not cooling adquately. High- and low-side pressures are within 30 psi of each other.
    Mechanic A states the control valve is defective. Mechanic B states the compressor may be stuck in the low mode.
    Who is right?
    a. Mechanic A.
    b. Mechanic B.
    c. Both Mechanics A and B.
    d. Neither Mechanic A nor B.

17 SERVICING AIR CONDITIONING COMPRESSORS/COMPONENTS

After studying this chapter, you will be able to:
* Summarize common A/C compressor problems.
* Explain how to service common A/C compressor clutch problems.
* Describe how to service common A/C component problems.

INTRODUCTION

This chapter concentrates on the most common problems and repairs of air conditioning compressors and components. Some compressors can be rebuilt. Common practice is to replace the compressor instead of rebuilding it in the field. Some compressors, such as the R4, cannot be rebuilt due to their design. Most A/C compressor work is limited to replacement of the front seal, clutch bearing, and clutch coil assembly.

COMPRESSORS

When a clicking or knocking noise is audible after the A/C clutch engages, the bearings inside the compressor may be faulty. Internal compressor leakage is caused by worn piston rings/cylinder walls, broken reed valves, or a blown cylinder head gasket. When the compressor is unable to maintain the necessary pressures, suspect internal leakage. Insufficient compressor output, faulty bearings, or a seized compressor calls for replacement.

Compressor seizure

Compressor seizure, due to lack of lubrication, is when the compressor shaft is locked or cannot turn. A severely-burned clutch is good indication of a seized compressor. However, there is the possibility of a *false compressor seizure.* The internal parts momentarily "ring" or stick together after long periods of nonoperation. This makes the compressor appear to have seized.

To check for false seizure, attempt to rock the compressor shaft back and forth by hand. If the compressor rotates after the attempted rocking, it is a false seizure. The compressor should now be considered operational.

COMPRESSOR SHAFT SEALS

A refrigerant oil leak is indicated by an accumulation of dirt (smudge). A compressor shaft seal leak will be in the front area of the compressor and may spray oil on the underside of the hood. An accurate check can be made with an electronic leak detector. There are basically two different types of front seals used on compressors today. One type is the ceramic-seat seal, Fig. 17-1. The other type is the lip seal, Fig. 17-2.

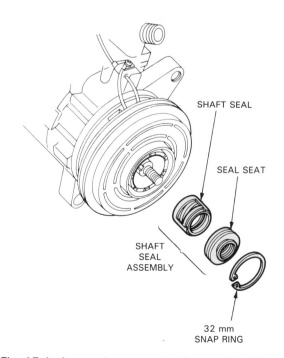

Fig. 17-1. A ceramic seat and seal assembly. (Honda)

189

Fig. 17-2. Lip seal encased by steel shell. (Oldsmobile)

Ceramic-seat seal

The *ceramic seat* provides a nonwearing surface for the seal to ride against. The spring-loaded seal rotates with the compressor shaft, Fig. 17-3. The snap ring holds the seal and ceramic seat in place.

Lip seal

The lip seal, Fig. 17-2, is similar to the type used on rotating engine shafts. The lip seal does not rotate with the shaft, it remains stationary. The lip seal does not use a ceramic seat.

COMPRESSOR SHAFT SEAL SERVICE

Leaking compressor shaft seals must be replaced. When replacing either type seal, always discharge the A/C system first. The clutch plate must first be removed, Fig. 17-4, whether replacing a leaking front seal, a bad clutch bearing, or a defective clutch coil.

Ceramic-seat seal service

With the clutch plate removed, extract the dust seal, Fig. 17-5. This allows access to the snap ring. Remove the snap ring with a pair of internal snap-ring pliers. Then, engage the lip of the ceramic seat with the seat remover/installer tool, Fig. 17-6. Pull the ceramic seat out with a twisting motion. Make sure the O-ring around the outer diameter of the ceramic seat is removed with the seat.

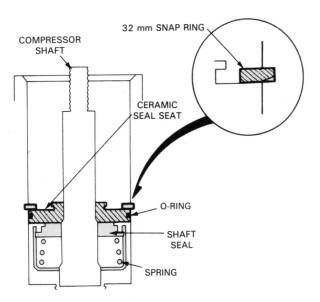

Fig. 17-3. Cross section view of ceramic seat and seal installed on compressor. (Honda)

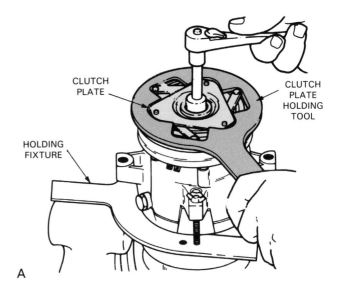

A

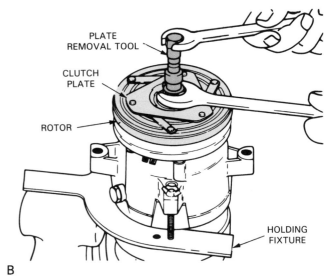

B

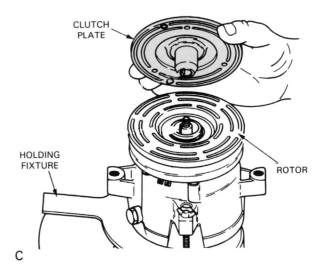

C

Fig. 17-4. Clutch plate. A—With clutch plate holding tool installed to clutch plate, the compressor shaft nut can be loosened or tightened. B—After removing the nut, a special tool is used to force the clutch plate off. After screwing removal tool in, the bottom wrench holds it stationary while the top wrench turns the tool. C—Lift off the clutch plate. (Oldsmobile)

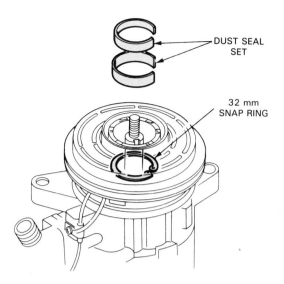

Fig. 17-5. Dust seal, which is usually made of felt, sits on top of snap ring. (Honda)

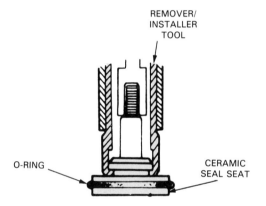

Fig. 17-6. The remover/installer tool grabs the lip of the ceramic seat. It is then pulled from the compressor. The O-ring fits around the outer diameter of the seat. The O-ring acts as a seal between the compressor and the seal seat. (Honda)

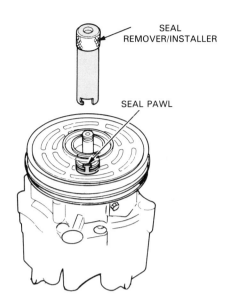

Fig. 17-7. Removing the seal requires a different special tool. Notches in the tool must engage the seal's pawls. Then, twist the tool to lock it to the seal's pawls. (Honda)

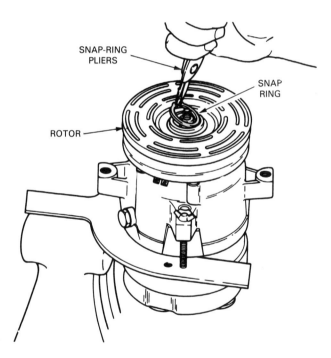

Fig. 17-8. Remove the snap ring.

If not, it will have to be removed from the compressor housing. Another special tool is needed to remove the seal.

Insert the seal remover/installer tool and, with a twisting motion, engage it with the seal pawl, Fig. 17-7. Pull the seal out. Insert a new seal on the remover/installer tool and push it in place. Install a new O-ring around the outer diameter of the ceramic seat. Make sure to lubricate the O-ring with refrigerant oil. Engage the lip of the ceramic seat with the remover/installer tool and push it in place. Reinstall the snap ring and the dust seal.

Lip seal service

With the clutch plate removed, the inner snap ring is then removed, Fig. 17-8. Insert the seal remover/installer tool into the seal. Pull the seal out with a clockwise twisting motion, Fig. 17-9.

With an awl-like tool, remove the O-ring from within the compressor, Fig. 17-10. The O-ring seals against the outer diameter of the lip seal steel shell. Make sure the

O-ring groove inside the compressor is clean. Lubricate the new O-ring with refrigerant oil and place it on the special tool. Insert the O-ring in its groove in the compressor, Fig. 17-11. Insert the new seal on the seal remover/installer tool, Fig. 17-12, and push it in place, Fig. 17-13. Reinstall the inner snap ring.

Compressor shaft seal leak test

A *compressor shaft seal leak test* determines if the compressor leaks refrigerant at the shaft seal. It should be performed after installing a new compressor shaft seal of either the lip or ceramic-seat type. Install the

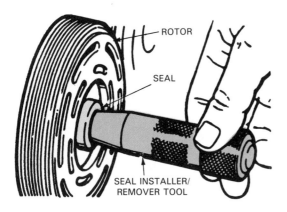

Fig. 17-9. Insert the seal remover/installer tool into the seal. Then, twist the tool while pulling the seal out. (Oldsmobile)

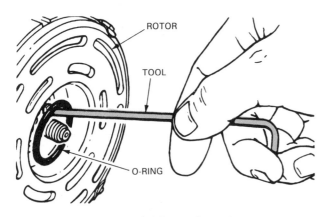

Fig. 17-10. Remove the O-ring from the compressor.

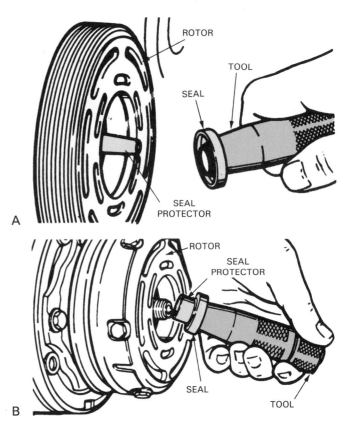

A

B

Fig. 17-12. Installing the lip-type seal. A—Insert seal protector over compressor shaft threads. Install lip seal on the special tool. B—The seal protector can be placed at the end of the special tool instead. Regardless of method selected, the seal protector prevents damage to the lip seal. (Oldsmobile)

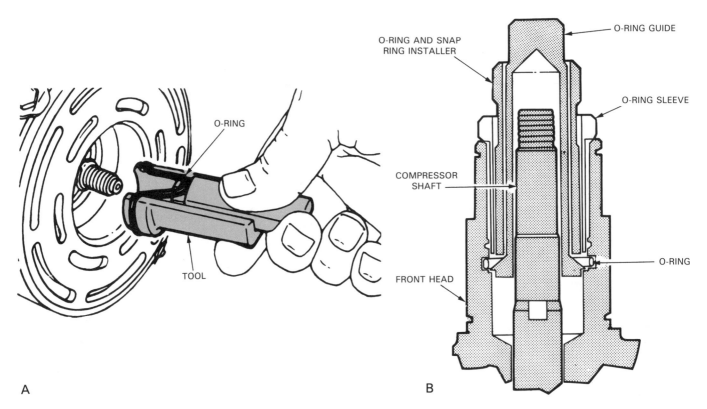

A

B

Fig. 17-11. Installing the O-ring. A—Inserting O-ring with special tool. (Oldsmobile) B—Cross-section view shows location of O-ring in its groove in compressor. (GMC)

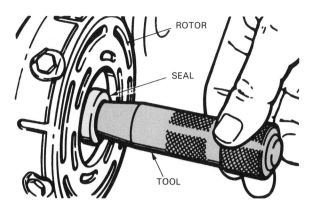

Fig. 17-13. Push the seal in place.

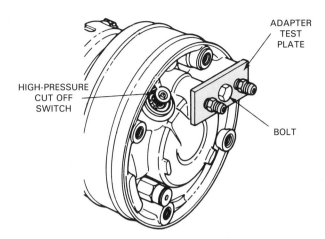

Fig. 17-14. Bolt the adapter test plate to the back of the compressor. (Oldsmobile)

adapter plate to the back of the compressor, Fig. 17-14. Connect the manifold-gauge set to the adapter plate, Fig. 17-15. Some compressors do not require the use of an adapter plate, Fig. 17-16.

Attach the center hose of the manifold-gauge set to a supply of refrigerant. Open the low- and high-pressure hand valve on the manifold-gauge set. This allows refrigerant to flow into and pressurize the compressor. Close both high- and low-side hand valves of the manifold-gauge set. Check the new seal for leaks with an electronic leak detector. Disconnect the center hose from the refrigerant supply. Open both low- and high-side hand valves of the manifold-gauge set. This will discharge the refrigerant from the compressor through the center hose of the manifold-gauge set. Reconnect the compressor to the A/C lines.

CLUTCH BEARING AND COIL

Knocking or clicking that seems to originate from the compressor area may be caused by a bad clutch bearing. This noise is most noticeable when the A/C system is off. An inoperative compressor clutch is due to a defective clutch coil or one of its controls. A blown thermal limiter or a defective/tripped high- or low-pressure cut off switch are some of the problems that can prevent the compressor clutch from operating.

The first step in checking an A/C clutch malfunction is to turn the ignition and air conditioning on. Determine if there is battery voltage at the clutch connector. Less

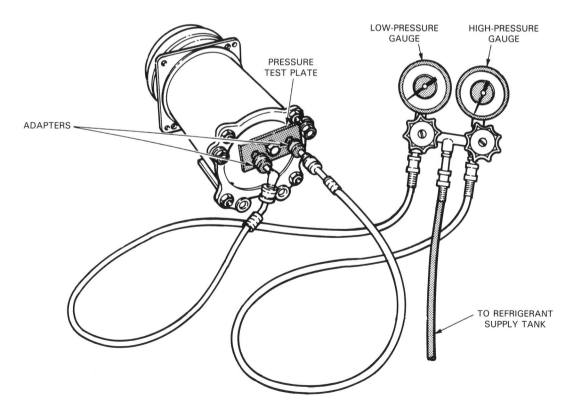

Fig. 17-15. Connect the manifold-gauge hoses to the adapter test plate. Connect the middle hose of the manifold-gauge set to a supply of refrigerant. Open the high- and low-side hand valves and, then, the refrigerant supply valve.   (Ford)

193

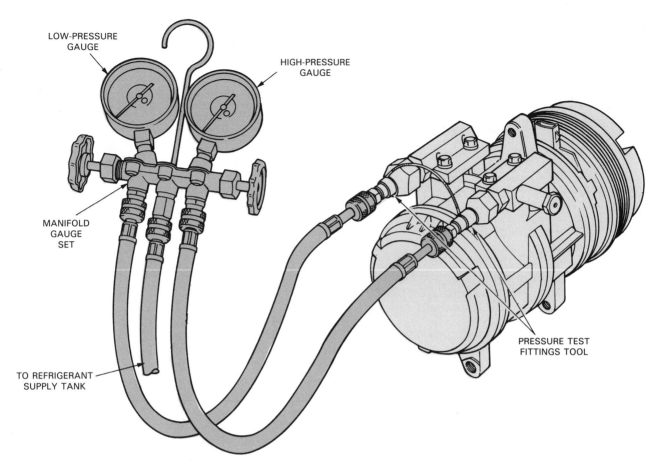

Fig. 17-16. Some compressors do not require the use of an adapter test plate. The manifold-gauge hoses screw on the Schrader service valves of the compressor. (Ford)

than 12 V indicates a weak battery or a corroded electrical connection between the battery and the A/C clutch coil. No voltage at the A/C clutch coil connection indicates an open circuit to the clutch (defective switch, disconnected wire). If battery voltage is at the electrical connector, the clutch coil must be replaced.

Clutch bearing service

Since the clutch plate has been removed, the clutch bearing can be replaced if needed. The outer snap ring is removed, Fig. 17-17. The rotor is then pulled off the compressor with a special tool, Fig. 17-18. Drive the defective bearing out of the rotor, Fig. 17-19. Flip the rotor over and press the new bearing in place, Fig. 17-20. Do not reinstall the rotor at this time.

Clutch coil service

The clutch coil can be replaced, if needed, before the rotor is reinstalled. Using a screw-type press, remove the clutch coil, Fig. 17-21. Position the new clutch coil on the compressor. Press the clutch coil in place, Fig. 17-22. Position the rotor over the clutch coil. Press the rotor in place, Fig. 17-23.

After the rotor is installed, position the clutch plate over it. Press the clutch plate in place, Fig. 17-24. Stop the screw press when a slight drag is felt on the feeler gauge, Fig. 17-25. The feeler gauge determines the air gap. The air gap is the distance between the rotor and

clutch plate. The *air gap* prevents the clutch plate from engaging the compressor when the A/C system is turned off. Install the compressor shaft nut and tighten it to

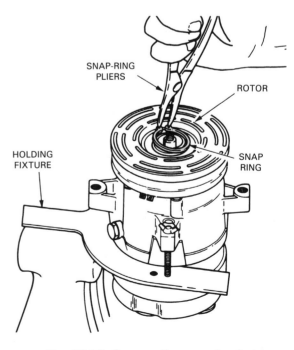

Fig. 17-17. Remove the snap ring first.

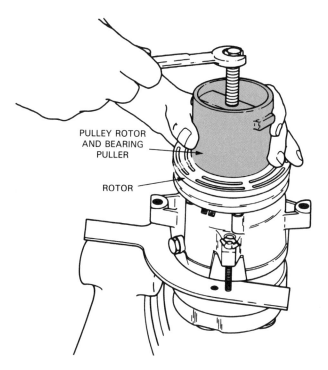

Fig. 17-18. Turn the bolt with a wrench while holding the special tool in place. This forces the rotor off the compressor. (Oldsmobile)

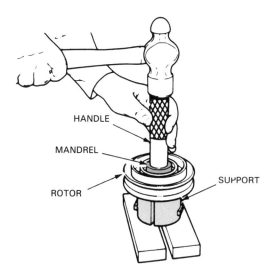

Fig. 17-19. Support the rotor face down. Position mandrel/handle and the rotor's support. Tap old clutch bearing out of the rotor.

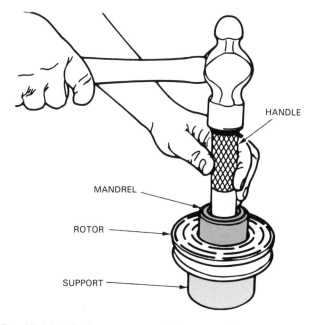

Fig. 17-20. Flip the rotor over so it faces up. Position the clutch bearing in the rotor. Tap the new clutch bearing in place with installer.

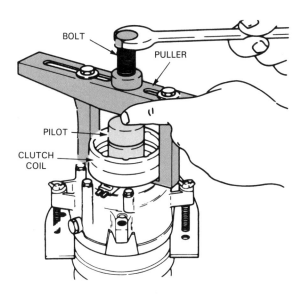

Fig. 17-21. Position the pilot and puller in place. Then, turn the bolt with a wrench while holding the puller with the other hand until the clutch coil is forced off the compressor. (Oldsmobile)

specifications once the proper air gap is obtained, Fig. 17-4A.

Other car makers control the air gap with shims, Fig. 17-26. If the air gap is not correct, the clutch plate must be pulled off and shims added or deleted to obtain the desired air gap. The clutch plate is then pressed back on and the air gap rechecked. Install the compressor shaft nut and tighten it to specifications once the proper air gap is obtained, Fig. 17-4A.

NOTE: The special tools, procedures, and specifications vary. Always consult the appropriate service manual.

A/C COMPONENT SERVICE

When an expansion valve, orifice tube, evaporator, condenser, accumulator, receiver-drier, some pressure switches, valves, or any A/C hose is replaced, the A/C system must first be discharged. This is done through the manifold-gauge set and allows the high-pressure refrigerant to be released in a safe and controlled manner. Always discharge the A/C system slowly to prevent excess loss of refrigerant oil. The A/C system does not have to be discharged when servicing a pressure switch that fits over a Schrader valve.

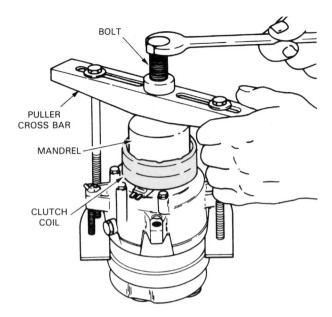

Fig. 17-22. Position the clutch coil on the compressor. Place mandrel inside clutch coil. Turn the bolt with the wrench while holding the puller with the other hand until the clutch coil is seated.

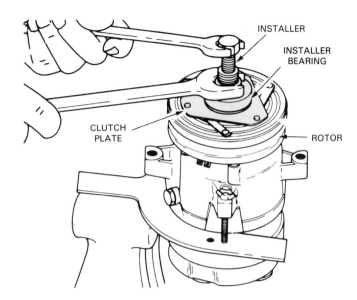

Fig. 17-24. Position the clutch plate over the rotor. Install bearing over clutch plate. Insert installer tool through the drive plate installer bearing. Hold bottom nut stationary, against the drive plate installer bearing, with a wrench. Turn the bolt with another wrench until desired air gap is obtained.

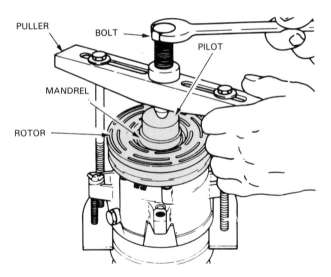

Fig. 17-23. Place rotor, pilot, and mandrel in position. Then, turn the bolt with a wrench. Hold the entire press with the other hand. Continue turning the bolt until the rotor is seated. (Oldsmobile)

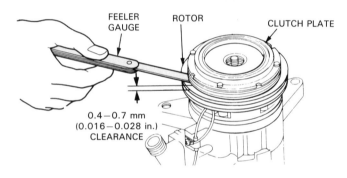

Fig. 17-25. Place feeler gauge between rotor and clutch plate to determine air gap. (Honda)

Evaporator/condenser service

Never attempt to repair a leaking condenser or evaporator by brazing, soldering, or welding. An evaporator or condenser that leaks refrigerant must be replaced with a new one.

An *internally plugged evaporator/condenser* contains debris that restricts refrigerant flow. This diminishes the transfer of heat, reducing the performance of the A/C system. The internally plugged evaporator/condenser can possibly be salvaged by flushing. *Flushing* is the removal of foreign debris with liquid refrigerant. Some evaporators, due to design, cannot effectively be flushed. When internal blockage is severe, the evaporator

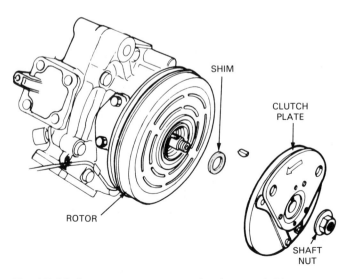

Fig. 17-26. Some compressors require the use of shims to control air gap. (Honda)

or condenser must be replaced with a new one.

An *externally plugged evaporator/condenser* often collects leaves and insects in its fins, restricting the airflow. This diminishes the transfer of heat and, therefore, reduces the performance of the A/C system. The debris can be blown out of the fins with compressed air. Bent fins may also reduce airflow through the condenser or evaporator.

NOTE: Bent fins can be straightened with a special tool.

Service valve service

There are two types of service valves. One type is the *stem service valve.* It is screwed in or out with a wrench to close or open the system. The *Schrader service valve* (similar to a tire valve) is the other type. When its core is depressed, the pressurized vapor or liquid escapes. The problem with either service valve is that they can leak.

The stem service valve is not easily serviced. Therefore, the entire assembly is usually replaced when defective. The Schrader service valve has a screw-in core. Replace only the core of a Schrader valve when defective.

NOTE: Screw-in cores used for tire and air conditioning valves are different and cannot be interchanged due to the higher operating pressures of the A/C system.

A/C line connections

The A/C line connectors attach A/C lines or components. O-rings are usually used at this connection point. This prevents the pressurized refrigerant from leaking. Age, heat, and vibrations cause the O-rings to deteriorate and leak refrigerant. When a refrigerant leak is detected at a line connection, discharge the A/C system. Disconnect the line fittings. Replace the leaking O-ring with a new one. Make sure the O-ring seat does not have a burr or dirt on it. This will cause the new O-ring to leak. Lubricate the new O-ring with clean refrigerant oil. Tighten the line fittings to specifications. Evacuate the A/C system and recharge it.

Valves-in-receiver service

All items in the valves-in-receiver (VIR) can be replaced, Fig. 17-27. Some VIR designs have a *moisture*

indicator ring visible through the sight glass. Excessive moisture is detected in the A/C system when the indicator ring turns from blue to pink.

A special tool is needed when removing either the POA or expansion valve from the VIR, Fig. 17-28. When replacing the expansion-valve capsule, and a moisture indicator is used, press the expansion valve onto the moisture indicator with your hands. Lubricate the expansion-valve capsule O-rings with clean refrigerant oil. Install the new expansion-valve capsule. The same procedure is used for the POA valve, except there is no moisture indicator ring.

A replacement POA valve may include a filter, Fig. 17-29. It protects the POA valve from foreign material circulating in the system. The filter installs over the POA capsule. The VIR inlet has a screen, Fig. 17-30. This screen should be cleaned or replaced when the VIR assembly is serviced.

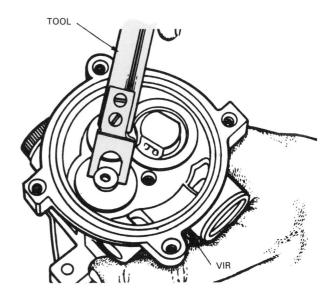

Fig. 17-28. Special tool is needed to remove either expansion or POA valve from VIR. (GMC)

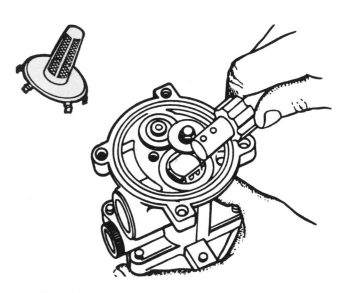

Fig. 17-29. The POA valve filter screen is not original equipment. It is found only in service kits.

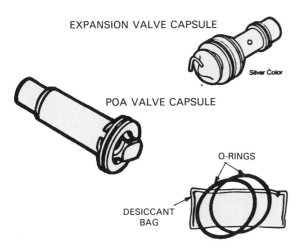

Fig. 17-27. Components found in VIR assembly. (Murray Corp.)

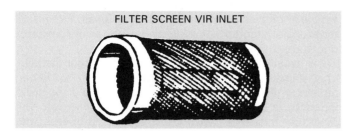

Fig. 17-30. The inlet of the VIR also has a filter screen. It should be replaced if torn. (Murray Corp.)

NOTE: The VIR assembly is removed from the car for servicing. This makes it easier to work on, due to the limited working space when it is on the car. Always replace the desiccant bag when servicing any of the other components in the VIR.

Accumulator service

An accumulator with physical damage (leaks refrigerant) or a plugged oil-bleed hole, Fig. 17-31, must be replaced. The *oil-bleed hole* regulates oil flow to the compressor. A plugged oil-bleed hole could cause insufficient compressor lubrication. This would cause the compressor to seize. If the A/C system is left open for any length of time, the accumulator must be replaced.

NOTE: After draining the refrigerant oil from the accumulator, cut the accumulator top off. Inspect the

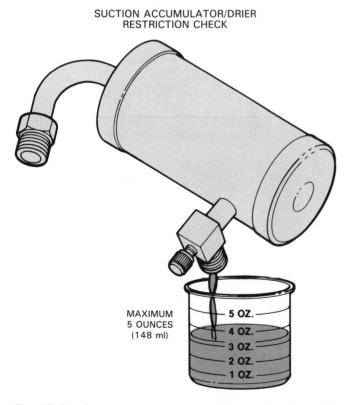

SUCTION ACCUMULATOR/DRIER
RESTRICTION CHECK

MAXIMUM
5 OUNCES
(148 ml)

5 OZ.
4 OZ.
3 OZ.
2 OZ.
1 OZ.

Fig. 17-31. Remove accumulator after discharging A/C system. Pour oil into the measuring glass. If more oil than specified is poured out of accumulator, its oil-bleed hole is plugged. This could result in poor cooling performance and/or a seized compressor. Replace the accumulator. (Ford)

dessicant bags. If they are torn, the a/c system must be flushed.

Other A/C component service

Problems with the expansion valve consist of sticking:
1. In the open position.
2. Partially open.
3. In the closed position.

The expansion valve inlet screen may also become plugged with debris. The inlet screen on an orifice tube can also become plugged or torn. Never reinstall an orifice tube once it has been removed from the A/C system.

The receiver-drier assembly can leak or become plugged. The receiver-drier becomes plugged from contamination circulating through the system. The desiccant can separate from its bag and circulate through the system, plugging orifices. A cold outlet line from the receiver-drier assembly indicates an internal restriction. Discharge the A/C system and replace the receiver-drier assembly. Evacuate and recharge the system.

SUMMARY

The most common repairs to an A/C compressor are replacing a front seal, clutch bearing, and clutch coil. A compressor may develop problems other than mentioned. When a compressor has worn pistons or rings/cylinder walls, it is not rebuilt by the technician in the field. The defective compressor is replaced with a new one. Some compressors, like the R4, cannot be rebuilt due to their design.

If the compressor has seized, try rotating the compressor shaft back and forth by hand. If the compressor shaft now turns, it was a false seizure. The internal parts momentarily "ring" or stick together. A false seizure may occur after a long period of nonoperation.

The front seal can be a lip type or ceramic-seat seal. Different special tools and procedures are required for servicing the two seal types. Whether a new seal, clutch bearing, or coil is needed, removal of the clutch is required. Always discharge the A/C system first before replacing either type of front seal. After making repairs, leak test the compressor. Check the air gap between the rotor and clutch plate when reinstalling the clutch plate.

Never attempt to repair a condenser or evaporator by welding, brazing, or soldering. Always replace a leaking evaporator or condenser with a new one. An internally plugged evaporator/condenser can usually be salvaged by flushing. An externally plugged evaporator/condenser can be cleaned with compressed air.

Service valves are of the stem or Schrader valve type. Either type service valve can leak. The entire stem-type service valve must be replaced. Only the core needs to be replaced on a Schrader-type valve.

When hose connections leak refrigerant, replace the O-ring with a new one. Lubricate the new O-ring with refrigerant oil and install. Make sure the O-ring seat does not have a burr or dirt on it or the new O-ring will also leak. Tighten the line connections to the specified torque.

Drain the oil from the accumulator when servicing the A/C system. If the amount of drained oil exceeds specifications, the oil-bleed hole in the accumulator is plugged. Replace the accumulator.

KNOW THESE TERMS

Compressor seizure, False compressor seizure, Ceramic seat, Lip seal, Compressor shaft seal leak test, Air gap, Internally plugged evaporator/condenser, Flushing, Externally plugged evaporator/condenser, Stem service valve, Schrader service valve, Moisture indicator ring, Oil-bleed hole.

REVIEW QUESTIONS—CHAPTER 17

1. Discharge the A/C system before replacing a front seal. True or false?
2. Components can be removed without discharging the A/C system if mounted on a/an:
   a. O-ring.
   b. Electronic control unit.
   c. STV valve.
   d. Schrader valve.
3. Parts that momentarily stick together after a period of nonoperation are referred to as:
   a. Brazed.
   b. Plugging.
   c. Welded.
   d. Ringing.
4. What items in the VIR are considered serviceable?
   a. Expansion tube, accumulator, and thermal limiter.
   b. Expansion valve, desiccant bag, and POA valve.
   c. Expansion tube, desiccant bag, and STV valve.
   d. Expansion valve, Schrader valve, and POA valve.
5. The condenser or evaporator can be repaired if it is leaking refrigerant. True or false?
6. What causes a compressor to seize?
7. If a line connection is leaking refrigerant, it may be corrected by:
   a. Overtorquing the line fitting slightly.
   b. Torquing the line fitting to specifications.
   c. Replacing and lubricating the O-ring.
   d. Both b and c.
8. The desiccant bag in the VIR should be changed:
   a. Whenever the A/C system is opened.
   b. Every 10,000 miles.
   c. Seasonally.
   d. Every year regardless of mileage.
9. Discharging the A/C system should be done slowly to prevent:
   a. Excessive loss of refrigerant oil.

   b. Moisture from entering the system.
   c. Seal damage.
   d. Desiccant loss.
10. Describe the two types of compressor shaft seals.
11. A clicking or knocking that originates from the compressor area is most noticeable when the A/C system is off.
    Mechanic A states the compressor bearings are bad.
    Mechanic B states the clutch bearing is bad.
    Who is right?
    a. Mechanic A.
    b. Mechanic B.
    c. Both Mechanics A and B.
    d. Neither Mechanic A nor B.
12. A clicking or knocking that originates from the compressor area is only noticeable when the A/C system is on.
    Mechanic A states the compressor bearings are bad.
    Mechanic B states the clutch bearing is bad.
    Who is right?
    a. Mechanic A.
    b. Mechanic B.
    c. Both Mechanics A and B.
    d. Neither Mechanic A nor B.
13. An inoperative compressor clutch may be caused by:
    a. A defective clutch coil.
    b. One of its controls that is defective or tripped.
    c. An electrical wiring problem.
    d. All of the above.
14. A compressor shaft seal leak test should always be performed after replacing the front seal. True or false?
15. Excessive oil in the accumulator indicates a:
    a. Leak somewhere in the A/C system.
    b. Plugged oil-bleed hole in the compressor.
    c. Plugged oil-bleed hole in the accumulator.
    d. All of the above.
16. An internally plugged evaporator/condenser may be salvaged by:
    a. Flushing it with liquid refrigerant.
    b. Blowing compressed air through its fins.
    c. Both a and b.
    d. Neither a nor b.
17. An externally plugged evaporator/condenser can be salvaged by:
    a. Flushing it with liquid refrigerant.
    b. Blowing compressed air through its fins.
    c. Both a and b.
    d. Neither a nor b.

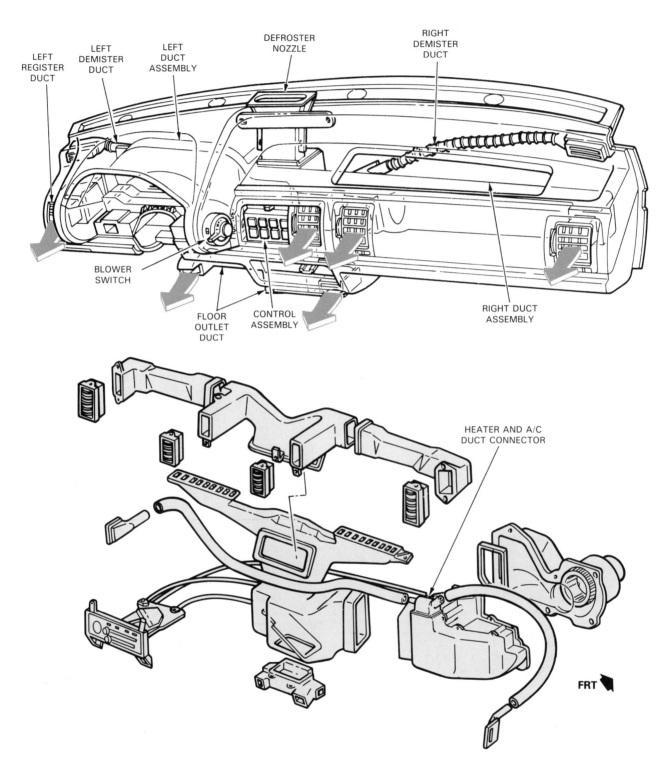

LEFT REGISTER DUCT

LEFT DEMISTER DUCT

LEFT DUCT ASSEMBLY

DEFROSTER NOZZLE

RIGHT DEMISTER DUCT

BLOWER SWITCH

FLOOR OUTLET DUCT

CONTROL ASSEMBLY

RIGHT DUCT ASSEMBLY

HEATER AND A/C DUCT CONNECTOR

FRT

Heating and ventilation airflow, at top, and components, at bottom.   (GM)

SERVICING HEATING AND VENTILATION COMPONENTS

18

After studying this chapter, you will be able to:
* List things that prevent the airflow from becoming heated.
* Relate engine cooling system problems affecting passenger compartment temperature.
* Summarize the factors affecting air distribution.
* Describe what affects the airflow volume.

NO/INSUFFICIENT HEAT

The *heating and ventilation system* adjusts the ambient air temperature once inside the heater/evaporator case, Fig. 18-1. The ambient temperature affects heater output temperature at the floor register, Fig. 18-2. If the temperature is too low, the problem may be: the airflow is not heated, the engine cooling system, airflow distribution, and/or insufficient airflow volume.

AIRFLOW NOT HEATED

The *temperature blend-air door* directs all or a portion of the airflow through the heater core, Fig. 18-1. Hot

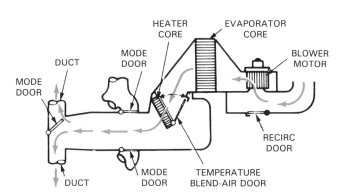

Fig. 18-1. Airflow enters heater/evaporator case. Mode doors, in color, direct airflow. Temperature blend-air door position determines how much air flows through heater core. (Oldsmobile)

TEMPERATURE REFERENCE CHART			
Ambient Temperature		Minimum Heater System Floor Outlet Temperature	
Celsius	Fahrenheit	Celsius	Fahrenheit
15.5°	60°	62.2°	144°
21.1°	70°	63.8°	147°
26.6°	80°	65.5°	150°
32.2°	90°	67.2°	153°

Fig. 18-2. To determine if the system is heating properly, insert a thermometer in the floor register. Turn the heater on maximum, set the blower speed on high, and roll up the windows. Outside or ambient temperature affects heater output temperature. The exact temperatures vary from car to car. (Chrysler)

engine coolant flowing through the heater core provides the heat.

Plenum chamber

The *plenum chamber* directs the incoming ambient airflow, Fig. 18-3A, through the heater/evaporator case to the passenger compartment. The plenum chamber is basically trouble free. However, the drain in the chamber could possibly become plugged with leaves or other debris that gets past the inlet screen. If severe, the debris could interfere with the airflow from becoming heated. Remove the windshield wiper blades and the screen, Fig. 18-3B. The debris can now be removed from the plenum chamber.

Water control valve

The *water control valve* regulates the hot coolant flowing to the heater core. A water control valve that sticks closed prevents the hot coolant from passing through the heater core. This results in the no heat when the heat mode is selected. The water valve is placed in the inlet heater hose, Fig. 18-4.

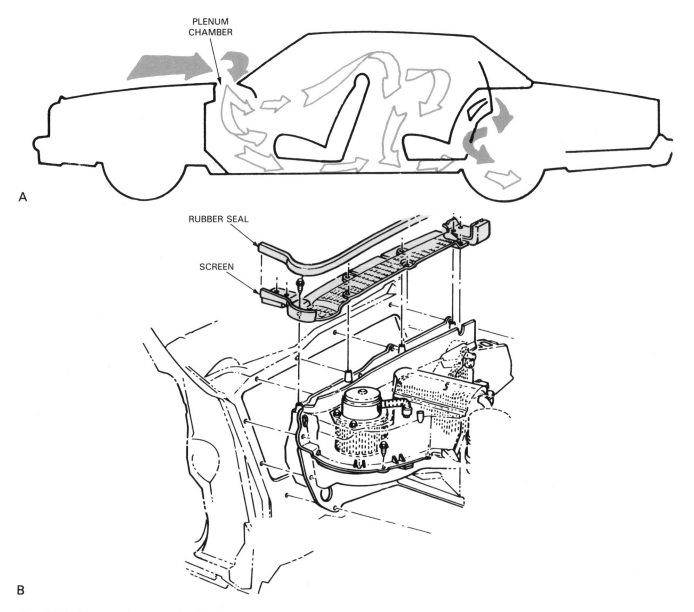

Fig. 18-3. Plenum chamber. A—Outside or ambient airflow enters plenum chamber. It is located on the outside, lower edge of the windshield. B—Remove the screen to gain access to the plenum chamber. (Oldsmobile)

The water control valve can be operated by vacuum or a Bowden cable. The vacuum control method depends on the mode selected. Selecting the heat, defrost, or A/C mode opens the water control valve, allowing coolant flow to the heater core. Selecting the MAX A/C mode or off position closes the water control valve, blocking coolant flow to the heater core.

When the water control valve is cable controlled, the temperature control lever position determines coolant flow to the heater core. The temperature control lever in the "cold position" closes the water control valve, blocking coolant flow to the heater core. The temperature control lever in the "hot position" opens the water control valve, allowing coolant flow to the heater core.

When the water control valve is open, the heater inlet hose before and after the water valve should be hot. If the heater inlet hose after the water valve is not hot, the water valve or one of its controls may be defective. The

vacuum hose to the water valve may be disconnected or pinched. A defective control head can block vacuum to the water valve. If the water valve is cable controlled, the cable may become misadjusted, kinked, or disconnected. Adjust or replace the cable.

Internally plugged heater core

An *internally plugged heater core* does not get hot and prevents the airflow from becoming heated. Deposits restrict coolant flow through it. This is the result of cooling system neglect (coolant not changed at prescribed intervals). Engine heat depletes the inhibitors in the antifreeze. Loss of inhibitors increases the temperature at which the engine coolant freezes. Depletion of the inhibitors also cause rust and scale deposits to form in the water jackets. When these deposits break loose, they circulate and are trapped in the small passages of the heater core and radiator. To prevent this from happening, drain the coolant at the recommended intervals.

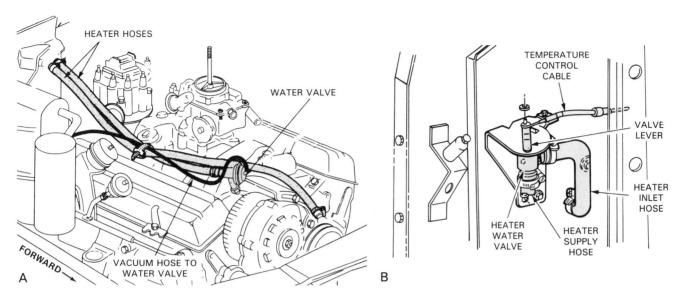

Fig. 18-4. Water valve. A—Vacuum-operated water valve. (GM) B—Cable-controlled water valve. (Ford)

Refill the cooling system with the recommended solution of new coolant.

A quick test determines if the heater core is internally plugged. Feel both the input and return heater hoses. A noticeable temperature difference between the two hoses indicate the heater core is internally plugged. The heater core may be salvaged by pressure flushing it. If this fails to correct the problem, a new heater core is needed.

> WARNING: Chemical cleaners are not recommended to dissolve an accumulation of deposits inside the heater core.

Externally plugged heater core

An *externally plugged heater core* has leaves and other airborne debris collect against its fins. This prevents the airflow from entering the heater. The heater core must be removed from its case and the debris blown out with compressed air.

Temperature blend-air door

The *temperature blend-air door position* determines if all or only a portion of the air flows through the heater core. All of the cold outside air is directed through the heater core when maximum heat is selected, Fig. 18-1. A stuck or binding temperature blend-air door may direct only a portion of the cold outside air through the heater core, Fig. 18-5.

A binding temperature blend-air door may cause no or insufficient heat, depending on the ambient temperature. If it is extremely cold, the complaint will be no heat inside the passenger compartment. However, if the outside temperature is moderately cold, the complaint will be insufficient heat inside the passenger compartment.

A manual heating/cooling system has a temperature blend-air door that is cable-controlled. The temperature blend-air door of a semiautomatic system is vacuum-motor controlled. The computerized automatic temperature control system temperature blend-air door is controlled with an electric motor. Troubleshooting the

semiautomatic or computerized automatic temperature control system requires the use of the appropriate service manual. A broken or kinked temperature blend-air door control cable prevents the desired temperature inside the passenger compartment.

Temperature blend-air door control cable

The *control cable* connects the temperature control lever (at the control head), Fig. 18-6, to the temperature

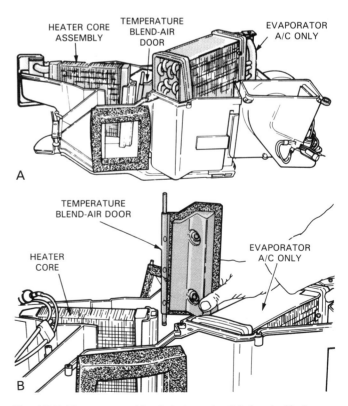

Fig. 18-5. Temperature blend-air door. A—It is located between heater and evaporator core inside heater/evaporator case. B—Removing or installing temperature blend-air door. (Chrysler)

203

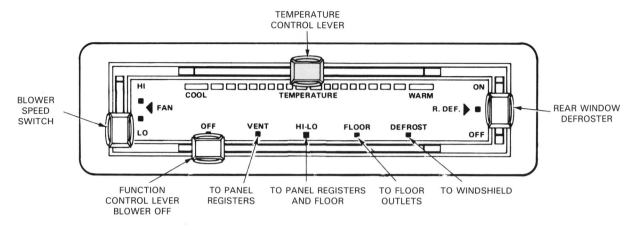

Fig. 18-6. Temperature control lever is adjusted by the driver to obtain the desired temperature inside the passenger compartment. Control cable connects to lever on back of control head. (Ford)

blend-air door. The control cable operates the temperature blend-air door. Replace the control cable when it becomes kinked or broken. When installing a new cable, it must be correctly positioned or the temperature blend-air door will not correspond to the desired temperature selection. Some cables must be adjusted prior to installation, Fig. 18-7. Other cables are self-adjusting, Fig. 18-8.

Evaporator/heater case seal

The evaporator/heater case seal that has become old and brittle leaks air from the engine compartment, Fig. 18-9. The air then enters the passenger compartment without being heated by the heater core. The heater/evaporator case must be removed to install a new seal.

ENGINE COOLING SYSTEM PROBLEMS

The engine cooling system affects heater output and the passenger compartment temperature. A low coolant level may be the cause. A low temperature thermostat

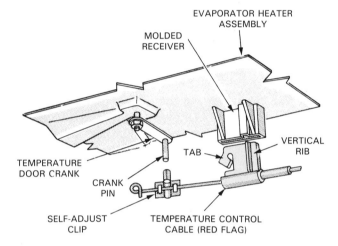

Fig. 18-8. Position the self-adjust clip on the crank pin. Push the tab into the molded receiver. This automatically adjusts the control cable position. (Chrysler)

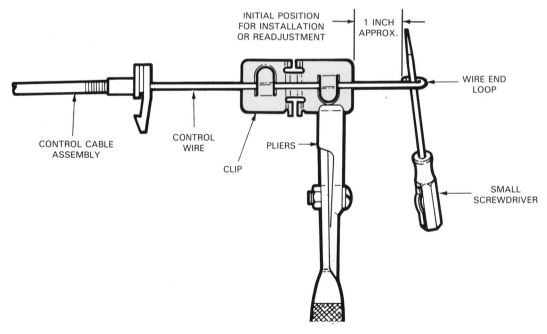

Fig. 18-7. Positioning clip on control cable. (Ford)

204

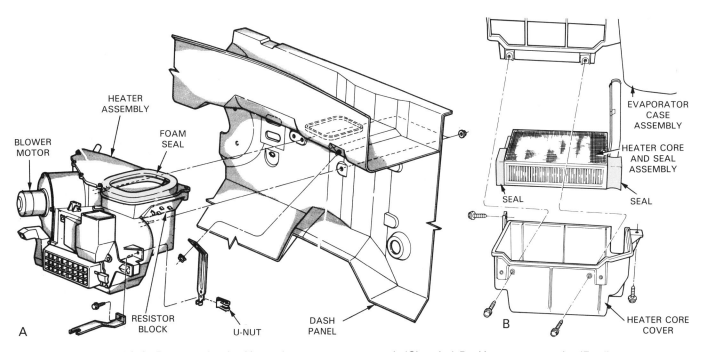

Fig. 18-9. Foam seals. A—Heater/evaporator case seal. (Chrysler) B—Heater core seals. (Ford)

or one that is stuck open lowers heater output. Air trapped in the cooling system can also be a cause of insufficient heater output.

Coolant level

A low coolant level also causes insufficient heater output. Air cannot retain and transfer heat as effectively as a liquid. A low coolant level is usually the sign of a coolant leak.

Thermostat

The *engine thermostat* regulates when the coolant is allowed to circulate through the radiator. Most thermostats are located in a housing under the top radiator hose. An engine thermostat that sticks open causes low heater output. This is due to the engine coolant being allowed to circulate through the radiator before it is hot. A replacement thermostat with a low-temperature rating or the thermostat removed has the same effect.

A quick thermostat test is to feel the upper radiator hose immediately after the car has been driven 5 to 10 minutes. The upper radiator hose should be extremely hot to the touch. Replace the thermostat if the upper radiator hose is only warm.

Trapped air

Air can become trapped in the cooling system. This can happen when coolant is added after repairs are made or coolant loss. The effect is reduced heater output. There are two methods of bleeding trapped air.

One method is to loosen the clamp that secures the heater hose to the heater inlet. Then, loosen the heater hose, but do not remove it from its connection. Start the engine. The trapped air escapes at the heater hose connection while the coolant circulates through the system. When coolant begins to leak out of the heater hose connection, the air has been purged. Retighten the heater hose clamp.

The other method of bleeding trapped air is to run the engine and allow the cooling system to purge itself. This method can be very lengthy. Maintain the proper coolant level while the engine is running. This prevents additional air from entering the cooling system. Always pressure-test the coolant system after making repairs to it. This ensures no coolant leaks out or air enters.

AIRFLOW DISTRIBUTION PROBLEMS

An *airflow distribution problem* is the interruption of airflow after it is heated. Loss of airflow through a desired outlet, whether it is at the dash, defroster, or floor register, is an air distribution problem. The control head regulates the mode-door motors, Fig. 18-10A. The motors open and close the mode doors, directing the heated airflow to the proper ducts, Figs. 18-1 and 18-10B. The ducts connect to the registers. The registers direct the airflow to the passenger compartment.

Mode doors

The *mode doors* direct the heated or cooled airflow from the heater/evaporator case to the proper ducts, Fig. 18-1. The mode doors can be operated by electric or vacuum motors. Electric motors are used on computerized automatic temperature control systems. Vacuum motors are used on manual and semiautomatic temperature control systems. Troubleshooting vacuum-operated mode doors requires the use of a vacuum pump and a vacuum gauge.

Start the engine and select the desired mode. Remove the vacuum hose from the suspect vacuum motor. Insert the hose from the vacuum motor into the vacuum gauge. Check the vacuum hose to determine if it is disconnected, pinched, or plugged if the gauge does not indicate the vacuum is present. Should the inspection not reveal a problem with the vacuum hose, the control

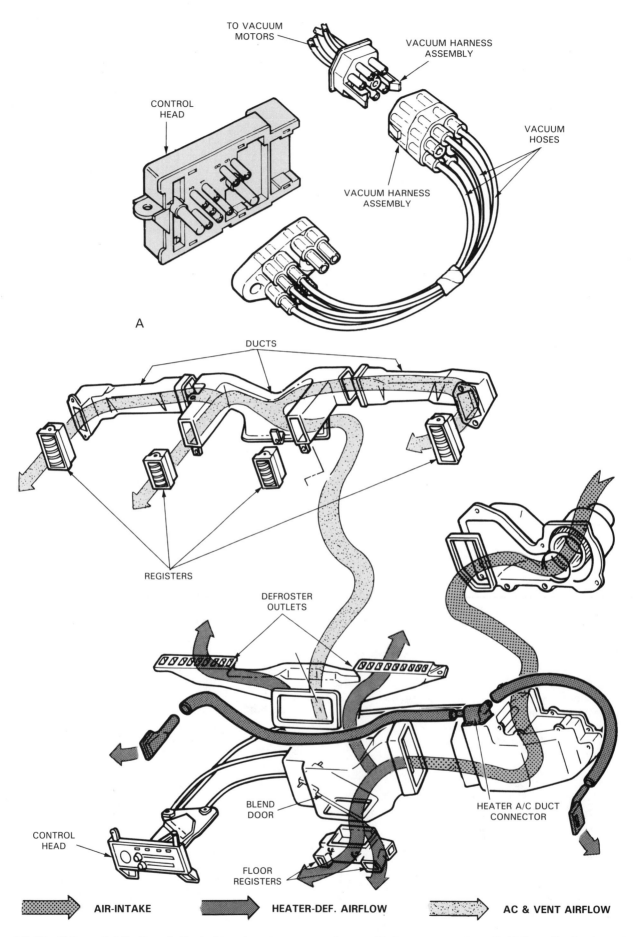

A

B

AIR-INTAKE ▶ HEATER-DEF. AIRFLOW ▶ AC & VENT AIRFLOW

Fig. 18-10. Airflow distribution. A-Control head routes vacuum to specified vacuum motors. B-Airflow distribution pattern.

head is defective, Fig. 18-10A. However, if the vacuum gauge initially registered the specified vacuum, test the vacuum motor.

Testing the vacuum motor requires the use of a vacuum pump. This can be done with the engine off. Connect the vacuum pump hose to the vacuum motor. Apply a vacuum to the motor. A vacuum motor that cannot maintain a vacuum is defective. Replace the vacuum motor and reconnect the vacuum hose to it.

Ducts

Ducts are tubing that connect the heater/evaporator case to the registers. Air discharged from only the floor register when the defroster is selected indicates a disconnected duct.

Registers

Registers direct the heated or cooled airflow from the ducts to the passenger compartment, Fig. 18-10B. Some are continually subjected to repositioning. As a result, they can become damaged or pushed out of place. Binding can also be a problem.

Some registers have a tab to hold them in place. They can be removed with a screwdriver, Fig. 18-11. Some use screws to hold the register in place. Others are held in place with a plastic retaining ring. This design requires removal of an applique prior to removing the plastic retaining ring, Fig. 18-12. Still another design uses spring clips that hold the register in place, Fig. 18-13.

INSUFFICIENT AIRFLOW VOLUME

The blower and ram air control the volume of airflow from the plenum chamber into the heater/evaporator case, Fig. 18-1. The *airflow volume* is the amount of air that is heated. Therefore, an *airflow volume problem* is an insufficient amount of airflow to the passenger compartment. This problem prevents the passenger compartment from becoming heated.

Common complaints are that the blower motor does not turn on, turn off, does not run at all speeds, or runs intermittently. These problems could be caused by a blown fuse, defective blower switch, blown resistor, blower motor burned out, and/or loose or corroded electrical connections, Fig. 18-14.

Blower motor noise

A noisy blower motor may be due to a faulty bearing, squirrel cage rubbing against the case housing, or an out-of-balance squirrel cage. The squirrel cage can be serviced separately from the blower motor, Fig. 18-15. Some blower motors are accessible without removing the heater/evaporator case.

WINDSHIELD FOGGING

Windshield fogging is caused by hot, humid air that condenses on the cooler temperature glass. While this is one cause, a leaking heater core or clogged evaporator drain can also have the same effect.

A leaking heater core allows engine coolant to accumulate in the heater/evaporator housing. A clogged evaporator drain allows condensed water vapor to also accumulate in the heater/evaporator housing. The condensed water vapor or coolant adds moisture to the airflow that is directed to the windshield resulting in fogging. The leaking heater core must be replaced or the evaporator drain cleared.

NOTE: Vehicles equipped with air conditioning have the air conditioner operating when the defrost mode is selected (except when ambient temperatures are below 40°F). This provides dehumidified (dry) air that speeds up the windshield defogging process.

SUMMARY

Basic heating and ventilating systems are similar in operation and design for all car manufacturers. Engine

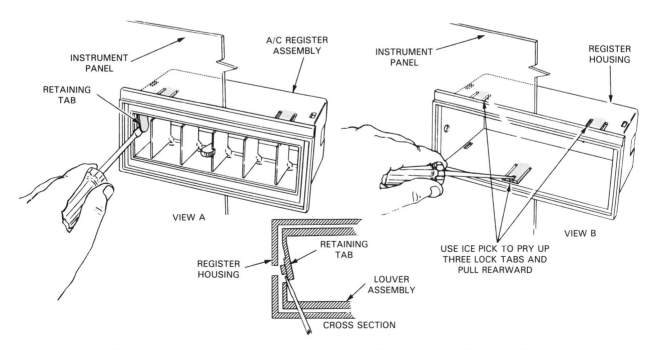

Fig. 18-11. Rectangular-shaped registers are held in place by retaining tab. (Ford)

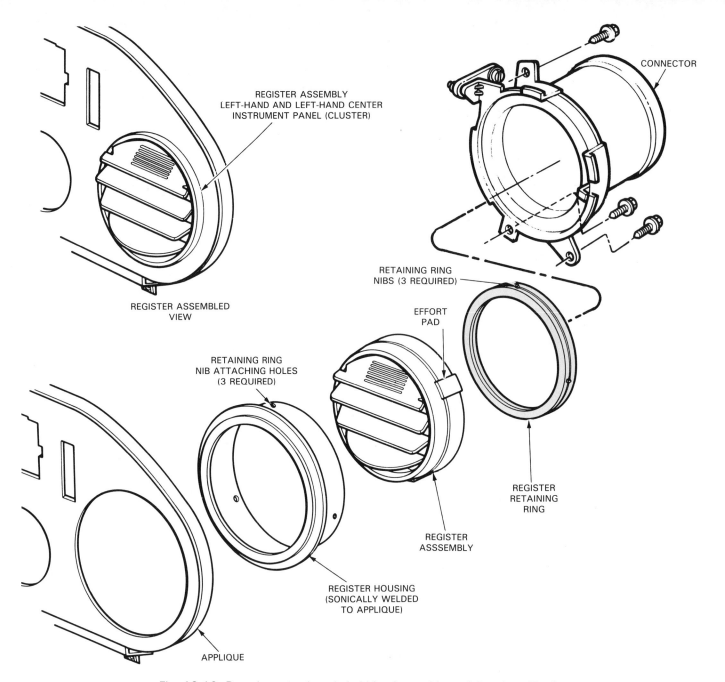

Fig. 18-12. Round-type register is held in place with retaining ring. (Ford)

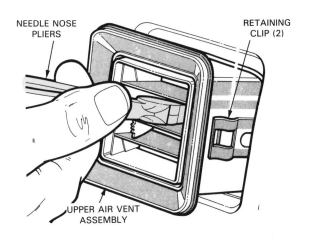

Fig. 18-13. Square-type registers are held in place with retaining clips. Grab vertical louver with needle-nose pliers and pull. (Chrysler)

coolant is used as a source of heat for the passenger compartment. A water valve regulates when the hot coolant enters the heater core. An internally plugged heater core may be salvaged by flushing. An externally plugged heater core must have the debris blown out of the heater core with compressed air.

Airflow problems consist of volume, temperature, and distribution. The factors involved with airflow volume are the blower and car speed (ram air). The components involved with air distribution are the mode doors, vacuum motors, vacuum lines, plenum chamber, ducts, and registers. The components affecting airflow temperature are the temperature blend-air door, control cable, heater core, and water valve. The engine thermostat, coolant level, and trapped air in the cooling system are problems that can affect heater output.

Windshield fogging is the moisture in the air that condenses on the cooler glass. A leaking heater core or

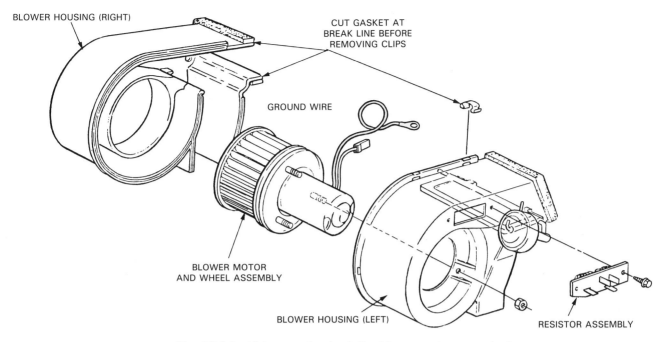

BLOWER HOUSING (RIGHT)

CUT GASKET AT
BREAK LINE BEFORE
REMOVING CLIPS

GROUND WIRE

BLOWER MOTOR
AND WHEEL ASSEMBLY

BLOWER HOUSING (LEFT)

RESISTOR ASSEMBLY

Fig. 18-14. Make sure to check the blower motor ground wire.

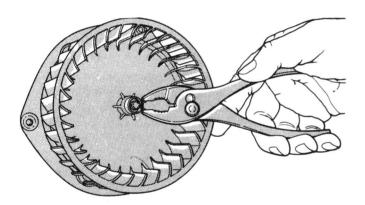

Fig. 18-15. Squirrel cage is serviced separately from the blower motor. An out-of-balance squirrel cage creates a loud hum or vibration. Remove it from blower motor. Then, reposition it on blower motor 180°. (Chrysler)

plugged evaporator drain can also cause the windshield to fog up.

KNOW THESE TERMS

Heating and ventilation system, Temperature blend-air door, Plenum chamber, Water control valve, Internally plugged heater core, Externally plugged heater core, Temperature blend-air door position, Control cable, Engine thermostat, Airflow distribution problem, Mode doors, Ducts, Registers, Airflow volume, Airflow volume problem, Windshield fogging.

REVIEW QUESTIONS—CHAPTER 18

1. Low coolant level can cause:
   a. Excessive heater output.
   b. Insufficient heater output.
   c. Windshield fogging.
   d. Heater core plugging.

2. The water valve is located in the inlet heater hose. True or false?
3. A temperature differential between heater inlet and outlet hoses indicate a/an:
   a. Engine thermostat stuck open.
   b. Defective water valve.
   c. Internally plugged heater core.
   d. Externally plugged heater core.
4. A temperature differential of the inlet heater hose before and after the water valve indicates a/an:
   a. Engine thermostat stuck open.
   b. Defective water valve.
   c. Internally plugged heater core.
   d. Externally plugged heater core.
5. Airflow distribution starts at the:
   a. Register.
   b. Ducts.
   c. Mode doors.
   d. Plenum chamber.
6. All temperature control cables must be adjusted prior to installation. True or false?
7. The engine coolant is changed on a regular basis to:
   a. Prevent freeze-up of the coolant.
   b. Prevent formation of cooling system deposits.
   c. Both a and b.
   d. Neither a nor b.
8. Windshield fogging can be caused by:
   a. Leaking heater core.
   b. Clogged evaporator drain.
   c. Both a and b.
   d. None of the above.
9. A defective evaporator/heater case seal causes:
   a. Excessive heat in passenger compartment.
   b. Excessive cold in passenger compartment.
   c. Both a and b.
   d. Neither a nor b.
10. Describe one method of releasing trapped air and why it must be performed.

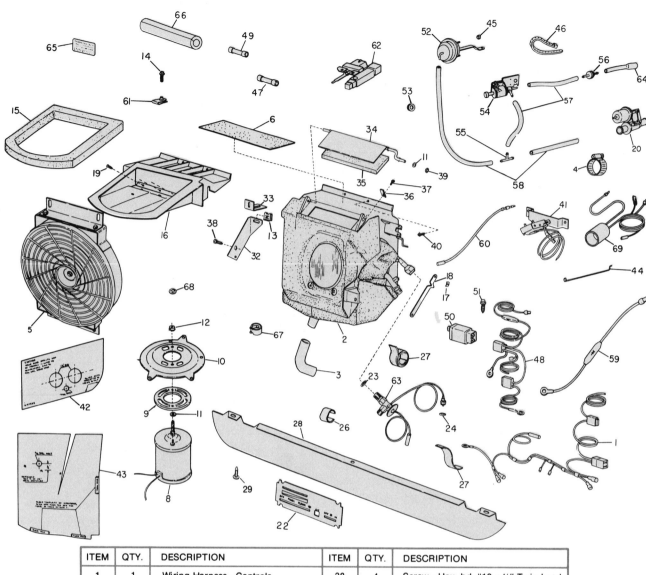

ITEM	QTY.	DESCRIPTION	ITEM	QTY.	DESCRIPTION
1	1	Wiring Harness - Controls	38	4	Screw - Hex. hd. #10 x ½" Twin Lead
2	1	Case Evaporator Assembly	39	1	Nut - Push-ons 3/16" Dia.
3	1	Drain Tube	40	7	Screw Hex. hd. #10 x ½"
4	2	Clamp - Hose	41	1	Switch - Thermostat & Brkt. Assy.
5	1	Fan & Bracket Assembly	42	1	Template
6	1	Insulation - Case Top	43	1	Template
8	1	Motor - 12V	44	1	Link - Thermostat Switch
9	1	Pad - Motor Mounting	45	2	Nut #6
10	1	Plate - Motor Mounting	46	7	Tie - Cable
11	2	Washer - Flat	47	1	Connector - Wire Butt - Yellow
12	2	Nut and Lockwasher Assy.	48	1	Wire Harness - Cooling Fan
13	1	Nut "U" #10	49	2	Connector - Wire Butt - Blue
14	1	Screw - Hex. hd. ¼-20 x ½"	50	1	Relay
15	1	Gasket	51	3	Screw - Hex. Wash. hd. #14 x ¾"
16	1	Duct - Air Inlet	52	1	Vacuum Motor
17	1	Nut - Push-on ⅛" dia.	53	1	Grommet
18	1	Link - Fresh Air Door	54	1	Solenoid Valve
19	3	Screw #8 x ⅝" Lg	55	1	Tee - Vacuum Line ⅛" x 3/16" x ⅛"
20	1	Water Valve	56	1	Vacuum Check Valve
22	1	Applique - Control Panel	57	1	Vacuum Hose 5/32" I.D.
23	2	"O" Ring - ½" Tube O.D.	58	1	Vacuum Hose 3/32" I.D.
24	1	"O" Ring - ¼" Tube O.D.	59	1	Wire & Diode Assy.
26	1	Bulb Clamp	60	1	Wire - Aux. Fan
27	1	Asphalt Tape	61	1	Nut - "U" ¼ - 20
28	1	Radiator Air Deflector	62	1	Blower Switch - HTR - A/C
29	3	Ratchet Fastener	63	1	Expansion Valve
32	1	Bracket - Unit Mounting	64	1	Hose - Vacuum (Reducer)
33	1	Bracket - Unit Mounting	65	1	Label - Refrig. Charge
34	1	Door Assy. - Fresh Air	66	1	Tube - Insulation
35	1	Seal - F.A. Door	67	1	Clip - Drain Hose
36	1	Bracket - F.A. Door Retainer	68	1	Push Nut
37	3	Screw - Hex. hd. #8 x ½"	69	1	Wire Harness - L.P. Switch

Fig. 19-1. Diagram shows what is included in basic kit.

19

INSTALLING AIR CONDITIONING SYSTEMS

After studying this chapter, you will be able to:
• Summarize the types of aftermarket A/C systems.
• Describe the many kits for installation of an A/C system.
• List the many modifications needed when adding an A/C system.

INTRODUCTION

Aftermarket air conditioning means an air conditioning unit is installed after delivery to the dealer or customer. While most new cars come equipped with air conditioning, some new car dealerships order cars without. The dealer may decide at a later date to upgrade a car in inventory by installing an air conditioner. The customer may decide at a later date, after receiving the car, that air conditioning is needed.

In most cases, the customer will request the new car dealer to install an A/C unit. The dealer will have a dealership technician install the A/C unit or sublet the job to an independent installer of A/C units. Experience gained by installing an aftermarket A/C system enhances the technician's skills. This chapter focuses on the procedure for installing an aftermarket A/C system.

TYPES

There are two types of aftermarket A/C systems available. One is the integral system that uses the existing heater housing and ventilation duct work. The other type is the hang-on unit that mounts under the instrument panel or dash. It contains the evaporator, blower, ducts, and controls in one unit. The hang-on units, as a rule, use an expansion valve. The integral system will be discussed in this chapter. However, many modifications and procedures are similar for both types.

KITS

The aftermarket A/C units commonly installed are the expansion valve or clutch cycling orifice tube (CCOT) systems. A typical basic kit, Fig. 19-1, includes the evaporator, refrigerant controls, and necessary accessories. The typical condenser kit, Fig. 19-2, contains the condenser and receiver-drier. The typical engine drive kit contains the compressor and clutch assembly, mounting brackets, idler pulley, and replacement pulleys (for the power steering pump and alternator), if required, Fig. 19-3. The carburetor fast-idle kit contains a solenoid, relay, and related parts, Fig. 19-4.

KEEP IT CLEAN

When working on an A/C system, keep the work area clean. Dirt is one of the worst enemies of an A/C system. A tiny speck of dirt can plug an orifice. Also, all components should remain capped until connected. This reduces the amount of moisture and the chance for dirt to enter.

MODIFICATIONS REQUIRED

A car may not be equipped to handle the additional cooling, electrical, and engine load following the installation of an aftermarket A/C system. Modifications are needed to make the difference between a well-performing A/C system and a marginal one.

Engine cooling system

A larger radiator is needed to handle the additional heat load from the condenser. A new fan shroud and fan spacer are also needed. Increasing the airflow at idle is required to dissipate the additional heat. This can be accomplished with the use of an engine fan with more blades and/or a larger diameter engine fan. A viscous fan clutch attached to the fan is used on rear-wheel-drive cars. This reduces the drag on the engine at highway speeds when the fan is not needed. An auxiliary fan may also be used in conjunction with the original engine fan. These parts are not usually included with the aftermarket installation kits, but may be recommended in the instructions.

211

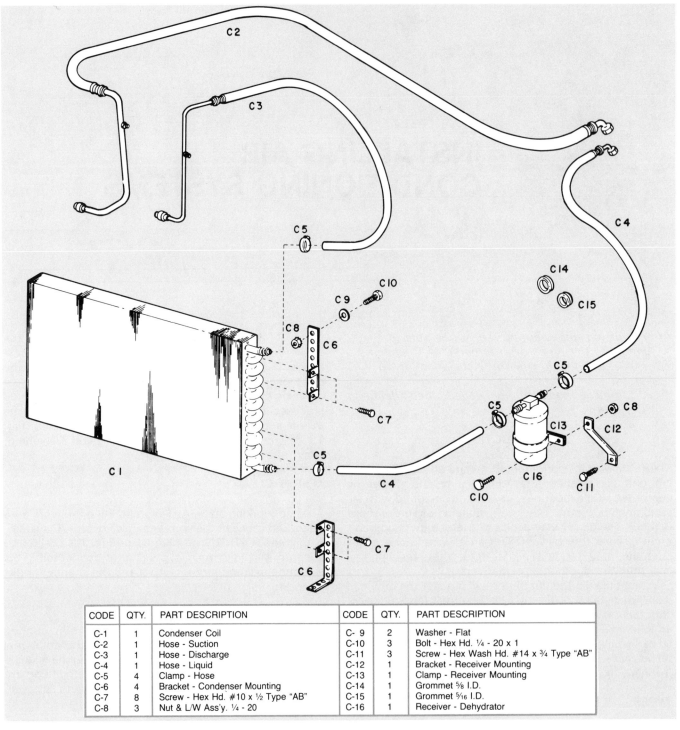

CODE	QTY.	PART DESCRIPTION	CODE	QTY.	PART DESCRIPTION
C-1	1	Condenser Coil	C-9	2	Washer - Flat
C-2	1	Hose - Suction	C-10	3	Bolt - Hex Hd. ¼ - 20 x 1
C-3	1	Hose - Discharge	C-11	3	Screw - Hex Wash Hd. #14 x ¾ Type "AB"
C-4	1	Hose - Liquid	C-12	1	Bracket - Receiver Mounting
C-5	4	Clamp - Hose	C-13	1	Clamp - Receiver Mounting
C-6	4	Bracket - Condenser Mounting	C-14	1	Grommet ⅝ I.D.
C-7	8	Screw - Hex Hd. #10 x ½ Type "AB"	C-15	1	Grommet ⁵⁄₁₆ I.D.
C-8	3	Nut & L/W Ass'y. ¼ - 20	C-16	1	Receiver - Dehydrator

Fig. 19-2. Parts that can be found in a condenser kit. (Ford)

Cooling fan override

Front-wheel-drive cars use electric fan motors. A coolant temperature sensor measures engine temperature and sends a signal to the computer. The computer energizes a fan relay when the coolant reaches operating temperature, which turns the fan motor on.

The engine fan must come on any time the air conditioner is turned on, regardless of coolant temperature. To make sure that this occurs, the electrical signal from the coolant temperature sensor is overriden at idle when coolant temperature is cold. By overriding the sensor signal, the engine is prevented from overheating at idle and slow speeds.

CAUTION: Route all electrical wiring away from hot manifolds, sharp edges, and fan blades.

Air dam

An air dam can be found on front-wheel-drive cars. This is due to the smaller grille opening. Some rear-

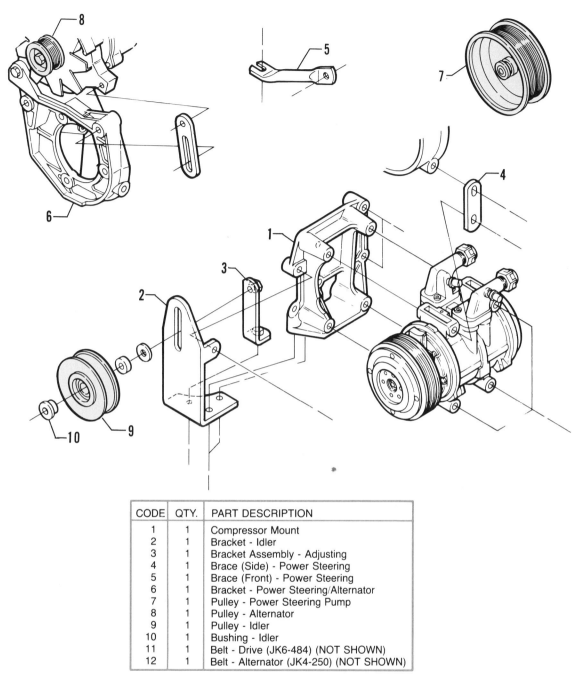

CODE	QTY.	PART DESCRIPTION
1	1	Compressor Mount
2	1	Bracket - Idler
3	1	Bracket Assembly - Adjusting
4	1	Brace (Side) - Power Steering
5	1	Brace (Front) - Power Steering
6	1	Bracket - Power Steering/Alternator
7	1	Pulley - Power Steering Pump
8	1	Pulley - Alternator
9	1	Pulley - Idler
10	1	Bushing - Idler
11	1	Belt - Drive (JK6-484) (NOT SHOWN)
12	1	Belt - Alternator (JK4-250) (NOT SHOWN)

Fig. 19-3. Engine drive kit contains pulleys and brackets. (Ford)

wheel-drive cars (police package only) also have air dams. An *air dam* directs the airflow, from under the front end, upward to flow through the radiator and condenser. This increases the airflow through the condenser and radiator at highway speeds. An air-conditioned front-wheel-drive car not equipped with an air dam could be subject to engine overheating at highway speeds on a hot, humid day.

Electrical system

Modifications are sometimes needed to the electrical system. The alternator, in some cases, should be replaced with one of greater amperage rating to handle the additional electrical demand.

A/C clutch diode

A diode must be installed between the A/C clutch wiring and ground when the ignition system is computerized, Fig. 19-5. The *A/C clutch diode* protects the computer from being damaged by electrical surges when the air conditioner is turned off.

Larger tires

With the added weight of an aftermarket air conditioner, many suppliers recommend replacing the tires with a larger size. This is important if it is a lightweight, compact car. Using larger tires increases the safety factor. The added weight of an aftermarket A/C system may be a contributing factor to accelerated tire wear.

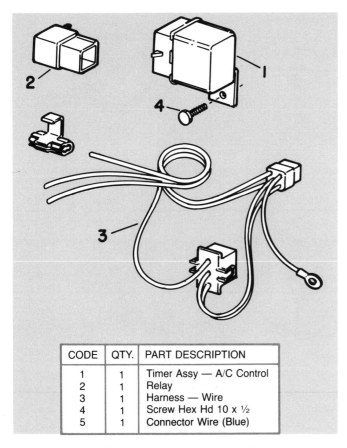

CODE	QTY.	PART DESCRIPTION
1	1	Timer Assy — A/C Control
2	1	Relay
3	1	Harness — Wire
4	1	Screw Hex Hd 10 x ½
5	1	Connector Wire (Blue)

Fig. 19-4. Fast-idle kit prevents engine stalling at idle when air conditioner is turned on.

PREPARATION

A step-by-step procedure for installing an aftermarket air conditioning kit follows. However, some preparation should precede installation. Check all parts in the kit against the parts list. This ensures no parts are missing. Disconnect the negative terminal from the car battery. This prevents an accidental electrical short circuit.

REMOVING PARTS

Remove and save the glove box assembly and its fasteners. Remove and discard the original air inlet duct

assembly, Fig. 19-6. Disconnect the wiring from the resistor block. Remove the blower motor assembly from its case. Separate the blower wheel from its motor. Save the blower wheel and gasket; discard the motor, Fig. 19-7. A new motor will be used during reinstallation with an increased amperage rating.

NOTE: The blower motor is not changed in some procedures.

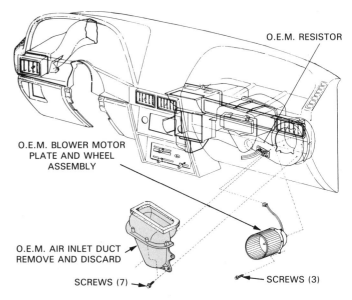

Fig. 19-6. The original inlet duct is discarded. (Ford)

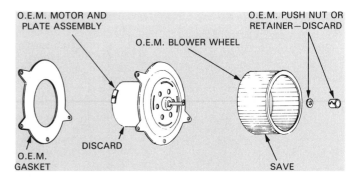

Fig. 19-7. Separate blower wheel from its motor. Throw away the original blower motor, but save the blower wheel.

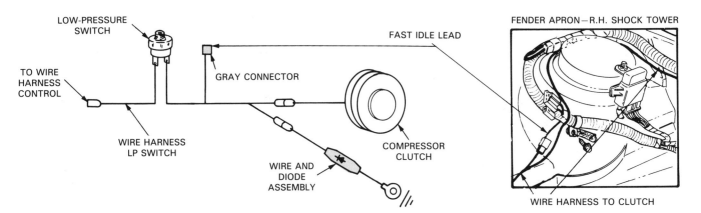

Fig. 19-5. Diode connected to A/C clutch wiring. (Ford)

Drill the drain hole

Pull back the floor carpeting. Position the template (provided in the kit) against firewall inside the passenger compartment. Drill holes in the firewall for the A/C hoses to pass through, Fig. 19-8. Then, lay back the floor carpet. Position the drain hole template, Fig. 19-8. Drill the drain hole.

> CAUTION: Make sure the engine side of the firewall is clear of fuel lines, brake lines, and wiring before drilling holes in the firewall. Also, use a reamer to remove all sharp edges and burrs from the drilled holes. Insert grommets in the drilled holes, Fig. 19-9.

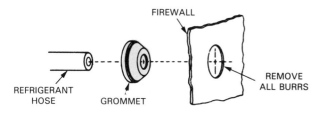

Fig. 19-9. Install grommet in drilled hole at firewall before A/C hose passes through it.   (Ford)

Remove the radiator

Drain the coolant from the radiator. Disconnect all lines and hoses from the radiator. Remove the fan shroud from the radiator. Remove the mounting fasteners attaching the radiator. Then, remove the radiator from the engine compartment.

Remove the control head

Remove and save the original control-head knobs. Disconnect and pull the control head away from the instrument panel. Remove and discard original blower switch. Peel applique from the front of the control head, Fig. 19-10.

INSTALLATION

Install the new blower and A/C on-off switch (in kit), Fig. 19-11. Peel backing from new applique (in kit). Carefully position it on the face of the control head, Fig. 19-11. Route wiring harness under the dash and through the firewall, Fig. 19-12. Make electrical connections at the control head. Reinstall control head assembly to instrument panel. Connect the wiring to the compressor, fan relay, diode, and auxiliary fan.

Blower motor

Install the original blower wheel on the new blower motor. Insert blower motor assembly in heater case. Plug

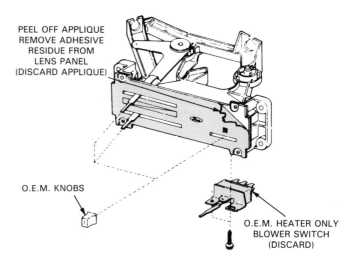

Fig. 19-10. Remove old applique and blower switch from control head and throw away.

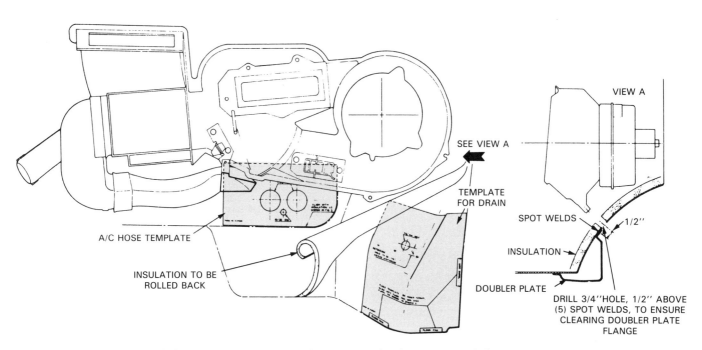

Fig. 19-8. Position of templates for drilling holes for drain and A/C hoses.   (Ford)

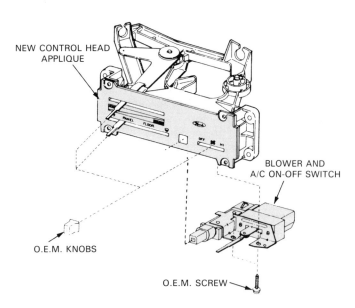

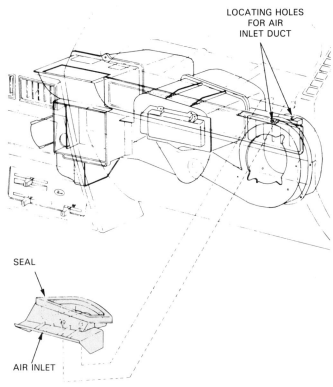

Fig. 19-11. Install new applique and blower switch to control head. (Ford)

Fig. 19-13. Install inlet duct, which is supplied with kit.

electrical connector to resistor. Install fresh air inlet duct to the top of heater case, Fig. 19-13.

NOTE: Thermostat capillary tube is inserted into the evaporator at the factory.

Thermostat control link

Locate the temperature blend-air door actuating rod, Fig. 19-14. Install the thermostat control link by positioning it on the actuator rod.

Evaporator case

Install the evaporator case, Fig. 19-15. Check the position of the evaporator case to be sure it is seated and seals properly. Also, check the fresh-air door location and operation. Install the evaporator case mounting brackets, Fig. 19-16. Route the drain tube from the evaporator case through the hole. Attach the evaporator drain elbow, Fig. 19-17.

NOTE: Press evaporator firmly against case while tightening front mounting bracket.

Water valve

Cut the heater inlet hose about 8-12 in. from the firewall. Install the vacuum-operated water valve in the heater hose line, Fig. 19-18. Arrow on water valve must point in the direction coolant flows.

Vacuum controls

Install the vacuum solenoid valve and route the vacuum hoses, Fig. 19-19. Cut the vacuum hoses to length and install vacuum control system. Install grommet around vacuum hoses going through firewall. Connect the terminal leads to the solenoid valve, Fig. 19-19.

CAUTION: Vacuum check valve must be installed with its vacuum side pointing to source of vacuum.

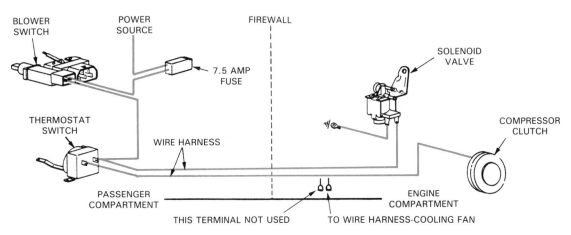

Fig. 19-12. Electrical components that must be wired to blower switch.

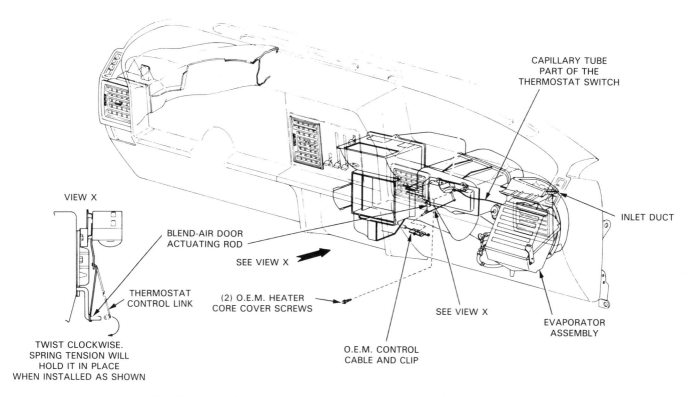

VIEW X

BLEND-AIR DOOR
ACTUATING ROD

SEE VIEW X

THERMOSTAT
CONTROL LINK

(2) O.E.M. HEATER
CORE COVER SCREWS

TWIST CLOCKWISE.
SPRING TENSION WILL
HOLD IT IN PLACE
WHEN INSTALLED AS SHOWN

CAPILLARY TUBE
PART OF THE
THERMOSTAT SWITCH

INLET DUCT

SEE VIEW X

O.E.M. CONTROL
CABLE AND CLIP

EVAPORATOR
ASSEMBLY

Fig. 19-14. Installing thermostatic link and blend-air door actuating rod.

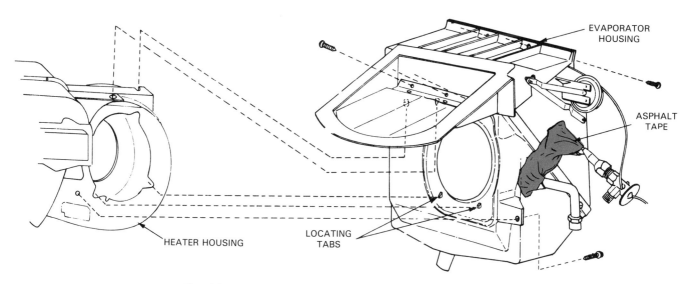

EVAPORATOR
HOUSING

ASPHALT
TAPE

HEATER HOUSING

LOCATING
TABS

Fig. 19-15. Mount evaporator housing to heater housing.

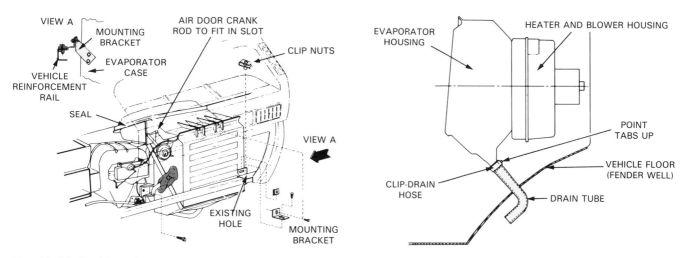

VIEW A

MOUNTING
BRACKET

EVAPORATOR
CASE

VEHICLE
REINFORCEMENT
RAIL

SEAL

AIR DOOR CRANK
ROD TO FIT IN SLOT

CLIP NUTS

VIEW A

EXISTING
HOLE

MOUNTING
BRACKET

Fig. 19-16. Position of evaporator case mounting brackets.

EVAPORATOR
HOUSING

HEATER AND BLOWER HOUSING

POINT
TABS UP

VEHICLE FLOOR
(FENDER WELL)

CLIP-DRAIN
HOSE

DRAIN TUBE

Fig. 19-17. Location of evaporator-case drain. (Ford)

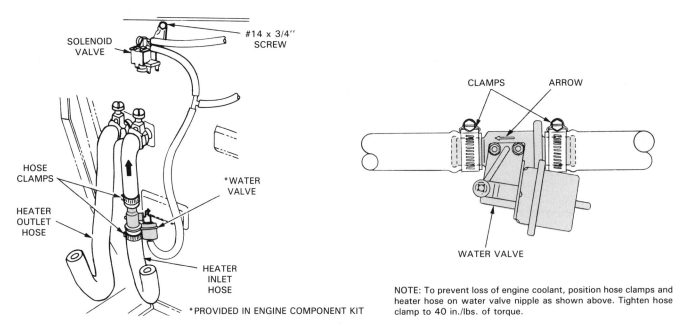

Fig. 19-18. Position of arrow on water valve must coincide with direction of coolant flow. (Ford)

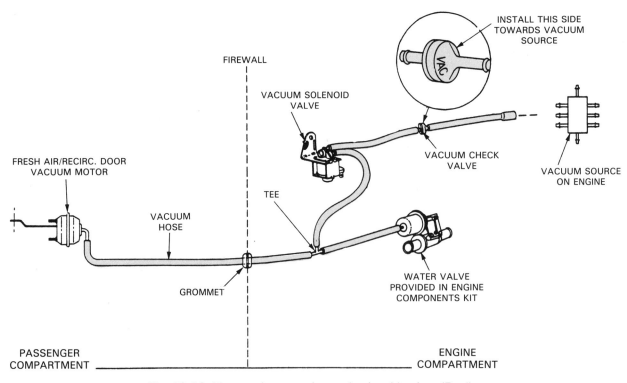

Fig. 19-19. Vacuum hose routing and solenoid valve. (Ford)

Fittings

Route A/C hoses through grommets, Fig. 19-9. connect evaporator fittings. Recommended torque:

Fitting size	Thread size	Torque
3/8 in.	5/8-18	15-19 Ft. Lbs.
1/2 in.	3/4-16	21-27 Ft. Lbs.
5/8 in.	7/8-14	25-31 Ft. Lbs.

CAUTION: Use two wrenches when tightening fittings. This prevents twisting of lines.

Asphalt tape

Wrap all exposed metal parts of the high-pressure line and expansion valve with asphalt tape. Slot in evaporator case must also be sealed, Fig. 19-20. All metal parts must be clean and dry for tape to adhere.

FINAL COMPONENTS

This section deals with the installation of major components under the hood. The condenser, A/C hoses, aux-

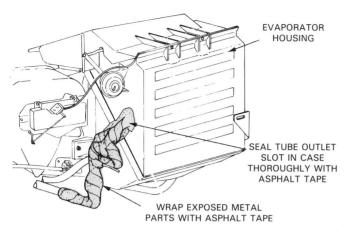

Fig. 19-20. Asphalt tape, supplied in kit, is wrapped around metal A/C lines and components.

iliary fan, compressor, air dam, and final assembly procedure complete this chapter.

Condenser

Trim the deflector, Fig. 19-21. Then, install it in the radiator opening. Drill holes in the lower support structure. The condenser mounts directly in front of radiator opening. Secure condenser bottom brackets with fasteners provided in kit. Install the radiator using the original hardware. There must be approximately 3/4 in. to 1-1/4 in. air gap between the condenser and radiator. This ensures proper performance of the condenser. Install the receiver-drier with the hardware provided in the kit.

A/C hoses

Determine A/C hose length required. Keep ends of hose square when cutting. Lubricate fittings with a few drops

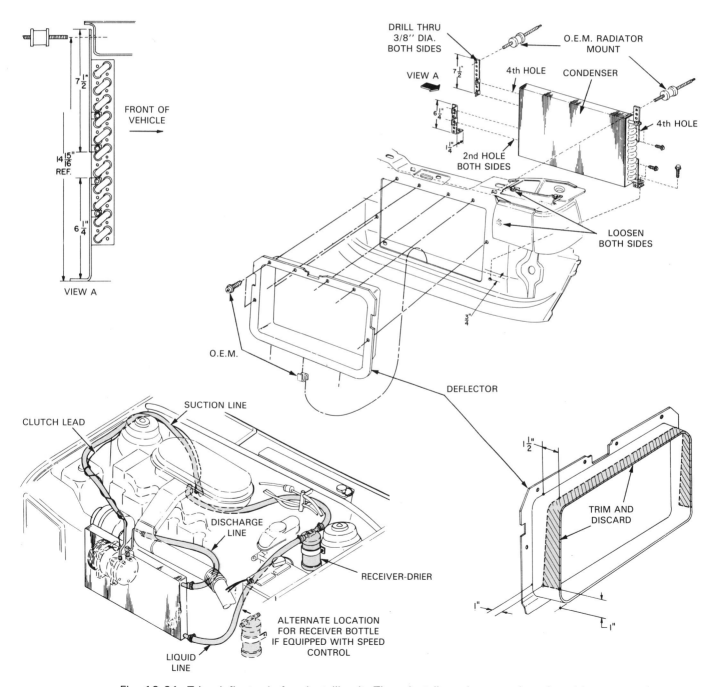

Fig. 19-21. Trim deflector before installing it. Then, install condenser and receiver-drier.

of refrigerant oil. Push the hose over the fitting with a twisting motion. Slide hose clamps over the hose. Position clamps over end of hose, Fig. 19-22. Tighten the hose clamps to ensure a leak-proof seal.

Auxiliary fan

While some kits provide a larger diameter fan and/or fan with more blades, other kits provide a second fan and motor. Either option increases airflow through the condenser and radiator at idle.

Remove existing screw at ''X,'' Fig. 19-23. Position auxiliary fan between the grille and radiator support. Mount auxiliary fan with screw ''X.'' Using fan bracket assembly as a guide, drill remaining three holes. Install the #10 hex head screws. Drill a hole in radiator support. Attach ground eyelet to radiator support and connect wiring, Fig. 19-23. Use tie cables to secure electrical wire to hood cable. Splice electrical wiring, Fig. 19-24, to connect auxiliary fan motor, Fig. 19-25, to existing relay.

NOTE: Auxiliary fan will energize when air conditioner or main engine fan is on.

Compressor

Install compressor clutch on compressor. Drain shipping oil from compressor. Add specified amount of new oil as stated in service manual. Remove and discard

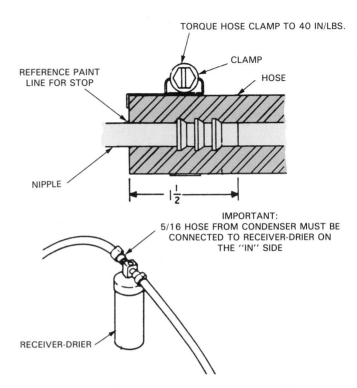

Fig. 19-22. Relationship of A/C hose, nipple, and hose clamp is critical.

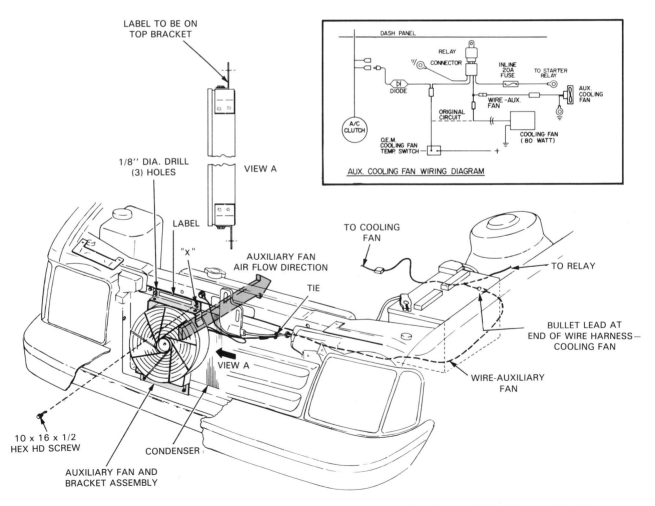

Fig. 19-23. Auxiliary fan mounts between condenser and grille. Note inset wiring diagram. (Ford)

1. Cut and strip wires 0.3'' (7.6 mm).

2. When joining (3) wires, twist together leads of heavy gauge with lighter gauge.

3. Insert into crimp barrel.

4. Crimp using crimp tool for pre-insulated crimps.

5. Heat shrink with heat gun until tubing shrinks and adhesive flows from each end.

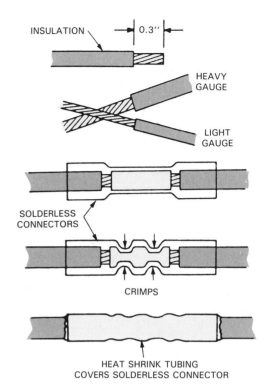

Fig. 19-24. Splicing electrical wires when using solderless connectors. (Ford)

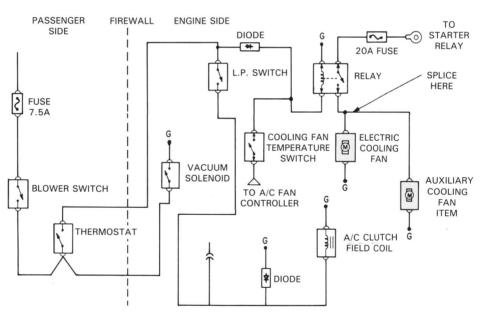

Fig. 19-25. Wiring diagram of aftermarket A/C system.

original pulleys and alternator belt. Install brackets from engine kit, Fig. 19-26. Then, attach compressor to engine mounting bracket. Install the new pulleys and drive belts from kit. Tighten compressor and bracket bolts to the proper torque specification.

NOTE: Pulleys must align to prevent abnormal belt wear.

Air dam

Loosen the heat shield fasteners. Position air dam on front frame crossmember, Fig. 19-27. Attach the air dam with fasteners provided in kit. Retighten heat shield fasteners.

Final assembly

Replace the glove box, carpet, and radiator grille. Wrap the A/C low-side hose inside the car with insulation. Secure it in place with cable ties. Reconnect the battery ground cable. Install refrigerant charge label provided in kit. Evacuate the A/C system and charge it with the specified amount of refrigerant. Leak test the A/C system and correct any leaks found. Run the engine for a

221

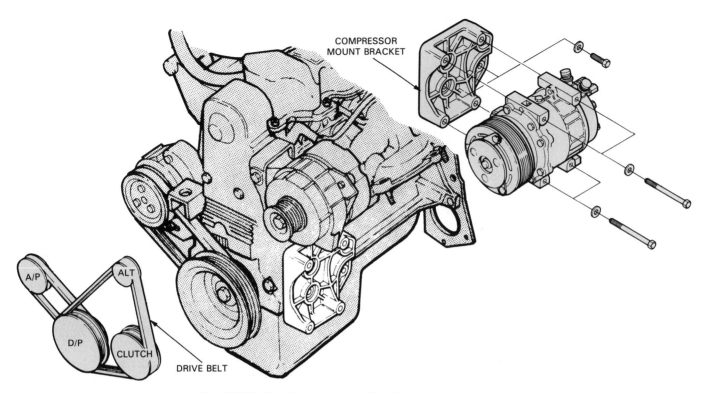

Fig. 19-26. Positioning pulleys, brackets, and drive belts.

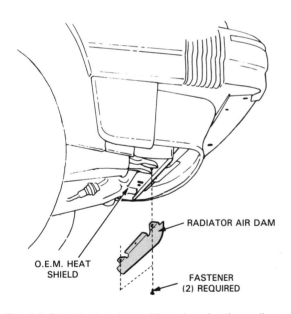

Fig. 19-27. Air dam is positioned under the radiator.

period of 10 minutes. Retension the drive belts if necessary. Install the coolant recovery system if not already equipped. Add coolant to the proper level.

Run the A/C system and check all controls, blower speeds, function, and temperature control responses. Check the discharge air temperature at panel outlets for proper cooling.

COMPUTERIZED A/C SYSTEM

Today, many cars have computer controlled fuel and ignition systems. Computers also control some electrical accessories as well. This may include the air conditioner. The kit may provide instructions on integrating the computer with the air conditioner controls. Each electrical system and computer are different. It is beyond the scope of this book to include specific information for each application.

SUMMARY

There are two types of aftermarket air conditioning systems in use today, integral and hang-on units. The integral type uses the existing heater housing, ventilation, and heating ducts. The integral kits may be furnished with an expansion valve or a clutch cycling orifice tube (CCOT). Aftermarket A/C systems do not have as many driveability controls as factory installed units.

The hang-on unit is an assembly that mounts under the instrument panel. It consists of the evaporator, blower, ducting outlets, and controls in one unit. The hang-on unit generally uses an expansion valve.

Aftermarket A/C systems come in kit form. Instruction sheets, which are enclosed, should be followed to the letter. Study the instructions each time before installation. Running changes are often made to the cars, kits, and instructions.

All air conditioning work requires the work area be kept clean. Air conditioning components must remain capped until connected. This ensures that no contamination enters the system. OBSERVE ALL SAFETY PRECAUTIONS WHEN WORKING ON AN AIR CONDITIONING UNIT.

KNOW THESE TERMS

Aftermarket air conditioning, Integral system, Hang-on unit. Basic kit, Condenser kit. Engine drive kit, Fast-idle kit. Air dam. A/C clutch diode.

REVIEW QUESTIONS—CHAPTER 19

1. Cars equipped with air conditioning require a larger radiator to handle extra heat from the:
   a. Car interior.
   b. Condenser.
   c. Engine.
   d. Evaporator.
2. When installing the same A/C kit repetitively, you must:
   a. Rely on previous installation experience.
   b. Repeat exact procedure used in the last installation.
   c. Read instructions to see if any changes have been made.
   d. None of the above.
3. List the different kits needed to install an aftermarket A/C unit.
4. Modifications that may be needed, but not included in the kits are:
   a. Larger tires, engine fan, and radiator.
   b. A fan clutch (rwd cars only) or air dam (fwd cars only).
   c. An increased amperage alternator.
   d. All the above.
5. A good grade of SAE 10W-40 oil should always be used to lubricate hoses and O-rings during installation. True or false?
6. Rubber grommets should always be used:
   a. To hold hoses in place.
   b. Under hose clamps.
   c. To protect hoses and tubing.
   d. In conjunction with sealant to seal holes in the firewall.
7. Explain the two different aftermarket A/C system designs.
8. Who is the customer for an aftermarket A/C system?
   a. The owner of a car.
   b. A new car dealer.
   c. Both a and b.
   d. None of the above.
9. Why is it necessary to disconnect the battery ground cable prior to working on a car?
10. Proper pulley alignment is necessary to prevent abnormal belt wear. True or false?
11. When installing an A/C system, it is important to:
    a. Maintain cleanliness.
    b. Read a book called "Zen and Automotive Air Conditioning."
    c. Both a and b.
    d. None of the above.

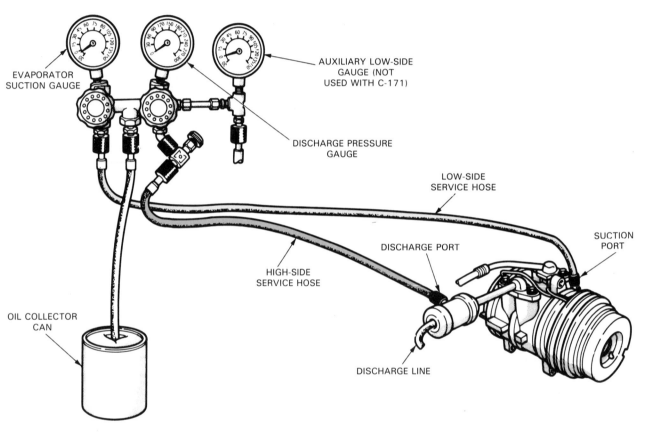

EVAPORATOR
SUCTION GAUGE

AUXILIARY LOW-SIDE
GAUGE (NOT
USED WITH C-171)

DISCHARGE PRESSURE
GAUGE

LOW-SIDE
SERVICE HOSE

SUCTION
PORT

DISCHARGE PORT

HIGH-SIDE
SERVICE HOSE

OIL COLLECTOR
CAN

DISCHARGE LINE

Fig. 20-2. After the service hoses are connected to the A/C system, the center service hose is placed inside a can. (Chrysler)

20

DISCHARGING, EVACUATION, AND CHARGING

After studying this chapter, you will be able to:
* *Explain when and why an A/C system is discharged.*
* *Describe the refrigerant recovery and recycling process.*
* *Relate when and why an A/C system is evacuated.*
* *Give examples of when and why an A/C system is flushed.*
* *List the various methods of charging an A/C system.*

INTRODUCTION

This chapter provides the final step in servicing an air conditioning system. It deals with the discharging, evacuation, flushing, and charging of the A/C system. Handling refrigerant presents the greatest exposure to dangers and hazards associated with refrigerant. The technician must observe and comply with all safety rules, Fig. 20-1.

DISCHARGING THE A/C SYSTEM

Discharging is the separation of refrigerant from its system. Prior to repairing or replacing an A/C component, the refrigerant must be completely discharged from the system. The pressurized refrigerant is discharged from the A/C system through the use of a manifold-gauge set. This makes it a safe procedure and possible to control the rate of refrigerant discharge. Discharging the A/C system slowly minimizes compressor oil loss.

Discharging to the atmosphere
Connect the manifold gauge hoses to the A/C system service valves, Fig. 20-2. Open both hand valves slightly by turning each in a counterclockwise direction. If oil starts accumulating inside the can, reduce the rate the refrigerant is discharged. This is accomplished by turning each hand valve slightly in a clockwise direction. The refrigerant escapes from the can and into the atmosphere.

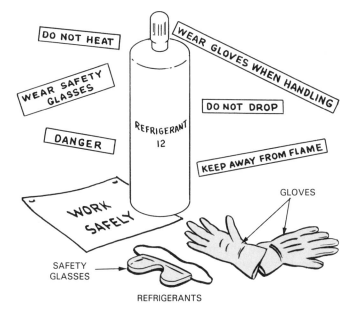

Fig. 20-1. Always think safety when working with refrigerant. (Deere and Co.)

Scientists have found that chlorofluorocarbons (CFCs), such as R-12, deplete the ozone layer. Ozone protects the earth from the sun's ultraviolet rays. Laws forbidding discharge of R-12 into the atmosphere may soon become effective. Some new car dealerships have installed systems to recover the refrigerant.

RECOVERING REFRIGERANT

The *refrigerant recovery method* involves routing discharged refrigerant from the A/C system to a storage tank through a special machine, Figs. 20-3 and 20-4. This machine is called the *air conditioning refrigerant recovery/recycling* (ACR3) *station.* It recovers and then

Fig. 20-3. The air conditioning refrigerant recovery/recycling or ACR3 station. (Oldsmobile)

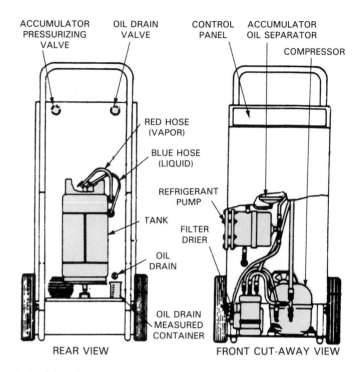

Fig. 20-4. Location of the various components of the ACR3 station. (Oldsmobile)

recycles the refrigerant instead of discharging it to the atmosphere. This prevents damage to the environment.

Preparation for recovery

A tank that captures the discharged refrigerant is placed on a scale at the rear of the ACR3 station, Fig. 20-4. The tank is pressurized with nitrogen. This keeps the tank clean during shipping. Discharge the nitrogen from the tank prior to placing it on the scale.

Connect the red hose, from back of ACR3 station, to a vacuum pump. Connect the blue hose, from back of ACR3 station, to the port on the tank marked LIQUID. Open the valve on the tank marked LIQUID. Turn the vacuum pump on for 10 minutes. This removes any air and moisture from the tank. Disconnect the red hose from vacuum pump. Then, connect the red hose, from back of ACR3 station, to the VAPOR port on the tank. Open the valve on the tank marked VAPOR. The blue hose, from back of ACR3 station, remains connected to the LIQUID port at the tank. The valve marked LIQUID remains open. Preparation is now complete.

Recovery of the refrigerant

Connect the manifold-gauge set to the vehicle A/C system service valves. Then, attach the center hose from the manifold-gauge set to the ACR3 station, Fig. 20-5. Turn the MAIN POWER switch on, which is located at the control panel, Fig. 20-6. Then, push the COMPRESSOR START button, also located at the control panel. The COMPRESSOR ON lamp should now glow. The compressor will automatically shut off when refrigerant recovery is complete. Observe the high- and

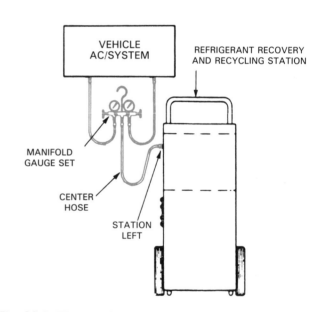

Fig. 20-5. The manifold service hoses are connected to the A/C system. The center service hose connects the manifold gauges to the ACR3 station. (Oldsmobile)

low-side pressure gauges for at least two minutes. If pressure increases within two minutes after the compressor stops, push the COMPRESSOR START button again.

Next, open the ACCUMULATOR PRESSURIZING VALVE located at rear of the ACR3 station, Fig. 20-4. This will drain compressor oil from the accumulator. Close the valve immediately when the oil stops draining. This prevents the accumulator from completely depressurizing. The technician may choose to recycle the refrigerant after each job or wait until the tank is full.

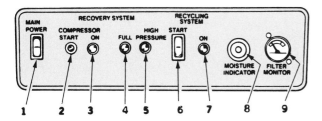

1—MAIN POWER SWITCH—MUST BE ON TO RECOVER OR RECYCLE
2—COMPRESSOR START BUTTON
3—COMPRESSOR ON INDICATOR LIGHT
4—RECOVERY TANK FULL INDICATOR
5—HIGH VEHICLE SYSTEM PRESSURE INDICATOR
6—RECYCLING SYSTEM START SWITCH
7—RECYCLING INDICATOR LAMP
8—MOISTURE INDICATOR—YELLOW = MOISTURE GREEN = DRY
9—FILTER MONITOR—RED ZONE = REPLACE FILTER

Fig. 20-6. A close-up view of the ACR3 control panel. (Oldsmobile)

The FULL light, at the control panel, will glow informing the technician the tank is completely filled.

Recycling the recovered refrigerant

Recycling refrigerant is the removal of moisture and air from the recovered refrigerant. This allows the same refrigerant to be reused. Push the START button, which is located under the words RECYCLING SYSTEM on the control panel, Fig. 20-6. Refrigerant can now be seen going through the MOISTURE INDICATOR also located at the control panel. When bubbles cannot be seen through the MOISTURE INDICATOR, the refrigerant pump is operating at peak efficiency. When the MOISTURE INDICATOR appears green, the moisture has been removed from the refrigerant. The recycling operation is now complete. Turn off the machine.

However, if the MOISTURE INDICATOR appears yellow when refrigerant first flows through it, the recycling time may take two hours. This amount of time is needed to remove all moisture from the refrigerant. Should the MOISTURE INDICATOR remain yellow after two hours, the filter is saturated with moisture. Replace the filter. A plugged filter is indicated if the needle in the FILTER MONITOR (at control panel) moves to the red zone. The filter should be replaced after recycling 300 lbs. of refrigerant as preventive maintenance.

NOTE: A/C hoses from the manifold gauges do not need to be purged when using the ACR3 station. Air is automatically vented from the tank during recycling operation.

EVACUATING THE A/C SYSTEM

Moisture is a major enemy of an air conditioning system. It combines with the refrigerant to form hydrochloric acid, which corrodes the metal parts of the A/C system. This can cause failure and/or erratic operation of the refrigerant controls. Moisture can also gather at the expansion valve and freeze. This blocks the refrigerant flow.

Evacuation removes air and moisture from within the A/C system. This is accomplished by attaching a vacuum pump to the A/C system, Fig. 20-7. The A/C system is placed under a vacuum (less than atmospheric pressure)

for a given period of time. Vacuum is measured in inches of mercury (in. Hg). A complete vacuum is 29.92 in. Hg. Placing the A/C system under vacuum accomplishes two things. It causes moisture inside the A/C system to boil at lower temperatures, Fig. 20-8, and then pulls the water vapor from the A/C system.

The system MUST be evacuated after it is opened for any reason (usually repairs). An improperly evacuated system can result in repeated component failure. Single evacuation in many cases is sufficient. However, if excessive moisture is indicated (expansion valve frozen and/or light internal corrosion of metal parts), triple evacuation is needed. Triple evacuation eliminates almost all moisture.

Single evacuation

A *single evacuation* removes a slight amount of moisture that was allowed to enter the A/C system during repairs. The A/C system must be fully discharged of refrigerant prior to evacuation. Pulling refrigerant through a vacuum pump may damage it. Use the following sequence:

1. Connect center hose of manifold-gauge set to vacuum pump. Connect high- and low-pressure hoses to their respective service valves, Fig. 20-7.
2. Open the low-pressure hand valve on the manifold-gauge set. Start the vacuum pump.

NOTE: Evacuating an A/C system transfers the water vapor (moisture) to the vacuum pump where it condenses and mixes with the vacuum pump oil. Therefore, vacuum pump oil should be changed after evacuating an A/C system. Type of oil is specified by manufacturer of the vacuum pump.

3. Evacuate the system until a reading of 25-30 in. Hg is obtained on the low-side gauge. Continue evacuating the A/C system for approximately 20 to 30 minutes. If the desired vacuum cannot be obtained, a leak exists. If a leak is indicated, see step 7.
4. Turn the vacuum pump off. Close the low-pressure hand valve on the manifold-gauge set.
5. Observe the low-pressure gauge for five minutes. If the vacuum drops less than one in. Hg in five minutes, the system does not have any leaks. Proceed with charging the A/C system.
6. If the vacuum drops one in. Hg or more within five minutes, a leak exists. See step 7.
7. If a leak is indicated, charge the A/C system with refrigerant. Use a leak detector to find the leak. Then, discharge the A/C system and make the needed repairs. Evacuate the A/C system once again, then, recharge it.

NOTE: It is necessary to check the manifold-gauge set itself for leakage. Service hoses are plugged with threaded plugs. Then, apply a vacuum to the manifold-gauge set using the vacuum pump. This determines if the manifold gauges and hoses can hold a vacuum. If a vacuum cannot be maintained, a leak exists. Locate the source of the leak and make the needed repairs or obtain another manifold-gauge set.

Triple evacuation

Triple evacuation involves evacuating the A/C system

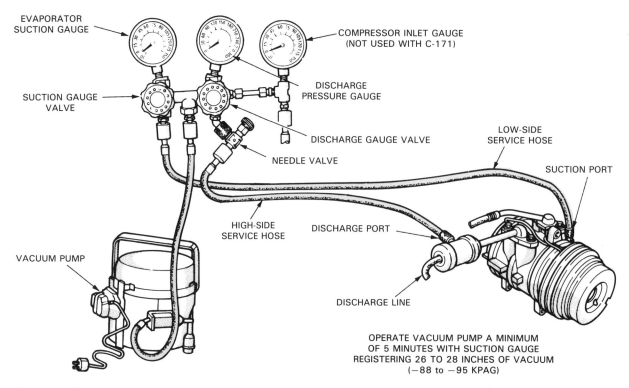

Fig. 20-7. With the manifold service hoses properly installed to the A/C system, the middle service hose connects the manifold gauges to the vacuum pump. (Chrysler)

BOILING POINT OF WATER UNDER A VACUUM	
SYSTEM VACUUM (INCHES MERCURY)	BOILING POINT (TEMPERATURE °F)
24.04	140
25.39	130
26.45	120
27.32	110
27.99	100
28.50	90
28.89	80
29.18	70
29.40	60
29.66	50
29.71	40
29.76	30
29.82	20
29.86	10
29.87	5
29.88	0
29.90	−10
29.91	−20

Fig. 20-8. As the vacuum increases, the temperature at which water boils is reduced. (Ford)

1. FIRST PULL DOWN REMOVES 90% OF THE MOISTURE.
2. FIRST PURGE MIXES WITH REMAINING 10% OF MOISTURE.
3. SECOND PULL DOWN REMOVES 90% OF REMAINING MOISTURE.
4. SECOND PURGE MIXES WITH REMAINING 10% OF MOISTURE.
5. THIRD PULL DOWN DRAWS OUT PRACTICALLY ALL REMAINING MOISTURE.

Fig. 20-9. Triple evacuation. Pull down refers to evacuation. After first and second pull down, the A/C system is charged with refrigerant. The refrigerant mixes with the remaining moisture. The A/C system is then discharged and evacuated again. (Ford)

FLUSHING

Flushing is the removal of foreign matter from the A/C lines, condenser, and evaporator with liquid refrigerant. A badly contaminated A/C system must be flushed. This is indicated when the A/C system contains liquid water, sludge, heavy internal corrosion of metal parts, desiccant (when it breaks loose), black thick refrigerant oil, and/or compressor failure (metal chips circulating through system).

If the compressor has failed or the refrigerant oil has turned black and thick, drain the refrigerant oil from the compressor. Refrigerant oil that has turned black and thick is acidic (acid-based). Flush the A/C components. Replace the receiver-drier or accumulator. The orifice tube should be replaced when the A/C system is flushed or the expansion valve cleaned. If the A/C system is not properly serviced during flushing, repeated problems/

three times to progressively remove almost all of the moisture. Following each evacuation, the A/C system is charged with refrigerant to mix with the remaining moisture, as described in Fig. 20-9. Triple evacuation is performed when there is an indication of moisture in the system. The use of triple evacuation is preferred to flushing because it is less costly and less time-consuming. However, flushing should be done in cases where it is difficult to determine whether the A/C system can be salvaged by using triple evacuation.

failures can be expected. Refill the compressor with new refrigerant oil.

NOTE: Never flush a compressor, receiver-drier, or accumulator.

Refrigerants for flushing

A *flushing agent* is a refrigerant with a high vaporization point. A refrigerant must remain in a liquid state to effectively wash away contaminants (vapor will not wash away contaminants). Two refrigerants can be used as flushing agents. Both R-11 and R-113 have high vaporization points, Fig. 20-10. This ensures both refrigerants remain a liquid at room temperature.

The low closed-container pressure of R-11 and R-113 reduces the dangers of rupturing containers. However, when a refrigerant has a low closed-container pressure, a propellant or pump is needed to circulate the flushing agent through the evaporator, condenser, and lines.

Flushing procedure

The most commonly used flushing kit consists of a cylinder (for the flushing agent), Schrader valve, connecting hose, and a nozzle to inject flushing agent, Fig. 20-11. The following is a preparation for flushing a contaminated A/C system:

1. Make certain hose connections at the flushing cylinder outlet and nozzle are tight.
2. Fill the flushing cylinder with one pint of R-11 or R-113. Make sure the valve assembly at top of cylinder is tightened securely.
3. A refrigerant hose and special dispensing valve connects the can of R-12 to the cylinder filled with the flushing agent. The refrigerant acts as a propellant to push the flushing agent through the A/C components. Make certain the valve on the can is closed and all connections are tight.
4. After discharging the A/C system, disconnect all A/C hoses and lines from the A/C components.
5. Remove the compressor from vehicle, if needed.
6. Remove the expansion valve or orifice tube. Blow the expansion valve clean or install a new orifice tube, if used. Also remove the receiver-drier or accumulator and replace it.
7. Flush the evaporator, condenser, and A/C lines with flushing agent, Figs. 20-12 and 20-13. Catch the contaminated flushing agent in a container.
8. Purge all A/C lines, condenser, and evaporator of

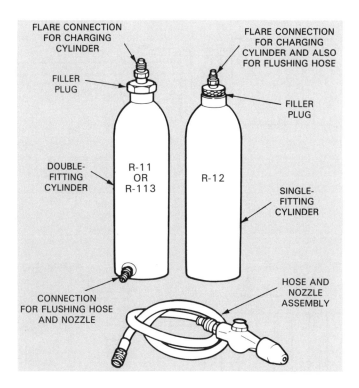

Fig. 20-11. A typical flushing kit. The separate container of R-12 connects to the container of R-11 or R-113. This forces the flushing agent through the A/C system. (Ford)

flushing agent with vaporized nitrogen or R-12.
9. Install the new receiver-drier or accumulator.
10. Add the amount of oil, as specified in the service manual, to the evaporator, condenser, receiver-drier or accumulator, and compressor. Reconnect all A/C lines to their components.
11. Evacuate the A/C system for 30 minutes.
12. Charge the A/C system with the prescribed amount of refrigerant.

ADD REFRIGERANT OIL

When you replace or flush an A/C component (evaporator core or condenser), refrigerant oil must be added to the unit before reinstallation. The refrigerant carries refrigerant oil with it. The refrigerant oil collects inside each component after the system is turned off.

REFRIGERANT FLUSHING INFORMATION CHART

Refrigerant	Vaporizes @ °F**	Approximate Closed Container Pressure @					Adaptability
		60°F	70°F	80°F	90°F	100°F	
R-12	−21.6°F	57 PSI	70 PSI	84 PSI	100 PSI	117 PSI	Self-propelling
R-11	74.7°F	8 in. Hg	3 in. Hg	1 PSI	5 PSI	9 PSI	*Pump needed
R-113	117.6°F	22 in. Hg	19 in. Hg	16 in. Hg	13 in. Hg	8 in. Hg	Pump needed
*R-11 is also available in pressurized containers. This makes it suitable for usage when special flushing equipment is not available. However, it is more toxic than R-12.							
**At sea level atmospheric pressure.							

Fig. 20-10. The boiling points and closed-container pressures of some refrigerants. (Ford)

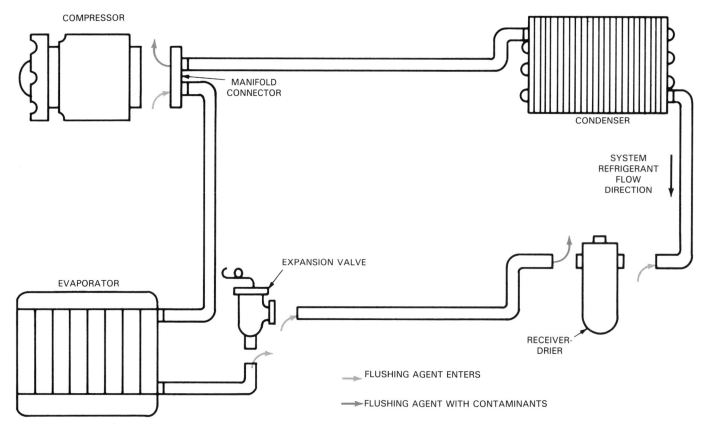

Fig. 20-12. Expansion valve system. With the A/C lines removed, the flushing agent is introduced into the lines, evaporator, and condenser. The flushing agent exits with contaminants. Catch the contaminated flushing agent in a container.

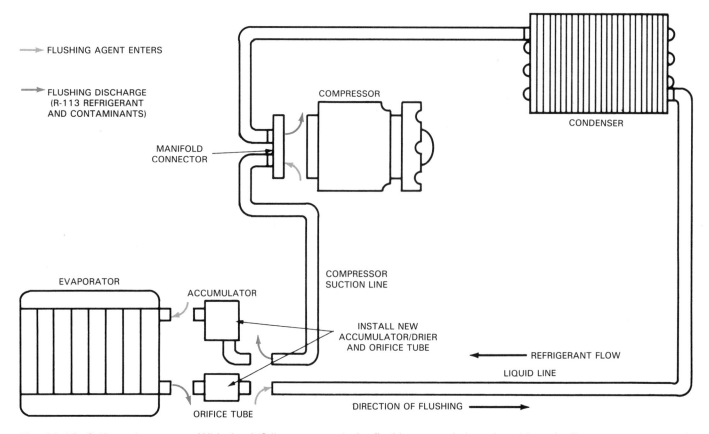

Fig. 20-13. Orifice tube system. With the A/C lines removed, the flushing agent is introduced into the lines, evaporator, and condenser. The flushing agent exits with contaminants. Catch the contaminated flushing agent in a container.

Replenishing the oil supply ensures there is adequate lubrication for the compressor.

If specifications cannot be found in the service manual, the amount of refrigerant oil added to each component is as follows: two ounces to the condenser; one ounce to the receiver-drier or accumulator; two ounces to the evaporator. Assemble all connections using new O-rings lubricated with refrigerant oil.

Minor refrigerant oil loss, usually due to a small refrigerant leak, can be compensated for when charging the A/C system. Oil charge comes in pressurized cans and is added using a charging kit in the same manner as adding refrigerant. Using a can of oil charge eliminates the need for the A/C system to be opened up.

CHARGING AN A/C SYSTEM

Charging is the addition of refrigerant to the A/C system. Before charging the A/C system, obtain the refrigerant capacity of the system from the decal on the compressor. The decal may be located at some other point under the hood. Tolerance must be held accurate to +4/−0 ounces of the specified amount of refrigerant. The larger capacity systems are less sensitive to charge levels that do not fall within the tolerance range.

The accurate charging of an A/C system is of extreme importance to its performance and service life. Failure to accurately charge an A/C system will have a negative effect on performance and may damage the system.

Undercharged A/C system

An *undercharged A/C system* has an insufficient amount of refrigerant. This leads to inadequate cooling and may cause the clutch to cycle on and off too fast. A slightly undercharged A/C system may function satisfactorily in moderate ambient conditions. However, it will fail to cool satisfactorily under extreme heat load conditions and may be difficult to diagnose.

Overcharged A/C system

An *overcharged A/C system* has an excess amount of refrigerant. This also results in inadequate cooling, because the evaporator is flooded with liquid refrigerant. The liquid refrigerant cannot vaporize fast enough to carry the heat with it. Higher than normal liquid level in the A/C system can cause refrigerant control malfunctions. It can also be a cause of a noisy or inoperative compressor.

CHARGING METHODS

There are several methods of charging an A/C system with refrigerant. The preferred method is to use a charging station, due to its convenience, speed, and accuracy. Another accurate method is to use a manifold-gauge set with weigh scales. This ensures proper charge quantities.

Charging stations

Charging stations, Fig. 20-14, can discharge, evacuate, charge, and performance-test an A/C system. The charging station includes manifold gauges, vacuum pump, a place for a 30 lb. drum of refrigerant, and a graduated charging cylinder for the liquid refrigerant. Some may also include a leak detector or a place to store

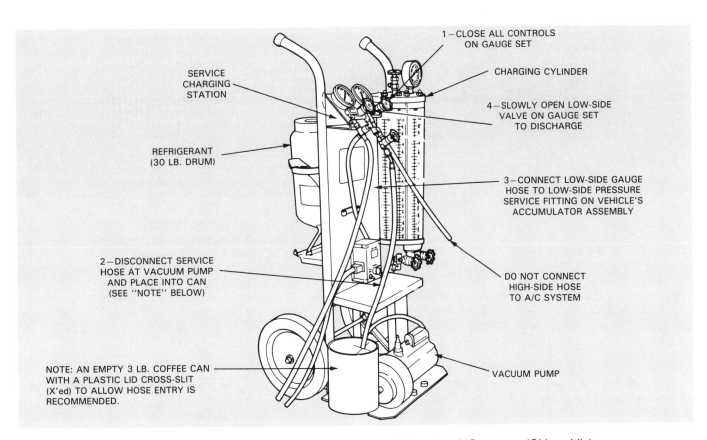

Fig. 20-14. Charging station with sequence for discharging A/C system. (Oldsmobile)

231

it. An internal heater heats the drum of refrigerant to 125 °F (51.6 °C). This speeds the charging process. Some charging stations have an oil injector (adds specified amount of oil to A/C system during charging). Temperature probes are also included that measure ambient and A/C system temperatures.

NOTE: Some electronically controlled refrigerant dispensing units permit the technician to dial in the precise amount of refrigerant charge desired. The equipment adds the specified amount of refrigerant to the auto A/C system, then shuts off automatically.

Charging with a 30 lb. drum

Many repair shops charge automotive A/C systems with refrigerant from a 30 lb. drum, used in combination with a weigh scale (usually electronic) and a manifold guage set. Fig. 20-15 shows placement of the drum on the scale. This is the most popular charging method, because of the economy possible through buying refrigerant in large quantity. It eliminates the expense of a charging station. This is an accurate method, since the electronic scale shows precisely how much refrigerant has been added to the auto A/C system.

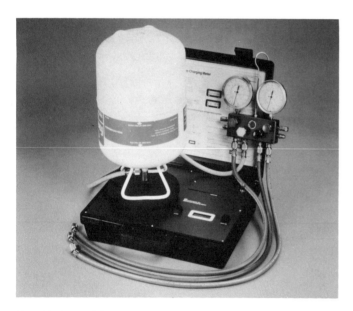

Fig. 20-15. A 30 lb. drum of refrigerant is inverted and placed on an electronic scale. (TIF)

Charging with 14-ounce cans

Another method of charging an A/C system is with disposable cans of refrigerant, Fig. 20-16. Since each can contains 14 ounces of refrigerant, it is impossible to provide an accurate partial charge (for example, five ounces). Only an approximation can be assumed.

Liquid charging

When charging the A/C system with 14-ounce cans or 30 lb. drum, the position of the can or drum determines if a liquid or a vapor is dispensed, Fig. 20-17. If liquid refrigerant enters the compressor, it can cause a hydraulic lock that can severely damage the compressor. Liquid charging, which is faster, can be used on A/C

systems with an accumulator. The liquid refrigerant vaporizes in the accumulator.

NOTE: Never add liquid refrigerant to the low-pressure side on a system that uses a receiver-drier.

CHARGING PROCEDURE

The following procedure for charging can be used regardless of whether a charging station, 30 lb. drum and weigh scale, or the 14-ounce can method is used:

1. Attach center hose from manifold-gauge set to refrigerant supply. The container of refrigerant can be placed in a pan or container of hot water. This speeds up the charging operation (water temperature not to exceed 125 °F).
2. Place the refrigerant supply and pan of hot water on an accurate scale and note the weight.
3. Subtract the weight of required refrigerant charge for the specific A/C system from current scale reading. Charging the a/c system decreases the weight of the refrigerant in its container. When the scale is at the desired reading, the A/C system is fully charged.
4. Purge center hose of the manifold-gauge set. This step is not done when an ACR3 station is used.
5. Open the low-pressure gauge hand valve when the engine and air conditioner are both turned on and running.

CAUTION: Never charge the A/C system through the high side by opening the high-side hand valve. The high-pressure refrigerant would overpressurize the container, causing it to explode.

6. Close the low-pressure hand valve and the dispensing valve at the refrigerant supply.
7. The sight glass (if so equipped) should be clear after the specified amount of refrigerant has been drawn into the A/C system.
8. Turn off the A/C system and engine.
9. Disconnect the manifold hoses at the service valves.

CAUTION: Never disconnect a service hose at the manifold gauge assembly. This will discharge the refrigerant from the A/C system.

10. Check the A/C system for leaks.
11. Performance test A/C system.

NOTE: Most A/C systems use a low-pressure cutout switch, or in some cases a thermal limiter, to prevent compressor operation when the refrigerant level is low. A jumper wire is needed to bypass these devices, Fig. 20-18. This allows compressor operation during the charging process. The compressor must be operational so that refrigerant can be drawn into the A/C system.

PERFORMANCE TEST

Once the A/C system has been charged and leak tested, check the readings of both high and low-pressure gauges. Also, insert a thermometer in the center register to determine the discharge air temperature, Fig. 20-19. This check will determine if any problems exist in the A/C

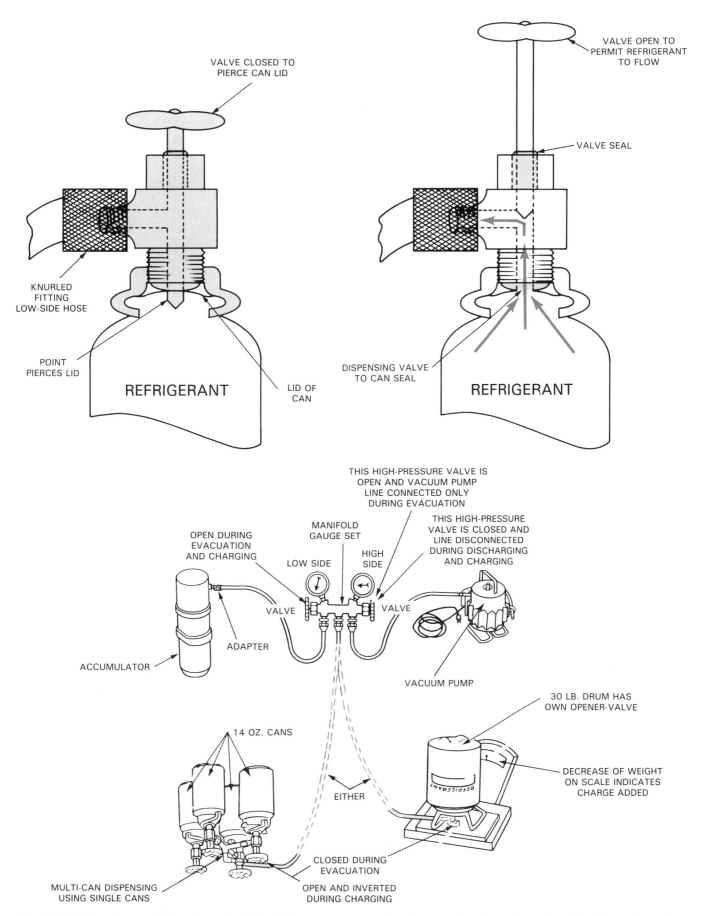

VALVE CLOSED TO
PIERCE CAN LID

KNURLED
FITTING
LOW-SIDE HOSE

POINT
PIERCES LID

REFRIGERANT

LID OF
CAN

VALVE OPEN TO
PERMIT REFRIGERANT
TO FLOW

VALVE SEAL

DISPENSING VALVE
TO CAN SEAL

REFRIGERANT

THIS HIGH-PRESSURE VALVE IS
OPEN AND VACUUM PUMP
LINE CONNECTED ONLY
DURING EVACUATION

THIS HIGH-PRESSURE
VALVE IS CLOSED AND
LINE DISCONNECTED
DURING DISCHARGING
AND CHARGING

OPEN DURING
EVACUATION
AND CHARGING

MANIFOLD
GAUGE SET

LOW SIDE

HIGH
SIDE

VALVE

VALVE

ACCUMULATOR

ADAPTER

VACUUM PUMP

30 LB. DRUM HAS
OWN OPENER-VALVE

DECREASE OF WEIGHT
ON SCALE INDICATES
CHARGE ADDED

14 OZ. CANS

EITHER

CLOSED DURING
EVACUATION

MULTI-CAN DISPENSING
USING SINGLE CANS

OPEN AND INVERTED
DURING CHARGING

Fig. 20-16. Charging an A/C system. A—Using 14 ounce cans requires the use of a dispensing valve. The dispensing valve punctures the can lid of refrigerant. B—The 30 lb. drum of refrigerant or multi 14 ounce can dispensing unit can also be used. (GMC)

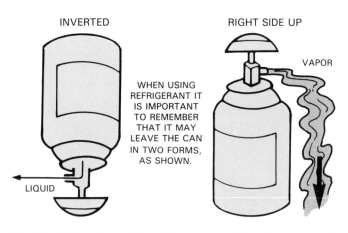

INVERTED

RIGHT SIDE UP

VAPOR

LIQUID

WHEN USING REFRIGERANT IT IS IMPORTANT TO REMEMBER THAT IT MAY LEAVE THE CAN IN TWO FORMS, AS SHOWN.

Fig. 20-17. Position of the refrigerant container determines if a liquid or vapor is dispensed. (Volkswagen)

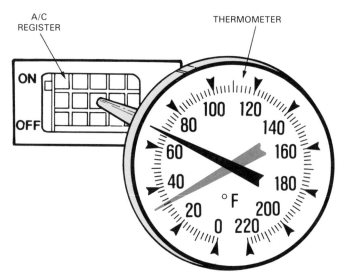

A/C REGISTER

THERMOMETER

ON

OFF

°F

Fig. 20-19. A thermometer is placed in the register. This determines discharge air temperature, which should be between 20° and 40 °F cooler than ambient air temperature, depending on humidity. (Volkswagen)

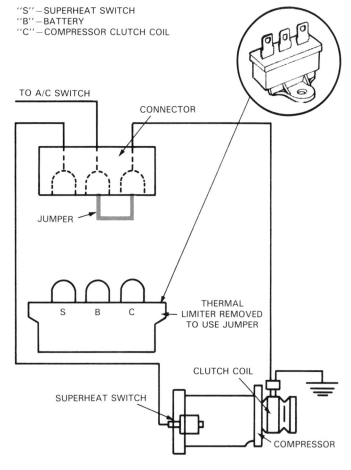

"S"—SUPERHEAT SWITCH
"B"—BATTERY
"C"—COMPRESSOR CLUTCH COIL

TO A/C SWITCH

CONNECTOR

JUMPER

S B C

THERMAL LIMITER REMOVED TO USE JUMPER

CLUTCH COIL

SUPERHEAT SWITCH

COMPRESSOR

Fig. 20-18. The thermal limiter must be removed and a jumper wire inserted between electrical connections B and C, so that compressor is operational.

system. If there are any performance problems with the A/C system, the problem should be corrected prior to returning the car to the customer.

SUMMARY

Discharging, flushing, and charging are all procedures that expose the technician to the dangers of refrigerant.

Discharging is the removal of refrigerant from the A/C system. Discharging is required prior to opening or removing a component from the A/C system. Discharging should be into a can or preferably through a refrigerant recovery station.

Evacuation is the pumping down of the system to remove air and moisture. The technician must make a judgment call as to whether a single or triple evacuation is required, or if flushing is necessary.

Flushing is the removal of foreign matter from the A/C lines, condenser, and evaporator. Flushing agents are refrigerants that have high vaporization points. Flushing an A/C system is performed when liquid water, sludge, heavy internal corrosion of metal parts, black thick refrigerant oil, or loose desiccant are noted, or when a compressor has failed.

Charging is the addition of refrigerant to the A/C system. Charging an A/C system is absolutely critical for optimum performance and acceptable service life. The tolerance is critical. Therefore, it is necessary to charge the system within a tolerance of $+4/-0$ ounces.

The charging supply may be 14-ounce cans or a 30 lb. drum of refrigerant. The charging station requires a 30 lb. drum and is the preferred method for charging an A/C system. The operator can program the exact amount of refrigerant required for any given system. This ensures the charge of refrigerant will be within the specified tolerance. Another method is using a manifold-gauge set, 30 lb. drum, and weigh scales. This requires the technician to weigh the refrigerant container and mathematically determine the final scale weight. An alternate method uses the manifold-gauge set with 14-ounce cans of refrigerant. It is impossible to determine a partial quantity when using a 14-ounce can. Liquid charging is faster, but can only be done on systems using an accumulator.

At the completion of the evacuation and charging process, it is customary to leak test and conduct a performance test. This ensures the A/C system is operating within the manufacturers specified limits.

KNOW THESE TERMS

Discharging, Refrigerant recovery method, Air conditioning refrigerant recovery/recycling station, Recycling refrigerant, Evacuation, Triple evacuation, Flushing, Flushing agent, Charging, Undercharged A/C system, Overcharged A/C system, Charging station.

REVIEW QUESTIONS—CHAPTER 20

1. When and why is the A/C system discharged?
2. A vacuum pump can be used for checking A/C system leaks. True or false?
3. The process of evacuation is used to remove:
   a. Only moisture from the system.
   b. Only air from the system.
   c. Air and moisture from the system.
   d. Debris and metal particles.
4. Liquid charging is done with the refrigerant supply in the upright position. True or false?
5. To salvage a badly contaminated A/C system, it must:
   a. Have a single evacuation.
   b. Have a triple evacuation.
   c. Be flushed out.
   d. Be blown out with nitrogen.
6. The sight glass should be clear after charging. True or false?
7. To properly evacuate an A/C system, a vacuum of 25-30 in. Hg must be obtained for:
   a. 10-15 minutes.
   b. 15-20 minutes.
   c. 5-10 minutes.
   d. 20-30 minutes.
8. The A/C system should be discharged slowly. This minimizes:
   a. Moisture from entering the A/C system.
   b. Refrigerant oil loss.
   c. Compressor shaft seal damage.
   d. Damage to the vacuum pump.
9. A pan of hot water is helpful when charging an A/C system. Why?

10. If high- and low-side pressure readings increase after the refrigerant has been recovered using an ACR3 station, what action needs to be taken?
11. Name the two methods for discharging refrigerant.
12. After flushing a contaminated system, it is necessary to:
    a. Evacuate the system.
    b. Replace the accumulator or receiver-drier.
    c. Purge system with refrigerant vapor.
    d. All of the above.
13. Refrigerant is charged and discharged through the _____ hose of the manifold-gauge set.
14. List the causes for replacing a filter of the ACR3 station.
15. When should the A/C system be evacuated?
16. After the condenser, evaporator, and lines are flushed and purged, it is necessary to evacuate the A/C system. True or false?
17. The reduced pressure (vacuum) in the A/C system during evacuation:
    a. Removes refrigerant oil.
    b. Removes foreign matter.
    c. Eliminates the flushing process.
    d. Causes moisture to vaporize and be drawn off.
18. List the causes for flushing the components of an A/C system.
19. If the high-pressure hand valve were to be opened while charging the A/C system when it is operating, what could result?
20. To accurately charge an A/C system, a 30 lb. drum of refrigerant and manifold-gauge set must be used in conjunction with a:
    a. Weigh scale.
    b. Pan of warm water.
    c. Both a and b.
    d. None of the above.
21. The charging station is the most accurate and fastest method of charging a system. True or false?
22. Never remove the service hose from the manifold gauge assembly. True or false?
23. What is a flushing agent?

AMC TECHNICAL SERVICE MANUAL

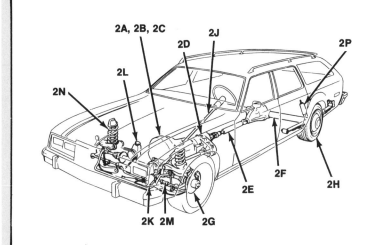

PART 1 POWER PLANT

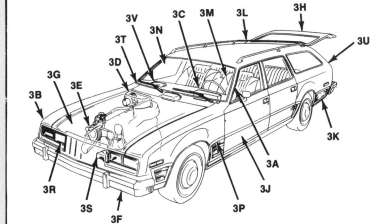

PART 2 CHASSIS

PART 3 BODY

Fig. 21-1. A table of contents lists the different sections of the service manual. Each section contains many topics. (Chrysler)

USING MANUALS AND REPAIR ORDERS

After studying this chapter, you will be able to:
* *Explain the differences between a service and repair manual.*
* *Describe how to use a flat rate manual.*
* *Relate how to fill out a repair order.*
* *Summarize the difference between diagnosis charts.*

INTRODUCTION

In earlier chapters, you have learned theory and repair procedures for servicing automotive A/C systems. Modern air conditioning systems are complex and varied. Manuals must be used for specifications when troubleshooting or repairing the A/C system.

TYPES OF MANUALS

There are two types of manuals. One type is the service manual. Some manufacturers refer to this as a shop manual. The other type is the repair manual. Information on specifications and repair procedures are contained in each type.

Service manuals

All car manufacturers produce their own *service manuals.* They contain specifications, diagnosis, and repair procedures for all systems of a specific car model. A service manual is published for each car model the manufacturer produces every year. Specifications, diagnosis, and/or repair procedures may change each year. Car manufacturers also produce ''specialized service manuals'' which cover repair and specifications for specific components.

The service manual also changes every year to reflect changes and modifications. Components, systems, service, test procedures, and specifications frequently change from year to year. Therefore, use only a service manual for the specific model and year of the car you are working on.

Service manuals are divided into sections to make the information easier to find. See Fig. 21-1. The general information section includes data relating to all models of that car manufacturer. Vehicle identification number, belt tension, general maintenance, maintenance schedules, lubrication, fluid capacity and specifications, bolt torque, bolt grade classification, towing procedures, and lift points are some of the things found in the general information section.

An important topic in the general information section is the vehicle identification number (VIN). The VIN is located on the top left side of the instrument panel and can be seen through the windshield, Fig. 21-2A. The VIN contains 17 digits. Each digit, or series of digits, provides data about the car, Fig. 21-2B. Most car makers also locate the VIN on the Federal Safety Certification Label that is located on the driver's door, Fig. 21-3. The *Body Identification Plate* may also be located on the driver's door. It contains data on the exterior paint color and interior trim, Fig. 21-3.

The other sections of the service manual contain very specific information on the topic. A technician can perform tests and make a diagnosis based on this data. The repair or replacement procedure of the failed component is also covered. Service manuals show many exploded views of the parts, Fig. 21-4. Service manuals also include vacuum and wiring diagrams that are sometimes needed for the troubleshooting process, Fig. 21-5.

Repair manuals

Repair manuals are published by companies other than by the car maker (Chilton, Mitchell, and Motor). Repair manuals are not as detailed as service manuals. A repair manual provides information for only the most common types of repair work. They cover more than one car manufacturer, make, and model for a seven-year time span. Due to the cost of each individual service manual (not to mention the space all the service manuals require), most independent garages buy repair manuals.

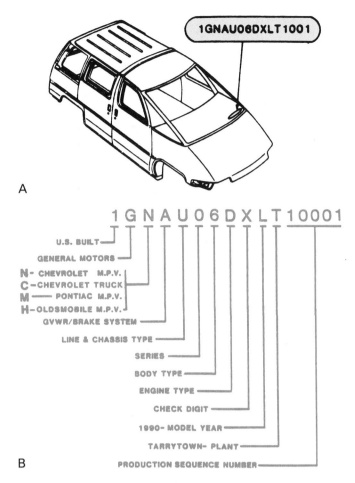

A

B

```
1 G N A U 0 6 D X L T 1 0 0 0 1
U.S. BUILT
GENERAL MOTORS
N- CHEVROLET M.P.V.
C- CHEVROLET TRUCK
M- PONTIAC M.P.V.
H- OLDSMOBILE M.P.V.
GVWR/BRAKE SYSTEM
LINE & CHASSIS TYPE
SERIES
BODY TYPE
ENGINE TYPE
CHECK DIGIT
1990- MODEL YEAR
TARRYTOWN- PLANT
PRODUCTION SEQUENCE NUMBER
```

Fig. 21-2. Vehicle identification number. A—VIN can be seen through the windshield on all vehicles. B—The service manual contains the information needed to decipher the VIN. (Oldsmobile)

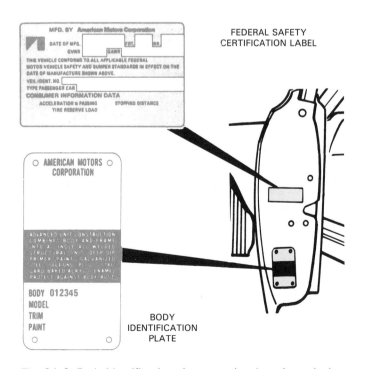

Fig. 21-3. Body identification plate contains data about the internal and external paint color used on the car.

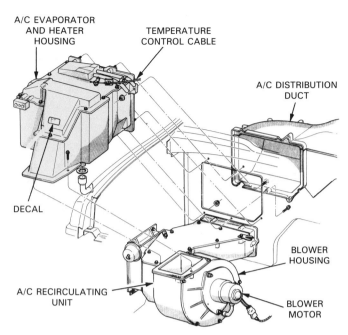

Fig. 21-4. Service manuals contain illustrations. This gives the technician a better understanding of how a part is assembled. Exploded view shows the evaporator/heater case removed from the blower motor housing and distribution duct. (Chrysler)

Separate repair manuals must be purchased for domestic and import models.

DIAGNOSTIC CHARTS

Service or repair manuals both contain diagnostic charts. The diagnostic chart guides the technician in a logical step-by-step testing sequence in finding the problem. Diagnostic charts can be either the logic tree or block chart type.

Logic tree

The *logic tree diagnostic chart* shows each diagnostic step branching out from the problem (tree), Fig. 21-6. Also, each main branch has its own smaller branches of test procedures leading to the solution. While there are many branches, only one will accurately lead to the solution of the problem.

Block charts

A *block diagnostic chart* lists the symptoms and probable causes in column form, Fig. 21-7. A block diagnostic chart can be read from left to right or from top to bottom, depending on the chart.

SPECIAL TOOLS

A *special tool* is designed for one specific operation that a normal hand tool cannot perform. Service and repair manuals state when a special tool is needed to perform a specific repair and show a line drawing or photo of the special tool in use. The part number for the special tool is usually shown in the illustration. Several different companies make special tools. Consult the local auto parts store or service department at the new car dealership for details.

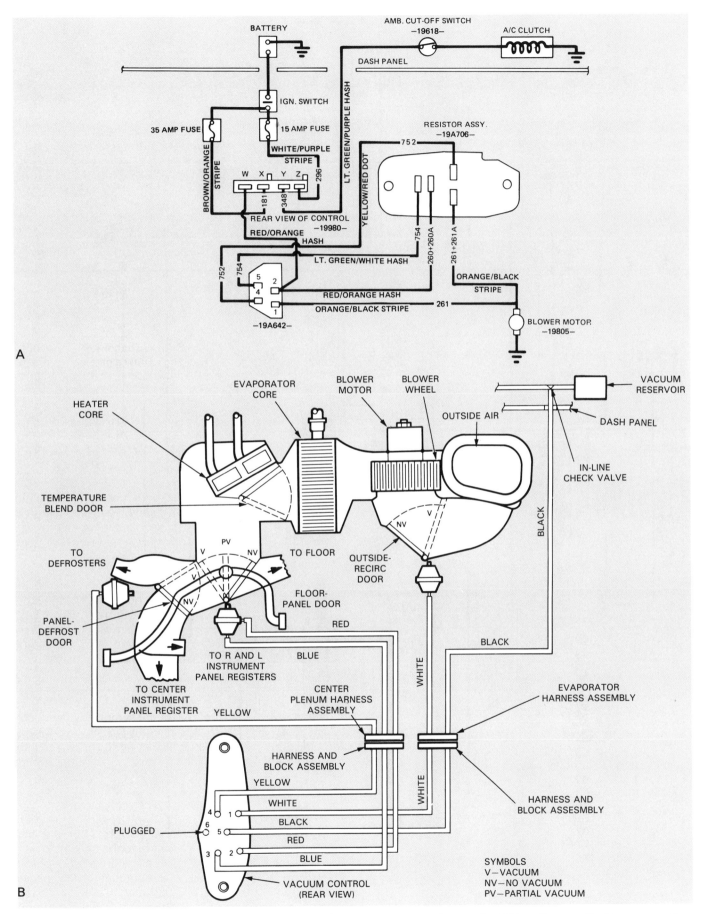

Fig. 21-5. Service manuals also contain diagrams needed to troubleshoot problems. A—Wiring diagram. B—Vacuum routing diagram. (Ford)

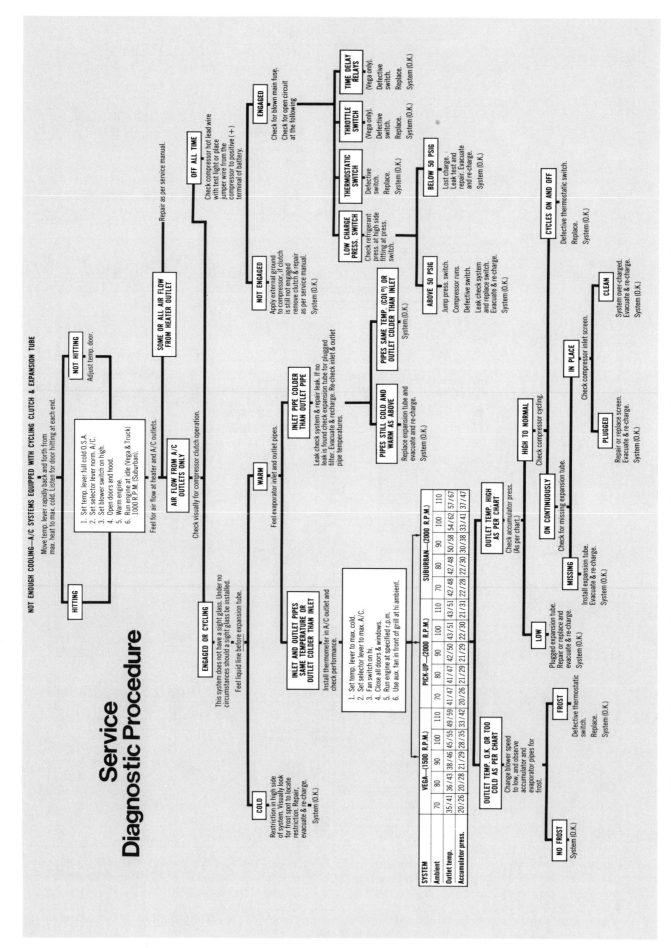

Service
Diagnostic Procedure

NOT ENOUGH COOLING—A/C SYSTEMS EQUIPPED WITH CYCLING CLUTCH & EXPANSION TUBE

Fig. 21-6. Logic tree diagnostic chart has problem stated at the top. Following the logical sequence or branch leads to the solution. (GM)

HIGH (DISCHARGE) PRESSURE	LOW (SUCTION) PRESSURE	CLUTCH CYCLE TIME			COMPONENT — CAUSES
		RATE	ON	OFF	
HIGH	HIGH	CONTINUOUS RUN			CONDENSER — Inadequate Airflow
HIGH	NORMAL TO HIGH				ENGINE OVERHEATING
NORMAL TO HIGH	NORMAL				AIR IN REFRIGERANT. REFRIGERANT OVERCHARGE (a) HUMIDITY OR AMBIENT TEMP. VERY HIGH (b).
NORMAL	HIGH				FIXED ORIFICE TUBE — Missing. O-Rings Leaking/Missing
NORMAL	HIGH	SLOW	LONG	LONG	CLUTCH CYCLING SWITCH — High Cut-In
NORMAL	NORMAL	SLOW OR NO CYCLE	LONG OR CONTINUOUS	NORMAL OR NO CYCLE	MOISTURE IN REFRIGERANT SYSTEM. EXCESSIVE REFRIGERANT OIL
		FAST	SHORT	SHORT	CLUTCH CYCLING SWITCH — Low Cut-In or High Cut-Out
NORMAL	LOW	SLOW	LONG	LONG	CLUTCH CYCLING SWITCH — Low Cut-Out
NORMAL TO LOW	HIGH	CONTINUOUS RUN			Compressor — Low Performance
NORMAL TO LOW	NORMAL TO HIGH	CONTINUOUS RUN			A/C SUCTION LINE — Partially Restricted or Plugged (c)
NORMAL TO LOW	NORMAL	FAST	SHORT	NORMAL	EVAPORATOR — Low Airflow
			SHORT TO VERY SHORT	NORMAL TO LONG	CONDENSER, FIXED ORIFICE TUBE, OR A/C LIQUID LINE — Partially Restricted or Plugged
			SHORT TO VERY SHORT	SHORT TO VERY SHORT	LOW REFRIGERANT CHARGE
			SHORT TO VERY SHORT	LONG	EVAPORATOR CORE — Partially Restricted or Plugged
NORMAL TO LOW	LOW	CONTINUOUS RUN			A/C SUCTION LINE — Partially Restricted or Plugged. (d) CLUTCH CYCLING SWITCH — Sticking Closed
LOW	NORMAL	VERY FAST	VERY SHORT	VERY SHORT	CLUTCH CYCLING SWITCH — Cycling Range Too Close
ERRATIC OPERATION OR COMPRESSOR NOT RUNNING		—	—	—	CLUTCH CYCLING SWITCH — Dirty Contacts or Sticking Open. POOR CONNECTION AT A/C CLUTCH CONNECTOR OR CLUTCH CYCLING SWITCH CONNECTOR. A/C ELECTRICAL CIRCUIT ERRATIC — See A/C Electrical Circuit Wiring Diagram

ADDITIONAL POSSIBLE CAUSE COMPONENTS ASSOCIATED WITH INADEQUATE COMPRESSOR OPERATION

- COMPRESSOR CLUTCH Slipping • LOOSE DRIVE BELT
- CLUTCH COIL Open — Shorted, or Loose Mounting
- CONTROL ASSEMBLY SWITCH — Dirty Contacts or Sticking Open
- CLUTCH WIRING CIRCUIT — High Resistance, Open or Blown Fuse

ADDITIONAL POSSIBLE CAUSE COMPONENTS ASSOCIATED WITH A DAMAGED COMPRESSOR

- CLUTCH CYCLING SWITCH — Sticking Closed or Compressor Clutch Seized
- SUCTION ACCUMULATOR DRIER — Refrigerant Oil Bleed Hole Plugged
- REFRIGERANT LEAKS

(a) Compressor may make noise on initial run. This is slugging condition caused by excessive liquid refrigerant.
(b) Compressor clutch may not cycle in ambient temperatures above 80°F depending on humidity conditions.
(c) Low pressure reading will be **normal to high** if pressure is taken at accumulator and if restriction is downstream of service access valve.
(d) Low pressure reading will be **low** if pressure is taken near the compressor and restriction is upstream of service access valve.

Fig. 21-7. Block diagnostic chart is in column form. The chart is read from left to right. High- and low-pressure readings, along with clutch cycle time, are the symptoms. Column at far right shows the solution(s).   (Ford)

ABBREVIATIONS

Abbreviations are shortened forms of a long word or several words. They save space in publications. Mechanics and parts specialists usually use the abbreviated part name. Abbreviations may be explained the first time they are used in the text, or may be listed in the front or back of the service manual, Fig. 21-8.

FLAT RATE MANUAL

The *flat rate manual* is a book that aids in calculating how much labor, in terms of hours, to charge for a specific repair. The exception to this is when the technician troubleshoots electrical problems. The actual time spent on diagnosis is clocked and recorded on the repair order.

LIST OF AUTOMOTIVE ABBREVIATIONS WHICH MAY BE USED IN THIS MANUAL

A/C—Air Conditioning
ACCEL—Accelerator
ADJ—Adjust
A/F—Air Fuel Ratio
AIR—Air Injection Reaction System
ALDL—Assembly Line Diagnostic Link
Alt—Altitude
AMP—Ampere(s)
ANT—Antenna
APS—Absolute Pressure Sensor
ASM—Assembly
AT—Automatic Transmission/Transaxle
ATDC—After Top Dead Center
Auth—Authority
Auto—Automatic

BARO—Barometric
Bat—Battery
Bat+—Battery Positive Terminal
Bbl—Barrel
BCM—Body Control Module
BP—Back Pressure
BTDC—Before Top Dead Center

°C—Degrees Celsius
Calif—California
Cat. Conv.—Catalytic Converter
CCC—Computer Command Control
CCOT—Cycling Clutch Orifice Tube
CCP—Controlled Canister Purge
CID—Cubic Inch Displacement
CL—Closed Loop
CLCC—Closed Loop Carburetor Control
CO—Carbon Monoxide
Coax—Coaxial
Conn—Connector
Conv—Converter
CP—Canister Purge
CPS—Central Power Supply
Crank—Crankshaft
CTS—Coolant Temperature Sensor
CV—Constant Velocity
Cyl—Cylinder(s)
C³I—Computer Controlled Coil Ignition

DBM—Dual Bed Monolith
Diff—Differential
DIS—Direct Ignition System
Dist—Distributor
DVDV—Differential Vacuum Delay Valve
DVM—Digital Voltmeter (10 meg.)

EAC—Electric Air Control
EAS—Electric Air Switching
ECC—Electronic Climate Control
ECM—Electronic Control Module
ECU—Engine Calibration Unit (PROM)
EECS—Evaporative Emission Control
    System
EFE—Early Fuel Evaporation
EFI—Electronic Fuel Injection
EGR—Exhaust Gas Recirculation
EGR/TVS—Exhaust Gas Recirculation/
    Thermostatic Vacuum Switch
ELC—Electronic Level Control
ESC—Electronic Spark Control
EST—Electronic Spark Timing
ETR—Electronically Tuned Receiver
EVRV—Electronic Vacuum Regulator
    Valve (EGR)
EXH—Exhaust

°F—Degrees Fahrenheit
FED—Federal (All States Except Calif.)
FWD—Front Wheel Drive

GAL—Gallon
Gen—Generator
Gov—Governor
g—gram

Harn—Harness
HC—Hydrocarbons
HD—Heavy Duty
HEI—High Energy Ignition
Hg—Mercury
HiAlt—High Altitude

IAC—Idle Air Control
IC—Integrated Circuit
ID—Identification
    —Inside Diameter
IGN—Ignition
ILC—Idle Load Compensator
INJ—Injection
IP—Instrument Control
IPC—Instrument Panel Cluster
INT—Intake

km—Kilometer
km/h—Kilometer per hour
kPa—KiloPascals
KV—Kilovolts (thousands of volts)

L—Liter
lbs. ft.—pounds foot
lbs. in.—pounds inch
LF—Left Front
LH—Left Hand
LR—Left Rear
LS—Left Side
L-4—In-line four-cylinder engines

MAF—Mass Air Flow
MAN—Manual
MAP—Manifold Absolute Pressure
MAT—Manifold Air Temperature
MEM-CAL—Memory and Calibration Unit
Max—Maximum
M/C—Mixture Control
Min—Minimum
mm—millimeter
MPFI—Multi-Port Fuel Injection
MPG—Miles Per Gallon
MPH—Miles Per Hour
MT—Manual Transaxle/Transmission
MV—Millivolt

NC—Normally closed
N•m—Newton Meter
NO—Normally open
NOx—Nitrogen, Oxides of

OD—Outside diameter
OHC—Overhead Camshaft
OL—Open Loop
O₂—Oxygen

PAIR—Pulse Air Injection System
P/B—Power Brakes
PFI—Portable Fuel Injection
PRESS—Pressure
PROM—Programmable Read Only Memory
P/N—Park/Neutral
P/S—Power Steering

PSI—Pounds per Square Inch
Pt.—Pint
Pri—Primary
PWM—Pulse Width Modulated

Qt—Quart

REF—Reference
RF—Right Front
RFI—Radio Frequency Interference
RH—Right Hand
RPM—Revolutions per Minute
RPO—Regular Production Option
RR—Right Rear
RS—Right Side
RTV—Room Temperature Vulcanizing
RVB—Rear Vacuum Break
RVR—Response Vacuum Reducer
RWD—Rear Wheel Drive

SAE—Society of Automotive Engineers
Sec—Secondary
SES—Service Engine Soon
SFI—Sequential-port Fuel Injection
SI—System International
Sol—Solenoid
SPEC—Specification
Speedo-Speedometer
SYN—Synchronize

TAC—Thermostatic Air Cleaner
Tach—Tachometer
TBI—Throttle Body Injection
TCC—Trasmission/Transaxle
    Converter Clutch
TDC—Top Dead Center
Term—Terminal
Thermo—Thermostatic Air Cleaner
TEMP—Temperature
TPS—Throttle Position Sensor
TRANS—Transaxle/Transmission
TV—Throttle Valve
TVRS—Television & Radio Suppressioin
TVS—Thermal Vacuum Switch

U-Joint—Universal Joint

V—Volt(s)
VAC—Vacuum
VIN—Vehicle Identification Number
V-ref—ECM reference voltage
VRV—Vacuum Reducer Valve
VSS—Vehicle Speed Sensor
V-6—Six-cylinder "V" engine
V-8—Eight-cylinder "V" engine

w/—With
w/b—Wheel base
w/o—Without
WOT—Wide Open Throttle

Fig. 21-8. Abbreviations may be listed in the service manual. (Oldsmobile)

The flat rate manual lists the number of hours to perform each repair for most every year, make, and model car made in a seven-year time span. Separate flat rate manuals are published for import and domestic car models. The specified amount of time for each repair is charged whether the technician takes less or more time than allotted.

Using the flat rate manual

Multiply the shop's hourly labor rate by the time indicated in the flat rate manual for the specific repair to determine the dollar amount. For example, the flat rate manual may specify that it takes four hours to remove and replace (R & R) the evaporator core for a specific car. If the shop's labor rate is $50.00 per hour, the cost to R & R the evaporator is $200.00. The price of the evaporator is not included and must be added to the labor. Do not forget to add other operations not included in the R & R of the evaporator, such as labor for

evacuation and charging the A/C system.

Most flat rate manuals also list the part numbers and prices. This will enable you to estimate the cost of the job prior to performing it. Some states require that you give the customer a written estimate before performing the needed repairs. If the actual cost exceeds the written estimate, the shop may have to absorb the difference.

REPAIR ORDER

The *repair order* (R.O.) contains space for the name and address of the customer along with information on the car. The repair order serves as a document that records the problem described by the customer. It also serves to record the parts and repairs needed to correct the problem. The repair order acts as the needed authorization for the repair. Describe the problem, insufficient cooling in this case, on the first line under the labor heading, Fig. 21-9.

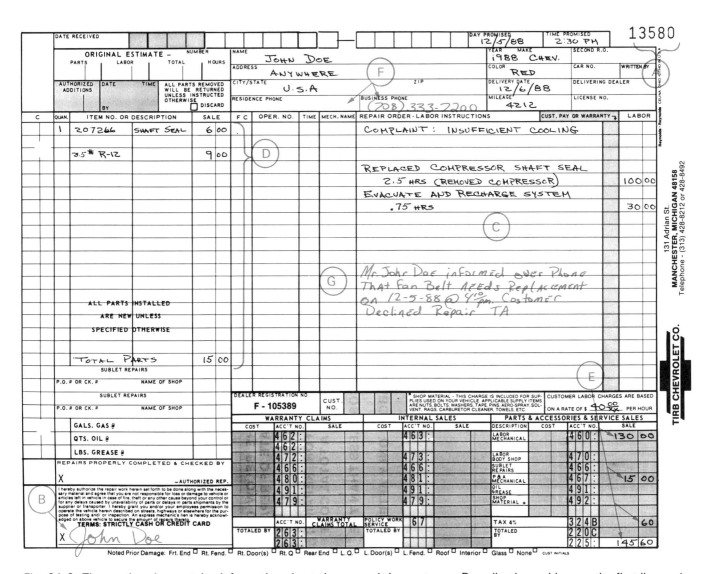

Fig. 21-9. The repair order contains information about the car and the customer. Describe the problem on the first line under the labor column. A—Control number. B—Customer signature. C—Labor operation performed by mechanic to correct the problem. D—Parts needed by mechanic to correct the problem. E—Add the total parts, labor, and tax together. This is the amount customer pays. F—Phone number where customer can be reached during working hours. G—Document the repair order with other problems found. Include the problem and the date and time the customer was informed, along with customer's decision. Initial the statement.

Repair order control number

The *control number,* Fig. 21-9A, is a sequential number listed on all repair orders (warranty and nonwarranty) and allows easy tracking of all repair orders. The control number ascends on each repair order. The service manager is responsible for each repair order. There cannot be such a thing as a "lost repair order." If a repair order cannot be accounted for, it may be assumed the shop is using questionable practices.

Signature on the repair order

The repair order must be signed by the customer before the technician attempts any repairs, Fig. 21-9B. This relieves the shop and mechanic of any responsibility should anything happen to the car beyond their control (fire and theft). It also implies that the customer consented to the repairs should there be any legal conflicts.

Repair order labor column

Once the mechanic determines the problem with the car, the repairs are made. The labor column on the repair order provides a space for the mechanic to write down what repairs were made to correct the problem, Fig. 21-9C. The service manager then looks up the allotted time for the repairs in the flat rate manual. The service manager then multiplies the flat rate time by the hourly rate, $40.00 per hour in this case. The dollar amount for labor is then entered on the repair order next to each repair.

Repair order parts column

The parts column on the repair order provides a place for the parts department to list the parts used to make the needed repairs, Fig. 21-9D. The part number, description, quantity, and price must be listed separately for each part. The total parts dollar amount is written at the bottom of the parts column, since some states tax only the parts and not the labor.

Total amount due on the repair order

The dollar amount for all parts and labor is entered at the lower right hand section of the repair order. A place for the tax is also included. Add the labor, parts, and tax together. Place this amount at the very bottom of the column. This is the amount the customer must pay, Fig. 21-9E.

PROTECT YOURSELF AND THE SHOP

While making the needed repairs, the mechanic may find other problems with the car. The technician should phone the customer immediately at the number indicated on the repair order, Fig. 21-9F. Inform the customer of the problem and estimate the additional repairs. Write down the problem you found on the repair order and indicate the date and time you talked with the customer, Fig. 21-9G. Also, write down whether the customer agreed to or declined the repairs. Always initial this statement on the repair order. Failing to inform the customer of other problems, or not documenting the problems, can cause the customer to initiate a lawsuit.

The customer may agree to the additional repairs, but forget about the verbal agreement when paying the bill.

The service manager can show the date and time the customer was contacted, and by whom, when it is documented on the repair order. If additional repairs are made without the customer's consent, the shop may have to absorb the expense for the repairs.

The customer may decline to correct the other problems found by the mechanic. If the car breaks down at a later date, due to the declined repairs, the customer may want to take legal action against the shop. However, since the problem was documented on the repair order stating the customer was warned, the customer has little (if any) legal recourse.

SUMMARY

Service manuals are precisely written technical guides that explain how to diagnose and repair one specific make and year of car. Included in the manuals are specifications, diagrams, illustrations, wiring and vacuum schematics, and step-by-step procedures for maintenance and repair of each car model.

Repair manuals cover a wide variety of car models for a seven-year period. However, repair manuals only cover the most common diagnosis and repair procedures. Separate repair manuals are needed for domestic and import car models.

Flat rate manuals list the allotted time for each repair for most car makes and car models made in a seven-year time span. The flat rate manual does not cover the time to diagnose electrical problems. The specified repair time is multiplied by the hourly rate charged by the shop. Separate flat rate manuals are needed for domestic and import car models.

Diagnostic charts are used to solve problems that occur on cars. Diagnostic charts can be of a logic tree or block form. The logic tree chart has many different branches. The block type is read from left to right or top to bottom, depending on the chart. Both charts use a logical step-by-step approach.

A repair order is a written log of the work performed on the car and the parts needed to correct the problem. The repair order contains a control number that allows tracking of each and every repair order. The service manager is responsible for every repair order. The customer must sign the repair order prior to the technician making the needed repairs. The repair order contains separate columns for parts and labor. Add the parts total to the total labor. Place this amount, plus any tax, at the lower right-hand corner of the repair order. This is the amount the customer must pay. Document on the work order any other problem observed on the car. Documentation includes the nature of the problem, the date and time the customer was informed, and whether the customer approved or declined the repairs.

KNOW THESE TERMS

Service manuals, General information section, Vehicle identification number, Body identification plate, Repair manual, Logic tree diagnostic chart, Block diagnostic chart, Special tool, Abbreviations, Flat rate manual, Repair order, Control number.

REVIEW QUESTIONS—CHAPTER 21

1. Explain what information can be found in a service manual.
2. Explain what information can be found in a repair manual.
3. What is the difference between a service manual and a repair manual?
4. Where can the VIN be found on the car?
5. Where can information be found to decipher the VIN?
6. What is the difference between a logic tree diagnostic chart and a block diagnostic chart?
7. A book that determines how much labor to charge for repairs is called a:
   a. Service manual.
   b. Repair order.
   c. Flat rate manual.
   d. Repair manual.
8. To determine the dollar amount for a specific labor operation, multiply the shop hourly rate by the time listed in the repair manual. True or false?
9. What is a control number and where can it be found?
10. Why must the customer sign the repair order prior to the mechanic making the needed repairs?
11. A car comes into the shop because the air conditioner is not working. While troubleshooting the A/C system, you notice the water pump is leaking engine coolant. What should you do?
    a. Replace the water pump.
    b. Overlook it, since the customer did not bring the car in for this reason.
    c. Call the customer and explain the situation, then document it on the repair order, along with the customer's decision.
    d. None of the above.

SUCCEEDING IN AUTOMOTIVE HEATING AND AIR CONDITIONING

After studying this chapter, you will be able to:
- *Explain why a technician must keep up with technology.*
- *Describe what is meant by quality work.*
- *Define what is meant by work speed.*
- *List the different ways a technician can be paid.*
- *Summarize the shop types.*
- *Relate why cooperation is important.*

INTRODUCTION

New technology presents a constant challenge to auto technicians. Therefore, it is necessary that a technician is constantly reading and learning. Work quality and speed are also important to any auto technician's success.

KEEPING UP WITH TECHNOLOGY

An auto technician must keep up with the changing technology for survival. A good technician must constantly read service manuals and trade journals to stay current. This keeps the technician knowledgeable of new systems and other advancements. If the technician does not know how the system components work, servicing will be impossible.

Automotive trade journals provide information on technical advances in the automotive field. *MOTOR, Automotive News, Chilton's Motor/Age,* and *Automotive Engineering* are excellent sources of information. *MOTOR* and *Chilton's Motor/Age* are published monthly and aimed at the technician level. *Automotive News* is published weekly and contains articles on technical advances. However, most of the articles are aimed at the business end of the automotive industry. *Automotive News* also contains a classified section that lists the various automotive-related jobs available throughout the United States. *Automotive Engineering* is published monthly by the Society of Automotive Engineers (SAE).

It is aimed at the engineering and theory level of technical advances in the automotive field.

Concentrate on learning about changes in the automotive field. Staying knowledgeable about the design and component changes will make your work enjoyable. It will also give you a sense of pride, satisfaction, accomplishment, and increase your value as a technician.

Avoid the pitfall of thinking you know everything about your job. This only leads to trouble, and you will be quickly left behind by the new technology.

QUALITY WORK

Quality work is the ability to make correct repairs the first time. This is a primary concern of the mechanic, shop owner, and the customer. Always adhere to factory specifications.

When a technician sacrifices quality for speed, the result is an increase in *comebacks* (the same repair must be repeated free-of-charge). The consequence is that everyone loses: the technician loses time that could be spent on new money-producing repairs, the shop owner also loses money, the car owner loses use of the vehicle while repairs are done over.

Experience shows that a dissatisfied customer will tell other people of your poor quality work. These people will tell more people. This will have an undesirable effect on your job.

WORK SPEED

Work speed is the rate at which the assigned work is finished. This is a very important factor in the technician's success. Many work on a percentage or straight commission. The incentive here is to work faster and complete more jobs to make more money. If the technician is paid on an hourly basis, emphasis on work speed is less, since the pay is based on the number of hours worked and not the number of jobs completed.

It is necessary to increase work speed without affecting work quality. As an example, a new or different repair technique should be considered to save time. This comes only from experience. A positive attitude is very important in order to improve your skills. The result is using your time well and becoming more productive. Electric and pneumatic tools properly used also increase the work speed without adversely affecting work quality.

EARNINGS

Three basic methods are used to pay auto technicians: hourly rate, straight commission, and commission plus parts. The method used depends on the technician's position and the shop policy.

Hourly rate

A technician on an *hourly rate* receives a specified dollar amount per hour worked. The hourly method of pay generally results in a lower overall income than commission rate.

Straight commission

Most shops use this method. The *commission* method pays a technician a percentage of the hourly rate the shop charges the customer. For example, if the shop charges $60 per hour and the technician's commission is 30 percent, the technician earns $18 per hour.

The "per hour" charge the technician receives is not always an accurate description. The *flat rate manual* (a book that lists the number of hours a job should take) may state that it takes two hours to replace an A/C compressor. If the technician can replace the compressor in one hour, the technician still receives pay for two hours labor. The technician can then move on to the next assignment. However, if it takes the technician three hours to replace the compressor, the technician still only receives pay for two hours labor.

Commission plus parts

The *commission plus parts* method pays the technician commission plus a small percentage of the cost of the parts used in the repair. This method provides the technician with an incentive to check additional parts during the repair. Make sure the parts are legitimately worn or defective.

TYPE OF SHOPS

The type of shop you choose to work in dictates the scope of work, benefits, compensation, and advancement opportunities. New car dealerships, independent repair shops, service stations, and franchised auto repair centers all employ technicians.

New car dealerships

New car dealerships must be able to service the car while it is under warranty. Dealerships can also service the car after it is out of the warranty period. Small dealerships may require each technician to service all areas of the car. Large dealerships have one or two technicians that specialize in servicing each area of the car. This means a large dealership can have as many as 8 to 16 technicians. This does not include the body shop technicians, service writers, service manager, or shop supervisor.

Independent repair shops

An *independent repair shop* does not handle new car warranty repairs. Some independent repair shops specialize in servicing only one area of the car. If the shop is reputable and has plenty of work, it can also be a good place in which to work. The shop owner controls the work atmosphere and conditions.

Service station

A *service station* sells gasoline and also has service bays in which to make minor car repairs. The work, for the most part, is *quick service* (repairs that only take an hour or two). This involves such jobs as replacement of belts, tune-ups, brake jobs, exhaust system work, engine cooling system repairs, charging and starting system repairs, and minor A/C repairs.

Franchised auto repair center

A *franchised auto repair center* is similar to a service station, except it does not sell gasoline. Most repair centers also limit their work to quick-service repairs. Sears, Goodyear, and Firestone are examples of franchises that have auto repair centers.

BENEFITS

Benefits include health insurance, life insurance, vacation pay, uniform rentals/cleaning, and a retirement plan at little or no cost to the employee. When applying for a job, you should always inquire about the benefits. Employers have diverse benefit packages.

APPEARANCE

Appearance is very important. Work clothing or uniforms must be comfortable, fit well, and pleasing to the eye. Most people expect the technician to be slightly dirty due to the nature of automotive repair work. However, keep your work clothes as clean as possible. Change your work clothes every day.

The technician's appearance may reflect attitude and mechanical abilities. A dirty and sloppy look creates an impression the technician does not care about work quality. Always maintain a professional image.

COOPERATION

Cooperation is the ability to work well with other people. This is essential for auto technicians. Many jobs require a "third hand." Some operations involve one technician in the car and another outside the car. Always keep a good working relationship with other technicians by helping them when needed. Then, they will be glad to assist when you need help. Maintain good working relationships with the service manager, shop supervisor, service writers, and the parts department.

ADVANCEMENT

There are many opportunities in automotive related fields. Many opportunities open up after the proper schooling and/or experience. These include:

1. Auto instructor in school or for an auto manufacturer.
2. Service manager.
3. Auto repair shop supervisor.
4. Technical representative for an auto manufacturer.
5. Technical representative for an auto aftermarket company.
6. An auto aftermarket salesperson.
7. Automotive technician.
8. Auto repair shop owner.
9. Technical writer.
10. Test and development engineer.

Special training may be required for some of these positions. Attending college or taking specialized courses may be necesary to qualify for some of these jobs. Experience in auto mechanics will provide an edge over a competitor seeking the same position. Auto manufacturing and repair fields are among the largest employment areas in the nation. Success depends upon initiative, diligence, and willingness to learn.

SUMMARY

There are many challenges and rewards for the auto technician in today's world. The rewards will depend upon the willingness to develop skills, cooperation with employers and fellow workers, and keeping abreast with technological changes.

An auto technician will be expected to work efficiently and rapidly while turning out quality work. Compensation will depend on the shop and the technician's position. The technician may be paid hourly, straight commission, or commission plus a percentage of parts installed.

The type of shop you choose to work in affects your advancement opportunities, benefits, and compensation. Large auto dealerships, in most cases, pay well, have good benefits, and afford opportunities for advancement. Independent repair shops pay well, but have limited opportunities for advancement. Service stations and franchised auto repair centers are a good place to gain initial experience.

Auto mechanics can be rewarding in itself and provide a basis for advancement into other automotive-related jobs. Some jobs may require the auto technician to attend college or other specialized courses.

KNOW THESE TERMS

Automotive trade journals, Quality work, Comebacks, Work speed, Hourly rate, Commission, Flat rate manual, Commission plus parts, New car dealerships, Independent repair shops, Service station, Quick service, Franchised auto repair center, Benefits, Cooperation.

REVIEW QUESTIONS—CHAPTER 22

1. Why must a technician keep up with technology?
2. What is meant by quality work?
3. What is meant by work speed?
4. What methods are used for paying a technician?
5. Give a brief description of each shop type.
6. Why is it important that a technician cooperate?
7. Define the term "comeback."

23 PREPARING FOR CERTIFICATION

After studying this chapter, you will be able to:
- *Explain the purpose of the certification testing program.*
- *List the ASE certification test categories.*
- *Describe the ASE testing procedures.*

CERTIFICATION

Certification tests provide a method of measuring whether a technician is competent to service a specific system of a car. The tests consist of multiple choice questions to evaluate the technical knowledge of technicians working in the field. ASE is a national organization that conducts the auto service technician certification.

ASE (NIASE)

ASE stands for Automotive Service Excellence. It was shortened from *NIASE* or the National Institute for Automotive Service Excellence. ASE is a nonprofit, nonaffiliated (no ties to industry) organization. ASE helps assure that high standards in the automotive service field are maintained.

ASE is under the guidance of a 41-member board. Six of these members are on its board of directors. These members represent all areas of the automotive industry: educators, shop owners, consumer groups, government agencies, aftermarket parts suppliers, and automotive manufacturers. This group of experts guides the certification testing program, keeping it in touch with the needs of the auto industry.

VOLUNTARY TESTING

ASE tests are voluntary and do not have to be taken. The tests do not license technicians. In the United States, technicians take ASE tests for personal benefits. Also, this exhibits to employers and customers that they are qualified to work on a particular area of a car. ASE

statistics currently show that over 300,000 technicians have passed certification tests.

ASE TESTS

There are eight test categories for automotive service technicians:
1. Engine repair.
2. Automatic transmission/transaxle.
3. Manual drive train and axles.
4. Suspension and steering.
5. Brakes.
6. Electrical systems.
7. Heating and air conditioning.
8. Engine performance.

Most certification tests ask 40 questions, Fig. 23-1. However, the engine repair and engine performance tests each have 80 questions. You can take any one or all of these tests. Only four certification tests can be taken during one test session. In addition, ASE provides testing for heavy-duty truck repair technicians, auto body service technicians, and automotive engine machinists.

ASE test requirements

The certification requirements consist of two years on-the-job experience or one year on-the-job and one year of preapproved educational courses. It is possible to take the ASE test without any of the experience requirements. However, test scores will be sent without a certification or shoulder patch. Then, after you obtain the mandatory experience, ASE will furnish a certificate and shoulder patch.

Some schooling can be substituted for on-the-job experience. Credit for formal training will be granted by one or a combination of the following types of schooling:
1. Three full years of high school training in auto mechanics may be substituted for one year of work experience.
2. Two years of post-high school training in a public

HEATING AND AIR CONDITIONING

TEST SPECIFICATIONS FOR HEATING AND AIR CONDITIONING (TEST 7)

Content Area	Number of Questions in Test	Percentage of Coverage in Test
A. A/C System Diagnosis and Repair	12	30.0%
B. Refrigeration System Component Diagnosis and Repair	10	25.0%
1. Compressor and Clutch	(4)	
2. Evaporator, Condenser, and Related Components	(6)	
C. Heating and Engine Cooling Systems Diagnosis and Repair	7	17.5%
D. Operating Systems and Related Controls Diagnosis and Repair	11	27.5%
1. Electrical	(5)	
2. Vacuum/Mechanical	(4)	
3. Automatic and Semi-Automatic Heating, Ventilating and A/C Systems	(2)	
Total	**40**	**100.0%**

Fig. 23-1. Most ASE tests have 40 questions. This reference shows the breakdown of the number of questions devoted to diagnosis and also repair within this one test. (Courtesy of ASE)

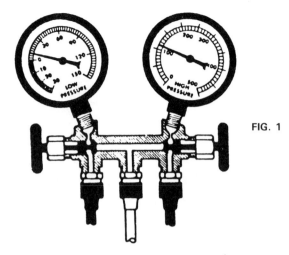

FIG. 1

1. The readings in FIG. 1 are taken with the A/C system operating at an ambient (outside) temperature of 85 °F. What do the readings indicate?
   - **(A)** Normal operation
   - **(B)** Low refrigerant level
   - **(C)** A restriction in the high side
   - **(D)** Broken compressor reed valves

2. A vacuum operated heater control valve has been installed backwards in a heating system. Technician A says that this can cause the engine to overheat. Technician B says that this can cause cold air output at the heater. Who is right?
   - **(A)** A only
   - **(B)** B only
   - **(C)** Both A & B
   - **(D)** Neither A nor B

3. All of these statements are true about a factory installed A/C-heater system EXCEPT:
   - **(A)** air flows through the evaporator before going through the heater core.
   - **(B)** inlet air can come from the outside or from the inside of the vehicle.
   - **(C)** air flow through the evaporator is controlled by the position of the blend door.
   - **(D)** outlet air temperature is controlled by the position of the blend door.

Fig. 23-2. All questions on ASE tests are multiple choice. Note the key word EXCEPT in this sentence. (ASE)

or private facility can be substituted for one year of work experience.
3. Two months of short training courses can be substituted for one month of work experience.
4. Successful completion of a three- or four-year apprenticeship program is substituted for two years of on-the-job training.

In order to substitute schooling for work experience, it is necessary to send a copy of the school transcripts, a statement of the training received, or a certificate to verify the training and/or apprenticeship. This information should accompany the registration form and fee payment.

ASE test location and date

ASE administers tests twice a year in over 300 locations across the United States. Test sites are usually community colleges, high schools, or training centers. Tests are given in May and November. Most tests are given on weeknights, after normal working hours. Contact the ASE for specific test dates and locations.

ASE test taking

All ASE tests have multiple-choice questions, Fig. 23-2. It is necessary to read the statement carefully evaluate the question, and then select the most correct answer. Tests primarily cover diagnosis, service, and repair. It is not necessary to remember specifications, unless they apply to all makes and models.

Here are some hints to help you while taking the test:
1. Read each question carefully. You may want to read it twice so that you fully understand it.
2. Analyze the statement or question.
3. Think carefully of all possible situations and use common sense when choosing the most correct answer.
4. When two technicians give statements concerning a problem, you should try to decide if either statement is incorrect. If both are valid statements, mark that both technicians' statements are correct.
5. If the statement does not allow you to conclude that one answer is better than another, then both answers are correct.
6. Generally, your first thoughts about which answer is correct is usually the accurate response. Do not think about the question too long, as you could read something into it that is not there.
7. Do not waste time on any one question. It is important that you have time to answer all test questions.

8. Visualize the diagnostic or repair procedure when attempting to answer questions. This will help in accurate problem-solving.
9. The questions refer to generic automotive service work and problems. The questions do not refer to a specific car make or model.

ASE test results

Test scores are mailed out within a few months. The test results are mailed directly to your home address. Only you will know the results. If you failed the test, it indicates that more study may be needed.

BENEFITS OF ASE CERTIFICATION

Successfully passing the certification test entitles the technician to wear the shoulder patch on the work uniform. The shoulder patch, Fig. 23-3, is mailed with the test results. "Automotive Technician" appears under the blue logo when one or more tests are passed or "Master Auto Technician" when all eight tests are passed. The technician also receives a certificate. It states the areas in which the technician is certified and the expiration date. Shops that employ certified auto technicians can display a sign to the public, Fig. 23-4.

The ASE patch will serve as good public relations. It indicates to the public that a technician is well-trained.

Fig. 23-4. This sign indicates the shop employs certified auto technicians. (ASE)

Fig. 23-3. The shoulder patch indicates this auto technician is certified. This provides confidence for the consumer. (ASE)

It also indicates to employers that extra effort has been expended. This may lead to advancement and more income.

RECERTIFICATION

The automotive technician must take a recertification test every five years. *Recertification* ensures the technician is keeping current with technical advances. The recertification tests are given each May and November. Each recertification test usually asks only 20 questions (one-half the number of the initial certification). The same type of questions that are on the initial certification tests are asked on the recertification tests.

FOR MORE INFORMATION

Additional information can be obtained by writing ASE. Ask for the test registration and/or the ''ASE preparation guide to ASE automobile test booklet.'' The address is:

ASE
13505 Dulles Technology Drive
Herndon, VA 22071-3415

SUMMARY

A national certification program under the guidance of ASE (Automotive Service Excellence) tests auto technicians on a voluntary basis. The testing program measures the competence of auto technicians in eight different categories. A technician may take any one or all of the tests. Successfully passing the test entitles the technician to a certificate and shoulder patch.

There are eight test categories that a technician can take. A technician needs only to pass one area to become certified. If the technician passes all eight areas, he or she becomes a certified master automotive technician. The auto technician must also meet prerequisites of training and education established by a board of directors.

KNOW THESE TERMS

Certification, ASE, NIASE, Recertification.

REVIEW QUESTIONS—CHAPTER 23

1. List the eight categories of tests offered by ASE.
2. Certification and recertification tests are given in the months of _____ and _____ each year.
3. ASE stands for _____ _____ _____.
4. You must have either two years of on-the-job training or one year of approved educational courses and a year of on-the-job training. True or false?
5. ASE is:
   a. A federal testing program which licenses auto technicians.
   b. A voluntary testing program that certifies mechanics.
   c. Affiliated with the automotive industry.
   d. None of the above.
6. How often must an auto technician be recertified?
7. How many questions does the initial certification usually ask for each test?
8. How many questions does the recertification ask on each test?
9. The certification and recertification tests ask essay-type questions. True or false?
10. You must be a college graduate before taking the ASE test. True or false?

ACKNOWLEDGEMENTS

The authors would like to extend special thanks to the companies and individuals that helped make this book possible.

AMERICAN AUTO MANUFACTURERS
American Motors Corporation; Buick Motor Car Division; Chevrolet Motor Car Division; Chrysler Corporation; Ford Motor Company; GMC Truck and Coach Division; Oldsmobile Car Division; Pontiac Motor Car Division.

FOREIGN AUTO MANUFACTURERS
Honda Motor Co.; Nissan Motor Corporation; Mitsubishi Motor Co.; Subaru of America, Inc.; Toyota Motor Co.; Volkswagen of America, Inc.

AUTOMOTIVE-RELATED COMPANIES
AC-Delco; Kent Tool; Harrison Radiator Divison of GM; Snap-On Tool Corporation; TIF Instruments; John Deere & Co.; Ford Diversified Products; National Institute for Automotive Service Excellence; A-Z Auto Center; Lab Safety Supply.

A special thanks to Bob Hansen (Tirb Chevrolet); Judson Goltra, Ken Brooks, and Bob Witt (Ford Diversified Products); Jeff Powell and Fred Worden (Faist-Morrow Chevrolet/Buick/Olds); Hugh Mann (Moehn Chevrolet/Honda); Al Hand (Cooper Volkswagen); Frank Schossau (F.G.S. Radiator and Air Conditioning Service); Joe Dutcheshen (Mitsubishi Motor Company); Richard Kuntz.

To our wives, Jocelyn and Nancy, for their patience and encouragement, and to our sons Chris, Jeff, Bruce, and Corey for their assistance.

INDEX